Globalization and Institutions

NEW HORIZONS IN INSTITUTIONAL AND EVOLUTIONARY ECONOMICS

Series Editor: Geoffrey M. Hodgson
Research Professor, University of Hertfordshire Business School, UK

Economics today is at a crossroads. New ideas and approaches are challenging the largely static and equilibrium-oriented models that used to dominate mainstream economics. The study of economic institutions – long neglected in the economics textbooks – has returned to the forefront of theoretical and empirical investigation.

This challenging and interdisciplinary series publishes leading works at the forefront of institutional and evolutionary theory and focuses on cutting-edge analyses of modern socio-economic systems. The aim is to understand both the institutional structures of modern economies and the processes of economic evolution and development. Contributions will be from all forms of evolutionary and institutional economics, as well as from Post-Keynesian, Austrian and other schools. The overriding aim is to understand the processes of institutional transformation and economic change.

Titles in the series include:

Employment Relations and National Culture
Continuity and Change in the Age of Globalization
Ferrie Pot

Institutions and the Role of the State
Edited by Leonardo Burlamaqui, Ana Celia Castro and Ha-Joon Chang

Marx, Veblen, and Contemporary Institutional Political Economy
Principles and Unstable Dynamics of Capitalism
Phillip Anthony O'Hara

The New Evolutionary Microeconomics
Complexity, Competence, and Adaptive Behaviour
Jason D. Potts

National Competitiveness and Economic Growth
The Changing Determinants of Economic Performance in the World Economy
Timo J. Hämäläinen

Conventions and Structures in Economic Organization
Markets, Networks and Hierarchies
Edited by Olivier Favereau and Emmanuel Lazega

Globalization and Institutions
Redefining the Rules of the Economic Game
Edited by Marie-Laure Djelic and Sigrid Quack

Globalization and Institutions

Redefining the Rules of the Economic Game

Edited by

Marie-Laure Djelic

Sociologist and Professor, ESSEC Business School, Paris, France

and

Sigrid Quack

Sociologist and Research Fellow, Wissenschaftszentrum Berlin für Sozialforschung (WZB), Berlin, Germany

NEW HORIZONS IN INSTITUTIONAL AND EVOLUTIONARY ECONOMICS

Edward Elgar

Cheltenham, UK • Northampton, MA, USA

Published by
Edward Elgar Publishing Limited
Glensanda House
Montpellier Parade
Cheltenham
Glos GL50 1UA
UK

Edward Elgar Publishing, Inc.
136 West Street
Suite 202
Northampton
Massachusetts 01060
USA

A catalogue record for this book
is available from the British Library

Library of Congress Cataloging in Publication Data
Globalization and institutions : redefining the rules of the economic game / edited by Marie-Laure Djelic and Sigrid Quack.
    p. cm. — (New horizons in institutional and evolutionary economics series)
   Includes bibliographical references.
   1. International economic relations. 2. Globalization—Economic aspects. 3. Free trade. I. Djelic, Marie-Laure. II. Quack, Sigrid. III. New Horizons in institutional and evolutionary economics

   HF1359 .G58275 2003

2002034713

ISBN 1 84064 975 5
Printed and bound in Great Britain by MPG Books Ltd, Bodmin, Cornwall

We should strive for ideals while taking stock of the real
Jean Jaurès

Contents

Figures

Tables

Contributors

Ainamo, Antti University of Tampere, Finland

Ali-Yrkkö, Jyrki The Research Institute of the Finnish Economy, Finland

Bensedrine, Jabril ELM Research Associates and University of California Berkeley, United States

Dacin, M. Tina School of Business, Queen's University, Canada

Djelic, Marie-Laure ESSEC Business School, France

Huolman, Mika LTT Research Ltd, Finland

Kleiner, Thibaut Merger Task Force, DG Competition, European Commission, Brussels, Belgium

Lehmkuhl, Dirk Center for International Studies, Zürich University, Switzerland

Lilja, Kari Helsinki School of Economics, Finland

McKenna, Christopher Said Business School, Oxford University, United Kingdom

McNichol, Jason University of California Berkeley, United States

Midttun, Atle Norwegian School of Management, Sandvika, Norway

Moen, Eli Institute for Culture Studies, University of Oslo, Norway

Omland, Terje Norwegian School of Management, Sandvika, Norway

Plehwe, Dieter Wissenschaftszentrum Berlin für Sozialforschung – WZB, Germany

Pulkkinen, Matti LTT Research Ltd, Finland

Rupérez Micola, Augusto Norwegian School of Management, Sandvika, Norway

Quack, Sigrid Wissenschaftszentrum Berlin für Sozialforschung – WZB, Germany

Szyliowicz, Dara Texas Tech University, United States

Tainio, Risto Helsinki School of Economics, Finland

Ventresca, Marc J. Kellog School of Management, Northwestern University, United States

Vescovi, Stefano Federal Department for Foreign Affairs, Switzerland

Whitley, Richard Manchester Business School, United Kingdom

Ylä-Anttila, Pekka The Research Institute of the Finnish Economy, Finland

Acknowledgments

This book is the crystallization of a collective undertaking that started in July 2000 as a subtheme in the Helsinki colloquium of the European Group for Organization Studies (EGOS). Each adventure has its beginnings and we would like to acknowledge the role of Kari Lilja, who was instrumental in bringing us together. Kari had suggested that the two of us should jointly run a subtheme at EGOS. In retrospect this was a good match indeed and our collaboration has been both extremely fruitful and pleasant.

A second meeting followed in the fall in Lisbon, Portugal. This second meeting took place within the framework of the European Summer Research Institute (ESRI). ESRI was a three year program (1999–2001) funded by the European Science Fundation (ESF), the Copenhagen Business School, the Danish Research Academy and the Danish Social Science Research Council. It sponsored regular research workshops and also involved the yearly running of a PhD Summer School on Comparative Economic Sociology. We thank the Steering and Scientific Committees of ESRI for giving us the opportunity to bring contributors together a second time. This has been critical, we found, and the Lisbon workshop has allowed us to move towards a tightly-knit volume. We would like to extend our special appreciation to Marianne Risberg and Peer Hull Kristensen for taking on the heavy load of organizing the logistics for that workshop. The Lisbon workshop was a highly stimulating intellectual event and we are grateful to all participants for making it so.

All along in our job as editors, we have been aided by a great group of contributors. They have patiently dealt with long and repeated sets of detailed comments that we sent them. They agreed to follow the 'rules of the game' as we had defined them – work towards and craft a tightly-knit and homogeneous volume.

Work for this book would never have been possible without the support of a number of institutions. We have already mentioned ESRI, the European Science Foundation and the Copenhagen Business School. We would also like to acknowledge the support we received from our own institutions – ESSEC and the WZB – in the form both of time and resources. Our appreciation extends to the Sociology Department at Stanford University where one of the editors spent a six month sabbatical and found a highly congenial environment to work on this book. The list would be too long but behind all chapters to this volume there are one or several institutions that, directly or indirectly, contributed important resources.

Ultimately, however, in intellectual endeavours of this sort the greatest debts are to individuals. Along the way, we were helped by a number of scholars and colleagues who provided us with advice, reacted and commented on parts of the manuscript, shared their own work, engaged with us in discussions apparently unrelated yet still highly useful, or were supportive in any other way. Our special appreciation goes to John Meyer. We would also like to thank, in alphabetical order, Jose Luis Alvarez, Rolv Peter Amdam, Jennifer Bair, Nils Brunsson, Haldor Byrkjeflot, Steven Casper, Anita Engels, Lars Engwall, Neil Fligstein, Marion Fourcade-Gourinchas, Michal Frenkel, Henrik Glimstedt, Michel Goyer, Mark Granovetter, Peer Hull Kristensen, Georg Kruecken, Christel Lane, Arie Lewin, Ray Loveridge, Peter Mendel, Glenn Morgan, Dieter Plehwe, Woody Powell, Kerstin Sahlin-Andersson, Ayse Saka, Diana Sharpe, Arndt Sorge and Richard Whitley. We also acknowledge the collective input of research seminars where parts of the manuscript were presented – the Globalization Seminar at Stanford University, the Doctoral Seminar at HEC in Paris, and the Organization and Employment Research Seminar at the WZB in Berlin.

At Edward Elgar, we benefited from the professionalism of Francine O'Sullivan and Bob Pickens, who were of great help through all stages. We also appreciated the support of Geoffrey Hodgson, Editor of the series 'New Horizons in Institutional and Evolutionary Economics'.

Finally, we dedicate this book to our daughters, Alma, Milena and Nepheli, thanking them for being patient and for 'sharing' us with this book, which none of them will be able to read for quite a number of years still!

Acronyms

ACME – Association of Consultants and Management Engineers
ACT – Automated Confirmation Transaction System
ADM – Archer–Daniels–Midland
AG – Aktiengesellschaft
AGF – Assurances Générales de France
APX – Automated Power Exchange
ARCCO – Association des Régimes de Retraite Complémentaires
ASEAN – Association of Southeast Asian Nations
ASFFI – Association des Sociétés et Fonds Français d'Investissement
ATS – Automated Trading System
BCCI – Bank of Credit and Commerce International
BEUC – Bureau Européen des Unions de Consommateurs
BKW – Bernische Kraftwerke AG
BNP – Banque Nationale de Paris
BPIF – British Printing Industries Federation
BSE – Bovine Spongiform Encephalopathy
CCF – Crédit Commercial de France
CENTRAL – Centre for Transnational Law
CEO – Chief Executive Officer
CEPI – Central European Power Index
CER – Community of European Railways
CIAA – Confédération des Industries Agro-alimentaires de l'Union Européenne
CIOS – Comité International de l'Organisation Scientifique
CLECAT – Comité de Liaison Européen des Commissionnaires et Auxiliaires de Transport
CM – Council of Ministers
COB – Commission des Opérations de Bourse
COGECA – Comité Général de la Coopération Agricole de l'Union Européenne
COPA – Comité des Organisations Professionnelles de l'Union Européenne
CPE – Coordination des Paysanne Européenne
DB – Deutsche Bahn AG
DHL – Dalsey, Hillblom and Lynn
DNA – Deoxyribonucleic Acid
DPWN – Deutsche Post World Net

EASDAQ – European Association of Securities Dealers Automated Quotation
EBRD – European Bank for Reconstruction and Development
EC – European Commission
ECJ – European Court of Justice
ECK-SA – Electrocieplownia Krakow SA
ECSC – European Coal and Steel Community
EdF – Electricité de France
EEC – European Economic Community
EFTA – European Free Trade Agreement
EGOS – European Group for Organization Studies
EIM – European Rail Infrastructure Managers
ENA – Ecole Nationale d'Administration
EnBW – Energiewerk Baden Württemberg
ENEL – Energia Elettrica
EP – European Parliament
EPU – European Payments Union
ERISA – Employee Retirement Income Security Act
ESIS – Energy Settlements and Information Services Limited
ESRI – European Summer Research Institute
ESTAG – Energie Steiermark AG
EU – European Union
EVA – Economic Value Added
FAO – Food and Agriculture Organization
FDA – Food and Drug Administration
FEACO – Federation of Associations of Consultants
FEDIOL – Fédération des Industriels de l'Oléagineux
FFE – Freight Forward Europe
FIBV – Fédération Internationale des Bourses de Valeurs
GATT – General Agreement on Tariffs and Trade
GdF – Gaz de France
GM – Genetically Modified
GMO – Genetically Modified Organisms
GTC – Groupement des Transports Combinés
HEC – Ecole des Hautes Etudes Commerciales
HESE – Helsinki Stock Exchange
HQ – Headquarters
IASB – International Accounting Standards Board
IASC – International Accounting Standards Committee
IBA – International Bar Association
IBE – International Business Environment
IBRD – International Bank for Reconstruction and Development (World Bank)
ICC – International Chamber of Commerce

IFC – International Finance Corporation
IFCI – International Financial Risk Institute
IMAB – International Market Advisory Board
IMF – International Monetary Fund
INCOTERMS – International Commercial Terms
INSEAD – Institut Européen d'Administration des Affaires
IOMA – International Options Market Association
IOSCO – International Organization of Securities Commissions
IR – International Relations
IRU – International Road Union
ISG – Intermarket Surveillance Group
JMC – Joint Marketing Committee
LJK – Liikkeenjohdon Konsultit
LSE – London Stock Exchange
MAF Law – Loi de Modernisation des Activités Financières
MATIF – Marché à Terme d'Instruments Financiers
MBA – Master of Business Administration
MNC – Multinational Corporations
MNE – Multinational Enterprises
MOU – Memorandum of Understanding
MVA – Market Value Added
NAFTA – North American Free Trade Agreement
NASD – National Association of Securities Dealers
NASDAQ – National Association of Securities Dealers Automated Quotation
NESA – Nordsjaellands Elektricitets- og Sporvejs Aktieselskap
NGO – Non Governmental Organization
NIMI – Nasdaq International Market Initiatives
NYSE – New York Stock Exchange
OECD – Organisation Européenne pour la Coopération et le Développement
OMEL – Operadora del Mercado Español de Electricidad
OMGUS – Office Military Government for Germany–United States
PG Paperboard – Product Group Paperboard
PWG – Presidents Working Group
RASTOR – Rationalization, Standardization and Organization
R&D – Research and Development
REC – Regional Electricity Companies
RWE – Rheinisch Westfälisches Elektrizitätswerk
SBF – Société des Bourses Françaises
SEC – Securities and Exchange Commission
SEP – Samenwerkende Elektricitets Producenten
SGAM – Société Générale Asset Management
SNCB – Société des Chemins de Fer Belges

SNCF – Société des Chemins de Fer Français
SWEP – Swiss Electricity Price Index
TEN – Trans European Networks
TICON – International Committee on Newsprint
TIR – Transport International Routier
TNT – Thomas Nationwide Transport
TAP – Third Party Access
TRIPS – Trade Related Aspects of Intellectual Property
TSE – Toronto Stock Exchange
UAP – Union des Assurances de Paris
UCITS – Undertakings for Collective Investment in Transferable Securities
UETR – Union Européenne des Transporteurs Routiers
UIRR – Union of International Road Rail Transports
UN – United Nations
UNCITRAL – United Nations Commission on International Trade Law
UPS – United Parcel Service
USAID – US Agency for International Development
USDA – United States Department of Agriculture
USSR – Union of Soviet and Socialist Republics
VEBA – Vereinigte Elektrizitäts und Bergwerks Aktiengesellschaft
VEW – Vereinigte Elektrizitätswerke
VIAG – Vereinigte Industrie-Unternehmen AG
WFSE – World Federation of Stock Exchanges (formerly FIBV)
WZB – Wissenschaftszentrum für Sozialforschung Berlin
WTO – World Trade Organization

Introduction: Governing globalization – bringing institutions back in

Marie-Laure Djelic and Sigrid Quack

The image of a 'runaway world' (Giddens 2000) – a very fast train without drivers going along the tracks of market and technological evolutions – will probably remain associated with the 1990s. During that decade, this image triggered essentially three kinds of reactions.

First were the believers – those who observed, predicted and championed an intensifying and accelerating movement of globalization, understood as an unavoidable, ahistorical, neutral and progressive force. Then came the sceptics for whom the nation-state remained a robust structuring principle. Without denying processes of internationalization, sceptics pointed at the most to a regionalization of exchanges around three poles – Europe, Asia and the Americas. From that perspective, ideas of a 'borderless world' or of a 'global village' (McLuhan 1968; Ohmae 1990, 1995) were mere utopias. Finally, one found the critics – those who agreed that globalization was a reality in the making but did not see it as progressive. Critics pointed to the negative externalities associated with globalization, in terms of inequalities, durable growth, ecological conditions and also in terms of the reduction or destruction of diversities.

Naturally those three groups had quite different ideas on how to deal with this 'runaway world'. For believers, forces such as market competition, techno-logical change and rationalization were bringing along wealth, development and social, if not moral, progress. Those forces hence should be set free and liberated. Political and regulatory intervention created particularly problematic hurdles and obstacles from that perspective. Globalization would not progress and push along its benefits if the polity did not wither away.

For sceptics this was naive wishful thinking. From their perspective, the nation-state remained extremely robust as a locus of structuration and organization of social and economic life. This vouched for the persistence of differences, made convergence unlikely and in itself this strength of the polity at the national level set limits and constraints to the process of globalization.

As for critics, they identified the whithering away of the polity, particularly in its national dimension, as indeed a process associated with globalization. They saw it as one of the negative externalities of a globalizing world that

1

should be countered. A rallying cry of part of the anti-globalization movement
has been the issue of governance. The argument went that, if left to its own
devices, globalization could have destructive consequences – particularly on
the weak, the marginal, the minorities, the diverse and the different. The polity
could play in that context the role of a buffer and filter and each state should
act as a counter power on its own territory.

   Another and complementary side of the call for governance has had to do
with the space in between – the international arena. Generally, that space has
been viewed and described as an anomic and apolitical sphere, a space of non-
law largely unregulated and leaving free play to market, financial and economic
logics. Pleas for curbing the power and strength of those logics in that space
have become not only more widespread but also more mainstream at the turn of
our millennium. A witness to that is the importance granted to the issue of the
'governance of globalization' by the 2002 World Economic Forum held in the
aftermath of the September 11, 2001 drama and which took place symbolically
in New York. Political and economic leaders have tended to appropriate either
the discourse on and/or the project of reining in globalization and working
towards its 'governance'.[1] There, too, the polity would seem to have an important
role to play – the role of the 'driver' of this runaway world, may be, which was
absent and unnecessary in the eyes of the 'believers'. The ambiguity appears to
be much greater, however, in that context, as to the meaning of the term 'polity'.

RECONCILING EMBEDDEDNESS AND CHANGE: A REINTERPRETATION OF 'GLOBALIZATION'

This volume starts with a different understanding of the relationship between
economic globalization and institutions. We do not treat the economy and the
polity as two separate spheres of social life, each with its own autonomous
logic in interaction – and competition – with the other (Parsons 1949, 1951;
Alexander 1985). Instead, the contributors to this book all embrace a conception
of economic (but also political) action as being deeply embedded in larger institutional schemes. Working from within an institutionalist tradition, we see
institutions as the fabric or frame shaping, constraining, embedding, orienting,
facilitating and allowing actions and interactions including those of an economic
nature (Weber 1978; Veblen 1904; Polanyi 1944; Granovetter 1985, for a more
systematic discussion see Chapter 1). Hence, when trying to account for changes
in the French asset management industry (Kleiner in this volume) we look at
the organizations, structures, norms and rules that control but also orientate and
facilitate the behaviour of actors in this industry. We have to focus, furthermore, on the interplay between local or preexisting national frames and

challenger ones with foreign origins and transnational scope. When taking stock of the emergence of an integrated, European-wide truck transport industry (Plehwe with Vescovi in this volume) we also have to look at the ways in which national and transnational organizations, structures, norms or rules conflict, converge or interact leading to partial hybridization.

While we share a number of assumptions about what constitutes institutions with the sceptics identified above, we differ from them, however, quite significantly in essentially two ways. First, we see those institutional fabrics or frames as being malleable under certain conditions and through certain types of processes that we identify in the chapters of this volume. National institutions are robust and durable but we argue and provide evidence that they can change. We reinterpret globalization as contributing to that process of change – not destroying national institutional frames but rather pushing along their evolution and transformation (Part I of this volume).

A second manner in which we differ from the sceptics is that we acknowledge the need to take into account seriously the space in between nations, the transnational arena, as economic organization and coordination increasingly reach across national borders. Markets, we know, are or reflect institutions (Fligstein 2001). This is true of national markets and of regional markets of the European Union type (Fligstein and Mara Drita 1996). From the perspective we adopt that any kind of economic activity is embedded in a wider institutional frame, this is also true of transnational markets in the larger sense of the word. Hence we argue that globalization of economic activity reveals and means processes of institutionalization in the transnational space. Globalization, we claim, is not only about adaptation and change of national institutions. It is also about institution building in the transnational arena (Part II of this volume) – a space traditionally and typically pictured and described as anomic and adversarial.

TOWARDS AN HISTORICALLY BOUNDED UNDERSTANDING OF 'GLOBALIZATION'

We take stock of the fact that institutional frames and fabrics as we know them today are tightly connected with the process of state and nation building that marked the modern era. However, that connection is historically contingent (see Whitley in this volume). Economic activity before the nation-state was structured and framed both locally (at a sub-'national' level in today's terms) and trans-locally, going well beyond national boundaries as they are defined today (Berman 1983; Greif 1992; Spruyt 1994 and Lehmkuhl in this volume).

The 'nationalization' of processes of institutionalization started around the seventeenth century with a progressive extension of the scope and reach of those national institutions that left little space to other than non-national rules (see Lehmkuhl in this volume). There were periods, during this era of the nation-state, when transnational exchanges were extremely limited – the most extreme case of that being the 1930s and early 1940s (James 2001). There were periods, on the other hand, when transnational activity particularly of an economic nature picked up significantly. This was the case for example in the last decades of the nineteenth century but also during the 1920s until the Great Depression (Murphy 1994; Williamson 1996; James 2001).

Our focus in this volume is on the latest such episode of significant internationalization of economic activity, which we see starting after the end of World War II (McKenna et al.; Whitley and Lehmkuhl in this volume) and accelerating significantly from the 1980s on (all other contributions to this volume). This episode we call 'globalization'. We therefore create historical boundaries and situate precisely both the term and the phenomenon of globalization instead of treating them as is often done as universal and/or historical concept and evolution (Bartlett and Ghoshal 1998; Ohmae 1990, 1995; Guillén 2001).

One of the objectives of this book was to get at an understanding of what, if anything, may be unique and different in this latest episode of internationalization of economic activity, called here 'globalization'. Economic historians have argued on the whole that our contemporary episode of globalization and internationalization at the turn of the twentieth century do not differ so much. Figures show that foreign trade was 18.2 per cent of British GDP in 1890, 27.7 per cent in 1913 and 21.2 per cent in 1994. Foreign trade represented 6.5 per cent of US GDP in 1890 and 8.9 per cent in 1994 (Krugman 1995). If anything, economists have pointed to even denser flows of exchange in the earlier period with respect to labour and people or even capital.

Internationalization at the turn of the twentieth century did correspond with an intense period of migration, away from Europe – about 60 million people left the old continent and 40 million alone went to the US – but also within Europe mostly from the South to the North (Williamson 1996; Cohen 2002). It was also associated with high levels of capital flows (Wilkins 1989; Hirst and Thompson 1996; Obstfeld and Taylor 1997; Berger 2002). In some countries, capital flows were even higher then in proportion to national wealth than they are now, as documented in Table I.1. If defined as an internationalization of exchanges of goods and services coupled with factor mobility (Ohmae 1995) the contemporary period of globalization therefore appears as neither new nor fundamentally distinct from earlier episodes of internationalization of economic activity.

We start, however, from another understanding of globalization in this volume and our focus on institutions and processes of institutionalization does lead us to make different conclusions. Periods of internationalization of economic activity in the nineteenth and early twentieth centuries were characterized, we argue, by what Whitley calls in this volume a 'particularistic logic'.

The background was a Westphalian system of largely independent nation states. British hegemony, the Gold Standard and a series of bilateral agreements between leading trading nations were stabilizing factors. In that context, connections, exchanges, cooperation and the management of uncertainty but also the resolution of disputes relied typically on the preexistence and structuration of transnational networks and on relatively ad hoc, isolated and case by case mechanisms (McKenna et al.; Whitley; Lilja and Moen and Lehmkuhl in this volume, see also van der Pijl 1998). These networks often had a very personal dimension – reflecting friendships, deeply embedded trust and even kinship or family links (see Bouvier 1992; Autin 1983; Fargette 2001 or Chernow 1990 for the case of banking and particularly of the merchant banking industry).

Table I.1   Capital flows as per cent of GDP, 1870–1996

	Argentina	France	Germany	Great Britain	United States
1870–89	18.7	2.4	1.7	4.6	0.7
1927–31	3.7	1.4	2.0	1.9	0.7
1947–59	2.3	1.5	2.0	1.2	0.6
1974–89	1.9	0.8	2.1	1.5	1.4
1989–96	2.0	0.7	2.7	2.6	1.2

Source: Obstfeld and Taylor (1997).

Getting somewhat ahead of ourselves, probably one of our main collective findings in this book is that the logic behind the recent episode of globalization has been different and we would even argue qualitatively different. We find and provide evidence of increasing formalization, structuration, codification, standardization and depersonalization of the rules of the game in the transnational space (all contributions to this volume and particularly Part II). Hence, we see a clear evolution from interpersonal networks to institutional rules of the game as the background and basis of the internationalization of economic activities. Besides state agencies and a small number of elite personal networks, we point to the involvement of other types of actors in the process of transnational rule making. We document an increasing density of organizational actors – private corporations, business or professional associations, unions, NGOs, consumer or citizens' groups – that are taking part in that process in one way or another.

The result is institutional rule making with a transnational scope. In certain circumstances, the institutional backbone or set of rules of the game crystallizes from preexisting transnational networks (Lilja and Moen in this volume, see also van der Pijl 1998). Sometimes it reveals the transfer of a dominant national set of rules and its adaptation and stabilization at the transnational level (Tainio et al.; Kleiner; McKenna et al. in this volume). In other cases, it reflects processes of negotiation between competing sets of rules or it can even represent an entirely emergent and new rule system (Plehwe with Vescovi; Ventresca et al.; McNichol and Bensedrine; Lehmkuhl in this volume).

Altogether, we thus find that while the national arena remains important for the structuration of economic activities and interactions, the consequence of this episode we call 'globalization' is that the transnational space has also become an important purveyor of institutional 'rules' for the economic game. This evolution started in the immediate aftermath of World War II (Djelic 1998; Whitley; McKenna et al.; Lehmkuhl in this volume). But it has become more obvious and more rapid since the 1980s (all other contributions to this volume). The complexity and interrelatedness of various and often decentralized mechanisms of transnational rule formation together with the diversity and multiplicity of actors involved are two defining characteristics of the contemporary period of globalization. Interestingly, those transnational rules of the game are having an impact on the way the economic game is being played at the international level but they are also having an impact on the way it is being played within particular national arenas. Contributions to this volume provide evidence of that and specify some of the mechanisms by which transnational rules are reflecting back on national spaces (see also Djelic and Quack in the conclusion to this volume).

GLOBALIZATION AS INSTITUTIONAL CHANGE AND INSTITUTION BUILDING

A key suggestion of this volume is that globalization should be reinterpreted as a double process of institutional change and institution building. Globalization, we argue, is in fact and deeply about governance – it is about a transformation of governance systems or institutional rules of the game in many nation-states. It is also about the building, structuration and stabilization of new governance systems in the transnational space.

The logics sustaining those new governance systems are sometimes so different from what we traditionally mean and understand by governance that we might misinterpret or even miss them altogether. A number of chapters show that these new understandings or practices of governance may be impacting and reflecting back on the way we do governance nationally and hence on the features of what we could call traditional democratic spaces (see Djelic and Quack in the conclusion to this volume). We argue therefore that globalization does not mean the fading away of national polities and national institutional systems – it probably means, however, at least their partial reinvention.

Bringing institutions back in does make for a richer debate on globalization. Instead of appearing as an ahistorical, impersonal and neutral force, globalization is situated as a particular episode of internationalization with multiple and contextual, highly embedded expressions or dimensions. The significance and specific features of this recent episode of internationalization of economic activity are brought to the fore and they have to do, we argue, with a sustained level both of institutional change in the national context and of institution building in the transnational space. In contrast, discussions about the internationalization of exchanges, flows of goods, money, technology, practices, organizations and people across borders generally associated with debates on globalization (for example Ohmae 1990; Sassen 1998; Giddens 2000; Guillén 2001) appear less fundamental.

At the very same time, pointing to the tight connections between institutions and globalization also allows us to make a contribution to the institutionalist literature. The process here is clearly one of cross-fertilization between debates on globalization and discussions about institutions. There has been widespread agreement over recent years that issues of institutional change and emergence are weak points of institutionalist arguments in general (Brinton and Nee 1998; Clemens and Cook 1999). By taking globalization seriously and pointing to its institutional dimension, we contribute to reconciling the idea of institutional embeddedness with processes of change and emergence and we open new venues for the institutionalist perspective. The following chapter looks into greater details at the treatment of issues of change and emergence in the institutionalist literature, pointing in the process to the ways in which the connection between globalization and institutions opens up new directions.

Institutional Change at the National Level

This volume points to the transformative impact of the process of globalization on national institutional systems (especially Part I). With respect to national systems change, institutionalist perspectives have tended to oppose two extreme alternatives – rare episodes of radical, abrupt and highly consequential change versus incremental and, on the whole, benign and non-transformative evolutions. In this book we suggest that, in certain circumstances, incremental change may be highly consequential – we call that the 'stalactite' model of change (for more see Djelic and Quack in the conclusion to this volume). This type of change may lead in time and progressively to a profound and qualitative transformation of the core institutional order or at least to a transformation of some of its key dimensions. Our 'stalactite' model of change is one where change is seen as both incremental and consequential – where change is in fact the aggregation and crystallization through time of a multiplicity of smaller processes of transformation. We position this 'stalactite' model of change as complementing rather than displacing other perspectives.

In particular, we build upon the idea of institutional change as a combination of processes of de-institutionalization and re-institutionalization (Jepperson 1991; Tolbert and Zucker 1996). We take it that institutional durability can be reinterpreted as a succession of processes of reproduction, disruptions and reactions to disruptions (Clemens and Cook 1999). But we see this succession of processes as also potentially leading to change and even quite consequential change. Change, we find and we add, will be more likely when the system opens up somewhat, that is for example when the national institutional frame gets in contact and collision with non-national challenging frames. Hence we focus on the points of interface between transnational and national spheres as deserving special attention.

Globalization, we argue, means a questioning of preexisting institutional arrangements and behavioural patterns. And this largely reflects an increasing awareness about alternatives precisely at the points of interface between the national and the transnational (for cases and empirical examples see the contributions by Tainio et al.; Kleiner; McKenna et al.; Lilja and Moen; McNichol and Bensedrine in this volume). Globalization is also about processes of re-institutionalization that have to do either with 'bricolage' and the recombination of different preexisting principles (Douglas 1991) and/or with the diffusion and concomitant hybridization of behavioural patterns and institutional arrangements that were until then characteristic of different societal fields or societies.

Transnational Institution Building

A complementary argument of this book is that globalization is also about institution building in the transnational arena. The transnational level is a space in itself where interactions take place and behavioural patterns get structured. This is particularly true and interactions are particularly dense in periods when cross-border processes of exchange, competition and cooperation intensify. As such, the transnational space is bound to give way to processes of institutionalization or institution building – and in time also naturally to processes of institutional change through aggregated movements of de-institutionalization and re-institutionalization.

Social actors playing at the transnational level still often build upon resources, frames of references and strategic orientations that they bring with them from their institutional arenas of origin. And the latter often have a national scope. However, the multiplicity of such actors and their interactions can lead to innovative combinations of various elements and to a fair degree of institutional bricolage. In some cases, the multiplicity of actors and the diversity of the pool of institutional elements from which those actors draw is such that the result can really be something entirely new, unexpected, unanticipated and emergent. Political actors and agencies can play important roles in these processes of transnational institution building but it is even more apparent than within national arenas that they are only one amongst many actors involved.

LINKING INSTITUTIONAL CHANGE AND INSTITUTION BUILDING

Changes in national institutional frames reflect, we argue, at least in part, processes of institution building at the transnational level. But those processes of institution building in the transnational space cannot be understood without reference to national or subnational sets of actors and rules and their dynamics. We propose that this circular interplay is, in a deep and essential way, what globalization is all about. The first part of this volume focuses on institutional change at the national level and the impact there of the transnational. The second part bears upon transnational institution building, linking it, however, to national frames, actors and dynamics. In the conclusion, we go back more systematically and more theoretically to the interplay between the two spheres or levels of analysis – the national and the transnational.

Institutional Change at the National Level – the Transnational Impact

In Part I of this volume, we claim that interfaces between the national and the transnational may be key sources of challenge for national rule systems. Changes can be pushed along in an incremental but consequential manner either by foreign actors carrying challenger rules or by domestic actors acquiring new experiences and habits abroad. Earlier studies have looked at multinational firms as bridging the gap between the national and the transnational (for example Ghoshal and Westney 1993; Kogut 1993; Morgan et al. 2001).

Our focus in this first part is on complementary actors – professional service firms and transnational financial communities. Recent studies and work in progress point to the importance of those types of actors. Dezalay and Garth (1996) have looked at law firms. Institutional investors and the financial community are starting to be scrutinized (O'Sullivan 2000; *Economy and Society* 2000; Pilhon and Ponsard 2002). In the first part of this volume we take up this particular category of actors, applying and leveraging the specific theoretical framework described above. Our original contribution is to ask about and assess the impact of this type of actors on national or societal institutional frameworks and rule systems.

Part I tends to show that professional service firms and transnational financial communities often have common origins – they are Anglo-Saxon if not

American. Another common finding is that those actors are able to challenge existing national rules only if they find local relays. The case studies provide evidence that foreign actors and their logics find their way into the local or national arena through coalition building, often at the periphery of the national system and with what we call 'fringe' players. The chapter by Tainio et al., for example, shows that the influence of foreign investors in Finland was strongest originally on high-tech companies that were a few years ago clearly at the periphery and not at the core of the Finnish national business system. In the case of the French asset management industry, analysed by Kleiner, the first relays were also 'fringe' players and central or core domestic players were converted to the new logic only progressively and in a second stage.

The diffusion of challenger rules promoted by foreign entrants often went hand in hand with a strengthening of those actors that had previously been weak and located at the periphery. In some circumstances the diffusion of those challenger rules also led to the setting up of entirely new organizational fields. The chapter by McKenna et al. illustrates that with respect to the field of consultancy. The chapter by Kleiner does the same for the French asset management industry.

Chapters in this section thus point to the potentially strong impact of foreign rules on particular and isolated industries, organizational fields or subsocietal spheres. Those chapters also provide evidence that changes within particular industries, organizational fields or subsocietal spheres may spill over – impacting neighbouring fields or subsocietal spheres or even reverberating on national level rule systems. In the chapter on institutional investors in Finland, for example, changes in corporate governance triggered and stimulated a reevaluation and transformation of industrial relations. Those changes have also contributed to bringing about a new polarization of economic sectors in Finland and ultimately a deep redefinition of the Finnish national business and innovation system. The structuration of asset management or consultancy fields in France has had a radiating impact on the corporate governance, financing and structuration of major national industrial actors. It has also contributed to bringing about significant transformations in local patterns of elite selection, reproduction and professionalization.

Another common lesson from chapters in Part I is that the arrival of foreign actors and challenger logics has never been uncontested. All contributions underscore the role of domestic resistance or opposition in shaping the extent and the form in which challenger rules imposed themselves in particular sub-societal fields and eventually spilled over.

Institution Building at the Transnational Level – National Components

Part II of this volume takes on globalization as revealing processes of institutionalization – institutional emergence or institution building – in the transnational sphere, in an arena traditionally described and depicted as anomic. This second part deals essentially with two types of institution building. Chapters 6 to 8 focus on rule making within a strong and formally structured supranational construction, the European Union. Chapters 9 to 11 look at processes of institution building that take place in wider, more decentralized and fluid arenas.

A common finding is that a significant number of those actors involved in rule making at the transnational level remain influenced by their embedding national environments. It is from there that they extend their strategizing, their logics and their behaviours into the international sphere. But contributions in Part II also point to what is still more a common tendency than a common reality – the progressive transnationalization of a few actors, strategies and logics. This evolution, naturally, has not gone as far everywhere. In the European arena, it seems to be more true in the pulp and paper industry studied by Lilja and Moen than in the transport sector that is the focus of the contribution by Plehwe with Vescovi. In the electricity sector, analysed by Midttun et al., this evolution is barely perceptible. The importance and role of transnational actors, strategies and logics is altogether much more visible in the studies on GMO regulation by McNichol and Bensedrine, on exchange-traded markets by Ventresca et al. or on private commercial arbitration by Lehmkuhl. Even there, however, national components remain major building blocks of processes of negotiation and transnational rule making.

Another common direction taken by contributions in Part II is to underscore the increasing importance of private actors and the multilateral nature of institution building in the transnational arena. The role of private actors – firms and business associations – is key in the story told by Lilja and Moen on the pulp and paper industry. In a case study of the European transport sector, Plehwe with Vescovi provide evidence of multidirectional sets of influences where national states and European agencies play a role but where private firms, associations and business lobbies are also very much involved. McNichol and Bensedrine look at transnational rule making around the issue of genetically modified soy. There again state agencies and European Union institutions have been involved. But they also underscore the role of a great variety of economic and political but also societal actors such as consumer groups, some of which achieved considerable influence as 'institutional entrepreneurs'. The contribution by Lehmkuhl that looks at private commercial arbitration and the structuring of dispute resolution in transnational trade also points to the multiplicity and variety of private, semi-private and public actors involved.

This increasing role and place of private actors in rule making at the transnational level does not mean, however, that emerging institutional arrangements become completely disconnected from nation states and national government agencies. Nation-states or national government agencies remain important actors at various stages – during the process of rule making itself but also when it comes to legitimizing and enforcing the rules and arrangements that have been negotiated and agreed upon. This appears very clearly in all contributions in Part II.

Finally, while trying to document how various national components contribute to transnational institution building, chapters in Part II also point in the direction of reverse effects and impacts. Negotiated or emergent transnational rules can come to reverberate upon and challenge national institutions or rule systems in two ways. Transnational rules can become binding to the nation states associated with their production. They'll be implemented in a top-down manner, from transnational rule-making authorities to national government agencies that will then be in charge of national implementation. This, naturally, does not exclude the articulation of local or national opposition. Transnational rules can also become disseminated more indirectly through their institutionalization in specific industries, organizational fields or subsocietal spheres. We go back here, in a circular manner, to processes described in Part I. Both patterns or paths of reverberation are likely to generate, as chapters in Part II indicate or suggest, quite consequential transformations in national institutional frameworks or rule systems.

Working Towards a Synthesis: the Institutionalization of Global Governance

In the conclusion, we draw together the theoretical insights that emerge from the systematic comparison and confrontation of those empirical cases. We also go further in our specification of institutional change and institution building as two defining dimensions of contemporary globalization. Globalization, we propose, contributes in a very essential way to a significant redefinition of the institutional rules of the economic game.

This reinterpretation of globalization leads us to take up again the issue of the governance of globalization. We do not have to choose, we propose, between globalization and institutions. Globalization is about complementary processes of de-institutionalization and re-institutionalization. Globalization is in fact about governance and this volume is a step towards understanding precisely what type of governance.

NOTE

1. A striking illustration of that is provided by a speech of the French President, Jacques Chirac, on February 6, 2002 right after the World Economic Forum in New York and the World Social Forum in Porto Alegre: 'The desires and strivings of participants at Porto Alegre resonate with some of the fights our country and Europe have taken up for many years. We want a globalization – which does bring along freedom and growth – more closely associated

with solidarity and regulation, we want to build a worldwide governance system for global-ization that would be both efficient and democratic. In other words we want to humanize and control globalization.'

REFERENCES

Alexander, Jeffrey (1985), *Neo-functionalism*, Thousand Oaks, CA: Sage.

Autin, Jean (1983), *Les Frères Pereire*, Paris: Librairie Académique Perrin.

Bartlett, Christopher and Sumantra Goshal (1989), *Managing Across Borders: The Transnational Solution*, Boston, MA: Harvard Business School Press.

Berger, Suzanne (2002), 'La France et ses deux mondialisations', *Séminaire CONDOR*, February 7, Paris.

Berman Harold (1983), *Law and Revolution*, Cambridge, MA: Harvard University Press.

Bouvier, Jean (1992), *Les Rothschild*, Paris: Editions Complexe.

Braithwaite, John and Peter Drahos (2000), *Global Business Regulation*, Cambridge, UK: Cambridge University Press.

Brinton, Mary and Victor Nee (1998), *The New Institutionalism in Sociology*, Russell Sage Foundation.

Chernow, Ron (1990), *The House of Morgan*, New York: Atlantic Monthly.

Clemens, Elizabeth and James Cook (1999), 'Politics and institutionalism: explaining durability and change', *Annual Review of Sociology*, **25**, 441–66.

Cohen, Daniel (2002), 'La France et ses deux mondialisations', *Séminaire CONDOR*, February 7, Paris.

Dezalay, Yves and Brian Garth (1996), *Dealing in Virtue*, Chicago and London: The University of Chicago Press.

Djelic, Marie-Laure (1998), *Exporting the American Model*, Oxford: Oxford University Press.

Douglas, Mary (1991), *Wie Institutionen denken*, Frankfurt/Main: Suhrkamp.

Economy and Society (2000), *Special Issue on Shareholder Value*, **29** (1).

Fargette, Guy (2001), *Emile et Isaac Pereire*, Paris: L'Harmattan.

Fligstein, Neil (2001), *The Architecture of Markets*, Princeton, NJ: Princeton University Press.

Fligstein, Neil and Iona Mara-Drita (1996), 'How to make a market: reflections on the attempt to create a single market in the European Union', *American Journal of Sociology*, **102** (1), 1–33.

Ghoshal, Sumantra and Eleanor Westney (eds) (1993), *Organization Theory and the Multinational Corporation*, New York: Palgrave.

Giddens, Anthony (2000), *Runaway World*, New York: Routledge.

Granovetter, Mark (1985), 'Economic action and social structure: the problem of embed-dedness', *American Journal of Sociology*, **91**, 481–510.

Greif Avner (1992), 'Institutions and international trade: lessons from the commercial revolution', *The American Economic Review*, **82** (2), 128–33.

Guillén, Mauro (2001), 'Is globalization civilizing, destructive or feeble? A critique of five key debates in the social science literature', *Annual Review of Sociology*, **27**, 235–60.

Hirst, Paul and Grahame Thompson (1996), *Globalization in Question*, Cambridge, UK: Polity Press.

James, Harold (2001), *The End of Globalization: Lessons from the Great Depression*, Cambridge, MA: Harvard University Press.

Jepperson, Ronald (1991), 'Institutions, institutional effects, and Institutionalism', in Walter Powell and Paul DiMaggio (eds), *The New Institutionalism in Organizational Analysis*, Chicago: University of Chicago Press, pp. 143–63.

Kogut, Bruce (ed.) (1993), *Country Competitiveness*, Oxford: Oxford University Press.

Krugman, Paul, (1995), 'Globalization and the inequality of nations', working paper series no. 5098, Cambridge, MA: NBER.

Lane, Christel (2000), 'Understanding the globalization strategies of German and British multinational companies: is a "societal effects" approach still useful?' in Marc Maurice and Arndt Sorge (eds) (2000), *Embedding Organizations*, Amsterdam and Philadelphia: Benjamins, pp. 189–208.

McLuhan, Marshall (1968), *War and Peace in the Global Village*, New York: Bentam Books.

Morgan, Glenn, Peer Hull Kristensen and Richard Whitley (eds) (2001), *The Multinational Firm*, Oxford: Oxford University Press.

Murphy, Craig (1994), *International Organization and Industrial Change*, Cambridge: Polity Press.

O'Sullivan, Mary (2000), *Contests for Corporate Control*, Oxford: Oxford University Press.

Obstfeld, Maurice and Alan Taylor (1997), 'The Great Depression as a watershed: international capital mobility in the long run', working paper series, no. 5960, Cambridge, MA: NBER.

Ohmae, Kenichi (1990), *The Borderless Economy*, New York: Harper.

Ohmae, Kenichi (1995), *The End of the Nation State*, London: Harper Collins Publishers.

Parsons, Talcott (1949), *The Structure of Social Action*, Glencoe, IL: Free Press.

Parsons, Talcott (1951), *Toward a General Theory of Action*, Cambridge, MA: Harvard University Press.

Pilhon, Dominique and Jean-Pierre Ponsard (eds) (2002), *La Montée en Puissance des Fonds d'Investissement*, Paris: Documentation Française.

Polanyi, Karl (1944), *The Great Transformation*, Boston, MA: Beacon Press.

Sassen, Saskia (1998), *Globalization and its Discontents*, New York: The New Press.

Spruyt, Hendrik (1994), *The Sovereign State and its Competitors*, Princeton, NJ: Princeton University Press.

Tolbert, Pamela and Lynne Zucker (1996), 'The institutionalization of institutional theory', in Stewart Clegg, Cynthia Hardy and Walter Nord (eds), *Handbook of Organization Studies*, London: Sage, pp. 175–90.

Van der Pijl, Kees (1998), *Transnational Classes and International Relations*, London: Routledge.

Veblen, Thorstein (1904), *The Theory of Business Enterprise*, New York: C. Scribner's Sons.

Weber, Max (1978), *Economy and Society*, Berkeley, CA: University of California Press.

Wilkins, Mira (1989), *The History of Foreign Investment in the United States to 1914*, Cambridge, MA: Harvard University Press.

Williamson, Jeffrey (1996), 'Globalization, convergence, history', *Journal of Economic History*, **56** (2) (June), 277–306.

1. Theoretical building blocks for a research agenda linking globalization and institutions

Marie-Laure Djelic and Sigrid Quack

The objective of this chapter is double. First, we take stock of the ways in which the institutionalist literature deals with issues of institutional change and institutional emergence. Then, we try to show how the connection we make between globalization and institutions opens up new theoretical directions.

Under the label 'institutionalism' or 'institutional theory', one finds a rather heterogeneous body of literature originating from different disciplines and based on rather distinct ontological assumptions about human behaviour. Building upon Hall and Taylor (1996) and Djelic (2001) we identify three main and distinct perspectives on institutions that we label respectively 'rational choice', 'cultural' and 'historical'.

TOWARDS A TYPOLOGY OF INSTITUTIONAL ARGUMENTS

The 'rational choice' perspective is found predominantly amongst economists and political scientists – particularly for the latter group in the international relations literature. This perspective tends to focus on formal and structural political and economic institutions. The existence of institutions is accounted for in an essentially functionalist way – institutions are there because they solve problems for actors. Institutional order is seen as arising from negotiations between rational actors pursuing preferences or interests that will in a particular case be better served through coordinated and institutionalized action (Crouch and Streeck 1997). Self-interested actors make decisions and create institutions which they believe most efficient in a particular situation (North 1981; Williamson 1985). From this perspective, both the origins of those frames and action within them reflect a 'logic of expected consequences' (March and Olsen 1998).

'Cultural' and 'historical' perspectives have roots in classical and more particularly Weberian sociology (Weber 1978). In the cultural perspective,

Table 1.1   Towards a typology of institutional arguments

	'Rational choice' institutionalism	'Cultural' institutionalism	'Historical' institutionalism
Definition of institutions	Formal and structural economic and political frames	Wider cultural and symbolic patterns	Formal and structural political, legal, societal frames backed up by coercive mechanisms
Origins	Rational interest of actors, calculus	Long term evolution – external reality	Nationally-shaped path dependencies – external reality
Logic of action	Rational interest of actors, calculus	Appropriateness	Constraint

institutions are 'wider cultural and symbolic patterns', increasingly with a 'global' or transnational scope, that shape and to a large extent determine organizations, structures or actors and script behaviours and interactions (Scott, Meyer et al. 1994; Jepperson 2000a). Institutions, from this perspective, are not produced – they are external 'realities', they are givens and determining constraints to which actors, structures, organizations or even nation-states conform give or take a degree of decoupling (Meyer et al. 1997). In the long run, those institutions are on an evolutionary path leading towards greater rationalization and this the world over, naturally with standardizing and homogenizing effects (Scott, Meyer et al. 1994, pp. 2–4). The origins of this evolutionary path are to be found in cultural schemas provided by Christendom and in the structuration of the modern system of nation-states (Jepperson 2000b). From this type of perspective, action reflects normative patterns. The logic of 'action' can be described using March and Olsen's terms (1998) as a 'logic of appropriateness' – knowing, however, that 'action' here cannot be understood as 'free agency'.

From an historical perspective, institutions are frameworks essentially of a political, legal and societal nature. These frameworks are made up of organizations and formal rules and regulations often backed by coercive mechanisms and structures. This perspective insists on the particular significance of nation-states historically for the emergence and structuration of those frameworks. Those national institutional frameworks create powerful constraints at the national level and they lay out path dependencies that explain variations across countries in patterns of action, organization and interaction (Fligstein 1990; Whitley 1992, 1999; Hollingsworth and Boyer 1997; Hall and Soskice 2001). Those path dependencies also explain the robustness of national institutional frameworks – each of which is articulated in fact as a system (Whitley 1999; Maurice and Sorge 2000; Hall and Soskice 2001). From that perspective, the origins of institutional frames are external to actors for whom they essentially represent constraints and coercive mechanisms. And indeed action follows in that perspective what we call a 'logic of coercive constraint'.

Table 1.1 brings together in summary form and contrasts those three perspectives on institutions. For the purposes of this volume, we are moving towards our own type of institutional argument (see also Djelic 1998) that combines elements of all three perspectives and more particularly of the 'cultural' and 'historical' ones in an attempt at cross-fertilization (Djelic 2001).

DEFINITION OF INSTITUTIONS

In this volume, we use an umbrella definition of institutions as consisting of both structures and formal systems on the one hand and normative and cognitive frames on the other that altogether provide stability and meaning to social behaviour (Scott 1995, see also Djelic and Quack in the conclusion to this volume). These sets of institutions owe their survival to self-activating social processes of reproduction (Jepperson 1991). In our view, institutions have both a structural dimension, including formal and informal rules and systems and an ideational dimension, including normative and cognitive patterns. Whereas these two dimensions have always been treated and approached separately and by different streams of the institutional argument, we believe that in order to understand processes of institutional change and emergence both dimensions should be brought together and investigated simultaneously (see also Campbell 1998; Djelic 1998).

We also combine the 'culture' and 'historical' perspectives in a different manner. We acknowledge the need to take into consideration together and at the same time the two levels of analysis that characterize each of these perspectives – 'global' or transnational for the cultural perspective and national for the historical one. As we will see below, one way to reconcile institutional arguments with issues of change and emergence is precisely to look at the interplay and interface between these two spheres or levels of analysis.

Another way in which to bring in issues of change and emergence is to take some distance from descriptions of institutions as constraining or even determining behaviours – which is predominantly what institutional analyses do both in the cultural and in the historical stream. We need to think also of the enabling functions of institutions. It is necessary to investigate, in other words the ways in which actors creatively recombine and extend the institutional principles at their disposal to devise new institutional solutions to their problems (Sewell 1992; Campbell 1997; Clemens and Cook 1999; Caspar 2000, Kristensen 2000; Lane 2001; Sharpe 2001). It is necessary in other words to think of the conditions for 'institutional entrepreneurship' (Fligstein and Mara-Drita 1996). Actors, here, are not the 'free agents' of the rational choice perspective but neither are they merely an aggregation of cultural scripts as suggested in the cultural perspective. We will show below that such recombination is much more likely in situations where different institutional frames enter into collision. One place, undeniably, where such collision is significant today is at the interface between national and transnational spheres.

In the following, we look more systematically into the treatment of change and emergence in the institutionalist literature. This naturally comes together with the correlative issues of institutional persistence and its conditions. We point, in the process, to the main building blocks of our own theoretical framework underscoring the ways in which it differs from existing perspectives.

INSTITUTIONAL CHANGE AND PERSISTENCE

A core insight behind institutional theory is that the patterning of social life is not produced solely by the aggregation of individual and organizational behaviours but also by institutions that structure actions through regulative instruments as well as normative and cognitive frames. Institutions and social action are thus seen as being inextricably linked and as reciprocally and mutually constituting each other. Institutional accounts, particularly those fitting under the label 'historical' used above, have tended to emphasize the stability and durability of institutions. These accounts are based on an understanding of institutional arrangements where the latter are internally coherent and externally fitted. They tend to focus, furthermore, on the constraining or even determining effects of institutions on social behaviour rather than on potential converse and reciprocal effects.

Conditions of Institutional Persistence

There are two main ways in which institutions can constrain social behaviour – either through external control and sanctioning or through persuasion, voluntary appropriation or socialization. Those institutional arguments that centre on states – their structures and constituent organizations – hence 'historical' institutionalism in our typology, tend to underscore the importance of control and sanctioning processes. In those arguments, the nation-state or state agencies have the capacity to establish rules, monitor conformity and exert sanctions if necessary. The power to sanction and control, however, does not have to be restricted to the nation-state and its agencies. Other societal bodies such as private firms and agencies or non-governmental organizations can exert authority based on their control over or access to resources and this may even extend beyond the borders of a particular nation-state with the potential risk of conflicting with or even undermining state authority (Strange 1996).

A second way in which institutions constrain behaviour is through processes of persuasion that operate in the absence of formal and centralized sanctioning authorities. These processes reflect essentially normative and cognitive logics and we identified 'culture' institutionalists as focusing more particularly on these types of logics. Norms and values become appropriated and internalized by individuals, groups or organizations, which motivates them to respect and defend the status quo even in the absence of controls or sanctions. Educational and professional organizations are good examples of societal bodies relying on these types of logics to ensure homogeneity and stabilization of behaviours.

Naturally, in situations where diffused rule setting is effected apparently through persuasion, it is much more difficult to identify and/or recognize power and power relations. It seems reasonable, nevertheless, to differentiate between those situations where a number of actors have privileged access to some resources that allow them to promote and push their own normative and cognitive frames and those situations where actors have more equal access to resources and get to develop collectively shared understandings and frames out of mutual interaction and dialogue.

The constraining power and dimension of institutions can explain their persistence and robustness over time. The motives of social actors to support existing institutions and oppose change can reflect the articulation of two complementary rational logics – the fear of sanctions for subordinates and the desire to defend vested interests for dominant groups. These motives can also reveal successful socialization and internalization that led actors to believe that existing institutions are the best, the only or the most efficient solutions.

We propose that the stability, robustness and self-reproducing character of institutions will be all the more pronounced that regulative pressures and systems of control combine with normative and cognitive frames and reinforce each other. Legal institutions, for example, would hardly be as effective if they were not strengthened by actors' internalized beliefs of what is 'right' and 'wrong', of what is 'honesty' and 'fraud', and so on. The view that institutions articulate into systems – particularly at the national level – naturally makes stability and robustness even more likely. The homogeneity and coherence of the whole is assumed to have an impact on the preservation and reproduction of the parts (Burns and Flam 1987; Jepperson 1991; Whitley 1999; Maurice and Sorge 2000; Hall and Soskice 2001).

The Nature of Institutional Change

The extreme picture of a self-stabilizing, self-reproducing and tightly fitted system of constraints, characteristic in particular of historical institutionalism, leaves little place in this form to the idea of institutional system change or to the consideration of institutional emergence.

With respect to change of institutional systems, particularly those institutional systems of a national scope, institutionalist perspectives have tended to do one of three things. A number of these perspectives have de-emphasized change, pointing at the most to small, progressive or non-consequential steps. This has particularly been the case for the historical stream of institutional arguments. Instead of change, these perspectives have underscored the enduring stability and resilience of national institutional frameworks or systems even in the face of significant pressure for change, as stemming for example from processes of internationalization (D'Iribarne 1989; Whitley 1999; Maurice and Sorge 2000; Zeitlin and Herrigel 2000; Hall and Soskice 2001). Some of the resilience of national institutional systems has been related to what can be called their inherent 'flexibility for stability'. These are mechanisms and properties which enable societal systems to adapt and readjust to changes in their environment without breaking with the overall system logic (Burns and Flam 1987; Offe 1995; Pempel 1998; Quack and Morgan 2000).

Alternatively, some institutional arguments have acknowledged the possibility of a transformation of national institutional frameworks but essentially as a dramatic and rupture-like process, often implying a major crisis (Westney 1987; Djelic 1998). This suggests a picture of punctuated equilibria – a Kuhnian-type succession between periods of stability and moments of paradigm shift (Kuhn 1996; Krasner 1984).

A third approach has pointed to a long-term evolutionary process whereby a world-society carrying standardized and rationalized cultural and normative patterns was building up. In time, national institutional systems were coming to reflect those patterns becoming in the process increasingly homogeneous (Meyer et al. 1997; Jepperson 2000a). This has defined the cultural stream of institutional arguments. Beyond the evolutionary trajectory, there is little specification in that approach of the concrete ways in which this world-society institutional frame is building up and being structured, or of the concrete mechanisms through which it is reverbating and translating into institutional system change at the national level.

From our perspective, a dichotomous opposition in the form of extreme alternative between radical and incremental change is not satisfying. Rupture-like change processes are assumed to have the potential to effect a radical transformation of the core institutional order of a society such 'that we can speak of a change in type of society' (Lockwood 1964, p. 244). Incremental institutional change, in contrast, is expected to be path dependent and rarely consequential by definition. Indeed, preexisting institutions constrain the ways in which actors perceive and choose alternative solutions when earlier arrangements become challenged and, as a consequence, the core institutional order of society remains in place, unchanged or, at the most, only slightly modified (North 1990; Campbell et al. 1991; Whitley and Kristensen 1997; Whitley 1999; Maurice and Sorge 2000; Hall and Soskice 2001).

In fact, even in situations of rupture-like change, quite a number of institutional principles will carry over from one period to the next. Campbell (1997, p. 28), for example, concludes from his collaborative work on institutional transformation in Central and Eastern Europe that dichotomies 'such as these convey the impression that fundamental institutional change is a discontinuous process when even ostensibly revolutionary changes often embody significant evolutionary qualities'.

On the other hand, incremental models of change may be largely overestimating the continuity of institutional arrangements over the long run. In this book we suggest that, in certain circumstances, incremental change may be highly consequential – we call that the 'stalactite' model of change (for more see Djelic and Quack in the conclusion to this volume). This type of change may lead in time and progressively to a profound and qualitative transformation of the core institutional order or at least of some of its key dimensions. Our 'stalactite' model of change is one where change is seen as both incremental and consequential – where change is in fact the aggregation and crystallization through time of a multiplicity of smaller processes of transformation. We position this 'stalactite' model of change as complementing rather than displacing other perspectives.

Loci and Triggers of Institutional Change

According to Tolbert and Zucker (1996) the emergence of institutions is a process in three stages. First, actors develop through recurrent and regular interactions patterned reactions to problems to which shared meanings and understandings become attached (see also Berger and Luckmann 1967). This is in fact a pre-institutionalization stage.

Then these particular meanings and understandings become generalized beyond the specific context in which they crystallized. This second stage can be called the objectification stage and goes together with the stabilization of a consensus among social actors about the value of the behavioural patterns and of their associated meanings and understandings. This consensus can translate into preliminary structures and rules that on the whole remain fragile at this semi-institutionalized stage and can still be revised or challenged.

The third and last stage of institutionalization is what Tolbert and Zucker (1996) call 'sedimentation'. It is characterized both by an even wider spread of patterned behaviours and meanings and by the solidification and perpetuation of structures. It is during this last stage that institutions can potentially acquire the 'quality of exteriority', that is, become taken for granted and develop a reality of their own.

The logical sequencing goes from habitualization to sedimentation. However, it is possible in a number of situations to skip the first stage – the habitualization stage. The diffusion of institutional rules preexisting in a different context represents such a short cut with a direct move into the objectification stage (Tolbert and Zucker 1996). Following DiMaggio and Powell (1983), there are three main channels for such a process of diffusion – the coercive, the mimetic and the normative. All three types of channels may be operative simultaneously thus reinforcing each other. They may also alternate or follow each other – the coercive channel being supported over time or even replaced by mimetic and normative ones (Djelic 1998).

Moving from institutions to institutionalization and thinking about the latter as a set of sequential stages – habitualization, objectification and sedimentation – suggests that the level of embeddedness and robustness of institutional rules will vary. Certain patterns of social behaviour – those that are semi-institutionalized or still at stage one or two – will be more likely to become subject to critical evaluation, modification and elimination than others – those that are fully institutionalized. Or as Jepperson (1991) puts it, degrees of institutionalization are best conceived in terms of relative vulnerability to social intervention.

Within a given society, varying patterns of behaviours will coexist that situate themselves at different stages of institutionalization. Instead of considering the systemic nature of institutional arrangements, we should take in this internal diversity and differentiation and the contradictions that it may generate (Sewell 1992; Clemens and Cook 1999). We should also look at border points or points of interface through which, we have suggested, alternatives may appear. In this volume, we focus in particular on those points of interface that put in contact the national and the transnational. Together, those are the cracks in the system – or at its boundaries – that are likely to make it more vulnerable. Those cracks or weaker points indicate the more obvious potential loci for change. We argue that external pressures can act as triggers. Major shifts in the environment, such as long-lasting alterations in markets or radical changes in technology may play a role. Internationalization, we add, is also in itself a source of pressure (see also Westney 1987; Campbell 1993; Djelic 1998; Boyer et al. 1998; Lane 2001). Our claim in this volume is that we should combine a focus on internal loci of disruptions and opportunities with an argument on external triggers of change. We point to institutional change as emerging where and when internal challenges and spaces of opportunity combine with and are being reinforced by external triggers and alternatives. Globalization is in part about the multiplication of configurations of that type.

Agents of Change: Foreign versus Domestic, Dominant versus Fringe Players

The understanding of institutions presented here as not only constraining but also enabling points to the role and significance of actors, sometimes characterized by the labels 'strategizing actors' or 'institutional entrepreneurs'. Institutional change comes about when certain groups or networks of actors develop new patterns of interaction, from scratch or through bricolage, when certain groups or networks seize upon patterns existing elsewhere and promote them as superior to existing arrangements, working to mobilize as large and significant a support as possible for that project.

The challenge to institutionalized rule systems can best be understood, we argue, when we have a clear picture of the impact different actors can have. From the perspective we develop here that the national/transnational interface is important to understand changes in national rules of the game, we differentiate between dominant and fringe actors but also between foreign and domestic actors. The following categorization, summarized in Table 1.2, is schematic and should be taken as identifying ideal types rather than as real life description.

Table 1.2   Actors of change – foreign or domestic, dominant or fringe

	Domestic	Foreign
Dominant	Resistant/Driving force	Missionaries
Fringe	Activists/Agitators	Absent

Dominant actors are those who hold a central position in terms of power and social status, based on privileged access to resources. Dominant foreign players will have the strength and resources to push along their own rules of the game well beyond their traditional boundaries of activity. They can become 'missionaries' of institutional change. Dominant local players will tend to do one of two things – either to resist change or else be its driving force.

In periods of relative stability, they will tend to resist institutional change. Dominant local players are likely then to have vested interests in existing institutions. Their perception of the world also has a tendency to remain structured by just these institutions. In periods of crisis, radical rupture or acute challenge, dominant local actors can turn however into active promoters of institutional change and in fact become its main driving force. The case of Nokia in Finland perfectly illustrates that (Tainio et al. in this volume). Other examples can be found in the Eastern part of the European continent.

One should add here the particular case of the transnational firm where a dominant actor is neither fully domestic nor entirely foreign but somewhere in between. There will be a tendency for these types of actors to be unsatisfied with the preexisting institutional conditions characteristic of their country of origin. These actors will then possibly turn into active promoters of institutional change – the case of Nokia once again illustrates that but one thinks also of Vivendi in France or Daimler Benz in Germany. Another possible reaction will be for those hybrid, a-national actors to flee their country of origin and set up their headquarters elsewhere – Swedish multinationals have tended to follow that path.

On the other side, one finds fringe players. Fringe players are located at the periphery of a particular institutionalized area. They tend to have little power, low social status and limited access to resources. Fringe players from foreign contexts will tend on the whole to be absent from the local scene. For the most part, local fringe players will also be relatively powerless and passive. The few that may take the initiative, however, may be quite innovative. In relatively stable periods, local fringe players can have more incentives than dominant players to experiment with new solutions since such experiments are less costly to them in terms of reputation. They are also less likely to be sanctioned by central players for violating rule systems, and if successful they will gain increased power and social status from institutional change. Fringe players have been identified as critical actors for developing alternative practices at the micro level which were in contradiction with existing institutions at the macro level. Leblebici et al. (1991) show how fringe players changed the governance structure of an inter-organizational field such as the US broadcasting industry (see also Jones 2002). Stearns and Allan (1996) refer to fringe players as successful challengers of existing practices in inter-firm coordination in the US whose innovation then became legitimized and institutionalized, through adoption and adaptation by dominant players, as a market for mergers and acquisitions.

Fringe players can challenge existing arrangements either at the level of discourse or at the level of practice – a combination of both being in fact quite likely. This challenge could remain localized and lead nowhere. In certain circumstances, it could also come to arouse wide support and it could possibly become appropriated, adopted and adapted, by dominant players. The new solution will thus be advocated as superior until it becomes taken for granted. Institutional innovation through fringe actors is therefore more likely to take the bottom-up road and to operate through mimetic and normative pressures since these actors usually do not have the means to institutionalize their solutions through coercion and sanction from above.

In the context of globalization, we see another path as being particularly operational. This is the direct or indirect alliance between foreign dominant actors pushing their own rules of the game and a few local fringe players that find an interest in sponsoring those alternative rules (all contributions in Part I, see also Djelic 1998; Djelic and Ainamo 1999). This kind of alliance appears to take the champions and partisans of status quo and stability through a pincer movement.

INSTITUTION BUILDING IN THE TRANSNATIONAL SPACE

A central claim of this volume, we have seen, is that the transnational level is one important purveyor in today's world of alternative rule systems that may contribute to the transformation of subsocietal or societal institutional arrangements. Those alternatives may themselves be rules that are dominant in foreign subsocietal or societal institutional spheres. They may also be, and this is we believe another major claim of this volume, rule systems in the making with a transnational scope or dimension. This process of structuration of a space traditionally conceived as anomic translates into institution building and institutional emergence at the transnational level. It is a marker and defining characteristic, we propose, of the recent episode of globalization.

Institutional Emergence – the Transnational Dimension

Even though there may have been cases, historically, when actors created social institutions from scratch and in a 'vacuum', the genesis of institutions in contemporary societies unfolds in general in a form that is closer to 'bricolage' than to ex nihilo generation (Offe 1995; Hall and Taylor 1996; March and Olsen 1998). Actors build upon, work around, combine, reinvent and reinterpret logics and institutional arrangements that either function elsewhere or with which they are familiar. This goes, we propose here, for institution building in the transnational space.

Within the context of nation-states, the creation of new institutions is likely to be influenced by the existing institutional environment. Interests and identities of social actors that engage in institution building, coalitions and conflicts between groups with similar and competing interests as well as the cognitive templates that actors use are shaped by the preexisting sets of institutional arrangements in which those groups of actors inscribe themselves. The state, in the form of political actors or agencies, does play a particularly significant role in that process of institution building at the societal level (Clemens and Cook 1999) but this should not blind us to the impact and significance of other actors.

A lot of these features translate, we argue, at the transnational level. Institution building in the transnational sphere brings in a multiplicity of actors or groups of actors. The interests and identities of those actors, their characteristic patterns for entering conflicts and coalitions as well as the cognitive templates that define them, reflect to a great extent the preexisting institutional arrangements in which they set themselves. Very often, those have a societal or national character (Morgan 2001a, b). Hence a number of national actors extend their national contextual rationalities into the international sphere and through their repeated interactions they become involved in institution building in a newly emerging transnational sphere (see for examples McNichol and Bensedrine or Ventresca et al. in this volume). Or they may become involved in reforming, renegotiating and changing existing international institutional arrangements as motivations, power relations and conditions change over time (see Lilja and Moen or Lehmkuhl in this volume).

Through time, repeated interactions and the building up of a transnational frame, actors are emerging that have transnational – in the sense of not purely national – identity and sense of selves. Hence the interplay between well known national structures and logics and more emergent transnational patterns and rationalities is a key direction for institutional analysis. This is a path on which we engage in this volume.

The Missing Links – Institutionalization as a Process in the Transnational Space

We have proposed above to talk about institutionalization as a process rather than about institutions. And building upon the work of Tolbert and Zucker (1996) we have differentiated between three moments – that fit in fact on a continuum and are not discrete or separate stages. This differentiation between moments of habitualization, objectification and sedimentation is particularly valuable, we believe, for looking at institution building in the transnational space. And a focus on institutionalization as a process rather than on institutional systems also makes particular sense when looking at the transnational space.

Such a perspective makes it possible to overcome the limits and shortcomings that are characteristic of existing debates. A first and quite significant advantage is that this perspective makes it possible to navigate between the Charybdis of under-determination and the Scylla of over-determination. The literature on and around the transnational arena has tended to cluster at two extremes.

On the one hand, the mainstream of the International Relations (IR) tradition pictures the transnational space as essentially anomic – a shapeless and structureless arena. Agents are essentially free and rational, maximizing their own interests with little burden being put on them by the space in which their action takes place. Krasner (1999, p. 72), for example, his recent book on sovereignty still questions the impact of institutions in the international sphere and argues that in this sphere a logic of consequence usually will prevail over a logic of appropriateness (see also Gilpin 2000). Other writers, such as Ruggie (1993, 1998), have given more weight to international organizations and drawn a more complex picture of the interdependencies between domestic and international power structures. Heterodox writers within the IR tradition go even further by directing attention to the structuration of social networks across borders. Neo-Gramscian scholars, in particular, focus on processes of transnational class formation and the emergence of 'historical blocks' of public and private authorities (Cox 1983, 1987). Transnational social networks are regarded as central mechanisms through which ideologies and worldviews – and hence structures and institutions – enter in conflict and contradiction and hegemonies come and go (van der Pijl 1984, 1998).

On the other hand, cultural neoinstitutionalism – the one strand of institutional theory taking the transnational space seriously – has underscored the thickness and highly determining nature of the transnational institutional system. The transnational space is made up of a dense web of cultural rules and patterns, symbolic constraints that shape and determine organizations and structures but also social action and actors themselves. 'What actors do', in the words of key proponents of this theoretical perspective, 'is inherent in the social definition of the actor himself. The particular types of actors perceived by self and others and the specific forms their activity takes reflect institutionalized rules of great generality and scope' (Meyer et al. 1994, p. 18).

This volume will point to a path somewhere in between – where the web of institutional constraints is multilayered and in the making, malleable and changing. Actors are neither free, independent or discrete, nor fully and only rational in the classical sense. The idea of social networks is useful but what emerges once again is the multiplicity and multidirectionality of those networks as well as their undeniable embeddedness in multiple and more or less over-lapping institutional frames.

Our perspective in this volume and our take in particular on institutional-ization allows us to avoid another simplistic and extreme alternative. This alternative has to do with the type of 'rationality' that can be found within the transnational space. The clear opposition here is between the idea of a universal or global rationality – neutral and theoretical that would point in fact to something like the 'end of history' or to the 'best of all possible worlds' – and the conviction on the other hand that rationalities are plural and that when they express themselves in the transnational space they tend to reflect in fact national embedding institutional systems. National systems do emerge as important in shaping actors and organizations' rationalities, however we do not rule out the possibility for the emergence of transnational bases of rationalities, in the process of transnational institution building.

A number of heterodox writers situated between the two extremes of tradi-tional International Relations and cultural neoinstitutionalism have identified elements of such processes of transnational institution building which can be integrated in our research agenda. What these authors find is an increasing blurring of border lines between political and private authority in the trans-national sphere and increasingly overlapping 'spheres of authority' (Rosenau 1997) and 'webs of influence' (Braithwaite and Drahos 2000). These emerging transnational arenas of institution building are populated by increasingly multiple and heterogeneous groups of agents, ranging from multinational companies and other private corporate actors (Stopford and Strange 1991; Strange 1996; Cutler et al. 1999) over representatives of social movements (Held et al. 1999; Boli and Thomas 1999; O'Brien et al. 2000) to the national political actors which prevail in traditional IR theory (for a critical review of the role of the latter actors in the project of building a European Union see Sandholtz and Stone Sweet 1998).

Finally, the perspective we propose makes it possible to avoid falling in the evolutionary trap. Institution building is not a simple and linear process. And this may be particularly true in the transnational space. The continuum of the three moments – habitualization, objectification and sedimentation – is analyti-cally useful but only if it is not used and understood at face value. The fact that we can differentiate between those three moments does not (indeed, far from it) say that those three moments necessarily follow each other in a linear and systematic manner in real life. Nor does it say that there is an evolutionary and unavoidable path going from pre-institutionalization or habitualization to the full stabilization of institutional rules of the game. On the contrary, those three categories can allow us to think of circular paths, ruptures and discontinuities. Institution building in the transnational space proceeds at varied pace according to the 'layer' that we look at. Such institution building remains highly fragile, particularly during the first two moments, which makes ruptures, discontinuities or even backlashes highly possible. The kaleidoscopic or multilayered nature of the institution building process in the transnational space also makes it possible and even likely that there will be shortcuts. Rather than starting from scratch and the progressive aggregation of and negotiation between behaviours, institution building in a particular layer can get inspiration from rules of the game and institutional patterns already stabilized in a neighbouring layer.

TRICKLE-UP AND TRICKLE-DOWN TRAJECTORIES – BRIDGING LEVELS OF ANALYSIS

We have argued above that processes of de-institutionalization and re-institutionalization are particularly likely to emerge at the interface of national and transnational rule systems. We have made suggestions of how we could use this interface as a starting point for our exploration into globalization as a process of institution building and institutional change, particularly looking at the confrontation between different national actors and between foreign and domestic, dominant and fringe players. But under which conditions do changes in actors' rule systems at the micro or subsocietal level become relevant for other arenas and for higher order rules at the societal or even transnational level? And in which circumstances do changes in macro level rules – at the transnational or national level – diffuse to the micro level and become relevant for the behaviour of individual economic actors?

Some of the debates and disagreements around the likelihood and degree of institutional emergence and change in relation to globalization can be explained by the fact that scholars place themselves at different levels of analysis without attempting to create a link. Whereas many studies of institutional change and institutional evolution are situated either at the organizational field level or at the transnational level, work that highlights stability and durability of institutions is predominantly focused on the nation-state level (Knill and Lenschow 2000). In order to reconcile change with stability, we need a better understanding of how those different levels of institutionalization are linked together. We need to investigate the processes through which institutional change in particular subsocietal systems contributes to the transformation of higher level institutional orders – both at the national and transnational level – and vice versa.

With regard to institutional change within national societal spaces, two types of processes are important here. First, transnational institution building can effect upon national institutional systems directly, in a top-down way, leading dominant actors to redefine national regulations or other forms of institution-

alized patterns of economic organization. The passing of a new European legislation relating to transport, for example, forced national governments, business
corporations and trade associations within the different European member states
to redefine their national rule systems and patterns of cooperation (see Plehwe
with Vescovi in this volume). Secondly, transnational institution building can
also have an indirect impact on national institutional systems if actors at the
subsocietal level start to introduce new and challenging rules of the game.
Cumulative changes of that type eventually lead to ambiguities and uncertainties that initiate bottom-up processes of change resulting in redefinitions of
higher level rules and principles. Examples are initially 'minor' changes in the
rules governing the French asset management industry (Kleiner in this volume)
or in foreign investment in Finnish corporations (Tainio et al. in this volume)
which in fact and together with other minor changes became a source of pressure
on the wider national systems of corporate governance and elite production and
reproduction.

These two forms of institutional change are what we will refer to as trickle-
down and trickle-up trajectories in the conclusion to this volume. Building on
the empirical contributions that make up this volume, we will propose in this
last chapter a more analytic and systematic description of those mechanisms
linking changes in the international business environment to different forms of
institutional change in national societal spaces. The focus here will be clearly
on transnational institution building as a trigger for national institutional change.

In turn, when analysing institution building in the transnational sphere, the
national origins and components of this process should not be lost from sight.
From this perspective, transnational institution building can be analysed as
processes of reinterpretation, recombination and bricolage of institutional
fragments from different contextual origins. We suggest that there are basically
three different modes in which the rubbing, contestation and combination of
different institutional fragments can take place at the transnational level.

In the dominant mode, the building of institutions at the transnational level
simply reflects one dominant local or national model. This is illustrated by the
diffusion of American economic rules of the game such as the logic of 'shareholder value' through international financial market actors to other countries
(see Tainio et al., Kleiner and McKenna et al. in this volume).

A second mode of transnational institution building is negotiation. In this
case, institution building in the transnational sphere comes about as the result
of confrontation, debate and bargaining between actors coming from different
national rule systems. Examples are the negotiation of unified legal frameworks
for specific sectors of economic activity within the European Union (see Plehwe
with Vescovi and Midttun et al. in this volume) or the bargaining between the
USA and the European Union leading to a multilateral agreement on labelling
of genetically modified soy (see McNichol and Bensedrine in this volume).

A third form of transnational institution building is the emergent mode. It tends to involve actors with less clear and often more transnational identities. It tends to take place at the borders of multiple rule systems and to be of a high complexity which makes outcomes rather unpredictable. These three modes will be, based on the empirical chapters of this volume, described in a more systematic manner in the conclusion.

Overall, we suggest that in order to understand the complexities involved in the link between globalization and institutions we should investigate more closely the interplay between transnational institution building and changes in national institutional systems. The interactions between these two types of processes over time can create a reinforcing cycle of institutional change and transnational institution building. With such an understanding of globalization, a lot of work still remains to be done. The contributions in this book represent attempts to study globalization from the conceptual viewpoint outlined above. They attempt to capture parts of the overall interplay between globalization as institutional change at the national level and globalization as institution building in the transnational sphere. They do this by focusing on specific sectors, countries, points and periods in time. Whereas contributions in Part I analyse how globalization has become a trigger for institutional change within the national space, contributions in Part II analyse processes of institutionalization in the transnational sphere. Taken together, the contributions to this volume provide rich evidence for the repeated, and often mutually reinforcing, interactions between institutional change at the national and institution building at the transnational level.

REFERENCES

Berger, Peter and Thomas Luckmann (1967), *The Social Construction of Reality*, New York: Doubleday.

Boli, John and George M. Thomas (eds) (1999), *Constructing World Culture. International Nongovernmental Organizations Since 1875*, Stanford, CA: Standford University Press.

Boyer, Robert, Elsie Charron, Ulrich Jürgens und Steven Tolliday (eds) (1998), *Between Imitation and Innovation*, Oxford, UK: Oxford University Press.

Braithwaite, John and Peter Drahos (2000), *Global Business Regulation*, Cambridge, UK: Cambridge University Press.

Burns, Tom and Helena Flam (1987), *The Shaping of Social Organization*, London: Sage.

Campbell, John (1993), 'Institutional theory and the influence of foreign actors on reform in capitalist and post-socialist societies', in Jerzy Hausner, Bob Jessop and Klaus Nielsen (eds), *Institutional Frameworks of Market Economies*, Aldershot: Avebury, pp. 45–67.

Campbell, John (1997), 'Mechanisms of evolutionary change in economic governance: interaction, interpretation and bricolage', in Lars Magnusson and Jan Ottosson (eds),

Evolutionary Economics and Path Dependence, Cheltenham: Edward Elgar, pp. 10–32.

Campbell, John (1998), 'Institutional analysis and the role of ideas in political economy', *Theory and Society*, **27**, 377–409.

Campbell, John, Leon Lindberg and Roger Hollingsworth (eds) (1991), *Governance of the American Economy*, New York: Cambridge University Press.

Casper, Steven (2000), 'Institutional adaptiveness, technology policy, and the diffusion of new business models: the case of German biotechnology', *Organization Studies*, **5**, 887–914.

Clemens, Elizabeth and James Cook (1999), 'Politics and institutionalism: explaining durability and change', *Annual Review of Sociology*, **25**, 441–66.

Cox, Robert (1983), 'Gramsci, hegemony and international relations: an essay in method', *Millenium Journal of International Studies*, **12** (2), 162–75.

Cox, Robert (1987), *Production, Power and World Order*, New York: Columbia University Press.

Crouch, Colin and Wolfgang Streeck (eds) (1997), *Political Economy of Modern Capitalism*, London: Sage.

Cutler, A. Claire, Victoria Haufler and Tony Porter (eds) (1999), *Private Authority in International Affaires*, New York: State University of New York Press.

D'Iribane, Philippe (1989), *La Logique de l'Honneur*, Paris: Editions du Seuil.

DiMaggio, Paul and Walter Powell (1983), 'The iron cage revisited: institutionalized isomorphism and collective rationality in organizational fields', *American Sociological Review*, **48**, 147–60.

Djelic, Marie-Laure (1998), *Exporting the American Model*, Oxford: Oxford University Press.

Djelic, Marie-Laure (2001), 'From a typology of neo-institutional arguments to their cross-fertilization', research document, Paris: ESSEC Business School.

Djelic, Marie-Laure and Antti Ainamo (1999), 'The coevolution of new organizational forms in the fashion industry: a historical and comparative study of France, Italy and the United States', *Organization Science*, **10** (5), 622–37.

Fligstein, Neil (1990), *The Transformation of Corporate Control*, Cambridge, MA: Harvard University Press

Fligstein, Neil and Iona Mara-Drita (1996), 'How to make a market: reflections on the attempt to create a single market in the European Union', *American Journal of Sociology*, **102** (1), 1–33.

Gilpin, Robert with Jean Millis Gilpin (2000), *The Challenge of Global Capitalism. The World Economy in the 21st Century*, Princeton: Princeton University Press.

Hall, Peter and David Soskice (eds) (2001), *Varieties of Capitalism*, Oxford: Oxford University Press.

Hall, Peter and Rosemary Taylor (1996), 'Political science and the three new institutionalisms', *Political Studies*, **XLIV**, 936–57.

Held, David, Anthony McGrew, David Goldblatt and Jonathan Perraton (1999), *Global Transformations*, Stanford, CA: Stanford University Press,

Hollingsworth, Rogers and Robert Boyer (eds) (1997), *Contemporary Capitalism*, Cambridge, UK: Cambridge University Press.

Jepperson, Ronald (1991), 'Institutions, institutional effects, and institutionalism', in Walter Powell and Paul DiMaggio (eds), *The New Institutionalism in Organizational Analysis*, Chicago: University of Chicago Press, pp. 143–63.

Jepperson, Ronald (2000a), 'The development and application of sociological neoinstitutionalism', working paper series, Florence, Italy: European University Institute.

Jepperson, Ronald (2000b), 'Political modernities: four main variants of the modern polity', working paper, Tulsa, OK: Tulsa University.

Jones, Candace (2002), 'Co-evolution of entrepreneurial careers, institutional rules and competitive dynamics in American film, 1895–1920', *Organization Studies*, **22** (6), 911–44.

Knill, Christoph and Andrea Lenschow (2000), '"Seek and ye shall find!" linking different perspectives on institutional change', preprints of the Max-Planck-project team 'Recht der Gemeinschaftsgüter', Bonn, 2000/6. Forthcoming in: *Comparative Political Studies*, **41** (2).

Krasner, Stephen D. (1984), 'Approaches to the state: alternative conceptions and historical dynamics', *Comparative Politics*, **16** (2), 223–46.

Krasner, Stephen D. (1999), *Sovereignty. Organized Hypocrisy*, Princeton: Princeton University Press.

Kristensen, Peer Hull (2000), 'Unbundling battles over bounded rationalities', keynote speech at the 16th EGOS Colloquium, Helsinki.

Kuhn, Thomas (1996), *The Structure of Scientific Revolutions*, Chicago, IL: University of Chicago Press.

Lane, Christel (2001), 'The emergence of German transnational companies: A theoretical analysis and empirical study of the globalization process', in Morgan, Glenn, Peer Hull Kristensen and Richard Whitley (eds) (2001), *The Multinational Firm*, Oxford: Oxford University Press, pp. 69–96.

Leblebici, Huseyin, Gerald Salancik, Anne Copay and Tom King (1991), 'Institutional change and the transformation of interorganizational fields: an organizational history of the U.S. radio broadcasting industry', *Administrative Science Quarterly*, **36**, 333–63.

Lockwood, David (1964), 'Social integration and system integration', in G.K. Zollschau and H.W. Hirsch (eds), *Explorations in Social Change*, Boston: Houghton Mifflin, pp. 244–57.

March, James and Johann Olsen (1998), 'The institutional dynamics of international political orders', *International Organization*, **52** (4): 943–69.

Maurice, Marc and Arndt Sorge (eds) (2000), *Embedding Organizations*, Amsterdam and Philadelphia: Benjamins.

Meyer, John, John Boli, George Thomas and Francisco Ramirez (1997), 'World society and the nation-state', *American Journal of Sociology*, **103** (1), 144–181.

Morgan, Glenn (2001a), 'Transnational communities and business systems', *Global Networks: a Journal of Transnational Affairs*, **1** (2), 113–30.

Morgan, Glenn (2001b), 'The development of transnational standards and regulations and their impacts on firms', in Glenn Morgan, Peer Hull Kristensen and Richard Whitley (eds), *The Multinational Firm. Organizing Across Institutional and National Divides*, Oxford: Oxford University Press, pp. 225–52.

North, Douglas C. (1981), *Structure and Change in Economic History*, New York: Norton.

North, Douglas C. (1990), *Institutions, Institutional Change and Economic Performance*, Cambridge: Cambridge University Press.

O'Brien, Robert, Anne Marie Goetz, Jan Aart Scholte and Marc Williams (2000), *Contesting Global Governance. Multilateral Economic Institutions and Global Social Movements*, Cambridge: Cambridge University Press.

Offe, Claus (1995), 'Designing institutions for East European transition', in Jerzy Hausner, Bob Jessop and Klaus Nielsen (eds), *Strategic Choice and Path-dependency in Post Socialism*, Aldershot: Edward Elgar, pp. 47–66.

Pempel, T.J. (1998), *Regime Shift*, Ithaca and London: Cornell University Press.

Quack, Sigrid and Glenn Morgan (2000), 'National capitalism, global competition and economic performance. An introduction', in Sigrid Quack, Glenn Morgan and Richard Whitley (eds), *National Capitalism, Global Competition and Economic Performance*, Amsterdam/Philadelphia: Benjamins, pp. 3–24.

Rosenau, James N. (1997), *Along the Domestic–Foreign Frontier*, Cambridge: Cambridge University Press.

Ruggie, John Gerard (ed.) (1993), *Multilaterism Matters. The Theory and Praxis of an Institutional Form*, New York: Columbia University Press.

Ruggie, John Gerard (1998), *Constructing the World Polity. Essays on International Institutionalization*, London and New York: Routledge.

Sandholtz, Wayne and Alec Stone Sweet (eds) (1998), *European Integration and Supranational Governance*, Oxford: Oxford University Press.

Scott, Richard (1995), *Institutions and Organizations*, London: Sage.

Scott, Richard, John Meyer et al. (1994), *Institutional Environments and Organizations*, Thousand Oaks, CA: Sage.

Sewell, William Jr. (1992), 'A theory of structure: duality, agency, and transformation', *American Journal of Sociology*, **98** (1), 1–29.

Sharpe, Diana Rosemary (2001), 'Globalization and change: organizational continuity and change within a Japanese multinational in the UK', in Glenn Morgan, Peer Hull Kristensen and Richard Whitley (eds) (2001), *The Multinational Firm*, Oxford: Oxford University Press, pp. 196–221.

Stearns, Linda and Kenneth Allan (1996), 'Economic behavior in institutional environments: the corporate merger wave of the 1980s', *American Sociological Review*, **61** (August), 699–718.

Stopford, John M. and Susan Strange (with John S. Henley) (1991), *Rival States, Rival Firms. Competition for World Market Shares*, Cambridge: Cambridge University Press.

Strange, Susan (1996), *The Retreat of the State. The Diffusion of Power in the World Economy*, Cambridge: Cambridge University Press.

Tolbert, Pamela and Lynne Zucker (1996), 'The institutionalization of institutional theory', in Stewart Clegg, Cynthia Hardy and Walter Nord (eds), *Handbook of Organization Studies*, London: Sage, pp. 175–90.

Van der Pijl, Kees (1984), *The Making of an Atlantic Ruling Class*, London: Verso.

Van der Pijl, Kees (1998), *Transnational Classes and International Relations*, London: Routledge.

Weber, Max (1978), *Economy and Society*, Berkeley, CA: University of California Press.

Westney, Eleanor (1987), *Imitation and Innovation*, Cambridge, MA: Harvard University Press.

Whitley, Richard (1992), *European Business Systems*, London: Sage.

Whitley, Richard (1999), *Divergent Capitalisms*, Oxford: Oxford University Press.

Whitley, Richard and Peer Hull Kristensen (eds) (1997), *Governance at Work. The Social Regulation of Economic Relations*, Oxford: Oxford University Press.

Williamson, Oliver (1985), *The Economic Institutions of Capitalism*, New York: Free Press.

Zeitlin, Jonathan and Garry Herrigel (2000) (eds), *Americanization and its Limits*, Oxford: Oxford University Press.

PART I

Globalization and National Institutional Change

2. Global investors meet local managers: shareholder value in the Finnish context

Risto Tainio, Mika Huolman, Matti Pulkkinen, Jyrki Ali-Yrkkö and Pekka Ylä-Anttila

INTRODUCTION

> Listing on the New York Stock Exchange in 1994 was a far more important step than we ever thought. But the access to capital was less important than the presence as such. (Jorma Ollila, President and CEO of Nokia, 28 March 2000)

There is no doubt that listing on the world's most demanding stock market is a significant step in the life of any company. But listing on less demanding local stock exchanges becomes an almost equally important step when stocks are traded there by foreign investors. In both cases, the company becomes part of global capital markets and is thus subjected to new rules of the game. These rules reflect the principle of shareholder value maximization (Williams 2000). The purpose of this chapter is to explore the ways in which these new rules of the game affect Finnish companies and the Finnish economy as a whole.

Companies may have different reasons for listing on a foreign stock exchange or inviting foreign investors. Usually they need cash to expand their business. Sometimes they are in the process of building a brand name and therefore need the public and media exposure. In practice, a public stock offering with an international dimension brings access to new sources of capital and shareholders. As indicated above, listing on the NYSE in 1994 provided capital for Nokia, but it also started the process through which the company went from being predominantly Finnish owned (60 per cent in 1994) to having a majority of American shareholders (55 per cent in 2000).

A mere presence on global capital markets seems to matter. The fact of being listed on a foreign stock exchange endows a company with legitimacy and gives it credibility. It also means publicity which can be helpful to strengthen the corporate image and differentiate the company from its competitors. It seems particularly important to be listed on one of the stock exchanges in New York (Ventresca et al. in this volume). A presence there spreads the visibility of a company beyond the financial experts to ordinary households. Since more than 51 per cent of American adults own stocks or mutual funds, listing in New York makes a company concrete and real to millions of Americans. This raises the company's profile, helps to build its brand name and eventually makes it well known throughout the world.

Most Finnish companies did not enter global capital markets before the mid 1990s. This, incidentally, is also about the time when foreign, and in particular American, service providers set up offices in Finland (McKenna et al. in this volume). At present, only six Finnish companies have listed in New York. Those are Nokia, UPM-Kymmene, Stora-Enso, Metso, Sonera and Eimo. However, throughout the 1990s foreign investors have actively bought shares in Finnish companies on the Helsinki Stock Exchange. At the end of 1999, foreign investors controlled 65 per cent of market capitalization on the HESE, and owned a third of all the stocks of Finnish companies. The influence of those investors over Finnish firms has increased rapidly and very significantly compared to what has happened elsewhere in Europe. This makes Finland an interesting research site for exploring the mutual influence of global investors and local managers and their combined impact on companies as well as on the national economy as a whole.

This chapter starts with a brief description of how foreign investors arrived in Finland and imposed themselves as key players. Then we focus on the ways in which these distant, dispersed and often faceless foreign investors exercise their influence in Finnish companies. Third, we look at interactions between investors and managers and how these reflect at the level of companies or even of the nation-state. Finally, we discuss emerging tensions and conflicts between foreign investors and local actors.

The empirical material for this chapter is drawn from a study of 16 major Finnish corporations and their evolution during the 1990s. The data on the channels of influence was gathered through in-depth semi-structured interviews with financial professionals (financial and investment analysts or money managers) and investor relations specialists. The share of foreign ownership was calculated by compiling official statistics and annual reports of the companies studied. The data on corporate restructuring was gathered from company reports and interviews with CEOs.

WHEN FOREIGN INVESTORS ARRIVED IN FINLAND

In the period following World War II, foreign ownership was tightly controlled in Finland. The legislation was particularly strict for the forest and transportation industries and for securities and real estate companies. Things started to change only towards the end of the 1980s, and in 1989 the government agreed in principle to welcome foreign investments. That same year the Ministry of Trade and Industry approved all 103 applications of foreign firms trying to acquire Finnish companies (Ojanen and Eriksson 1990). However the share of foreign ownership was still restricted at that time to 40 per cent of the equity and 20 per cent of the votes. A more liberal legislation was in the making, however, and in January 1993 foreigners could start to buy shares of Finnish companies without any restriction. This evolution was part of a process where Finnish laws were being harmonized with European Union legislation. This was a necessary and preliminary stage to European Union membership, which Finland finally obtained at the beginning of 1995.

The early 1990s was also a time when American institutional investors, with huge amounts of liquid capital, sought new investment targets all over the world (Useem 1996; Kleiner this volume). To allocate their money, these investors started relying more on company-level analyses rather than on national data. Instead of taking into consideration only country or regional risks, they focused instead on individual companies and their promises. Hence they were able to bypass a bleak national context to handpick what they felt were promising firms. After a long period of strong growth, Finland was, in 1993, at the bottom of a deep recession. The Finnish markka was weak and floating and stocks were highly undervalued. Thus some Finnish companies became attractive investment targets. The companies themselves were also active in reaching out to foreign investors. In their desperate need for money, they could still demonstrate a great potential for growth based in particular on well-established engineering skills.

Again Nokia is a good example of how foreign investors found Finnish companies in the early 1990s. In 1992, Nokia was in deep crisis. Its operating loss was significant and its business portfolio was diverse and dispersed due to the heavy over-investments of the 1980s. Nokia needed big money fast. The place to find such money was the USA. But American investors were not interested in the old Nokia that meant 'rubber, cables, paper and television sets'. The new management team at Nokia had to create a vision, a new story and a plan for the future of the company. The vision was summed up into four well-known words – focused, global, telecom-oriented and value-added. Investors were suddenly interested. Nokia did a private placement with a few American institutions in 1993 and it was listed on the NYSE in 1994. The rest is history. In five years, the stock of Nokia went up by 2300 per cent (*Fortune* 2000). At the moment, over 90 per cent of Nokia's stock is foreign-owned (55 per cent American, 10 per cent British and 25 per cent Swiss, Scandinavian and others).

An early success with Nokia meant that investors rapidly turned to other Finnish companies. At the end of 1995, the biggest foreign portfolio ownership in Finland after Nokia (68.5 per cent) was in Cultor, a biotechnology company (50.7 per cent). Then came Metsä-Serla, a paper and pulp company (45.6 per cent), Tieto, software (39.0 per cent), Pohjola, an insurance firm (31.5 per cent) and Valmet, a company producing paper machines (30.8 per cent). Those were followed by two major paper companies – Kymmene (28.5 per cent) and Repola-UPM (25.1 per cent) (Tainio 1999). All in all foreign ownership of Finnish stocks went from less than 10 per cent in 1993 to 65 per cent at the end of the 1990s (figures from Finnish Central Securities Depository). The predominant role of foreigners in these statistics is largely due to Nokia, naturally, since that company accounts for about two-thirds of market capitalization on the Helsinki Stock Exchange. Without Nokia, foreigners would own only 32 per cent of Finnish stocks (Karhunen and Keloharju 2001).

In the early 1990s, foreign investors provided Finnish companies with the capital they desperately needed. In general, the reaction to foreign capital was warm and positive. Foreign investors tended to be treated as saviours of Finland. A deep recession was not a time to debate the possible threats or dangers associated with foreign capital and the silence and courtesy continued, to a large extent, until the late 1990s. In that respect Finland was quite different from other countries like France where the role of foreign ownership in national development was widely discussed and debated (Maclean and Harvey 2001).

The positive atmosphere around foreign ownership was also held up in Finland by the news that foreign-owned companies actually performed better than domestically-owned companies in the 1990s. They were found to be more efficient in capital formation, value creation and even job creation (Ali-Yrkkö and Ylä-Anttila, forthcoming). Foreign investors can easily remain anonymous in Finland. Most of them are registered in the name of a nominee and their names are not publicly available unless their shares exceed 5 per cent (10 per cent until 1999) of the total voting rights and share capital of the company. This makes a dialogue between investors and local actors difficult and rare. This has also, to some extent, prevented an open debate about the role of foreign ownership in Finland.

It is nevertheless possible to find out from commercial data banks and stock exchange reports who the first foreign portfolio investors in Finland were. They consist of a relatively small group of well-known American investment and pension funds like Janus Capital, Franklin Research, Fidelity, Capital Research Management, Alliance Capital Management, Morgan Stanley and Merrill Lynch, and the two largest public pension funds, CalPERS and TIAA-CREF. These institutional investors have invested mainly in leading Finnish companies. Each of them has invested through several funds, which individually may have only small stakes (ranging from 0.1 per cent to 0.4 per cent) but together make up a significant share of ownership. In many cases American institutional investors are amongst the main owners of the companies in which they have invested.

Hence foreign investors control a fair share of capital by now in Finland. There is no doubt that they can make a difference in Finnish companies if they wish. The evidence from the USA suggests that they often do just that (Useem

1996). Public funds invest 'other people's money' and therefore have a legal obligation to promote the value of their investments. Investment companies are involved at the same time in fierce competition, which makes them active in pressing managers for better performance. In addition, both 'species' of investors have high, global standards for returns on investments (Steger 1998; Williams 2000). The entry of powerful and active foreign investors has challenged the old Finnish system, where companies were passively owned and CEOs were running the show.

THE CHANNELS OF INFLUENCE – EXIT, VOICE AND MORE INFORMAL PATHS

A common claim is that foreign investors who operate at arm's length exercise their influence mainly in two ways – through stock market action and personal influence. These patterns of influence can be labelled 'exit' and 'voice' following Hirschman (1970). The first refers mainly to selling or to the threat of selling the stocks on the market and the second to personal expression of advice or demands in formal meetings. Our evidence suggests that both channels are available to foreign investors in Finland but that they are used in slightly unconventional ways.

In general foreign investors have been relatively stable owners of Finnish companies. Levels of investments have, of course, varied over time but major foreign investors have been relatively patient, retaining or even increasing their holdings in Finnish companies (Veranen 1996). In investment terms, they have preferred to 'buy' or 'hold' rather than 'sell'. A relatively infrequent use of the exit strategy is probably related to the nature of the Helsinki stock market. The somewhat illiquid market makes it difficult for investors to sell (especially large stakes) without hurting themselves. On the other hand frequent small transactions become expensive and sometimes also risky in a remote local market. Some things may be changing, however, and there have been increasing signs of 'capital flight' during the last few years.

The 'voice' pattern of influence means that investors present their personal demands and wishes during formal meetings. The Finnish two-tier system of governance is quite similar to its German counterpart and owners are typically present on supervisory boards and at annual meetings of shareholders. Foreign investors seldom sit on supervisory boards in Finland. They have not concealed their critical view of that institution and more generally of the whole stakeholder view of corporate governance. They have publicly contended that supervisory boards are inefficient bodies, adding no value. And in fact they have played a central role in the process where the largest Finnish companies have suppressed supervisory boards or reduced their power.

Foreign investors have also usually been absent from annual shareholder meetings or, when present, they have remained silent. At most, they have reserved a right to intervene through their representatives if management needed backing. In its traditional form, the voice pattern of influence is thus seldom used by foreign investors in Finland.

Rare use of voice in the two major formal bodies does not mean, however, that foreign investors do not use their voice elsewhere. Investors and the top management of Finnish companies in fact meet informally both frequently and regularly. Top managers visit current and potential investors abroad and host them in Finland. These informal meetings and gatherings are important channels for the exchange of information, for delivering messages and for presenting demands and wishes. This type of interaction is generally called 'relational investing'.

Such informal discussions are naturally confidential and rarely shared with outsiders. Anecdotal evidence (Useem 1996; Bricker and Chandar 2000) and our interviews of both parties suggest, however, that on these occasions the following issues are often taken up – diversified business portfolios, large cash reserves, cross-shareholdings, the role of supervisory boards, state-ownership and expensive long-term investments. It appears quite obvious that foreign investors like focused business strategies, stock-based incentive schemes, abundant dividend policies, empowered boards of directors, efficient investor relations and innovations 'that may change the world'. They also stress the overall significance of market value in managerial thinking and action. There is evidence furthermore that initiatives and proposals of investors on these issues are usually implemented (Carleton et al. 1998).

There are a number of arenas or contexts where relational investing takes place. These arenas differ with respect to the kind of information that is exchanged and to the kind of influence that is being exercised. They vary from informal telephone calls to organized 'road shows', that is to official presentations of a company to investors. In between, there is a wide range of meeting places and negotiation fora where management and analysts meet, exchange information about the company and give advice to each other. The most common contexts for this kind of informal exchange are one-on-one meetings, informal group gatherings, company visits, capital market days in companies, and conference calls.

Our evidence indicates that relational investing tends to take place either in one-on-one meetings, in company visits or during road shows (Huolman et al. 1999). For these occasions, local managers need a story that catches the attention of investors. This 'good story' is, in the words of Matti Lehti, the CEO of Tietoenator:

short, clear, sensible, and interesting. It includes the business idea, strategy and future outlook. It needs to be reduced and compact – like your company. The story cannot promise too much or too little. It has to be accurate and plausible. It articulates what is possible in the local context. Investors hate first negative surprises and second surprises.

The story is not created or used only for investors. It is often also a guideline for top management and the entire personnel. As the story is repeated several times in front of investors it gradually becomes a promise. The words that may have been originally intended and told only to investors start turning into action and become a part of organizational reality (Tainio 1997).

Beside these kinds of informal channels, foreign investors in Finland also seem to be in need of an efficient formal channel to exercise their influence. The most obvious candidate would seem to be the board of directors. It is currently under renovation in a number of Finnish companies. American institutional investors have been especially active in promoting board reforms. They have contended that the old boards of directors have been too weak and ineffective in looking out for the interests of shareholders. Their members have been too dependent on top management and this has made them passive and inefficient.

Foreign investors have therefore been active in demanding changes in the composition of the boards in Finnish companies. From their perspective an effective board has the following features – independence, shareholder accountability and expertise (Lorsch 1995; Hirvonen et al. 1997). This means that good board members have only weak ties to the CEO, that they own a significant amount of company stocks and that they have the time, commitment and knowledge to work for the company. Finnish boards are also said to lack demographic and intellectual diversity. Currently they still seem to be dominated by old men with expertise from a distant past.

THE IMPACT OF FOREIGN INVESTORS ON FINNISH COMPANIES AND THE FINNISH ECONOMY

Foreign investors have the power, motives and channels to influence local companies and their management. It is, however, not clear when they exercise this influence and how they do it. Naturally investors do not directly restructure companies. This remains the prerogative and responsibility of management. Instead investors enable or constrain managerial action. As indicated above, investors can affect local companies through intervention on the stock market and through their voice as owners. Stock price is the ultimate outcome of that influence. Recently stock price has become a 'widely used currency' for management (Rappaport and Sirower 1999). By regulating the availability of that 'currency', investors shape the financial foundation of a company. They can open up new opportunities for management or limit the existing alternatives for the growth and renewal of a company.

Foreign Investors and Market Values of Companies

The natural starting point to illustrate the impact of foreign investors is therefore the stock price or more precisely the market capitalization of the companies studied. In Table 2.1, the market value levels and the share of foreign ownership in the companies studied are presented for 1999.

Table 2.1   Change in market values and foreign ownership in 16 Finnish companies in 1999

Company	Market value 31 December 1999	Market value 1st January 1999	Change in market value in 1999 (%)	Change and level of foreign ownership in 1999 (%)
Nokia	209.4	59.6	+ 250	+ 9.4 (86.0)
Sonera	49.1	10.9	+ 350	+ 18.0 (29.5)
Tietoenator	4.8	2.0	+ 134	+ 14.8 (60.5)
Eimo*	0.35	0.16	+ 119	+ 12.2 (12.2)
Stora-Enso	13.2	5.8	+ 127	+ 4.3 (70.1)
UPM-Kymmene	10.7	6.6	+ 61	+ 7.9 (57.5)
Metsä-Serla	1.6	0.97	+ 64	− 0.6 (40.0)
Outokumpu	1.8	0.98	+ 79	+ 2.1 (26.2)
Partek	0.66	0.38	+ 74	− 0.5 (3.7)
Raisio	0.68	1.54	− 59	− 20.3 (41.5)
Sanoma-WSOY***	1.8	0.67	+ 164	− 8.9 (1.9)
Alma-Media	0.49	0.44	+ 11	−5.0 (32.4)
F-Secure****	0.78	–	–	+ 8.4 (8.4)
Stonesoft**	0.69	0.08	+ 763	+ 8.2 (8.2)

Notes:
*   The figure for early 1999 is for 3/1999.
**   The figure for early 1999 is the figure for 4/1999.
***   The figure for early 1999 is the figure for WSOY.
**** F-Secure was listed on the Helsinki Stock Exchange in November 1999.

The level of foreign ownership indicates how closely the companies are tied to global capital markets. Two traditional and well established companies

(Partek and Sanoma-WSOY) and three recently listed smaller companies (Eimo, F-Secure and Stonesoft) seem to be only loosely connected.

Change in market value indicates how attractive the companies studied have been as investment targets. Finnish companies were on the whole very attractive in 1999, that year ending a long cycle of growth for the Finnish economy. In fact Raisio is the only notable exception. Nevertheless when it comes to the level of market value growth one can easily point to four distinct groups of companies.

A first group includes companies like Nokia, Sonera and Tietoenator that represent the 'new economy' and information technology sector. Eimo, a contract supplier of Nokia, also belongs to this group. The market values of these four companies increased rapidly in 1999. This was largely due to the highly optimistic expectations of investors on future prospects for these companies. Members of this group have been amongst the favourite companies of foreign investors during that particular year.

A second group of companies represents traditional industries like pulp and paper, steel or engineering (for transformations and evolutions within that group see Lilja and Moen in this volume). The market values of these companies have remained relatively low and the increase has been modest, particularly when compared to the first group. The Finnish paper (UPM-Kymmene, Stora-Enso and Metsä-Serla), steel (Outokumpu) and engineering (Partek) companies are all members of that group. These companies have performed very well and paid generous dividends but this has had only a weak impact on their market valuation. Raisio also belongs to a traditional industry – food. However that company emerges as an exception in that group. A radical innovation in 1995 attracted foreign investors. The share of foreign ownership increased from 10 per cent in 1995 to 50.9 per cent in 1996, to 58 per cent in 1997 and 61.8 per cent in 1998. The market value of that company skyrocketed until some marketing problems emerged, especially in the USA. Disappointed investors withdrew in 1999 and that movement is visible in the table.

In the third group, one finds two companies from the media and broadcasting sector – Sanoma-WSOY and Alma-Media. Sanoma-WSOY is a big, mostly family-owned company with a low level of foreign ownership. Its market value increased significantly in 1999 and the merger between Sanoma and WSOY can explain that. Investors reacted positively to the reconfiguration. Alma-Media, on the other hand, is partly owned by a Swedish family media group and it is a company from which foreign portfolio investors withdrew in 1999.

Finally, the fourth group is made up of young Internet companies (F-Secure or Stonesoft). Those companies were extremely appealing to investors in 1999. They were not strong on profits. However they developed promising concepts and attractive images and, as a consequence, they created high expectations. Investors are in a constant quest to invest in ideas 'that will change the world'.

Companies around the Internet business have raised high hopes in this respect. The stock market values of these companies have typically gone up exponentially during the 1990s. This has been the case for our two companies – F-Secure and Stonesoft. The share of foreign ownership in these two companies stayed at a relatively modest level for Finland in 1999 (8.5 per cent and 8.3 per cent) and this in spite of a huge increase in share prices. This is largely to be explained by the small size of those companies and by a limited availability of shares. The significant increase in stock prices seems to be mainly the consequence of domestic Internet euphoria.

Table 2.1 suggests that there is a positive correlation between the level of foreign ownership and change in market value – the more foreign ownership the greater the growth in market value of a company. Sonera and Nokia are good examples of this. The share of foreign ownership went up for each of these two companies respectively by 18 per cent and 9 per cent and stock prices in the meantime increased by 350 per cent and 245 per cent. At the other end, Raisio and Alma-Media are two examples of companies where a decline in foreign ownership appeared to be associated with a declining market value. In these companies foreign ownership dropped by 20 per cent and 5 per cent respectively and market values went down by 58 per cent for Raisio and up by only 11 per cent for Alma-Media. UPM-Kymmene emerges as a notable and interesting exception to this general rule. Although its share of foreign ownership went up significantly the increase in stock price remained quite modest.

Table 2.1 does not tell anything about the possible direction of causality in the connection between foreign ownership and market value. It does, however, suggest that investors in general, and foreign investors in particular, treat companies in different sectors differently, even in a year of overall growth. The outcome of their stock market action has been a gradual bifurcation of the economy. A huge amount of capital has been channelled into the information technology sector and the traditional, old-line companies have been, to a large extent, ignored and neglected. Investors have been looking for big gains and not so much for solid returns. Sectors are different in their potential for path-breaking discoveries, which makes them unequally attractive for investors. The latter's influence on market values of companies speeds up the overall restructuring of the Finnish national economy and shapes the future of the Finnish system of innovation.

Reciprocal Effects – Foreign Investors and Managerial Discretion

Foreign investors either enable or constrain managerial action in Finnish companies. A strong interest and a positive attitude towards a company increase the stock of available resources, open up new opportunities and make things easier for management. A negative attitude, on the other hand, tends to limit the range of managerial options and makes things difficult and more expensive for management. The behaviour of investors does not, by any means, determine managerial response and action, but it affects the repertoire of available alternatives and has an impact on the magnitude of efforts that are required for implementation.

In 1999, foreign investors generally extended or promoted managerial discretion in Finnish companies. They helped to build up and maintain a 'virtuous circle' in companies like Nokia, Sonera and Tietoenator. A virtuous circle starts when a sector or a company becomes, for some reason, attractive to investors. The latter provide initial or additional assets, which pushes up expectations for growth of the company and demand for its shares. This creates positive publicity, which further lifts the share price. The increased share price makes it possible for management to expand operations by acquisitions and/or R&D investments. This also brings management to restructure the company and to improve its competitive position. From this new position it is possible to dominate other players with new product market strategies. This accentuates the company's leading image, which makes it increasingly attractive to the best people. The new human and social capital opens up new perspectives for management and expands the repertoire of profitable businesses, which then brings in new investors. This in turn further enhances the demand for shares of the company. A virtuous circle is by definition something positive, something to pursue. It also has, however, risks and dangers that are related to an abundance of resources and a consequent temptation for over-investment.

In two companies, Raisio and Alma-Media, the situation and role of foreign investors were almost the opposite. Foreign investors constrained managerial action and decreased their discretion. Together they became involved in creating a vicious circle for these companies. A vicious circle starts when a sector or a company gets an unattractive investment image. This might stem from the company's unclear and diverse business portfolio, its protected ownership or some negative outcomes of managerial decision making. Declining interest on the part of investors leads to low demand for shares and a stable or falling share price. This means a loss of resources. Management lacks the 'currency' for R&D investments or acquisitions and this further weakens expectations about the company's future. The falling share price makes executive recruitment and compensation more difficult and expensive. Instead of stock options, a company has to offer more cash or restricted stocks, both of which have a negative impact on the bottom line. The best people start leaving. Problems escalate. This affects efficiency and the competitive strength of the company. Management has to lay-off people and downsize the organization. Investors see the smoke of impending crisis and the stock price falls even further. The deterioration of the financial and moral foundation of the company prevents a search for new resources and business ideas. The weak market value makes a company vulnerable to takeovers. This reduces motivation and reinforces the negative image of the company. This further slows down the demand for shares. A vicious circle amplifies negative developments. It tends to decrease resources and increases the risk of underinvestment.

Virtuous and vicious circles as described above illustrate how foreign investors and local managers together produce organizational outcomes. By extending or limiting managerial discretion foreign investors do not determine managerial response, but they influence the range of actual and potential behaviours available for management.

Reciprocal Effects – Shaping Managerial Practices

The interaction between foreign shareholders and managers does not have an impact only on share prices. Foreign investors and local managers also have personal and direct interactions. This occurs mainly at the level of top management and in the headquarters of the companies. The general message spread there by investors has to do with boosting the creation and maximization of shareholder value. This message has been delivered with varying degrees of determination, ranging from commands to the mere exchange of information (Tainio et al. 2001).

The response of management has obviously varied depending on the unique combination of business conditions and management personalities. The trend, however, is quite clear. Finnish managers have tended to restructure their companies by imitating companies that have been successful in global capital markets. As a result, leading Finnish companies and their managerial practices have become 'Americanized' or 'financialized' albeit to a varying extent (Tainio 2001).

In general, the companies studied have adopted those characteristics that foreign investors like and avoided those that they dislike. Shareholder-driven changes could be observed in the ways goals have been set and measured and dividends distributed. Finnish managers had not started experimenting with shareholder value-based performance measures like EVA and MVA before the mid 1990s and the arrival of foreign, and in particular American, investors.

Similarly, managerial incentive schemes and corporate governance structures have been constructed in accordance with shareholder interests. Although the first stock option schemes were introduced in Finnish companies in the late 1980s, they were not widely adopted before 1994 (Ikäheimo 1998). 'The lessons were learnt directly from America' says the CEO of Tietoenator. Finnish companies also looked at their American counterparts to find inspiration on corporate governance (Tainio 2001).

The success of the US economy during the late 1990s helped spread in Finland the popularity of shareholder value as a principle of corporate governance. Since American institutional investors were its main champions, their message and advice were taken seriously. This was amplified by the fact that their impact was strongest in a small group of flagship companies in Finland (Tainio 1999, and for the same phenomenon in Germany, Jyrgens et al. 2000). In a small country like Finland, these companies stand out as role models for all other companies. Nokia's role in particular is impressive in that respect. There is practically no executive training course or business book in Finland without a reference to Nokia. This does not mean that all Finnish companies will in the future follow Nokia's lead and replicate its managerial philosophy, but the Nokia case is a model through which other companies try to learn about the new game and its rules (for the central role of Nokia in the Finnish economy, see Ali-Yrkkö et al. 2000).

The principle of shareholder value is especially tempting and fashionable, since the companies that first adopted it in Finland have been quite successful. These positive results contrasted with the widespread inefficiencies that were common in the sheltered and regulated Finnish economy of the 1970s and 1980s (Pohjola 1996). Still nowadays, foreign-owned companies show better results than domestically-owned ones (Ali-Yrkkö and Ylä-Anttila forthcoming). But the demands from foreign investors remain high. For example, in the prosperous year of 1999, only four out of the 16 companies studied reached the 15 per cent ROCE target. These were Nokia, Tietoenator, UPM-Kymmene and Eimo.

This personal type of reciprocal influence between foreign investors and local managers is also important in understanding the evolution of managerial practices in Finnish companies. The repertoire of local managers in their response to demands or advice from investors may vary from obedient following of orders to active resistance. The outcomes of these discussions are very much dependent on the relative power of foreign investors and local managers (Tainio et al. 2001). This is, on the other hand, dependent on the financial strength and autonomy of the company as well as on the degree of fragmentation of ownership.

EMERGING TENSIONS BETWEEN FOREIGN INVESTORS AND LOCAL ACTORS

During recession years and while their companies were in crisis Finnish managers were unanimous about and receptive to the advice and guidance of foreign investors. Tensions between foreign investors and local managers started, however, to rise with economic recovery. On the one hand, the power of local managers increased along with the improving performance of their companies. On the other hand, the role of foreign investors became more controversial as the polarizing effects of their capital allocation were becoming more obvious.

Immediate short-term efficiencies created during the period of crisis could not hide fundamental contradictions between what foreign investors actually required and what the local product market allowed. Demands for shareholder value maximization were increasing with improving economic conditions. Shareholder value was created mainly from two sources – dividends based on operating profits and the appreciation of share prices. During the late 1990s, shareholder value emerged mainly from share-price appreciation and less from profit ratios (Froud et al. 2000).

This meant big problems for traditional industrial companies. In their golden age, in a production-driven world, it was enough to deliver solid and consistent returns to gain recognition from the stock market. In the finance-driven world investors, however, looked for big gains and extraordinary returns, which were exceptionally hard to achieve in old industrial companies. This made many Finnish old-line CEOs unhappy and frustrated. They could be characterized quite in the same way as their American counterparts. 'They are angry because they are working hard and not getting a lot of credit. They are fearful because they can now be cheaply bought by some dot-coms and they are envious because they want the valuation the technology companies have' (*Business Week* 2000).

But there was little local managers could do to lift the market value of their companies. They tried to sharpen the focus, to buy back stocks and to make the Internet central to their businesses. Nevertheless these moves were seldom reflected in share prices. The CEO of UPM-Kymmene expressed his frustration openly in a Finnish newspaper in 2000.

> Management should not comment on share prices, but I will. It is a big disappointment that when the company shows record profits, its future seems bright and promising and demand is growing fast, the only indicator which points down is the share price. It is difficult to understand! (*Kauppalehti* 2000)

The CEOs of the 'new economy' companies have, on the other hand, enjoyed steadily rising stock prices during the late 1990s. How much this was due to efforts of individual management can, however, be questioned, since the stock-exchange index of these 'growth companies' has risen steadily throughout the late 1990s. Rising stock prices, and consequent shareholder value, have thus been, to a large extent, dependent on the sectoral affiliation of companies. Sectors differed in their potential for returns and in how their value was appreciated. The differential treatment of industrial sectors by foreign investors has thus had wider implications for the Finnish economy as a whole (Laurila 1999). The old industrial engine of Finland, which for over a century has been based on large-scale, capital-intensive forest sector companies, has experienced a rapid and profound transformation during the 1990s (Lilja and Moen in this volume). At the same time, new growth industries, based mainly on advanced information and telecommunication technology, were becoming the emerging core of a reinvented Finnish economy (Lilja and Tainio 1996).

As argued above, the short-term effects of global capital markets have reflected a close interaction between foreign investors and some local managers. At the moment, however, the managerial elite is more split than ever. Opposition towards the blessings of shareholder value maximization seems to be growing.

Moreover, the creation of shareholder value is also dependent on the institutional context in which the companies operate. In Finland, foreign investors have not directly or in public intervened in discussions around institutional reforms. They have, however, pressed Finnish managers for higher returns and lower costs and the latter in turn have pressed state agencies, local authorities and interest groups for 'flexible' institutional arrangements (see also Useem 1996). This has created some new tensions between foreign investors and local communities, particularly around the potential effects on employment. Especially controversial have been events where extensive employee layoffs have immediately increased the stock price of the company. Episodes where announcements of layoffs coincided with announcements of generous management stock options have also created public protests. Sometimes they have also provoked strong opposition from trade unions and resistance from the shop floor and made customers threaten companies with a sales boycott. All this indicates that foreign investors have mostly indirectly pushed for changes in industrial relations, but local actors have actually produced the outcomes at the national level.

Stock options are one of the most concrete indications of the shareholder principle. The purpose of these compensation schemes is to align managers' interests tightly with market values and thus with the interests of owners. In Finland, stock options have created tensions in two ways. First, they have provoked criticism and debate on high executive compensation in a culture where 'equality' and a centralized wage negotiation system have been taken for granted. Second, stock options have been destroying traditional wage negotiation systems from within. They have shifted attention away from percents and pennies to the market values of companies. They have undermined the key role of unions and their shop floor representatives in the wage bargaining process and transformed the nature of industrial relations.

In pursuing shareholder value, managers often become engaged in divestment of businesses with a poor rate of return (Froud et al. 2000). This naturally creates significant problems for local communities. The short-term financial interests of companies often contradict long-term local interests. Since capital is more mobile than labour, local communities appear particularly vulnerable. Local communities and regions are not, however, entirely helpless victims of modern finance capital. They may sometimes proactively launch a search for new owners and new companies willing to acquire local units (Kristensen and Zeitlin 2001). They may also develop their own counter strategies to retain jobs and services.

Regarding the tensions between foreign investors and local communities, the most fundamental question for the future is what foreign investors and the shareholder view they represent can actually offer to people. In a recent extensive survey, people declared that the most important things in their lives were health, family and work. The effects of shareholder value will ultimately be judged against that background. The emerging opposition to what foreign investors stand for makes it difficult to predict the future. The tensions are indications of counter forces that may well change the direction and prevent investors' interests from becoming a part of reality. Various responses or various counter forces to 'globalization' or 'Americanization' make the outcomes quite unpredictable in the long run (Whitley in this volume, Djelic and Quack in the conclusion to this volume).

CONCLUSIONS

Entering global capital markets is indeed significant for any local company. It means access to a game with new rules. There the world is viewed from the vantage point of shareholders, mostly foreign institutional investors. The latter operate with a 'shareholder value'-driven set of goals.

The impact of this new game on local companies is by no means straightforward and clear. On the contrary, it was found that the relation between global financial markets and local companies is complex and mediated through various interdependencies tying together global investors and local managers.

Our evidence suggests that global capital markets have an impact on Finnish companies in the following ways. First, the new global game imposes new requirements on Finnish companies. This could be called a 'structural influence': the mere existence of the new game with its new rules is important. This structural influence becomes concrete and real through the influence of powerful key actors. This we call 'actors' influence'. It results from the interplay between foreign investors or their representatives and some key local managers. The outcomes of this reciprocal effect are most visible at the level of companies, but they are also identifiable at the national level. Local transformations aggregate and 'trickle-up' to the institutional level (see Djelic and Quack in the conclusion to this volume). The pressure on national institutions in turn can stabilize, reinforce and speed up transformations at the company or sector level (for an example of that see Kleiner in this volume).

We have shown in this chapter how structural influence has played out in Finland. During the second half of the 1990s, market value has become central in the functioning of companies. Strict requirements have emerged in the meantime around the issues of transparency and shareholder rights. We found that the larger the share of foreign ownership in a company, the more it was exposed to structural influence. However, even those companies with smaller shares of foreign ownership also appeared to be under this kind of structural influence. It seemed as if these companies were preparing themselves for the new game and were developing the features, characteristics and competencies that would likely be needed. This was mostly done through imitation of leading companies and by seeking advice and help from consultants and financial analysts.

With respect to the influence of actors we specified some of the interplays between foreign investors and local managers. We also described the ways in which this interaction played out in Finland. Foreign investors, as key actors in global capital markets, have exercised their influence on local managers in two ways – through their stock market action and through their personal presence. Through their stock market action they have enabled or constrained managerial action. Positive interest in a company increased the resources of that company. It opened new and wider opportunities for the future of that company and made many things easier for local managers. Negative interest, on the other hand, limited the range of options and made things more difficult and expensive for management. Investors' stock market action did not, by any means, determine managerial response and action, but it did affect the repertoire of alternatives and the efforts required for implementation. The importance of reciprocal effects was exemplified by the description of what we called vicious and virtuous circles. Both of these were clearly generated through the interplay and interaction between foreign investors on the one hand and local managers on the other.

Foreign investors also exercised their influence through their personal – physical or virtual – presence. They represented a new 'voice' in Finnish companies. We showed that this occurred mainly in the form of 'relational investing' through informal meetings and discussions between foreign investors or their representatives and local managers. During those informal interactions, foreign investors or their representatives presented their demands but also their recipes for creating shareholder value. Management, on the other hand, expressed what was possible, in other words what production and the product market would allow. The recipes proposed by foreign investors are well known, ranging from the introduction of financial performance measures to the restructuring of organizations and business portfolios. On the other hand, the repertoire of responses of local managers was quite broad. In the companies studied, responses varied from obedient following of 'orders' to rising criticism and resistance. There also, the interaction and reciprocal effect between foreign investors and local managers appeared to be the key to understanding actual changes in managerial practices.

The concrete consequences of this reciprocal influence have been quite significant at the level of companies in Finland. But by transforming companies investors and managers have ended up also having an impact on Finnish national institutions (for a similar process see Kleiner or McKenna et al. in this volume). Changes and economic efficiencies at the company level have had their social and institutional dimension – particularly with respect to industrial relations, management compensation, corporate governance arrangements and regulation, and the importance of the stock market as a financial channel. The interplay between foreign investors and local managers has led, we have shown, to a sectoral polarization of the Finnish economy. Base industries of the traditional Finnish business and innovation system have been somewhat marginalized. The information and telecommunications sector has imposed itself on the other hand as the new engine of the Finnish economy and innovation system. Throughout this process, the state has undeniably retreated to the background, leaving increasing ground to private initiative, actors and institutions. Labour market organizations have been pushed to experiment with flexible institutional arrangements. In a nutshell, foreign investors have also been busily involved in shaping or reshaping institutional rules of the game at the national level (Djelic and Quack this volume). Most of the time, however, they have done so at least in part indirectly, working through their local relays in Finland (for a similar argument see McKenna et al. this volume).

There is no denying that the tensions between companies and local communities and the tensions between companies and national institutions have gradually increased, particularly during the second half of the 1990s. Whether the penetration of 'shareholder value' principles will imply a profound and long-lasting transformation of Finnish institutional structures still remains to be seen. If that occurs, it is likely to set off a substantial discussion and debate, and also to trigger reaction and resistance from local forces. This means that the actual outcome of these battles will quite likely be Finland-specific (see also McKenna et al., Kleiner in this volume). Despite numerous claims that global capital markets produce integration and convergence between countries and regions, our observations point in a somewhat different direction. It is not a unidirectional causal power of foreign investors that is making the world more similar, but rather a reciprocal relationship between foreign investors and local actors that is simultaneously pushing for common rules and keeping the world diverse. When global investors meet local managers the strength of local forces cannot be entirely undermined. Local variation in the responses to common shareholder principles may even in the end perpetuate national and local differences or even generate more variation across countries and regions than is observable today.

REFERENCES

Ali-Yrkkö, J. and P. Ylä-Anttila (forthcoming), 'Globalisation of business in a small country – implications for corporate governance', *Management International Review*.

Ali-Yrkkö, Jyrki., Laura Paija, C. Reilly and P. Ylä-Anttila (2000), 'Nokia – a big company in a small country', *The Research Institute of the Finnish Economy – B 162 Series*, Helsinki: ETLA.

Bricker, R. and N. Chandar (2000), 'Where Berle and Means went wrong: a reassessment of capital market agency and financial reporting', *Accounting, Organizations and Society*, **25**, 529–54.

Business Week (2000), 'What's an Old-line CEO to do?', 27 March 2000.

Carleton, W.T., J.M. Nelson and M.S. Weisbach (1998), 'The influence of institutions on corporate governance through private negotiations: evidence from TIAA-CREF', *The Journal of Finance*, **53** (4), 1335–62.

Fortune (2000), 'Nokia's secret Code', 1 May 2000.

Froud, J., C. Haslam, S. Johal and K. Williams (2000), 'Shareholder value and financialization: consultancy promises, management moves', *Economy and Society*, **29** (1), 80–110.

Hirschman, Albert (1970), *Exit, Voice, and Loyalty*, Cambridge, MA: Harvard University Press.

Hirvonen Ahti, Heikki Niskakangas and Jari Wahlroos (1997), *Hyvä hallitustyöskentely* [Good Board Practice], Juva: WSOY.

Huolman, Mika, Matti Pulkkinen, Mia Rissanen, Risto Tainio and Sampo Tukiainen (1999), *Ulkomaisen omistuksen vaikutus yrityksen johtamiseen ja innovaatioihin* [The Impact of Foreign Ownership on Management and Innovations], Helsinki: LTT-Research Ltd.

Ikäheimo, Seppo (1998), 'Optiojärjestelyt Suomessa: teoria ja empiiriset havainnot' [Option Shemes in Finland: Theory and Empirical Evidence], Kirjassa Pekka Pihlanto-individuaali laskentatoimen tutkija (Kari Lukka toim), Turku: Turun Kauppakorkeakoulun julkaisuja, C: 1.

Jyrgens, U., K. Naumann and J. Rupp (2000), 'Shareholder value in an adverse environment: the German case', *Economy and Society*, **29** (1), 54–79.

Karhunen, J. and M. Keloharju (2001), 'Shareownership in Finland', *The Finnish Journal of Business Economics*, **2**, 188–226.

Kauppalehti (2000), 'UPM:n Niemelä pettynyt yhtiönsä kurssikehitykseen' [UPMs Niemelä disappointed with his company's stock price development], 14 August 2000.

Kristensen, Peer Hull and Jonathan Zeitlin (2001), 'The Making of a Global Firm: Local Pathways to Multinational Enterprise', in Glenn Morgan, Peer Hull Kristensen and Richard Whitley (eds), *The Multinational Firm*, Oxford: Oxford University Press, pp. 172–95.

Laurila, Juha (1999), 'Management in Finland', in M. Warner (ed.), *Management in Europe*, London: International Thomson Business Press, pp. 211–17.

Lilja, Kari and Risto Tainio (1996), 'The nature of the typical Finnish firm', in Richard Whitley and Peer Hull Kristensen (eds), *The Changing European Firm – Limits to Convergence*, London: Routledge, pp. 159–91.

Lorsch, J. (1995), 'Empowering the board', *Harvard Business Review*, **73** (1), 107–17.

Maclean, M. and C. Harvey (2001), 'Elites, ownership and internationalisation of French business', paper presented at the 17th EGOS Colloquium, 5–7 July 2001, Lyon, France.

Ojanen, E. and B. Eriksson (1990), 'Restrictions on foreign ownership in Finland', *Bank of Finland Bulletin*, **64** (1), 5–8.

Pohjola Matti (1996), *Tehoton pääoma* [Inefficient Capital], Porvoo: WSOY.

Rappaport, A. and M. Sirower (1999), 'Stock or cash', *Harvard Business Review*, **77** (4), 147–58.

Steger, Ulrich (ed.) (1998), *Discovering the New Pattern of Globalisation*, Ladenburg: Gottlieb Daimler-und Karl Benz-Stiftung.

Tainio, R. (1997), 'Does foreign ownership matter?', paper presented at the 13th EGOS Colloquium, 3–5 July 1997, Budapest, Hungary.

Tainio, Risto (1999), 'Ulkomaalaisomistuksen vaikutus suomalaisten yritysten johtamiseen ja rakenteeseen' [The impact of foreign ownership on the management and structure of Finnish companies], in Kauranen Pentti (toim.) *Suomalaisen Tiedeakatemian vuosikirja 1998* [Academia Scientiarum Fennica, Year Book 1998], Vammala, Finland: Vammalan Kirjapaino.

Tainio, R. (2001), 'Effects of foreign portfolio investors on Finnish companies and their management', paper presented at the 17th EGOS Colloquium, 5–7 July 2001, Lyon France.

Tainio, Risto, Mika Huolman and Matti Pulkkinen (2001), 'The internationalization of capital markets: how international institutional investors are restructuring Finnish companies', in Glenn Morgan, Peer Hull Kristensen and Richard Whitley (eds), *The Multinational Firm*, Oxford: Oxford University Press, pp. 153–71.

Useem, Michael (1996), *Investor Capitalism*, New York: Basic Books.

Veranen, Jyrki (1996), *Tuottoa vaativat omistajat* [Yield Demanding Owners], Porvoo: WSOY.

Williams, K. (2000), 'From shareholder value to present-day capitalism', *Economy and Society*, **29** (1), 1–12.

3. Building up an asset management industry: forays of an Anglo-Saxon logic into the French business system

Thibaut Kleiner

INTRODUCTION

The French asset management industry is an interesting case of business system dynamics, where institutional change at the national level comes through an interplay with transnational actors and a foreign logic. The story of that industry makes it clear that individuals may take initiatives to escape from the constraints of their national institutions. They can do so in particular by creating and structuring new spaces that will operate with radically different rules. Through both 'trickle-up' and 'trickle-down' trajectories (Djelic and Quack, in the conclusion to this volume), challenger rules coming from Anglo-Saxon countries progressively penetrated the French asset management business until they were eventually adopted by local actors and became the dominant rules of the game.

The business system perspective maintains that economic behaviour and dominant national institutions develop inter-dependencies, so that at the national level recurrent patterns may be observed (Whitley 1991, 1999). Thus global economic change will not cause national specificities to dilute or disappear in a global uniformity. Rather those specificities will be supported and possibly reinforced by institutional dependency and international specialization (Soskice et al. 1992; Crouch and Streeck 1997; Hall and Soskice 2001; Hollingsworth and Boyer 1998; Whitley 1999; Whitley and Kristensen 1996, 1997).

The French asset management industry, however, tells a somewhat different story. The activity of managing assets and funds used to be organized in France along what can be called here typically French patterns. But over a short period of time, starting around 1996, this sector experienced radical change and came to be structured by an Anglo-Saxon logic. In this small but important sector an island of the Anglo-Saxon business system was created. It was integrated within international networks and quite different from the rest of the French business system. The focus of this chapter is the series of events that led to this situation. We will show that national business systems are contested spaces where institutions do not automatically exert authority and where borders cannot be taken for granted. Significant change in a small sector of the French economy, such as asset management, may reveal and trigger wider transformations of the national business system. Individuals can take the initiative in changing the existing rules of the game, by opening new organizational spaces within which they are protected from existing institutions. They can introduce and establish challenger rules of the game. We will suggest that change and innovation, to be successful, must follow a strategy that suits or fits the structure of existing national institutions.

The chapter is based on fieldwork research – interviews, company data and documents, archives of newspapers and professional associations. Analysis through direct contacts covered a total of 16 firms that altogether controlled 71 per cent of overall market share for French asset management. The 16 firms can be divided into three categories – companies linked to retail banks, companies linked to insurers and independent firms. Secondary material was also used, and customers, finance professionals and consultants were interviewed to cover the entire organizational field (DiMaggio and Powell 1983). The methodology reflects a subjective approach to institutions (Parsons 1990), with a focus on actors who interact with those institutions. This has meant identifying and following coalitions[1] as they made sense of and enacted (Weick 1979, 1995) their business environment. This has meant looking at the strategies those coalitions adopted (Crozier and Friedberg 1977) to improve their positions in the field. This finally has also meant analysing coalitions reflexively and interpretatively (Giddens 1976), along political and cognitive dimensions. We followed Power (1992) in his analysis of consensus building in the accounting profession and Bourdieu (1992) in his analysis of the French literary field in the nineteenth century. This methodology led us to recognize how some coalitions were able to defeat others by imposing new rules of the game that led to a reinvention of the asset management activity in France.

THE TRANSFORMATION OF THE FRENCH ASSET MANAGEMENT INDUSTRY

In the mid 1980s, the activity of asset management in France was still very much structured by a logic that was highly consistent with the national business system. By the late 1990s, the rules of the game had changed in a radical way. The patterns of organization and behaviour of French asset management firms had become very similar to those of Anglo-Saxon firms.

Asset Management, a Brief Definition

Asset management is a financial service relating to investment. Asset management firms use their expertise in investing cash well to the benefit of their clients (British Invisibles 1997). Instead of managing their funds themselves, individuals, pension funds and corporations pay the asset management firm to do so. This activity calls for very good financial and technical expertise, and it requires an ability to gain the customers' trust.

In France as in most countries, firms must be officially registered and licensed before they can offer asset management services. Given its inherent risks the business is highly regulated, and therefore very dependent upon national institutions and more generally upon the state, which in the 1980s in France also owned most leading financial institutions. The management of assets and funds is also closely linked to the financial system and especially to national financial markets and contributory pension schemes. Anglo-Saxon countries, for this reason, have historically had a more developed asset management industry. But France also has a long tradition[2] in the investment field, and between 1980 and 2000 it was the fourth largest market in the world and the largest in continental Europe, thanks to its mutual funds. This business was organized in different but equally coherent ways in France and in the Anglo-Saxon countries.

Three categories of firms have been operating in French asset management. First, we find stock exchange companies and a few independent investment banks such as Rothschild and Lazard that historically were the original players. Then there are retail banks, which have the largest market share and sell mainly mutual funds to private customers and small- and medium-sized companies, with more dedicated capabilities for high-value customers. Finally, insurance companies also entered the game. They had started by managing only their own vast assets but in the late 1980s they moved to offer their services to third parties, selling in particular mutual funds via their life insurance products. We will argue below that French asset management emerged and structured itself as a new organizational field by gaining independence from traditional retail banks and insurance companies.

The French Model

Until about the mid 1990s, the management of assets and funds in France was done according to a consistent and dominant logic. This logic had essentially three key characteristics. First, asset management was not identified as a distinct business. Rather, it operated within universal banking and represented merely a service that was being offered through the retail bank network. In the structure of retail banks or insurance companies, it emerged only as a support-staff department.

Second, in terms of work organization and hierarchy, asset management was left to individual fund managers, that were each responsible for particular portfolios. Little corporate control was exercised over these fund managers and they had extensive discretion in organizing their work. Personnel matters were governed by a national collective agreement – careers relied exclusively on the internal labour market, there was little flexibility or horizontal mobility, and pay was indexed along essentially two dimensions, education and seniority.

Third, fund managers relied on their personal talent and on the exchange of information with a network of external partners, for example financial brokers, not so much on corporate norms and standards. In customer relationships primacy was given to personal contact, not to selection mechanisms.

Behind these characteristics, we recognize some of the classic components of the French business system, in particular a strong degree of concentration and centralization, the educational and corporate stratification with an impact on personnel matters and the importance of networks (Barsoux and Lawrence 1997; Crouch 1992; Lane 1989, 1995; Maurice et al. 1980, 1986, 1988; O'Reilly 1994).

A New Logic that Reflects Anglo-Saxon Rules of the Game

By the end of the 1990s, the patterns framing asset management activity had altered radically and French asset management firms behaved very differently. Asset management by then was recognized as a new business, a separate financial service and profession operated by autonomous subsidiaries with complete control over their resources and business strategy.

Work had come to be organized along an 'investment process', with division of labour and strict task definitions. Fund managers were being assisted by such other professionals as financial analysts and sales people. They had to confine themselves to their role and were tightly controlled by performance measurement tools. Human resource management was flexible and relied not on a national collective agreement but on company agreements. Pay had become linked to performance and on the whole it had significantly increased.

Fund managers were supposed to apply corporate rules and standards, not their individual intuitions. Customer relationships were being mediated through such selection contests as invitations to tender and commercial reporting and scrutiny by investment advisers and rating agencies.

This new logic obviously differs from the situation in the mid 1980s and it appears much closer in many ways to the Anglo-Saxon model, defined and understood as the patterns of organization and behaviour observed in the United States after the ERISA law of 1974 and in Britain after the Big Bang of 1986 (Kleiner 1999). Comparison would show that in 2000 the French configuration exhibits minor differences from that in the US or Britain (Salomon 1997). Differences are to be found especially in the relatively small number in France of independent asset management brands and in the persistence of the protective nature of labour laws (Kleiner 1999).

The key question, however, is how to explain such a radical and rapid move from one logic to the other. The timing of change is an important element of the story. The creation of autonomous asset management firms, which crystallized the adoption of the new model, occurred mainly after 1996. Some important and radical transformations – deregulation, the opening of borders, a deepening of the European logic – had had an impact on France as early as the mid and late 1980s, preparing the ground, it could be argued, for changes in the asset management industry. Around 1996, the role of some individuals and their ability to bypass 'incumbent rules of the game' (Djelic and Quack in the conclusion to this volume) and to impose instead the Anglo-Saxon logic became crucial.

TENSIONS AND REACTIONS

In the mid to late 1980s tensions and pressures in the environment were already starting to create challenges for the French model of asset management. However, the key protagonists in the industry did not agree on the best way for firms to adapt. There was in particular a clear dividing line between those coalitions that believed the evolution of the French financial system required an upgrading towards the Anglo-Saxon model, and those that continued to champion the French model.

Sources of Tensions in the Environment

Since about 1984, the asset management activity in France has had to contend with significant evolutions on the national financial scene. From that point on indeed the French financial system has been undergoing progressive but significant reengineering. Deregulation, liberalization, the opening of borders particularly under the process of Europeanization and the competition that came with it, the increasing role played by financial markets all combined to open the gates of the French scene to what can be called a more Anglo-Saxon logic. French actors involved in the management of assets and funds increasingly came to realize that the rules of their national game were quite different and not very compatible with the way the game was being played elsewhere, particularly by actors with a transnational or international dimension. There, the Anglo-Saxon model was dominant with undeniably an aura of 'best practice'.

The growing role of financial markets first modified the nature of the demand for asset management, by increasing the importance of institutional over private investors. This put some stress on the integrated French model which primarily targeted private clients, while the Anglo-Saxon model focused on pension funds. On the other hand, internationalization resulted in foreign competitors arriving in France at the end of the 1980s. Even though they were relatively weak if measured by market share, these foreign competitors (mainly British and American) employed their own rules of the game in France, as a way of entering the field to their own advantage. They introduced financial reporting norms and investment methods based on processes, not individual talent. They also attacked the integrated French distribution structures and the 'amateurish' work organization. This clearly came into collision with the French model (for similar processes see Tainio et al. and McKenna et al. in this volume).

On the other hand, the new environment also created opportunities outside France for French firms, in particular with Anglo-Saxon pension funds as clients. But this required French firms to comply with the expectations of these new clients, and therefore with their (Anglo-Saxon) rules of the game. All this combined with, and was being reinforced by, a growing awareness of and knowledge about the Anglo-Saxon rules of the game. The patterns of organization and behaviour characteristic of American and British firms were progressively becoming familiar in France (see also McKenna et al. in this volume). Actors making sense of the new situation therefore had to address the competitive threats facing French asset management firms in a changing environment. Given the nature of these changes, and given that the pressure was coming from abroad, sense making and problematization (Weick 1979) led to the idea that the French model had to be transformed to accommodate Anglo-Saxon patterns of organization and behaviour (compare Tainio et al.; McKenna et al.; Lilja and Moen in this volume for the same phenomenon in other sectors). More precisely, it led to an internal debate between those coalitions thinking that the Anglo-Saxon model was better for French asset management and those that had more qualms about it.

But although the environmental changes we described had started in the mid to late 1980s, this debate would only begin in 1996. Between 1984 and 1996, some adaptation and translation occurred within firms on a case-by-case and ad hoc basis, but with no impact on the industry as a whole. The investment bank Paribas adopted the Anglo-Saxon model in the late 1980s, when Paribas Asset Management was created following the sell-off of its American subsidiary AG Becker. Other French companies, such as Indosuez, CCF, UAP and AXA were also early adopters. These large firms adapted their structures and work organization to replicate the model they had observed in ventures abroad and in contact with international investment professionals. Their adaptation processes meant departing from the existing French asset management model. The incumbent rules of the game therefore became disconnected from the corporate strategies of some large firms, which were able to ignore these rules, in part because the system of corporate governance gave them relative autonomy (Goyer 2001).

Change, however, was not evolutionary, in the sense that the adoption of the Anglo-Saxon model was neither regular nor smooth. Rather, the movement went through a significant acceleration starting in 1996 when a few key individuals, very often from the firms we described as early adopters, were able to push along a more widespread, radical and thorough appropriation and implementation of the Anglo-Saxon model.

The Debate and Various Options

The tensions identified above triggered different reactions and several coalitions emerged, each having its own view on how French asset management could best compete. Eventually, this would result in the emergence of asset management as a distinct business, different from other financial services, in which challenger rules from Anglo-Saxon countries were to be endorsed.

Starting first with a reflexive and interpretative approach (Giddens 1976), we show how different coalitions supported particular arguments about the organization of asset management. To understand the struggles between those coalitions in the attempt to dominate an organizational field we followed Bourdieu (1992). To understand the confrontation between different rationalities and the eventual formation of consensus we followed Power (1992). Our investigation identified a number of coalitions, each representing groups of individuals, organizations or institutions, which championed the same discourses and occupied relatively similar positions in the field.

Second, to analyse the politics of consensus formation and understand the eventual dismantling of the French model, we focused on the one question that was at the centre of those politics: should French firms adopt the Anglo-Saxon model? We thus in the end positioned the opinions of the various coalitions along two main axes. First, we have a 'cognitive' axis, where a positive position means 'the Anglo-Saxon model is better than the French one'. This axis represents the opinions of the actors in the field on the intrinsic advantages of the Anglo-Saxon model, in terms of financial performance, costs, quality of service to customers and ethics. It corresponds to the classic 'economic efficiency' rationality.

A second axis is the 'political' one. There, a positive position means 'the Anglo-Saxon model is better for me'. This axis represents our assessment of the potential gains or losses for actors in the field in terms of power or financial rewards. The combination of the cognitive and political axes reflects our reflexive and interpretative approach and relates the 'interests' of actors to the socially constructed rationality they championed in the debate. Figure 3.1 allows

us to map the different competing positions around 1994–95 using as a grid
those two axes.

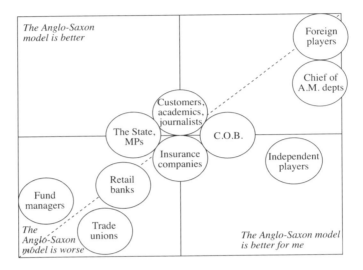

*Figure 3.1   Debate and coalitions in the French asset management
industry, 1995*

Champions of the Anglo-Saxon Model

One of the competing rationalities in the debate was defined by the idea that
French asset management should be upgraded by adopting Anglo-Saxon
patterns of organization and behaviour. We found two main coalitions in favour
of that argument both on cognitive and political grounds – foreign players on
the one hand, and the heads of asset management departments. A third coalition
had an opportunistic attitude – independent players became champions of the
Anglo-Saxon model mostly on political grounds because it could serve their
own interests.

Foreign players consistently advocated the Anglo-Saxon model. American
and British asset managers were world leaders and it seems natural that they
should believe in their own superiority. They thought their model better than
existing French practices, because it evoked clarity, transparency, good ethics
and quasi-scientific procedures. They had therefore a strong cognitive argument
in favour of their model. Moreover, we can assume that they had a strong
political interest in seeing the model expanded into France. Because of its
vertical integration within bank or insurance retail networks, the French market
was very difficult to penetrate for foreigners. The introduction of the Anglo-

Saxon model, in which asset management was an independent business, would mean breaking up the exclusive distribution arrangements within French financial institutions and opening up new opportunities to sell US or British investment services. Championing this model could also be used by foreign players as a strong marketing argument against their French competitors. Criticizing the French model was a way both to promote their own virtues and to attack the institutional barriers that were obstacles to their own growth.

For independent players, the situation was slightly different. Some interviewees in this category claimed that the Anglo-Saxon model was not necessarily superior. In particular, they insisted that investment processes did not bring better results. *B.* told us that the old-fashioned methods brought 'performances that are just as good as the firms using [investment] processes'. *M.* insisted that 'big firms are anonymous monsters' while *L.* believed that clients appreciated direct contacts with fund managers. Many of their arguments in fact supported, on a cognitive basis, the French model. However, some players used the Anglo-Saxon label to make their status of independent company more appealing. Carmignac Gestion presented itself as 'independent, *à l'Anglo-Saxonne!'* We can therefore interpret their support for the Anglo-Saxon model in terms of professional recognition. If independence became the norm French independent players would gain in terms of visibility, recognition and professional power. They would no longer be minor players in a sector dominated by retail banks and insurers, and in a business no-one pays attention to. They would become the core actors of a new business, asset management, as in the Anglo-Saxon model. Therefore we positioned this coalition in favour of the model, but mostly on opportunistic grounds.

The last and most prominent coalition in favour of the Anglo-Saxon model brought together the heads of asset management departments in large banking or insurance structures. This group probably understood best the market and its evolution, because they were at its core, with large market shares, resources and professional exposure. The consensus emerging among them was that to compete successfully a new business model was required, more precisely the adoption of what they considered the international reference point, the Anglo-Saxon model (Kleiner 1999, p. 57). There were also political reasons for them to favour the adoption of the Anglo-Saxon model. In the French model, each of these individuals was in charge of one not very big department in a large financial institution, either bank or insurance. Their business entered the category of support function and they had little if no professional recognition. As one of them underscored, 'the starting point was a total lack of recognition for the asset management business'. Within financial groups, their status and prestige were limited, despite their business being second in the world in terms of assets managed in mutual funds and despite growth ratios significantly higher than in other financial services.

If the Anglo-Saxon model came to be adopted, they would become CEOs of dynamic companies in a growing business, they would have their own resources and their own strategic plans and they would be recognized as a genuine profession. One can easily understand, therefore, that they would favour the adoption of the Anglo-Saxon model. Moreover, in the French model fund managers had a great deal of autonomy and organizational power, and the heads of asset management departments had trouble controlling them. By introducing Anglo-Saxon investment processes they would be able to control the fund managers better (compare Braverman 1974; Touraine 1955). In summary, for the coalition of asset management chiefs there was a strong case in favour of the Anglo-Saxon model.

The 'Nay' Sayers or the Resistance Coalitions

Another position in the debate was simply to maintain the existing situation. Three clearly identified coalitions opposed the adoption of the Anglo-Saxon model and were thus powerful sources of resistance – fund managers, trade unions and retail banks. Again, both cognitive and political motives were involved.

French fund managers were sceptical about the Anglo-Saxon model. They criticized the introduction of investment processes as a marketing gimmick, and as a way for the new heads of departments, many of whom were not genuine financial analysts, to take over control of investment decision making. One director of a leading French investment consultant, himself a former fund manager and SFAF-financial analyst, said:

> When one looks at performances and processes, one notices that the 'modern' process is in fact a loss of efficiency. Paradoxically, the financial houses that have the best performances are those with the most archaic processes, those that did not modernize, those that manage in a traditional fashion.

Fund managers also thought that the Anglo-Saxon model was no better than the French one, in terms both of performance and of customer relationships. Some insisted that in periods of market decline, clients would very much prefer talking to a fund manager rather than to a sales person. From a cognitive point of view, therefore, fund managers saw no superiority in the Anglo-Saxon model. From a political point of view, we would expect them to oppose it strongly, because an investment process in the American or British fashion would mean the end of fund managers' autonomy. Moreover, adopting the Anglo-Saxon model would jeopardize their financial rewards, because in a more divided and bureaucratized organization they could be replaced more easily. It was obvious that they would oppose any departure from the French model.

Trade unions representing asset management employees also opposed the adoption of the Anglo-Saxon model. First, an autonomous business would mean that workers would lose the privileges and protection of the national collective agreements in insurance and banking. These agreements favoured the workforce, while the Anglo-Saxon model would end the lifelong banking career for those in asset management. It would also mean introducing another type of career-track, one involving external mobility and, some even told us, greed. In 2000, Force Ouvrière, a leading trade union, distributed a leaflet saying, 'Investment professionals, we don't have the same corporate values!' to express the view that the new (Anglo-Saxon) model was undermining corporate loyalty and solidarity and favouring individualistic and money-oriented attitudes. From a cognitive point of view, therefore, trade unions opposed the introduction of a new model of human resource management that would destroy employees' commitment to their company. But it is also easy to understand why they would oppose it from a political point of view.

Autonomous subsidiaries operating outside the national collective agreement would be a direct threat to trade unions. Their rights to oversee redundancies, to protect employees against unfair practices, and to have a stake in many personnel management areas would be eliminated. It would also become possible for banks or insurers to create not only asset management subsidiaries but any other kind of subsidiaries and thus to destroy the relevance of collective agreements. And the trade unions were not ready to accept that.

Retail banks were a third coalition opposed to the Anglo-Saxon model. They were convinced that universal banking was a superior way to organize their business, as can be seen in reports from the Commissariat Général au Plan (France's governmental think-tank) on developments in French banking (Commissariat Général du Plan 1992). Universal banking meant that asset management was integrated within banking structures and not autonomous, in contrast to the Anglo-Saxon model. From a political point of view we would also expect retail banks to oppose strongly the adoption of this model. In the French model asset management was very profitable: clients were captive and had to pay high fees, and because of a lack of transparency they could not control how much the bank charged. With a quasi-lack of distinction between their own portfolios and those of their clients, banks had available colossal amounts of money they could play with (Story and Walter 1997, p. 286).

France's sui generis version of the German universal banking model meant that the *grand corps* heading retail banks had become an oligarchy, holding the levers of economic policy and of corporate governance in the boardrooms of major corporations (Story and Walter 1997, p. 218). Accepting the superiority of the Anglo-Saxon model would mean shooting themselves in the foot, by recognizing cracks in their ways of doing and by breaking up the stronghold of their economic power.

Somewhere in the Middle – those Coalitions Ready to be Convinced

In the debate on the French asset management model, there were other coalitions that did not seem to have strong views about the issue before 1994–95. Within these coalitions, we find the COB, the insurance companies and two broad categories we call the State and financial experts. We include them because they later helped to change the balance of power and to establish and institutionalize a new rationality.

Until 1996 the COB shared supervision of the asset management business with banking authorities. Although it did not have exclusive control over asset management firms, its role was critical in, for instance, the licensing of Undertakings for Collective Investment in Transferable Securities (UCITS). Since 1988 there were ethical rules about the management of UCITS, one of which was independence. The COB was therefore receptive to the Anglo-Saxon model, which would make it easier to control the relationships between promoters and managers of UCITS. But apart from that it did not have strong views about the Anglo-Saxon model. And the scandals involving Maxwell, BCCI, Barings and Morgan Grenfell, all of which afflicted the British scene in the early 1990s, were not strong incentives to implement that model in France. Moreover, the COB already had large responsibilities in the stock market and it is doubtful whether it was willing to take on an extra workload. As a result, it is difficult to identify any clear COB position in the debate on French asset management and the Anglo-Saxon model. The same can be said about insurance companies.

Insurance companies collect large amounts of funds through their life insurance and casualty activities, and because of this they have always had a stake in the asset management business. The Anglo-Saxon model could have some advantages for them. With autonomous subsidiaries, they could become more attractive as recruiters in the financial sector, and develop their market share at the expense of retail banks. However, because of the structure of their balance sheet they had a relatively discreet attitude until 1994–95. After all, most of their portfolios consisted of their own assets, not those of third parties. It is therefore understandable that insurers had no strong opinion about the adoption of the Anglo-Saxon model. To a large extent they regarded themselves as belonging to another organizational field, even though they were ready to seize any business opportunity.

Finally, we include in the debate two broad coalitions – the State and financial experts, this second group including customers, academics and journalists. These groups were rather indistinct and not effective operators – the second was anything but organized – but they represented the institutional level of the debate and were therefore quite significant. Before 1994–95, these two coalitions seemed to have rather different opinions about the asset management business. The French State, as already underscored, was a supporter of the

(German) universal banking model. However, from 1993 onwards there was some evolution in discourse. The Crédit Lyonnais fiasco was becoming increasingly obvious and in November 1993, Jean-Yves Haberer, its CEO, was sacked.

In July 1994, debates about the transposition of the European investment services directive started with the publication of a law proposal from the Senate. The financial commission of the Senate, under the presidency of Philippe Marini, a former financier, had drafted a text pointing in the direction of the Anglo-Saxon model, with a clear distinction between investment and credit activities. But as can be seen from the report to the Senate about the transposition of the Investment Services Directive, at first reading the French government did not accept this view and continued to support the universal banking model (Marini 1996, p. 18). In March 1996, therefore, the parliament and the government did not have clear views about the Anglo-Saxon model, and were neutral about any need to depart from the French model.

While some articles by financial experts emphasized the positive dimensions of Anglo-Saxon practices (*Option Finance*, 29 January 1996), others claimed that their reputation was largely overrated (*La Vie Française*, 13 December 1997). Some recognized that it offered more transparency (see the example of ARCCO, in *Option Finance*, 29 June 1998), while others were unconvinced by its merits (the SBF-Sofres survey in *L'Agefi*, 9 July 1996). More generally, the professional magazine *Banque* did not carry many articles about asset management, which suggests that public opinion was fairly neutral about the whole debate. The Caisse de Retraite (pension funds), French asset management's largest client, expressed mixed views about the Anglo-Saxon model.

INCUMBENT VS. CHALLENGER RULES – CONFRONTATION AND RESOLUTION

The initiative of a few key individuals, combined with the benevolent support of the French State, was able to move things along – leading to a quite radical transformation. In fact, a few key individuals acted as institutional entrepreneurs, and seizing upon a window of opportunity, they brought along the constitution of a new organizational field (for a similar combination leading to the structuration of the consulting industry see McKenna et al. in this volume). The core of that organizational field was the asset management activity which had been until then in France only a small, marginal and subordinate subpart of the banking and insurance organizational fields. After looking at the way in which these individuals got organized and created the context for collective agency[3] around 1994–95, we will show then how they seized the double historical opportunity of the transposition to France of a European directive and of the constitution in France of a formal working group to impose their views on the debate.

Collective Agency and Coalition Building

We showed above that heads of asset management departments were amongst the champions in France of an Anglo-Saxon logic. However, the concrete role played by some members of this coalition is not well known and deserves to be described in greater detail. In 1994–95, a small elite within this group, made up of the heads of those companies that had been operating or were about to operate as autonomous subsidiaries and which followed the Anglo-Saxon model, got together and set out to take collective initiative.

The main message of this elite of French asset managers was that France was in danger, that something had to be done in order to resist foreign competition. Times had changed and the French asset management industry, although large and apparently powerful, was in danger of losing out to international competition. Quotes from two influential members of the Asset Managers Club give an accurate and interesting picture of this process of collective entrepreneurship.

> We did some brainstorming together. We understood that the market had to evolve. The British sell the credibility of London; the Americans that of the USA. People have a certain image of credibility: Americans are regarded as good, safe, as having good products. ... We needed to establish the credibility of France and of French professionals. ... Times had changed. There had been a series of factors ... at a certain point, things were mature; there was some willingness. I created the Asset Managers Club, with 5 or 6 people, in 94–95, with XX, XX, XX and XX. We felt the time had come and that it was necessary to organize as a profession.
>
> We were some people who wanted to change the situation, we created a small Club, which was the starting point for the La Martinière report, in order to exchange our views and to make Members of Parliament, public administration, journalists and a series of people sensitive to the issue. This was driven by a number of people and we tried to sustain a collective action from rule-makers, public authorities, some clients, the press, the academic world and a number of personalities, so that people realize the obligation we had to change.

The individuals who took part in the creation of this Asset Managers Club had a number of common characteristics. All had been in contact with the Anglo-Saxon model (through careers in foreign investment banks and/or abroad). All belonged to networks of *Grandes Ecoles* (HEC, ENA, Polytechnique) and had been in contact with the administrative and political elite, by working in the Treasury, Finance Inspectorate or with professional associations (Asffi, in particular). Thus they represented a typical group of French business elites, as identified for instance by Barsoux and Lawrence (1997, pp. 135–65), with, however, the peculiarity of having been in contact with American and British business.

And they managed to articulate some rhetoric to sustain the argument that French asset management firms ought to adopt the Anglo-Saxon model, claiming that if France wanted to resist international competition it had no choice. Their collective agency was targeted at various institutional levels, and at the coalitions identified earlier. However, on its own this collective agency by the elites of the French asset management industry was not sufficient. It needed a catalyst, an historical opportunity. It needed more fundamentally, in France, to be endorsed in some way by the State.

MAF Law and La Martinière Report

The catalyst of the transformation of French asset management, the window of opportunity that would make possible the creation of a new business with rules of the game quite different from those of the French business system, had two sides to it. On the one hand, a key event was the transposition to France of the European Investment Services Directive (the MAF law). A second defining moment was the public communication of a report from a working group set up by Paris-Europlace (the association representing the Paris stock exchange and helping with its expansion). This report was known as the La Martinière report. Both of these occurred at the same time and they combined to create a momentum that would change French asset management radically and lastingly. Here we can see how a trickle-down trajectory, a directive from the European level, encountered on the ground a trickle-up trajectory, the agency of some individuals who represented key organizational actors. These two mechanisms combined, reinforcing each other naturally in the process.

The first determining event was the transposition to France of the European Financial Services Directive of 1993. This Directive aimed at establishing a European passport for investment services, in order to enable firms in any member state to offer their services in the whole Union. The objective included also establishing common definitions of basic investment services and investment vehicles. But as a Directive it had to be transposed into national law by the national parliaments. Debates first started in France in 1994, building upon a report from the financial commission of the Senate. Amid collective action from the Asset Managers Club, debates found a new life at the end of 1995, all the more since it had become clear by then that European Monetary Integration would take place.

The Madrid European Council of December 1995 had dispelled doubts and uncertainties about the project, with a strong commitment from Paris and Bonn to give birth to a single European currency on 1 January 1999 (*The Economist*, 17 October, 1998). The European Investment Services Directive had thus become extremely important, because an inadequate transposition would put the Paris Stock Exchange at risk of losing ground in a competitive market place (Marini 1996, p. 13). This was precisely also the time when Paris-Europlace set up a working group to examine the competitive situation of the asset management industry. Behind this initiative was one influential character in the French financial market – Gérard de La Martinière.

Gérard de La Martinière, an alumnus of the elite administration school ENA and of the Finance Inspectorate, worked for the French Treasury until 1986. Then, he became the first president of the MATIF, France's futures market. He became General Director and number three of the AXA Group at the time when AXA had just acquired UAP and had become the world's leading insurer. He also oversaw AXA's acquisition of the American Equitable in 1991 and therefore had a very good knowledge and understanding of the Anglo-Saxon logic and model. In 1995, he was also a board member of Paris-Europlace. At the beginning of 1996 he was asked by Europlace to investigate the French capital management industry and assess its competitiveness. He set up a working group, which met between March and October 1996. On 11 July 1996, at Paris-Europlace International Day, the group presented its preliminary conclusions (La Martinière 1996, p. 10). A week earlier, on 2 July 1996, the Modernization of Financial Activities Law (the MAF law) had been voted. The La Martinière Group was thus in operation at the same time as the Parliament was debating the transposition of the Investment Services Directive.

The members of the working group had close links with some of the coalitions identified earlier. The group included most members of the Asset Managers Club, and thus of the coalition representing the chiefs of asset management departments. But there were also independent players, foreign players and representatives of the insurance coalition – not least La Martinière himself. Journalists and a number of state officials were also included. Given the variety of profiles within the working group and the group's systematic use of external consultations, many of the coalitions identified above were drawn into discussions. The only exceptions were retail banks. On the whole, they were not well represented. Only a single bank manager was interviewed and no banking association or professional was in the group. To sum up, the comments we gathered suggest that the La Martinière group perceived itself as on a mission: to show that asset management was a genuine business with an existence of its own, different from retail banking.

Given the profiles of its members, the La Martinière report was therefore a catalyst that offered a forum to certain coalitions, especially the Asset Managers Club and the Anglo-Saxon players. It enabled them to be heard and provided a vehicle to legitimize them, especially against the retail banks. And it influenced and reinforced the re-definition of investment services taking place in the Parliament. Figure 3.2 shows the importance and influence of that group in a graphic manner.

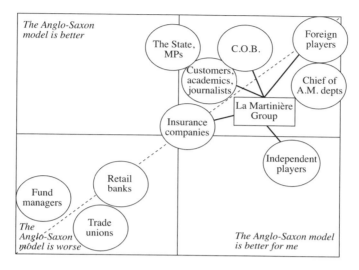

Figure 3.2   The La Martinière group as a catalyst in the debate

The MAF law was voted in July 1996 and the greater part of its second hearings occurred while the La Martinière working group was active. The law was the transposition in French law of the European investment services directive. It covered portfolio management, which was one of the investment services identified in the directive. In France, UCITS were covered through the 1989 law, which gave supervision to the COB. But asset management covered not only UCITS; it also covered mandates, by which investors' funds were managed individually in a separate account according to objectives defined in a written contract (the mandate). The final version of the MAF law turned out to display a surprising feature – neither expected nor specified in the European Directive. This partly accidental and unexpected feature would come to change the face of the organizational field (for a similar type of argument on unexpected consequences of legal acts see Fligstein 1990; Djelic 1998 on the Sherman Antitrust Act and McKenna et al. in this volume on the Glass Steagall Act).

We can assume that both collective agency and the proceedings of the La Martinière working group had some impact on parliamentary debates. The Asset Managers Club had lobbied actively, and the members of the group had connections with the political world. Members of the La Martinière group were invited to hearings in preparation of the preliminary report of April 1996 (Marini 1996). Their work was apparently well known and a member of the French

Senate even referred to it (Senate, session of 2 May 1996). Then a few events cast a new light on the issue of the separation between retail banking and asset management. There was for instance the Pallas Stern Bank scandal. The Pallas Stern Bank entered a bankruptcy procedure on 22 June 1995 and was liquidated in 1997, together with its parent company Comipar. Pallas Stern was a well-known player in the asset management business and its bankruptcy was the largest since World War II (*Les Echos*, 5 October 1995). Its troubles showed the dangers of vertical integration and how it could lead to a mismanagement of investors' portfolios and to a dangerous lack of transparency. It was a further blow, after Crédit Lyonnais, to the French model. But what led to the organic differentiation of asset management, and hence to its constitution as a new organizational field, was in reality something that could easily have seemed a mere technical point in the law.

During the last reading of the MAF law in the Senate, Senator Marini observed that the law lacked consistency and coherence. Portfolio management was recognized as a distinct financial service in the directive but there was no single legal vehicle for providing it: on the one hand there were UCITS, on the other hand many types of companies were allowed to manage individual portfolios. The La Martinière group too had criticized the lack of institutional and legal recognition of the distinctiveness of the asset management business. Marini proposed the creation of a new type of company: the Portfolio Management Company, which would be authorized to manage not only UCITS but also investment mandates. With this single legal entity, the structures would be more coherent. Eventually, the Parliament voted in favour of this new legal vehicle, and decided that the COB should be the only regulator of this new Portfolio Management Company. The MAF law, through these decisions, opened a new social space in the French financial sector: it created a unique legal entity supervised by a single authority. More importantly, if only implicitly, it ended the confusion between banking, insurance and asset management, and created borders between these three related organizational fields. It therefore specified that asset management on its own constituted a separate and distinct business. In other words, the French state had endorsed the position that the structures of the Anglo-Saxon model were appropriate.

INSTITUTIONALIZING A NEW ORGANIZATIONAL FIELD – ASSET MANAGEMENT IN FRANCE

We have seen how two specific events combined to promote the idea that asset management was a new business, distinct from retail banking and insurance. From that recognition, and because it was new, it was possible for that organizational field to structure itself in a social space that was characterized by few pre-existing institutional constraints. At the same time, it was able to take on new rules of organization and behaviour, which it found in the dominant Anglo-Saxon model.

A New Organizational Field, with New Rules at Hand

The MAF law and the La Martinière report were the catalysts establishing a new organizational field. While the law opened a new social space for asset management, the report provided it with new rules of the game.

First, asset management emerged as a new social space. The decision to create the Portfolio Management Company and to put it under the single supervision of the COB meant that asset management was considered a business separate from banking and insurance. It also meant that there was a new field dedicated to this specific activity, hence a new social space where practices related to asset management could develop autonomously. However, the law did not demand de-merger of asset management from existing banking or insurance units (to the difference of the Glass Steagall Act with consulting activities, see McKenna et al. in this volume). It specified few concrete requirements for the organization of the new business. But the La Martinière report and subsequent developments provided the virgin space with a set of rules, inspired by the Anglo-Saxon model.

The La Martinière report strongly recommended both the de-merger of asset management activities and 'the creation of a strong and powerful professional association' (La Martinière 1996, p. 13). More generally, it developed a blueprint for the organization of asset management, and suggested that the rules of the game should replicate the Anglo-Saxon model, in terms of work organization, performance measurement and customer relationship (La Martinière 1996, pp. 5–7, 11). Subsequent developments, in particular the creation of a single professional association (AFG-Asffi) in January 1997, pushed the restructuring of French asset management further along these lines.

Resistance and Institutionalization

However, it would be a mistake to believe that the structuration of French asset management as a new organizational field operating with Anglo-Saxon rules of the game was a smooth and hassle-free event. On the contrary, there was naturally significant opposition from the coalitions identified earlier as opposing the move (see also Tainio et al. and McKenna et al. in this volume). They tried to block its implementation, albeit unsuccessfully.

The fund managers attempted to resist internally the introduction of the Anglo-Saxon model, but their resistance was short-lived. The newly established asset management firms hired massively and the new recruits, often straight from university, were ready to accept the move and to compete against the old guard. Consequently, some fund managers were made redundant, some started their own funds and the remainder were integrated into the new structures. Trade unions tried to stop the de-merging process through lawsuits, in particular one against Société Générale. They tried to prevent SGAM, Société Générale's asset management subsidiary, from leaving the banking national collective agreement, arguing that de-merger was not lawful. However, the bank managed to convince the judges that the new entity was a proper firm, autonomous and involved in a different business. Consequently, trade unions failed to prevent subsequent de-mergers and a large number of autonomous asset management firms soon emerged.

The small and medium-sized banks opposed de-merger and tried to convince the COB to be lenient in implementing the MAF law. However, the COB put pressure on French retail banks to guarantee independence of their asset management activities. The COB was able to do this because the MAF law had put it in charge of approving the activity programmes of the new portfolio management firms as well as the resources available to them. This gave the COB effective leverage to ensure that the new firms had sufficient means of action and sufficient autonomy. In 1997, consequently, more than 100 portfolio management companies were created, and they operated using rules of the game that followed the Anglo-Saxon model.

Structuration of the New Organizational Field

The opportunity to create new firms dedicated to asset management activities made it possible to institutionalize the challenger rules of the game coming from Britain or the USA. Such transnational actors as consultants and pension funds supported this (see Tainio et al. and McKenna et al. in this volume). Ultimately, the resulting structuration of the new asset management business was bound to reflect on the French business system as a whole and at that level it could have a significant impact.

Many financial institutions hired Anglo-Saxon management consultants to design the new structures and organization of their asset management firms. These consultants, integrated in global networks, were able to introduce American or British practices into the new organizational field (for other stories of interplay and reinforcing interactions between business services providers see Tainio et al.; McKenna et al.; Whitley; and Lilja and Moen in this volume). In any case, the La Martinière report provided a blueprint for all French firms, and we saw that it advocated Anglo-Saxon patterns. Moreover, the whole process was witnessed and carefully monitored by such other institutional agents as Anglo-Saxon pension funds, investment consultants and rating agencies. All of these were part of the powerful international networks which made up the global financial markets community. Together they were able to influence the structuration (Giddens 1979, 1984) of the new organizational field and make sure that it complied with the patterns of organization and behaviour dominant in the Anglo-Saxon model.

By constituting asset management as a new organizational field and by providing new rules to operate it, it was possible to implement the Anglo-Saxon model, as a new (Anglo-Saxon) arena within the French national business system – a kind of Trojan horse scenario. Even though French national institutions had naturally not disappeared, French asset management was shielded from their effects because it was constituted and structured as a new organizational field and because of its links to international networks and institutions. It is also interesting that the changes in this small sector of the economy are actually having some impact throughout the French business system.

Asset management channels investment flows from investors and savings to private and public firms, through the financial markets. It therefore has a strong impact on the ways in which firms look for capital and on the rules governing this. The transformation of the French asset management business is consequently intimately linked with a series of developments in financial markets, concerning corporate governance, accounting standards and financial performance. And its adoption of the Anglo-Saxon model undeniably reflects upon the behaviour of large French companies. Since the 1990s and the liberalization of international capital flows, large French companies have seen the proportion of their shares held by US and other foreign investment funds grow steadily. According to a study by the Bank of France, foreign ownership in France represented around 35 per cent of the capitalization of the Paris stock market in 1997. Large French companies have become more like their international rivals and they have adopted stricter standards of accounting and corporate governance, as illustrated by TotalFinaElf, Vivendi-Universal and BNP-Paribas and by the recent campaigns for the rights of minority shareholders (*Financial Times*, 22 October 2001).

Moreover, recent analyses show that the country is moving away from interlocking and concentrated ownership structures and 'towards less complex, market-oriented structures, closer to the US and British models' (Morin 2000, p. 39). It appears that large French firms are changing the way they use their interlocking networks, which are the core of the so-called Latin model of capitalism (Scott 1997, pp. 156–62), and are starting to treat them as portfolios of assets, hence as investments potentially yielding financial revenues rather than shields against hostile takeovers. This change is illustrated by the attitude of the AXA-UAP group, which is managing its huge stock of French equities in line with profitability targets – as in the asset management business – and not primarily to foster strategic control. AXA-UAP could have used its cross-shareholdings or its own assets of 3500 billion francs to raise 60 billion francs and block the 1998 takeover of the French insurer AGF by its rival Allianz, but it did not intervene and thus allowed a foreign player to break the cross-share-holding network. In 2000, Euronext was created by the merger of the Paris, Brussels and Amsterdam stock exchanges and has its headquarters in Paris. After its subsequent acquisition of Liffe, the British derivatives market, some commentators praised Euronext as the leading contender in the race to become Europe's dominant stock exchange operator (*Financial Times*, 30 October 2001, see also Ventresca et al. in this volume). With asset management operating along international (Anglo-Saxon) standards and with a resolutely international stock exchange platform, French capitalism is bound to expand further the role of its financial markets.

These elements show that the French business system is potentially affected by the changes in the asset management business to the extent at least that the latter combine with and are being reinforced by a series of other parallel and similar changes in other parts of the French business scene (see Djelic and Quack in the conclusion to this volume). The country is indeed apparently moving away from the old French political economy model. As Hancké (2001) underlines, large firms have become central agents; but the state still has a role, even if it now focuses more on offering a social policy framework which furthers economic restructuring and competitiveness than on direct intervention.

CONCLUSIONS

Asset management is a peculiar business and the story we have told may have some anecdotal dimensions. It is nevertheless an important story, because asset management is a critical component of any developed financial market that channels savings to securities and definitely influences the shape of firms and economies. A French asset management industry organized in the American or British fashion undoubtedly has had and will have an impact on French capitalism as a whole. But our story also tells us something about our under-standing of business systems.

In a country often regarded as the ideal-type of state-centred capitalism, in which national institutions are expected to be powerful, some firms were able to start behaving in a way that differed from the dominant patterns character-istic of the national business system. In itself this result is not new; it is indeed consistent with other discrepancies observed within national economies, be it at the regional, sectoral or firm level (Maurice and Sorge 2000; Mueller and Loveridge 1997). This result is also consistent with Whitley's recognition that business systems require powerful institutions and display similar patterns only in sectors where national institutions actually have an impact (Whitley 1992).

But even this tells us that we should use the concept of system with caution in the comparative study of economic organization. National economies may well be a collection of disconnected spaces, some of which may combine into a coherent system, and some of which may deviate from, confront or even ignore the systems we define. In other words, even if the French asset management story is not a total surprise, it is a vivid reminder that in the comparative analysis of economic organization we should not dogmatically overstate or misjudge institutional effects.

The story we have told also opens up further research perspectives on institutional change. We showed that individuals fight over social spaces and for them: asset management won out over universal banking by imposing the view that it represented a different business. We showed that such a struggle operates at both a cognitive and a political level, where individuals and coalitions formulate rationalities that best represent not only their understanding but also their strategies. We also showed that the battle could be won only after the establishment of a new equilibrium, when some powerful actors (notably the State) had been convinced. The way we conducted the analysis should be noticed, and in particular how we were able to identify individuals' points of view and rhetorics (the cognitive axis) and interpret their strategies (the political axis). Analysing how particular rationalities articulated with particular positions in an organizational field required precise fieldwork analysis. But it also allowed us to identify the dialectic elements that sustain opposition and change and ultimately alter the positions of the coalitions involved in the debate.

Our third and last conclusion is the recognition that the dialectic developments which underlie business system consistence and transformation are to a large extent unique to their societal context. Change and innovation, to be successful, have to follow a strategy that suits the structure of existing national institutions. In the case of French asset management the path towards the new configuration of the industry employed traditional French activism to achieve institutional change. In fact, the message delivered by the French elites of the asset management business is almost exactly the same as that proposed by the *American Challenge* of Servan-Schreiber (1967). In 1967 and in 1995, the rhetoric of French elites is the same: in the face of international competition, in the face of the expected invasion by Anglo-Saxon competitors, it is necessary to change and to adopt the international dominant standard of organization. This would suggest, in agreement with Whitley (2000), that both the path towards innovation and the structure of debates and conflicts in the organizational field reflect and reveal societal legacies or properties.

NOTES

1. In this chapter, coalitions are defined following Pfeffer (1981). Coalitions are formed when individuals and groups seek to advance their own interests in the face of some perceived threat or in relation to some common goal. They involve intentional acts and strategies that enhance or protect the self-interests of the individuals or groups. To that extent, coalitions differ from other social groups because they relate to a precise goal or problem and because they can be defined in relation to it.
2. We should remember the importance of rent-owners in France until the First World War, as illustrated in Leroy-Beaulieu's book of 1906, *The Art of Investment.*
3. In this paragraph we use the term collective agency to define the various lobbying, influence, opinion and voicing from a group of individuals, who engage in a collective project and aim at the same objectives. We can contrast it with the concept of institutional entrepreneurship, as defined by Selznick (1954) and of collective action as defined by Olson (1965).

REFERENCES

Barsoux, Jean-Louis and Peter Lawrence (1997), *French Management: Elitism in Action*, London: Cassell.

Bourdieu, Pierre (1992), *Les règles de l'art*, Paris: Seuil.

Braverman, Harry (1974), *Labor and Monopoly Capital*, New York: Monthly Review Press.

British Invisibles (1997), *Fund Management*, City Business Series.

Commissariat Général du Plan (1992), *Prospective financière: banques, assurances, marchés*, Paris: La Documentation Française.

Crouch, Colin (1992), *Industrial Relations and European State Traditions*, New York: Clarendon Press.

Crouch, Colin and Wolfgang Streeck (1997), 'Institutional capitalism: diversity and performance', in Colin Crouch and Wolfgang Streeck (eds), *Modern Capitalism or Modern Capitalisms*, London: Sage.

Crozier, Michel and Erhard Friedberg (1977), *L'acteur et le système*, Paris: Seuil.

DiMaggio, Paul and Walter Powell (1983), 'The iron cage revisited: institutional isomorphism and collective rationality in organizational fields', *American Sociological Review*, **48** (April), 147–60.

Djelic, Marie-Laure (1998), *Exporting the American Model*, Oxford: Oxford University Press.

Fligstein, Neil (1990), *The Transformation of Corporate Control*, Cambridge: Harvard University Press.

Giddens, Anthony (1976), *New Rules of Sociological Method*, London: Hutchinson.

Giddens, Anthony (1979), *Central Problems in Social Theory, Action, Structure and Contradiction in Social Analysis*, London: The Macmillan Press.

Giddens, Anthony (1984), *The Constitution of Society*, Cambridge: Polity.

Goyer, Michel (2001), 'Corporate governance and the innovation system in France 1985–2000', *Industry and Innovation*, October 2001.

Hall, Peter and David Soskice (eds) (2001), *Varieties of Capitalism: The Institutional Foundation of Competitiveness*. Oxford: Oxford University Press.

Hancké, Robert (2001), 'Revisiting the French model: coordination and restructuring in French industry', in Peter Hall and David Soskice (eds), *Varieties of Capitalism*, Oxford: Oxford University Press.

Hollingsworth, J. Rogers and Robert Boyer (eds) (1998), *Contemporary Capitalism*, Cambridge: Cambridge University Press.

Kleiner, Thibaut (1999), 'The transformation of French asset management industry 1984–1999', *Les Etudes du Club*, 1999 (61), Jouy-en-Josas, France: Club Finance International.

La Martinière, Gérard (under the direction of) Groupe de travail Paris EUROPLACE (1996), *L'Industrie Française de la Gestion de Capitaux*, Novembre, Paris: Paris Europlace.

Lane, Christel (1989), *Management and Labour in Europe*, Oxford: Oxford University Press.

Lane, Christel (1995), *Industry and Society in Europe: Stability and Change in Britain, Germany and France*, Aldershot: Edward Elgar.

Leroy-Beaulieu, Pierre (1906), *L'art de placer et gérer sa fortune*, Paris: Garnier.

Marini, Pierre (1996), *Rapport fait au nom de la commission des finances, du contrôle budgétaire et des comptes économiques de la nation sur le projet de loi de modernisation des activités financières*, Sénat, session ordinaire de 1995–1996.

Maurice, Marc, Hiroshi Mannari, Yoshi Takeoka and Takenori Inoki (1988), *Des entreprises françaises et japonaises face à la mécatronique: acteurs et organisation de la dynamique industrielle*, Aix-en-Provence: Laboratoire d'Economie et de Sociologie du Travail.

Maurice, Marc, François Sellier and Jean-Jacques Silvestre (1986), *The Social Foundations of Industrial Power: A Comparison of France and Germany*, Cambridge: The MIT Press.

Maurice, Marc and Arndt Sorge (eds) (2000), *Embedding Organizations*, Amsterdam: John Benjamins.

Maurice, Marc, Arndt Sorge and M. Warner (1980), 'Societal differences in organising manufacturing units', *Organization Studies*, **1**, 63–91.

Morin, François (2000), 'A transformation of the French model of shareholding and management', *Economy and Society*, **29** (1), 36–53.

Mueller, Frank and Ray Loveridge (1997), 'Institutional, sectoral and corporate dynamics in the creation of global supply chains', in Richard Whitley and Peer Hull Kristensen (eds), *Governance at Work*, Oxford: Oxford University Press.

Olson, Mancur (1965), *The Logic of Collective Action: Public Goods and the Theory of Groups*, Harvard: Harvard University Press.

O'Reilly, Jacqueline (1994), *Banking on Flexibility: A Comparison of Flexible Employment in Retail Banking in Britain and France*, Aldershot: Avebury.

Parsons, Talcott (1990), 'Prolegomena to a theory of social institutions', *American Sociological Review*, **55**, 319–33.

Pfeffer, Jeffrey (1981), *Power in Organizations*, Marshfield, MA: Pitman.

Power, Mike (1992), 'The politics of brand accounting in the United Kingdom', *European Accounting Review*, **1** (1), 39–68.

Salomon, Daniele (1997), 'The problematic transformation of the banking sector in France', in Glenn Morgan and David Knights (eds), *Regulation and Deregulation in European Financial Services*, London: Macmillan.

Scott, John (1997), *Corporate Business and Capitalist Classes*, Oxford: Oxford University Press.

Selznick, Philip (1957), *Leadership in Administration, a Sociological Interpretation*, Evanston, IL: Row, Peterson.

Servan-Schreiber, Jean-Jacques (1967), *Le défi américain*, Paris: Denöel.

Soskice, David, Robert H. Bates and David Epstein (1992), 'Ambition and constraint: the stabilising role of institutions', *Journal of Law, Economics and Organisation*, **8**, 547–60.

Story, Jonathan and Ingo Walter (1997), *Political Economy of Financial Integration in Europe: The Battle of the Systems*, Manchester: Manchester University Press.

Touraine, Alain (1955), *L'évolution du travail ouvrier aux usines Renault*, Paris: Editions du CNRS.

Weick, Karl (1979), 'Cognitive processes in organization', *Research in Organisational Behaviour*, **1**, 41–73.

Weick, Karl (1995), *Sensemaking in Organizations*, London: Sage.

Whitley, Richard (1991), 'The social construction of business systems in East Asia', *Organization Studies*, **12** (1), 1–28.

Whitley, Richard (1992), 'Societies, firms and markets: the social structuring of business systems', in Richard Whitley (ed.), *European Business Systems*, London: Sage Publications.

Whitley, Richard (1999), *Divergent Capitalisms*, Oxford: Oxford University Press.

Whitley, Richard (2000), 'The institutional structuring of innovation strategies: business systems, firm types and patterns of technical change in different market economies', *Organization Studies*, **21** (5), 855–86.

Whitley, Richard and Peer Hull Kristensen (eds) (1996), *The Changing European Firm*, London: Routledge.

Whitley, Richard and Peer Hull Kristensen (eds) (1997), *Governance at Work*, Oxford: Oxford University Press.

4. Message and medium: the role of consulting firms in globalization and its local interpretation

Christopher McKenna, Marie-Laure Djelic and Antti Ainamo

INTRODUCTION

A century ago, management consulting as we now understand it did not exist. The management consulting industry emerged and structured itself in the twentieth century, growing very rapidly in the process. In today's capitalist landscape, the industry has become a significant actor (O'Shea and Madigan 1997). Historically, the changing needs of a stable group of large corporate clients drove the industry's growth. In time, however, growth also came from the exploration of uncharted territories – new clients, new industries and also new countries. From traditional engagements with private for-profit firms essentially involved in the manufacturing, marketing and distribution of goods, consulting firms have made inroads in the service and non-profit sectors and they have started working with semi-public and public organizations. Slowly from the mid 1960s and much more rapidly since the 1980s, consultants have also internationalized their activities from a mostly American base, often becoming in this process multinational, and increasingly global, firms.

Scholarly interest in management consulting has increased in relation to the weight of the industry in the economy. The role and legitimacy of management consultants are now key questions and emerging answers vary. Some scholars claim that management consultants fill in for a lack of internal expertise or competency. Alternatively, other scholars explain that consultants serve as scapegoats or hired guns in situations requiring difficult decisions (Greiner and Metzger 1995). They are also seen as carriers and brokers of knowledge and practices – or even of fads and fashions (Havelock 1969; Abrahamson 1991; Sarvary 1999). In the context of the internationalization of consulting activities, a particularly rapid phenomenon since the 1980s, the link between this role and the process of globalization has become an important research agenda (Kipping and Engwall 2002).

We would not deny that global consulting firms have become powerful channels for the diffusion of knowledge and practices on a worldwide level. The purpose of this chapter, however, is to show that there is both more and less to the impact of management consulting when it comes to globalization.

In questioning the origins of modern management consulting, the first part of this chapter describes the industry's emergence at the turn of the twentieth century as a constitutive institution in the infrastructure of American corporate capitalism. The modern consulting industry is one key feature in a particular set of 'rules of the economic game' (Djelic and Quack in this volume) that emerged in the United States. Thus we argue that there is more to the relationship between consulting and globalization than simply the diffusion of knowledge and practices. To better grasp the nature of this relationship, we believe that analysts should shift their attention away from the content to the form of consulting as a key institution of modern capitalism. Using a metaphor proposed by McLuhan (1964) in his work on media, the 'medium is the message' and from a focus on content or message, scholars should turn to the medium itself, the infrastructure behind the message. Modern management consulting plays a central role in the globalization process. More than simply through the diffusion of knowledge and practices, we argue that management consulting contributes to globalization by pushing new rules of the capitalist game in those countries where the industry becomes a significant player.

Modern management consulting expanded internationally during the second half of the twentieth century. There were two main moments in that transfer. The first was the 'American challenge' of the 1960s and the arrival *en masse* of American corporations and service providers in Western Europe. The second followed the fall of the Berlin Wall. Taking France and Finland to exemplify these two moments, we focus in sections two and three of this chapter on the respective processes through which modern management consulting came to each country. Both cases confirm the contribution of the industry to the re-definition of national rules of the economic game.

The two stories, however, also tell of differences and the respective historical accounts show that this transfer took place in unique conditions in each case. In the process, what had originally been a feature of American corporate and managerial capitalism was reworked, translated and transformed. As consulting spread around the world, the modern – originally American – form of management consulting has come up against national legacies and preexisting institutional constraints that act as filters to which it has had to adapt. This leads us to propose that there is also less to the impact of management consulting than a perfect convergence of practices and rules of the game. Again using McLuhan's framework, the medium is also the 'massage' perhaps even more than the 'message' (McLuhan and Fiore 1967). The massaging of the medium – in our case the originally American form of management consulting – to fit local conditions leads to partial appropriation and thus to a number of hybrid constructions. These hybrids have enough common features that they contribute to a degree of homogenization. They are nevertheless different enough to rule out full convergence.

MANAGEMENT CONSULTING – ORIGINS AND INSTITUTIONALIZATION

Management consulting did not, unlike Athena, emerge fully formed in its modern incarnation. Instead, in retracing the evolution of management consulting, we must clearly differentiate between two very different legacies best personified, respectively, by Frederick W. Taylor and J.P. Morgan. In the United States, prior to World War I, Taylor and Morgan both dominated not simply the market for, but the public perception of, corporate counsel (Kanigel 1997; Chernow 1990). Both men, as well, would define the rules of the game in American industrial relations for most of the twentieth century.

Between Shop Floor and Boardroom: the Two Traditions of American Business Counsel

Frederick Taylor, the leading advocate of scientific management, advised large industrial companies on the most 'efficient' means to speed up shop floor production (Aitken 1960; Nelson 1980). In contrast, John Pierpont Morgan, the senior partner of the most influential investment bank on Wall Street, oversaw the restructuring of the largest American corporations in order to increase their market value (Carosso 1987; Garraty 1957). Both Taylor and Morgan argued that their business methods led to more effective management, but the two men pursued vastly different means to achieve their common goal – while Taylor systematized the industrial shop floor, Morgan reorganized the corporate boardroom (Chandler 1977). Despite their apparent differences, however, modern management consulting owes its genealogy, both in ideological and institutional terms, to these two traditions.

Contemporary consultants, not surprisingly, have been more likely to acknowledge Taylor's legacy than Morgan's, since Taylor actually described himself as a 'consultant', while Morgan always considered himself a banker (Noble 1977). The well-known promoters of scientific management in America, including Frank Gilbreth, Harlow Person, Morris Cooke, Henry Gantt and Herrington Emerson, all acknowledged their intellectual debts to Frederick

Taylor, and between 1901 and 1915, they 'introduced scientific management in nearly 200 American businesses' (Nelson 1992). The influence of Taylorism, however, did not end on the American shop floor. As the market for scientific management declined in the United States after World War I, Taylorite consultants increasingly turned their attention to Europe and Japan for consulting contracts (Waring 1991). In their place a new generation of consultants, interested in 'management engineering' not 'industrial engineering', would come to dominate corporate counsel in the United States.

Scientific management was not the only form of corporate counsel to expand at the turn of the century, although it may have been the most controversial. More staid consulting engineers were well-known among business people for providing expert advice on the new electrochemical industries at the centre of the second industrial revolution. One was Arthur D. Little, founder of his eponymous chemical engineering firm, others were Charles Stone and Edwin Webster, founders of the Boston-based electrical engineering firm Stone & Webster, (Kahn 1986; Keller 1989). In tandem with the large civil engineering firms like Ford, Bacon & Davis, cost accounting firms like Arthur Andersen, and corporate law firms like Cravath, Swaine & Moore, these corporate professionals formed an institutional infrastructure that undergirded the rapid growth of big business in America (Larson 1977). It was the influential merchant bankers, however, who served, *primes inter pares*, to oversee and coordinate this network of corporate professionals for the benefit of the growing corporate giants.

From a modern-day perspective, J.P. Morgan as an archetype of the merchant banker combined the now separate functions of a commercial banker, stockbroker, management consultant and venture capitalist. In order to finance and organize such industrial giants at U.S. Steel, AT&T and General Electric, Morgan and his partners drew upon internal and external networks of advisors to help them evaluate, finance and subsequently reorganize the great industrial corporations (Carosso 1987). Indeed, many of Morgan's partners were not what we now think of as investment or commercial 'bankers', for as George Perkins, John Pierpont Morgan's 'right-hand man', readily admitted, ' I never went behind the counter or examined into the book-keeping end of the business. My job was to assist in the physical organization of the great industrial combines which Mr. Morgan was then engaged in financing' (Garraty 1957, p. 87). In the 1890s, as Morgan employed his internal staff to reorganize most of the American railroad network, he also drew upon external specialists, like the engineering firm Stone & Webster, to advise him on the sale of electrical generating facilities owned by General Electric (Daggett 1908; Keller 1989). The particular importance of the rapid growth of 'consulting engineering' (now better understood as 'management consulting') was not lost on the prominent economist Thorstein Veblen. Veblen explained that 'the ordinary duty of these consulting engineers has been to advise investment bankers as to the industrial and commercial soundness, past and prospective, of any enterprise that is to be underwritten' (Veblen 1921, p. 65). Veblen understood what management consultants later forgot: that the subsequent evolution of management consulting was tied less to Taylor's shop-floor efficiency than to Morgan's top-floor reorganizations.

Unintended Consequence of the Glass Steagall Act: the Birth of an Industry

Morgan's oversight of the functions of management consulting might have continued indefinitely in the United States had the American public not feared the extensive monopoly power of the 'Trusts' and the growing influence of Wall Street bankers (Brandeis 1914; Roe 1991). From the turn of the century on, the American Congress was increasingly distrustful of bankers' concentrated power and repeatedly investigated the role of the 'Money Trust' in the US economy (Carosso 1973). After the Great Crash of 1929, legislators – who blamed the stock market's decline on insider dealing by bankers – worked to curb Wall Street's broad influence by creating institutional checks on the national financial system. From the mid 1930s on, the Federal government required that listed companies hire independent auditors to file quarterly reports, that commercial and investment banking operate independently of each other and that management consulting be separate from commercial and investment banking (McKenna 1995). Where bankers had once acted as *de facto* knowledge brokers for the benefit of their commercial clients, in the mid 1930s management consultants – now independent of bankers – took over this vital economic role. After the passage of the Glass-Steagall and the associated Banking Acts, consultants served as the primary conduits for the exchange of managerial know-how.

The New Deal regulatory changes of the 1930s resulted in an explosion in the number of management consulting firms in the United States. Between 1930 and 1940, the number of management consulting firms grew, on average, 15 per cent a year from an estimated 100 firms in 1930 to 400 firms by 1940 (ACME 1964). By the 1940s, this rapid growth had slowed to 10 per cent annually, but this meant that by 1950 there were nearly 1000 separate management consulting firms in the United States, employing roughly 12 000 consultants. From 1950 to 1960, the growth rate slowed again, but the doubling in size of the average firms and the further doubling of the total number of management consulting firms meant that by the late 1950s there were nearly 50 000 people employed as consultants in the United States (Amon et al. 1958). As these numbers suggest, by the late 1940s and into the early 1950s, the critical problem for most consulting firms was not simply securing new clients or disseminating new management techniques, but simply institutionalizing the recruitment of high-quality people for the rapidly growing profession (Neukom 1975). The large and growing consulting firms, and in particular Marvin Bower of McKinsey & Company, responded to this personnel squeeze by expanding their recruitment to business school graduates, a decision that rapidly institutional-ized the flow of American MBAs into leading consultancies (Bower 1979).

Management Consulting Comes of Age: from Institutionalization to Expansion

Marvin Bower's decision to recruit at Harvard Business School, in the mid 1950s, had a lasting impact not only on McKinsey & Company, but also on the entire field of management consulting. By the early 1960s, the Harvard Business School had become the primary recruiting ground for new staff for elite con-sultancies, with heavy competition among leading firms for 'Baker Scholars', the top 5 per cent of a graduating class (*Career Guide* 1963). By 1961, the average starting salary for consultants graduating from Harvard was $8348, 12 per cent more than the $7500 starting salary for either accountants from Harvard or associates at top corporate law firms in New York (Galanter and Palay 1991; Bower 1963). By the early 1960s, it was increasingly clear to top business school graduates that one of the quickest ways to scale the corporate ladder was no longer through corporate training programmes at industrial companies like General Electric or Westinghouse. Instead, it seemed that the experience and cachet of elite consultancies like McKinsey & Co., Booz Allen or Arthur D. Little was the best insurance of a quick rise to the top (Higdon 1969). The large consultancies had diverted, if only for the first few years of their careers, the stream of the most promising business school students entering the job market.

During the 1950s, even as the senior partners of elite management consul-tancies were trying to institutionalize the flow of new recruits into their firms, they also began to look overseas at new markets for their services (Ryan 1953). Management consultants, unlike the earlier Taylorist consultants, had been slow to go to Europe. They had been busy, initially, keeping up with the surge in demand in the United States after the regulatory changes of the 1930s. They had also been quite unsure what services they might offer to European companies (Bower 1979). To American consultants it seemed that European managers would be particularly unlikely to pay hefty fees for American managerial know-how in the late 1940s and early 1950s when the American Marshall Plan presumably provided these same services for free (Locke 1996; Djelic 1998). In the late 1950s, however, as European managers and policy makers became convinced that American management techniques, perhaps even more than technology or labour, posed the fundamental challenge to European business expansion, European managers reached out to American management consulting firms for help in implementing American managerial innovations (Servan-Schreiber 1967). Leading American consultancies, which had initially followed American multinationals to Europe, quickly founded offices throughout Western Europe even where the latter did not need them. They offered European managers access to the same 'American' model of divi-sionalization that they were providing throughout America (Channon 1973). As a result, analysts would subsequently blame consultants, rightly or wrongly, for much of the Americanization of European business after 1960.

THE TRANSFER TO FRANCE

American management consulting firms began opening offices in France during the 1960s. Following their clients, consultants also rode the wave of a large-scale institutional transformation that had been redefining French industry since the late 1940s. Settling down, however, took time and proved difficult, requiring consultants to adapt to local conditions.

A Taylorist Precedent

Early in the twentieth century, Taylor's ideas had found a sounding board among a small group of French engineers. Before 1914, however, the rare attempts at actually implementing these ideas were on the whole quite contested and unsuccessful in France (Moutet 1997). Taylorism got a new lease of life after World War I, when Taylor's disciples set up offices in Paris. The first to do so were C.B. Thompson and W. Clark, who initially came to Europe to advise national governments. Paul Planus, an early collaborator of Thompson, soon followed and opened an office in Paris during the late 1920s. Within ten years, Planus' practice was quite successful and numbered roughly 35 profes-sionals. Charles Bedaux also opened an office in Paris in 1927. Born in France, Bedaux had emigrated to the United States in 1906, where he developed his own version of scientific management. By 1939, the Société Française Bedaux had 80 professionals and its system had been installed in about 150 firms (Christy 1985).

The ties linking these offices to local engineering and business communi-ties explain in part their relative success. The founders knew how to create and to leverage dense networks, enlisting the support of the small, but well organized, cadre of French Taylorite engineers (Moutet 1997; Kipping 1996). Well-anchored in the American tradition of scientific management but never-theless embedded in the local community, these Taylorite organizers structured the field during the 1930s of professional business counsel in France. Although limited to a few firms, their impact was significant, particularly given the cultural impediments consultants faced. To many French business owners, control – their own or their family's – remained throughout the interwar period a priority over efficiency and high levels of profit (Djelic 1998). Despite a natural French reluctance to external intervention, Taylorite organizers nevertheless managed to convince a few open minded and 'enlightened' business owners to let outsiders scrutinize their shop floors.

This was not yet, though, modern management consulting as we know it (McKenna 1995). Taylorite organizers specialized in time and motion studies, processes and work rationalization at the shop floor level. They did not work on issues of structure, strategy or control at the corporate level as McKinsey or Booz Allen & Hamilton were then doing in the United States. French boardrooms would remain out of reach for many years. It would take a remarkable transformation in the industrial landscape before outsiders would be let in.

Institutional Reengineering – a Necessary Precondition to Modern Management Consulting

The end of World War II created an opening as it came together in France with an acute sense of national crisis. For the new authorities the 'absolute necessity for national rebirth' called for radical transformation and the 'modernization' of economic structures (De Gaulle 1970; Commissariat 1946). A small group of national actors, around the key figure of Jean Monnet, coordinated this initial impetus. Their main referent was the American system of industrial production as an exemplar of the path to modernization (Monnet 1976; Fourquet 1980). This group of French modernizers controlled key institutions, and in particular the planning council, which gave them significant leverage over the national economy (Djelic 1998).

Starting in 1948, American foreign assistance initiative bolstered this French effort. Originally, Washington defined the Marshall plan as simply a programme of financial and material assistance, to provide for large-scale transfer of machinery and equipment. In reality, Marshall planners always had much greater ambitions. Their ultimate goal was to bring to Europe the 'rules of the economic game' as defined in the United States – to export the model of American corporate capitalism (Hoffman 1951; Hogan 1985; Djelic 1998). There was thus proximity and compatibility between the project of French 'modernizers' and American objectives. And in fact a cross-national network soon emerged that worked in close synergy.

One major common undertaking had to do with the small size of French firms and the continuing predominance of processes that left little space to mechanization, specialization and standardization. Both American Marshall planners and French modernizers championed mergers and concentration as a first step towards the modernization of ownership and organizational structures and a necessary condition to the importation of 'advanced' technologies and 'efficient' production methods. Using its access to American goods and its control over counterpart funds as an incentive, the French planning council fostered mergers, restructuring and mechanization in many industries (Djelic 1998).

Another common concern was the existence of cartels and restrictive practices that limited competition, rationalization and the search for efficiency. In 1953, a national antitrust act was enacted but it was not effective (Sélinsky 1979). Changes there would be more indirect, coming through the process of European construction. In 1951, Jean Monnet used American resources and support to integrate American-style antitrust provisions into the coal and steel treaty (Djelic and Bensedrine 2001). These provisions, which were subsequently incorporated in the Rome Treaty during the late 1950s, came to redefine, *de facto*, competition within the European Economic Community and later the European Union. They contributed to bringing closer the rules of the game in Europe to those then prevalent in the United States (Monnet 1976). Under the Rome Treaty, cartels were, in principle, outlawed which encouraged the growth over time of large corporations utilizing mass production and enjoying economies of scale and scope. The American philosophy of antitrust in which 'oligopolies, when policed by the vigorous enforcement of antitrust and anticartel laws as in the United States, yield pretty good results' was thus transferred to Europe (OMGUS Bd18).

Finally, the common cause of American and French 'modernizers' also targeted family capitalism and the 'conservative spirit' of most French business owners (Commissariat 1946). The nationalization of key industrial sectors represented a partial solution since it placed many French firms under the full and direct control of a technocratic elite that favoured large bureaucratic and mass producing hierarchies (Kesler 1985). The professionalization of management emerged as another solution. As part of the technical assistance programme, launched in 1949 within the framework of the Marshall plan, French business owners, engineers and workers were sent to the USA in large numbers to find direct inspiration in the American model. Teams of young experts were also sent to the USA, and they would later become trainers, consultants, and business school professors. A longer-term but parallel project was the construction of a national system of business education to socialize the emergent class of 'managers' (Boltanski 1982). In this case, once again, the recipe was a combination of French initiatives with American models and references, resources and support (Djelic 1998).

The American Challenge

Initially, public and semi-public actors and institutions oversaw this vast and multidimensional transformation. Rapidly, however, this came to be seen as only the first stage in the broader transformation of Europe. Americans in particular believed that these changes would not succeed if they remained state-led. Private initiative should be fostered in order to replace, in time, public intervention. In practice, this led to reorientation after 1953 of the American foreign assistance initiative. The Blair–Moody amendment increased the share, in the technical assistance programme, of direct loans to private companies for structural or technological transformations with a positive impact on productivity.

By the end of the 1950s, there were signs in France that things were indeed changing. In 1959, the French government justified its partial disengagement from the productivity drive by the fact that private initiative had regained sufficient vitality. The Rome Treaty, which had been signed two years earlier and was the second stage, after the coal and steel community, towards an open European market, only reinforced this trend by increasing competitive pressures on French firms. The preparatory work had gone far enough. Time was ripe for the 'American Challenge' (Servan-Schreiber 1967).

While they had been cautious before then, American private companies began moving in great numbers into France – and more generally into Europe – in the late 1950s. American foreign direct investment more than tripled between 1960 and 1973 (Jones and Schröter 1993, p. 10). In Europe, the number of American subsidiaries went from 150 in 1950 to nearly 1500 in the early 1970s (Delacroix 1993, p. 11). Large American companies were apparently the first to understand and seize upon the opportunities created by the structural and institutional transformations that marked Europe. In the wake of their clients followed American service providers, and in particular management consulting firms, which, by then, had become important actors in the United States. Booz Allen & Hamilton was the first to open an office in Paris in 1960. McKinsey arrived in 1964 while Arthur D. Little followed in 1967.

Initially, American consulting firms focused their activities in Europe on serving the American corporations pursuing internationalization. Consultants soon set up local offices, however, when they realized that there was also a domestic market for their services. In France, the mergers and reorganizations of the 1950s had resulted in the creation of large-scale companies for which the old organizational systems were ill suited. In the process, the networks, alliances and cartels through which French firms had previously shared information and maintained protective barriers were gradually weakened or destroyed. The new European regime, policed by a strict anticartel act, disturbed many French executives who were not used to competitive pressure. Changes in ownership structures also created greater need for professional managers both in state-owned and private firms. And many of these new managers had been exposed, in one way or another, to the American 'miracle'. Most of these managers were convinced that the only way French firms could fight the

'American challenge' was by becoming increasingly similar to their American competitors (Servan-Schreiber 1967).

French business counsel, however, was not up to the task of reorganizing French firms in the image of their American competitors, for French consultants did not have those skills. The problem with 'consulting centres' – direct heirs to Taylorite predecessors – was that they focused on shop floor practices and work rationalization; yet French companies now needed external experts who could help them think through strategic issues, implement mergers and move towards structural rationalization. American consulting firms offered just those kinds of services. American consultants were the repositories of 'modern' management knowledge and practices that consultants could transfer to these avid French firms. They were also the missing link bridging the gap, if only indirectly since collusion was becoming less acceptable, between competitors.

American Consultancies and Integration into the French Landscape

As a consequence, American consulting firms expanded rapidly during the 1960s and early 1970s even as firms that focused on scientific management and the shop floor level declined (Kipping 1996). This was true in France but also more generally within Europe. By 1969, McKinsey had six offices in Europe. The number of consultants working for these offices went from 15 in 1962 to 160 in 1969, when European revenues amounted to 35 per cent of McKinsey's worldwide revenues (McKinsey 1971). In France, McKinsey's assignments had to do mostly with helping emerging national 'champions' reorganize their structure. These were the golden years of the multidivisional form (Kogut and Parkinson 1993; McKenna 1997). The first oil shock, however, and difficulties in the process of European construction had a sobering effect. The 'phones stopped ringing' (McKenna 1997) and McKinsey even closed its Paris office for a while. The failure to adapt in spite of changing conditions could also explain, at least in part, the difficulties American consultants faced. As time had passed and the new generation of professional managers had appropriated the institutional and structural transformations of the postwar period, the French had developed their own version of corporate and managerial capitalism and French managers were far less ready than before to favour American consultants simply because they were American.

American consulting firms had to adapt before they could rebound in France. On the one hand, there was an effort at greater integration within the national landscape. American consultancies started recruiting locally, increasingly choosing to have French nationals as local directors. They understood, as American Taylorite organizers had before, that consultants had to be integrated within the networks of local elites. Hence, consultants recruited from the Grandes Ecoles. Interestingly, this did not lead them to compromise with what they saw as their mission and culture. And in many cases, American consultancies sent these French recruits to get MBAs in the US or at INSEAD. In the process, American consultancies undeniably reinforced the trend whereby managers with business school degrees came to play an increasingly significant role in France (Byrkjeflot 2000). Quite a number of former consultants went on to have successful careers as top managers, shaking up the traditional managerial class dominated by engineers and civil servants (Boltanski 1982). Another way in which American consultants adapted was through better responding to their clients' particular needs. The many years of 'one size fits all' solutions were gone and this was true not only within the French market.

Ultimately, the effort paid off. In France and more generally in Europe, the management consulting industry prospered during the 1980s and 1990s. The cumulative revenues of Booz Allen, McKinsey, A.T. Kearney and Arthur D. Little in Europe were over 21 million dollars in 1969, but by 2000, the consulting market in Europe was worth an estimated 25 billion euros (Feaco). The cost of success, however, has been that early American entrants – Booz Allen, McKinsey and Arthur D. Little – faced increasing competition. In the French market, competition came mostly from the US and in particular from the large accounting firms that developed consulting divisions. To a lesser extent, it also came from the transformation of a few local Taylorite organizers. The Gemini group, however, is the only example of a consultancy with French origins growing beyond its national boundaries. To this day, of the 20 largest consultancies in the world, 17 are headquartered in the US (Kennedy Information Research Group).

THE TRANSFER TO FINLAND

In Finland, the American model of management consulting arrived quite late, in the mid 1990s. Preparatory work had been intense, however, since the 1940s mostly due to the efforts of a handful of men. The work of this small network was constrained by local institutional patterns and by the structure of professional business counsel in the Finnish system. Leo Suurla, an industrial rationalization engineer, was the key figure. His right hand was Antero Kallio, a building construction engineer. L. Edward Scriven, an American expert, was the main bridge between Finland and American managerial knowledge. Henrik Virkkunen, Rector of the Helsinki School of Economics, also played a significant role by contributing to the creation of a local pool of managerial and professional talent (Ainamo and Tienari 2002).

The Roots of Business Counsel in Finland

Before the modern form of management consulting came to Finland, trade associations and commercial banks played the role of knowledge brokers and counsel on business issues. Finland's economic development started in the 1860s with the exploitation of wood. Finland was then a Grand Duchy of Russia. Foreign entrepreneurs led the movement, seizing upon the opportunities created by abundant forests, a large Russian market and the emerging railway tracks connecting Finland to Russia (Lilja et al. 1992). The capital-intensive nature of the forestry industry rapidly made it necessary to turn to commercial banks to finance investments. Another device to pool funds was the constitution of trade associations or cartels. In the forestry industry, cartels were also used to share knowledge and to provide individual firms with counsel on infrastructure projects – machine-making and power plants, workers' housing. Finally, cartels also sponsored the creation of bureaus that coordinated international sales (Koskinen 1987).

Trade associations, cartels and banks adapted to a context where a language dispute separated the educated class that spoke Swedish from working class who spoke Finnish. They survived the bloody Finnish civil war of 1917–18 but after Finland gained its independence, the new government became concerned by the country's strong dependence on forests (Laurila 1999, p. 215). Hence it sponsored the creation of a national industrial rationalization association (*Työtehollisuusliitto*) with the aim of fostering standardization, industrialization and growth in other more craft-based industries.

In 1947, the association hired Leo Suurla, a graduate in industrial organization from the Helsinki University of Technology to work on two 'national projects' – reconstruction and industrial exports. At the age of 25, Suurla became the assistant managing director and was granted a significant amount of autonomy and power (Suurla 1987). One of his early contributions was to persuade the Finnish association to join the international coordinating body for national scientific management and industrial rationalization associations – CIOS or Comité International de l'Organisation Scientifique (Ainamo and Tienari 2002).

The Rise and Fall of Local Firms

The 1948 Treaty of Cooperation, Friendship and Mutual Assistance between Finland and the Soviet Union, although in principle only a military treaty, *de facto* created special links with the Soviet sphere of influence (Tainio et al. 2000). Despite this, during Cold War years, Finland was not fully behind the 'wall' and the country managed to remain open to the West. This unique way of being in the middle was heavily criticized in Washington. In the 1970s 'Finlandization' or the Finnish attempt to 'maintain balance in the Cold War no man's land' (Kuisma 1998, p. 138) was highly suspect. The consequence was stringent regulation of American exports to Finland, in particular of 'strategic' technology. The objective was to exert pressure on Finland to sever its Eastern ties and move closer to American expectations, particularly in the economic sphere. In practice, the result was the converse: a nigh-isolation of Finland and a widening gap between that country's institutions and Western standards (Hobsbawn 1994, p. 251).

Behind the geopolitical game, the actions of a few individuals are key to understanding how Finland managed to keep many doors open to the West, particularly in the business and economic sphere. In the 1940s, industrial organization experts were still a highly regulated community in Finland, legitimated by the attribution of government licenses. Underscoring the need for 'messengers of free market economy', Leo Suurla vied for a liberalization of the profession. He engineered a transformation of the old industrial organization association into a local version of a modern consulting firm – RASTOR (Rationalization, Standardization and Organization). He channelled resources away from traditional industrial organization projects into 'company management – that is people management projects' (Suurla 1987). The 1952 Helsinki Summer Olympics revealed Finland to the rest of the world and triggered the interest of a few American and Western European companies in the country. Leo Suurla leveraged this interest to negotiate a $200 000 donation that would fund visits from American management experts into Finland. In this way, Finland was able to bypass, in part, its official exclusion from the American sponsored Marshall plan and technical assistance programme.

The first group of American experts to set foot in Helsinki had little impact, but the 1956 group included a man who would play a significant role in the transformation of the Finnish field of professional business counsel. L. Edward Scriven was an American who, in 1939, had opened the London office of Arthur C. Nielsen's market research branch to 'spread American management knowledge in Europe'. The war prevented him from opening offices in continental European countries and he went back to the United States. In 1956, he came to Finland and his ties with that country would be dense and long lasting (Scriven 2000).

The model Scriven was working from was the modern form of management consulting, as it had come to be institutionalized by the 1950s, in the United States. The focus was on planning and control at the managerial level. This was in stark contrast to the focus on skills at the shop floor level that reflected the prevailing German influence on consulting in Finland. It was also not the same as a more recent focus on leadership characteristics, triggered by the war. Finally, it was some distance away from the emerging interest for central planning and state control that was driven by Soviet connections. Working closely with Leo Suurla and Henrik Virkunnen, Scriven was a major factor behind the diffusion to Finland of a model of professional management that included as one of its key components modern management consulting. He also did a lot to open the 'black box' of the Finnish firm at the time. Scriven managed to convince Finnish managers that temporary outside help might sometimes be much more useful than trying to do everything alone or within a tight social network or cartel arrangement.

An indirect consequence of Scriven's work was that Finnish firms did not settle for local counsel when they pursued internationalization. Instead, they hired international management consultancies. All in all, the Finnish industry used in that period 20–30 foreign management consultants, including Stanford Research Institute and H.B. Maynard from America, EK Konsulterna from Sweden, and Habberstad from Norway. Naturally, their use of outsiders deterred the growth of a domestic consulting industry.

In 1961, Leo Suurla set up a Finnish association of management consultants (Liikkeenjohdon Konsultit or LJK) which joined the international coordinating body of national management consulting associations (Federation of Associations of Consultants or FEACO) itself founded that same year. Yet, by 1966, LJK had only 70 individual members – a good start perhaps but small in comparison to membership in other countries. To spur the growth of a management consulting industry within Finland, Leo Suurla decided to let a 'thousand flowers bloom'.

In 1968, Suurla merged Rastor and Mec – the Finnish subsidiary of H.B. Maynard – to form Mec-Rastor. In 1974, LJK organized the annual world meeting of FEACO in Helsinki. Despite an economic downturn from 1975 to 1977, Mec-Rastor managed to thrive. To offset declining prices, Mec-Rastor increased the number of its assignments, which focused principally on rationalization and downsizing. It also took advantage of state subsidies to diversify into assignments with small and medium-sized companies. Finally, Mec-Rastor advised Finnish companies competing with each other in the Soviet bilateral trade market, where volume and cost generally mattered more than quality. In the process, Mec-Rastor became known as 'the' Finnish national consulting firm. Mec-Rastor estimated its own market share in the 1970s at somewhere around 60–70 per cent of the domestic market (Malin 1989).

While Mec-Rastor dominated its home base then, it was also clear that it was a 'giant with feet of clay'. Even worse, H.B. Maynard was having its own problems and wanted out. Rastor's shareholders (mostly Finnish companies) bought Maynard's share in 1980 (Ainamo and Tienari 2002).

The Swan Song of the Finnish Model

In the 1980s and 1990s, four developments had an impact on management consulting in Finland. First, the Americanization of business and engineering schools had by then gone quite far. These schools were producing increasingly international-minded graduates who were able to discuss and thus disagree with dominant patterns of governance and cooperation. Secondly, Mec-Rastor failed in its attempt to internationalize. Thirdly, the country began to deregulate its economy. Finally, the Soviet Union collapsed.

The first major attack on dominant patterns and consensual institutions came from Nokia. Nokia was then the largest private sector corporation in Finland, a prominent actor in the forestry industry that also occupied a significant position in the electronics industry within Europe. In the mid 1980s, Nokia's CEO, Kari Kairamo, publicly proposed that Finland ought to bet on becoming an 'information society' instead of remaining dependent on 'smokestack industries' such as forestry (Lovio 1989; *Fortune* 2000). His direct collaborators in Nokia could not believe what he had said – forestry was for them a science-based, high-technology industry. To overcome resistance, Kairamo turned to the younger group of engineers within Nokia and hired a few outside recruits with international experience (*Fortune* 2000). Nokia's early move was soon reinforced by others and prompted the Finnish state to action. The state started with the deregulation of the telecom sector and cooperated with Nokia in its attempt to transform the national innovation system (Ainamo 1997). The deregulation of the banking sector soon followed. Finland's economy boomed and the gross domestic product grew quickly. By the mid 1980s, the country was often labelled the 'Japan of Europe' (Tainio et al. 2000, p. 278). As a sign that times were changing, one of the prominent forestry corporations withdrew from the national trade association that also played the role of a sales cartel (Lilja et al. 1992, p. 148). The outside world saw these developments as important signals and American consultancies in particular became increasingly interested in Finland. In 1988, Andersen Consulting and McKinsey set up offices in Helsinki.

This, naturally, represented a major challenge for Mec-Rastor, whose heels were at the same time being nibbled within the domestic market by smaller management consultancies. In the early 1980s, the new management at Mec-Rastor had started down the path to internationalization. The firm then aggressively sought to enlarge its Soviet operations and to exploit the growing Finnish–Swedish trade. History would show that Mec-Rastor bet on the wrong horse. By the end of the 1980s, the slow descent of the Soviet Union into economic decline was turning into outright economic catastrophe. With the collapse of the Soviet market, Finnish trade suffered. This was the end of the Finnish boom and the country entered a period of deep recession that came together with a banking crisis. Nokia had difficulties in consolidating its acquisitions in consumer electronics in Germany and Sweden. Large forestry corporations, one after the other, withdrew from the national trade association, prompting commentators to suggest that the old system was finished (Lilja et al. 1992, p. 148). Last but not least Mec-Rastor was in trouble. In the early 1990s, the company had to restructure in order to escape bankruptcy; in 1996, they sold themselves to Coopers and Lybrand.

The American Invasion

In the meantime, Andersen Consulting and McKinsey were becoming increasingly integrated into the local landscape. The managing director of the Finnish office of Andersen Consulting took it upon himself to follow in the footsteps of Leo Suurla who had retired in 1978. He received extensive media coverage, chaired LJK, proposed Andersen as the benchmark for other management consultancies in Finland, and introduced new products such as 'benchmarking', 'integrated transformation programmes' and 'outsourcing'. Soon, Andersen Consulting was the largest management consultancy in Finland (Ainamo and Tienari 2002). Ironically, though, Andersen's efforts also led to increased competition and foreign firms set up offices in Finland in rapid succession during the 1990s.

During that period, a number of other changes were radically redefining the Finnish business system. Most notably, Nokia became a global player in the digital telecommunications industry (Pulkkinen 1997; *Fortune* 2000). Finnish banks started losing their power over Finnish industry to global financial markets and in particular to American institutional investors (see Tainio et al. this volume). The call for 'deregulation' spread and became increasingly accepted throughout Finnish society. Finland became a full member of the European Union in 1995 and Finnish industry as a whole started to feel the 'need to Europeanize'. These developments reinforced the clout of global management consultancies in Finland.

Finnish managers were searching for new knowledge, 'best practices' and legitimate know-how which these consultancies proposed to sell. More importantly, management consulting emerged as itself an important element in the new rules in the economic game. Global consultancies were central mediating actors, bridging the gap between Finnish firms and their competitors – both the old, domestic type and the new, often global ones. In this bridging role, global consultancies were taking the place previously occupied in Finland by banks and cartel agreements. The same consultancies bridged the gap between Finnish firms and their new owners – often American institutional investors. Arguably, they also bridged the gap between Finnish firms and their own new managers who had been socialized to understand management as a profession where management consultancies were standard bearers and standard setters.

DISCUSSION AND CONCLUDING REMARKS

In its modern form, management consulting has a relatively short history. The consulting industry as we know it was born in the United States during the 1930s, partly as an unintended consequence of the Glass Steagall Act. American legislators wanted to limit the power of banks and after 1934 the latter's more narrow span of activities no longer included business counsel. This important role was taken over by new entrants who went through a period of rapid growth and managed to institutionalize business and corporate counsel as an industry unto itself. The new management consultancies focused on boardroom issues – organizational restructuring, strategy or control. This was quite different from Taylor's focus on the industrial shopfloor and the new firms were closer in fact to Morgan's understanding of corporate counsel.

In the emerging form of American corporate capitalism, the management consulting industry thus played a role that was played elsewhere – and had been played earlier in the US – by banks and cartels. The particular conditions, though, in which that industry took over the role of banks and cartels as knowledge brokers made for significant adjustments and led, one could argue, to the reinvention of that role.

Consulting as Institution

Modern management consulting emerged from the characteristically American preoccupation with concentrations of power. Its birthmark was to make transparent and independent an activity – business counsel – which until then had been used to serve private interests often to the detriment, it was believed, of the wider public. It reinvented in the process a form of corporate counsel that fitted with and even reinforced the stringent antitrust provisions that had come to structure American capitalism. In the 1930s and 1940s, modern management consulting rode on the wave of managerial professionalization then characteristic of the American industry. In time, it even became a key fostering mechanism of that process, along with business education institutions but also stock markets, the increasing size of corporations and the separation of ownership from control (Berle and Means 1932; Roe 2000; Roy 1997). American understanding of knowledge brokering in that context turned out to be quite removed from what it had been in the days of cartels and universal banking. Knowledge brokering was defined as open and encompassing rather than secretive and exclusionary. It was the broad and neutral diffusion of 'best' practices rather than the limited sharing of contextual and subjective information for essentially defensive purposes. It gave all actors equal opportunity in the competitive fight rather than limiting competition in the interests of a few.

In this way, the modern form of management consulting stands out as an important institutional component of the American form of corporate capitalism. It can be considered a constitutive element of its DNA – on a par with the large, multidivisional firm (Chandler 1977), public ownership and stock markets (Berle and Means 1932; Roe 2000), professional management and business education as well as antitrust legislation (Djelic 1998; Djelic and Bensedrine 2001).

Export and its Stages

Starting in the early 1960s, this American 'invention' began to export itself. American consultancies engaged an internationalization path, following in the footsteps of their large American corporate clients. The early destination was Western Europe where they realized, in surprise, that there was a local market for their services. In France, World War II shocked the existing system. Reconstruction became the pretext to radical transformations, which were quite disquieting to local actors. Behind these transformations, the USA loomed large as a model, the 'mystique' of which was effectively diffused in those years through a number of different channels (Djelic 1998). Unlike European consulting centres that had focused almost exclusively on personnel or labour policies and work rationalization, American consultants offered both boardroom level advice on structure, strategy and control and direct contact with the secrets of American know-how.

The second moment in the process of internationalization came in the 1980s with a rush of new entrants in the 'old' Western European markets – including some of local stock – and the assault on the Eastern border. The unique geopolitical position of Finland between 1940 and the 1990s allowed that country to keep many – often hidden – doors open to the West while the domestic market remained officially and formally closed to Western and in particular American firms and consultancies. The largest Finnish firms used consultants for their activities in Western countries. A small group of Finnish men with significant institutional leverage was in the meantime preparing the ground in Finland, working on the institutionalization of management education in the American tradition. So when the Soviet Union collapsed, triggering a national crisis, domestic actors were ready and able to question and shed off dominant institutions and practices. There were calls for changes in corporate governance, for a shift of power away from banks and towards the stock market. Foreign consultancies moved in, taking over with little difficulties the local market of professional business counsel.

Redefining National Rules of the Game?

The cases presented above suggest a new perspective on the worldwide expansion of modern management consulting. The rapid diffusion of knowledge and practices across national borders, for which this expansion is in part accountable, is only the tip of the iceberg. The more significant impact of modern management consulting is its contribution to the redefinition of the rules of the capitalist game in the countries where it comes to play a role. Modern management consulting is part of a 'package' – the unique version of capitalism that was originally, and partly accidentally, born in the United States. It is one piece of a puzzle that fits closely with other pieces, requiring them all to make sense. The structuration of a modern management consulting industry in a given country is bound, as we have shown in the French and Finnish case, to come together with the institutionalization of other elements of the 'package'. It may both follow and reinforce the constitution of large firms, the multiplication of joint stock corporations, the expansion of the role of the stock market, the enactment of strict antitrust rules and the professionalization of management.

In interaction with those other elements, the structuration of a management consulting industry thus becomes a powerful mechanism of change for national institutional systems – through time and in a clearly incremental kind of process (Tainio et al., Kleiner this volume). The progressive institutionalization of this combined set of elements creates, when it happens, a challenge for incumbent rules of the economic game. Consulting on its own may have little impact. But its interaction with changes in ownership structure or with a new definition of competition pushes forth a challenger model. The latter trickles up in a progressive and incremental manner, questioning in time national institutional legacies and rules of the game.

According to a recent survey of European top management consultants, deregulation and the ever-stricter implementation of antitrust legislation are key factors explaining the expansion of their industry (Garcia 1999). In this context, consulting firms emerge as an important – and the only legal – connecting link, a mediating institution between a company and its direct and indirect competitors. In the process, consulting firms spread further and contribute to the institutionalization, in the European landscape, of antitrust principles that forbid direct collusion between competitors. This questions and clearly contributes to threatening European traditions of cartelization and collusion (see also Lilja and Moen this volume).

Another important conclusion reached by European management consultants was that 'the relevance of strategic management consulting (was) strongly related to the systems of corporate control implemented by the firms' (Garcia 1999). More specifically, 'financial rationality based on the premise that management's goals concern the maximization of the value of the company translated into an increasing demand for management consulting' (Garcia 1999). Put differently, this tells us that management consultancies bridge the gap in Europe between local firms and 'new owners', mostly institutional investors of American origin (see Tainio et al. this volume). The latter have taken important positions, in recent years, on European stock markets, radically altering the ownership structure of a large number of firms. In the confrontation between two different worlds, two different paradigms, consulting firms emerge as a massaging interface, a smoothing mechanism (Lilja and Moen this volume). For American investors, consultancies serve as a form of corporate insurance; for European firms they are a legitimacy-enhancing device. For both, they serve as translator. In the process, consulting firms help in the promotion, diffusion and institutionalization of a form of ownership structure and corporate governance distinctly American in its heritage and quite foreign to European traditions – the public firm with dispersed ownership freely traded on stock markets (Roe 2000).

Last but not least, the strong presence and clout of management consultancies has had an impact on national power structures and elite systems (Pinçon and Pinçon-Charlot 1999). The consulting industry has naturally reinforced the trend, in most countries, towards a professionalization of management. More importantly may be the fact that consulting firms have tended to impose themselves as an alternate and legitimate – in worldwide standards – route to corporate power in many countries. They have disrupted in the process traditional social structures and local patterns of elite reproduction, contributing to the relative homogenization, across national borders, of business elites along a model that here again had clear American origins (Byrkjeflot 2000).

Globalization ... and its Limits

Even more than the knowledge it carries, the institution of management consulting as such thus appears to be a driver of homogenization and an agent of globalization. The historical narratives, though, and their comparison do not provide evidence of blind or full convergence. The stories we tell of management consulting in France and Finland reflect the impact of a common model, the American model. However, they also reflect the specific processes for each country through which this model was transferred. The stories point to unique networks of actors, historical accidents and locally grounded types of resistance, to unique and specific institutional and organizational legacies that structured the field of professional business counsel in each country before the transfer and acted as filters, sifters or deflectors to a greater or lesser extent.

Because American consultancies arrived early on in France, they had to face a fair degree of resistance – both active and passive – in that country, part of which was due to the lack of understanding of the purpose of consulting firms at the time. To grow and find a niche in the local ecological context, they had to understand it and adapt to quite an extent. Paradoxically, the great distance between local traditions and the foreign model in the French case and the solid structuration of a field of professional business counsel before the 1960s may have made it easier for a few local actors to survive. One of them at least – the Gemini Group – has become a success story in its own right and a rare case of a non-American consultancy playing on the international stage.

In any case, the process of adaptation and translation in the French case certainly went much further than in the Finnish case. American consultancies arrived in Finland quite late and their 'fame' had preceded their arrival. The largest of Finnish firms knew what management consultancies were; for they had already worked with them in the West. Even the Finnish public certainly knew more about global consultancies in the late 1980s, before they set up offices in that country, than the French elite had known in the 1960s. The consequence was that instead of an 'American challenge', the Finns faced an 'American invasion' and American consultancies entered the market with less need to adapt and little threat from local competitors.

Those different paths and the local 'massaging' processes they imply undeniably point to the limits of the homogenizing effects associated with globalization. Globalization appears to be indeed about new rules of the game transforming local incumbent frameworks – not necessarily radically but potentially quite significantly (Djelic and Quack in the conclusion to this volume). However, the specificity and unique character in each case of the encounter between a common 'dominant' model and multiple local legacies means that the end result remains open and leaves room for variability. By all means, the latter becomes all the more obvious that we go away from formal structures, rules or discourse and closer to practice and action.

REFERENCES

Abrahamson, Eric (1991), 'Managerial fads and fashions: the diffusion and rejection of innovations', *Academy of Management Review*, **16** (3), 586–612.

ACME (1964), *Numerical Data on the Present Dimensions, Growth, and other Trends in Management Consulting in the United States*, Association of Consulting Management Engineers, New York.

Ainamo, Antti (1997), 'The evolution of the Finnish system of innovation: the contribution of NOKIA', in Brian Fynes and Sean Ennis (eds), *Competing from the Periphery*, Ireland: Dryden Press.

Ainamo, Antti and Janne Tienari (2002), 'The rise and fall of a local version of management consulting: the case of Finland', in Matthias Kipping and Lars Engwall (eds), *Management Consulting: An Emerging Knowledge Industry*, Oxford: Oxford University Press.

Aitken, Hugh (1960), *Scientific Management in Action*, Princeton, NJ: Princeton University Press.

Amon, R.F. et. al. (1958), 'Management consulting', *Management Consulting Report Associates*, Boston, MA.

Berle, Adolf and Gardiner Means (1932), *Modern Corporation and Private Property*, New York: Macmillan.

Boltanski, Luc (1982), *Les Cadres*, Paris: Editions de Minuit.

Bower, Marvin (1963), 'Comments on fiscal 1963 profits', *Corporate Archives*, New York: McKinsey & Company.

Bower, Marvin (1979), *Perspective on McKinsey*, New York: McKinsey & Company.

Brandeis, Louis (1914), *Other People's Money and How the Bankers Use It*, New York: Frederick A. Stokes.

Byrkjeflot, Haldor (2000), *Management Education and Selection of Top Managers in Europe and the United States*, Bergen, Norway: Los-senter Rapport, 0103.

Career Guide (1963), *A Harvard Business School Student Publication*, vol. 2, no. 2, Boston, MA.

Carosso, Vincent (1973), 'The Wall Street money trust from Pujo through Medina', *Business History Review*, **47**.

Carosso, Vincent (1987), *The Morgans: Private International Bankers*, Cambridge, MA: Harvard University Press.

Chandler, Alfred (1977), *The Visible Hand*, Cambridge, MA: Harvard University Press.

Channon, Derek (1973), *The Strategy and Structure of British Enterprise*, Boston, MA: Harvard Business School Press.

Chernow, Ron (1990), *The House of Morgan*, New York: Atlantic Monthly.

Christy, Jim (1985), *The Price of Power: A Biography of Charles Eugène Bedaux*, New York: Doubleday.

Commissariat (1946), *Rapport Général sur le Premier Plan de Modernisation et d'Equipement*, Paris: Commissariat Général au Plan.

Daggett, Stuart (1908), *Railroad Reorganization*, Boston, MA: HMC.

De Gaulle, Charles (1970), *Discours et Messages, 1940–46*, Paris: Plon.

Delacroix, Jacques (1993), 'The European subsidiaries of American MNCs', in Sumantra Ghoshal and Eleanor Westney (eds), *Organization Theory and the Multinational Corporation*, New York: St Martin's Press.

Djelic, Marie-Laure (1998), *Exporting the American Model*, Oxford: Oxford University Press.

Djelic, Marie-Laure and Jabril Bensedrine (2001), 'Globalisation and its limits: the making of international regulation', in Glenn Morgan, Richard Whitley and Peer Hull Kristensen (eds), *The Multinational Firm*, Oxford: Oxford University Press.

Fortune (2000), 'NOKIA's Secret Code', Justin Fox, May 8.

Fourquet, François (ed.) (1980), *Les Comptes de la Puissance*, Paris: Encres.

Galanter, Marc and Thomas Palay (1991), *Tournament of Lawyers: The Transformation of the Big Law Firm*, Chicago, IL: University of Chicago Press.

Garcia, Clara-Eugenia (1999), 'Organizational innovations and management models: the role of consultancies in Europe', paper presented at the 1999 EGOS Colloquium in Warwick.

Garraty, John (1957), *Right-Hand Man: The Life of George W. Perkins*, New York: Harper & Brothers.

Greiner, Larry and Robert Metzger (1995), *Consulting to Management*, London: Prentice Hall.

Havelock, Ronald (1969), *Planning for Innovation*, Ann Arbor, MI: University of Michigan Press.

Higdon, Hal (1969), *The Business Healers*, New York: Random House.

Hobsbawn, Eric (1994), *The Age of Extremes*, London: Michael Joseph and Pelham Books.

Hoffman, Paul (1951), *Peace can be Won*, New York: Doubleday.
Hogan, Michael (1985), 'American Marshall planners and the search for a European neo-capitalism', *American Historical Review*, **90** (1).
Jones, Geoffrey and Harm Schröter (1993), 'Continental European multinationals, 1850–1992', in Geoffrey Jones and Harm Schröter (eds), *The Rise of the Multinational in Continental Europe*, Cheltenham, UK: Edward Elgar.
Kahn, Ely Jacques (1986), *The Problem Solvers: A History of Arthur D. Little, Inc.*, Boston, MA: Little, Brown.
Kanigel, Robert (1997), *The One Best Way: Frederick Winslow Taylor and the Enigma of Efficiency*, New York: Viking.
Keller, D.N. (1989), *Stone & Webster, 1889–1989, A Century of Integrity and Service*, New York: Stone & Webster.
Kesler, Jean-François (1985), *L'ENA, la Société, l'Etat*, Paris: Berger-Levrault.
Kipping, Matthias (1996), 'The US influence on the evolution of management consultancies in Britain, France and Germany since 1945', *Business and Economic History*, **25** (1), 112–23.
Kipping, Matthias and Lars Engwall (eds) (2002), *Management Consulting: An Emerging Knowledge Industry*, Oxford: Oxford University Press.
Kogut, Bruce and David Parkinson (1993), 'The diffusion of American organizing principles to Europe', in Bruce Kogut (ed.), *Country Competitiveness*, Oxford: Oxford University Press.
Koskinen, Tarmo (1987), *Tehdasyhteisö: Tutkimus tehtaan ja kylän kutoutumisesta tehdasyteisöksi, kudelman säilymisestä ja purkautumisesta*, University of Vaasa, Finland: Research Report, 123.
Kuisma, Markku (1998), 'A child of the Cold War – Soviet crude oil, American technology and national interests in the making of Finnish oil refining', *Historiallinen aikakauskirja/Historical Journal*, **96**, 136–49.
Larson, Magali Sarfatti (1977), *The Rise of Professionalism*, Philadelphia, PA: Temple University Press.
Laurila, Juha (1999), 'Management in Finland', in M. Warner (ed.), *Management in Europe*, Business Press/Thomson Learning.
Lilja, Kari, Keijo Räsänen and Risto Tainio (1992), 'The forest sector in Finland', in Richard Whitley (ed.), *European Business Systems*, London: Sage.
Locke, Robert (1996), *The Collapse of the American Management Mystique*, New York: Oxford University Press.
Lovio, Raimo (1989), *Suomalainen menestystarina*, Helsinki, Finland: Hanki ja jää.
Malin, Risto (1989), 'Maailma haastaa kansalliskonsultin', *Talouselämä*, **27**.
McKenna, Christopher (1995), 'The origins of modern management consulting', *Business and Economic History*, **24** (1), 51–8.
McKenna, Christopher (1997), 'The American challenge: McKinsey & Cie's role in the transfer of decentralization to Europe, 1957–1975', *Academy of Management Proceedings*, Boston, MA.
McKinsey (1971), 'Dollar distribution of total billings among industrial categories', *Corporate Archives*, New York: McKinsey.
McLuhan, Marshall (1964), *Understanding Media*, New York: McGraw Hill.
McLuhan, Marshall and Quentin Fiore (1967), *The Medium is the Message*, New York: Random House.
Monnet, Jean (1976), *Mémoires*, Paris: Fayard.
Moutet, Aimée (1997), *Les Logiques de l'Entreprise*, Paris: Editions de l'Ecole des Hautes Etudes en Sciences Sociales.

Nelson, Daniel (1980), *Frederick Taylor and the Rise of Scientific Management*, Madison, WI: University of Wisconsin Press.
Nelson, Daniel (1992), *A Mental Revolution: Scientific Management since Taylor*, Columbus, OH: Ohio State University Press.
Neukom, J.G. (1975), *McKinsey Memoirs: A Personal Perspective*, New York: Privately Printed.
Noble, David (1977), *America by Design*, Cambridge, MA: MIT Press.
O'Shea, James and Charles Madigan (1997), *Dangerous Company*, New York: Times Books.
OMGUS Bd18 (1947), *Bipartite Control Office, Economics Division and Decartelization Branch*, Koblenz, Germany, Bundesarchiv.
Pinçon, Michel and Monique Pinçon-Charlot (1999), *Nouveaux patrons, nouvelles dynasties*, Paris: Calmann-Lévy.
Pulkinnen, Matti (1997), *The Breakthrough of Nokia Mobile Phones*, Helsinki, Finland: Helsinki School of Economics and Business Administration.
Roe, Mark (1991), 'A political theory of American corporate finance', *Columbia Law Review*, **91** (10).
Roe, Mark (2000), 'Political preconditions to separating ownership from control', paper presented at the ESSEC Research Seminar, 14 March, Paris, France.
Roy, William (1997), *Socializing Capital*, Princeton, NJ: Princeton University Press.
Ryan, J.R. (1953), 'Consultant field shows big growth', *The New York Times*, 27 December.
Sarvary, Miklos (1999), 'Knowledge management and competition in the consulting industry', *California Management Review*, **41** (2), 95–107.
Scriven, L. Edward II (2000), Son of L. Edward Scriven, email communication with one of the authors.
Sélinsky, Véronique (1979), *L'Entente Prohibée*, Paris: Librairies Techniques.
Servan-Schreiber, Jean-Jacques (1967), *Le défi américain*, Paris: Denoël.
Suurla, Leo (1987), *Julkaisemattomat muistelmat*, Osat 1–13. Espoo, Finland.
Tainio, Risto, Kari Lilja and Matti Pohjola (2000), 'Economic performance after the Second World War: from success to failure', in Sigrid Quack, Glenn Morgan and Richard Whitley (eds), *National Capitalisms, Global Competition and Economic Performance*, Amsterdam: John Benjamins.
Veblen, Thorstein (1921), *The Engineers and the Price System*, H.B. Huebsch.
Waring, Stephen (1991), *Taylorism Transformed*, Chapel Hill, NC: University of North Carolina Press.

Online

FEACO: www.feaco.org
Kennedy Information Research Group, Consulting Central: www.consultingcentral.com

5. Changing transnational institutions and the management of international business transactions

Richard Whitley

INTRODUCTION

The comparative analysis of forms of capitalism has emphasized the institutionally structured nature of economic activities and outcomes (Hall and Soskice 2001; Hollingsworth and Boyer 1997; Whitley 1999). Variations in dominant institutions, such as those governing access to and use of capital and labour, explain the major contrasts in systems of economic coordination and control that have become established in twentieth century capitalism. They also help to account for continuing national differences in sectoral specialisation, technological development and performance (Soskice 1997; Quack et al. 2000; Whitley 2000). An important aspect of these contrasts concerns inter-firm relationships, especially how firms manage transactional uncertainty. Different institutional frameworks encourage owners and managers to deal with suppliers, customers and competitors in different ways across market economies, as the contrast of Japan and the UK exemplifies (see, for example, Sako 1992).

Many of these accounts of different patterns of economic organisation focus on the postwar nation state as the dominant unit of analysis and location of key institutions governing economic activities. As Djelic and Quack point out in their introduction to this book, the international business environment is typically regarded as anomic and adversarial, with weakly developed institutions that are limited in their effects on economic behaviour. However the dominant role of national institutions, and of the nation-state itself, in governing economic activities, is historically contingent, and various conventions for managing international business relationships have been developed in different industries and countries since the rise of industrial capitalism. While the global business environment as a whole may be best characterized as highly uncertain, this has not always been the case for particular sectors and companies where international cartels and similar arrangements were established (see Lilja and Moen in this volume).

The development of cross-border relationships between firms has been facilitated in the last decades of the twentieth century by the growth of regional trade agreements and other forms of economic and political cooperation across national boundaries, especially of course in the European Union. Together with the increasing harmonization and mutual recognition of transnational business regulation (Braithwaite and Drahos 2000), these developments suggest that international institutions are becoming more important in structuring business behaviour at the end of the twentieth century.

Additionally, the nature of the international regulatory regimes governing economic transactions may well be changing from being largely bottom up codification of existing business practices in leading world economies to a more mandatory imposition of standards. Braithwaite and Drahos (2000), for instance, claim that there has been a qualitative shift in the extent and type of global business regulation towards a more standardized and legalistic form. While debate about the significance of *lex mercatoria*, or law merchant, becoming a form of global law without a state (Teubner 1997 and Lehmkuhl in this volume) and the extent of institutionalization of international governance without government (Rosenau 1992, 1998; Ruggie 1993; Young 1992) continues, this view suggests that both the range of issues subject to, and the prevalent mode of implementing, transnational governance have changed in the last quarter of the twentieth century. This expansion of international 'spheres of authority' (Rosenau 1997) has been considerably affected by the proliferation of non-governmental organizations (NGOs), as exemplified by the disputes over genetically modified soya discussed by McNichol and Bensedrine in their chapter.

The growth in scope and intensity of international, if not truly 'global', business regulation together with the increasing variety of organizations and agencies involved in such governance, raise a number of questions about economic coordination and control in the twenty-first century, in particular, whether the international business environment (henceforth IBE) has become dominated by new kinds of global institutions and governance and, if so, of what type and with what consequences for distinctive forms of economic organization within and across national territorial boundaries? How do its principles, agencies and procedures differ from those of earlier periods and what are the results of these changes for business routines and practices in different environments?

In this chapter I consider these points by summarizing the key ways in which the IBE may be changing and how these changes are likely to affect cross-national business behaviour, especially the management of transactional uncertainty. First, I outline some of the major features of the IBE that have changed in the past few decades, and how these may herald the development of a different kind of institutional framework for transnational firm behaviour. I then discuss how these changes might be expected to affect the ways that firms deal with uncertainty in carrying out international business transactions, following the same general logic that governs relationships between institutional frameworks and inter-firm behaviour within domestic environments.

THE CHANGING INTERNATIONAL BUSINESS ENVIRONMENT

In contrast to national business environments where states monopolize, or at least dominate, political competition, control and mobilization, the IBE is characterized by a plurality of political units engaging in continuous cooperation and competition. Since these units vary considerably in their capacities and interests, the global system of nation-states has exhibited a high degree of pluralism in the structures and policies of political entities, especially with regard to the organization of economic relationships and ways of managing uncertainty. Principles, actors and routines concerning the regulation of economic activities vary greatly across national and regional borders so that the standardization and reliability of mechanisms for dealing with transactional uncertainty tends to be lower in the IBE than in many national ones. Indeed, to talk of *the* international business environment as if it were a single, coherent system is probably misleading.

Varieties of International Business Environments and their Particularistic Nature

This plurality of institutions, types of states and regulatory norms within and between territorial units has meant that firms have managed business transactions across national borders in much less standardized ways than those within most countries for much of the twentieth century. How different forms of uncertainty were dealt with varied considerably according to the nature and origin of the firms involved. This was also affected by the characteristics of the sector to which firms belonged and the existence of any transnational regulatory body for that industry, such as private standard setters or the world organizations discussed by Murphy (1994).

   In capital-intensive sectors where technological expertise was critical to competitive success, both capital costs and technical competence restricted industry entry and exit. As a result, the number of major companies operating internationally has been limited in these fields in much of the past century so that formal and informal agreements about production and market sharing or patent pooling, were relatively easy to develop and monitor (see Lilja and Moen in this volume).

This was especially so before the postwar internationalization of antitrust legislation (Arora et al. 1999; Glimstedt 2000; Djelic and Bensedrine 2001). Large firms in industries such as chemicals and electrical engineering were able to organize world markets through mutual self-interest and oligopolistic control over new technologies precisely because there was no effective transnational institutional order regulating firm behaviour. The weak institutionalized regulatory system governing business transactions allowed firms to develop their own idiosyncratic ways of managing uncertainty which meant that collusive cooperation – often under the leadership of a dominant company such as General Electric – could and did develop.

In contrast, where entry and exit were easier and technologies more widely available, the population of potential business partners was larger and more fluid. Accordingly, the identity of individual firms and their distinctive competencies were less easy to ascertain, and their behaviour was more difficult to monitor. In such sectors, the general weakness of cross-border institutions limited cooperation, as well as the ability of companies to develop strong collective standards governing corporate behaviour. Here, companies were more likely to rely heavily on their own experience and knowledge in selecting business partners. Such reliance on process-based trust encouraged firms to restrict their commitments to new business partners and to make longer-term connections directly dependent upon previous performance.

For most firms in the twentieth century, then, international regulatory regimes have been limited in their scope and effectiveness in governing cross-border business transactions. The collective organization of leading firms has been limited in degree and/or time at the international level and there were few international legal institutions solidly established. Formal certification mechanisms for evaluating the creditworthiness and/or competence of foreign firms, in the form of bank references or international standards, did exist, but were restricted in the range of countries where they could be relied upon. Similarly, the institutions governing authority relationships between economic actors across national boundaries remained rather limited in their scope and strength. On the whole, then, for most firms the IBE can best be characterized in similar terms to *particularistic* business environments.

This kind of business system has only weak formal institutions for managing risk and uncertainty and few autonomous collectivities between the individual family or wider kinship grouping and the state (Whitley 1999). Because of pervasive lack of trust in formal procedures and dispute resolution mechanisms, business owners in these kinds of social system are reluctant to delegate control to salaried managers and firms are typically run by families or by groups with whom the founder/owner has close personal ties. Additionally, the weakness of formal regulations and lack of strong collective organizations beyond kinship limit the institutionalization of collective standards and norms governing competence.

These features of the IBE as a whole have meant that the prevalent ways of managing international business transactions in much of the twentieth century have involved considerable reliance on personal and informal networks, especially for smaller firms in peripheral economies (Fafchamps 1996). Similarly, codification of agreements and reliance on contractual controls remain limited by the weakness of cross national legal institutions and the costs of enforcing compliance in foreign jurisdictions. The lack of strong international institutions encouraging lock-in effects between businesses in different countries likewise limited the extent of mutual commitment in cross border agreements, just as limited barriers to entry and exit internationally reduced the effectiveness of reputational control mechanisms.

Growing Formalization and Standardization in the Late Twentieth Century

This general view of environments facing most firms dealing with cross-border transactions in the twentieth century is being challenged by the recent growth of transnational business regulation. According to Braithwaite and Drahos, (2000, pp. 57–65, 84) not only has its extent increased considerably over the last quarter of the twentieth century but it has also altered in key respects, as symbolized by the Agreement on Trade Related Aspects of Intellectual Property (TRIPS) in 1994. While many agreements on how to regulate contracts across borders have developed in a bottom-up manner through reciprocal adjustment, TRIPS, and similar components of the WTO regime, are implemented in a more top-down fashion reinforced by economic coercion.

Furthermore, by enforcing a particular conception of property rights across all members of the WTO, TRIPS represents a stronger form of international regulation than standardizing contractual agreements and their implementation. Insofar as other aspects of cross-border business transactions are becoming governed by these kinds of rules and norms, and policed by similar enforcement processes and agencies, regulatory regimes may indeed be changing and a distinctive IBE becoming established. This embryonic regime is both broader in scope, covering for instance property rights and governance structures as well as contracting procedures, and stronger in degree than previous ones.

These changes have still to proceed as far as some suggest or would like. After all, the European Union has yet to standardize shareholding structures and voting rights (Becht and Röell 1999). In general it has failed to establish firm common rules of the game and governance structures in many markets, as the chapter by Midttun and Micola in this volume illustrates. These changes are also being strongly contested by some groups and countries, as in the case of intellectual property rights in the pharmaceutical industry. They do, however, herald a new kind of IBE in which a novel institutional framework might develop with significant consequences for transnational economic coordination and business behaviour.

One of the more striking features of this emerging IBE is the proliferation of actors. Not only have new kinds of regional political actors such as the European Union become important, but a wide variety of cross-national private business and non-business organizations have developed that monitor and attempt to influence corporate behaviour within and between countries. The range of groups and organizations engaged in constructing international business regulation thus includes: national and regional political associations and their agencies such as the IMF, World Bank and the WTO, cross-border business associations, ad hoc groups of large firms, financial intermediaries, international business service firms and model mercenaries, professional and technical societies, and campaigning NGOs.

The range of issues considered by these groups and organizations has expanded from the rules governing contracts and exchanges across national borders, and technical standards for managing transfers of goods and services, to the standards governing private property rights, corporate control and competitive behaviour (Fligstein and Mara-Drita 1996; Morgan 2001). If successful, these efforts could generate a common system of rules and procedures governing economic activities throughout the industrial capitalist world. However, it seems more likely that, given the quite different institutional frameworks of the USA, the European Union and Japan, as well as the wide variety of private actors involved, a continuing process of argument, bargaining and agreement will evolve, as different agencies and groups attempt to develop regulatory regimes that suit their own interests and rationalities (see McNichol and Bensedrine in this volume for an example).

Considering first the development of new regulatory regimes sponsored or co-sponsored by states, these are changing from the sorts of international unions agreed by national monopolies and ministries in Europe and North America to more transparent attempts to establish arms' length regulatory agencies overseeing specific areas of international economic activity. According to Braithwaite and Drahos (2000, p. 510), many of the nineteenth and early twentieth century coordinating bodies in industries such as posts, telecommunications and transport were 'rife with secret bilateral deals'. Such secrecy is not unknown today, but the combination of US firms seeking new markets abroad, and non-business NGOs seeking to influence global business standards, has both deregulated many national markets for new entrants and encouraged greater openness in regulatory regimes. The spread of antitrust legislation and agencies, at least formally, in Europe and Asia illustrates such processes.

A major factor behind this change has been the dominant role of the USA in the postwar world. Many of the initiatives and approaches to cross-national business regulation from the establishment of the Bretton Woods institutions onwards have reflected Anglo-American conceptions of economic organization, in addition to the interests of large multinational US companies (Braithwaite and Drahos 2000). This has become even more marked since the end of the Cold War. Many of the frameworks and assumptions underlying the legitimization and structure of such regulatory institutions stem from principles associated with the dominant institutions in *arms' length* business environments.

These kinds of institutional frameworks are characterized by much stronger formal institutions than occur in particularistic ones, but tend to be organized into discrete spheres of influence with little coordination between them. Institutional arenas are highly differentiated in terms of how conflict and competition are organized, and elite career paths are similarly separated between societal sectors. Social relationships tend to be regulated by formal rules and procedures that treat actors as discrete individuals pursuing their own, isolated, interests. Authority and trust relations are governed by formal institutions that limit mutual obligations to contractually specified duties. Collaboration between employers, unions and other groups is difficult to establish in such societies because collective actors are typically adversarial in their relations with each other and training systems tend to be fragmented. Firms here are relatively isolated from each other and rarely share risks or opportunities.

Such institutions can be contrasted with those characteristic of more collaborative, or coordinated, market economies (Hall and Soskice 2001; Whitley 1999). In these, economic activities are integrated by strong collective associations, within both industries and regions, which are encouraged by state agencies delegating some regulative functions to them. The more corporatist variants established in continental Europe have strong unions – often structured around industrial sectors rather than skills or employers – that are involved in policy development and implementation. Here, state agencies, employer associations, industrial groups and union federations typically engage in bargaining and negotiation with each other on a continuing basis with strongly institutionalized procedures limiting opportunistic behaviour. Such procedures depend on considerable trust between social partners and widespread beliefs in their joint dependence on cooperation for achieving group objectives.

One of the key principles enshrined in many international agreements that exemplifies this connection between emerging cross-national regulatory regimes and arms' length institutional frameworks is transparency of procedures and standards. In a number of industries, the decline of international coordinating bodies dominated by national agencies and their corporate clients has been paralleled by a growth in supranational agencies and norms that are more formally transparent in their operating rules and procedures, and often more open to legal and quasilegal challenges by outsiders. At least in principle, the international regulation of markets by continuous negotiation of terms and conditions of market access by national champions is being replaced by more harmonized and transparent rules developed and policed by international agencies, such as the WTO, that increasingly have to operate under more formal constitutions. Deregulation of national markets has thus been accompanied by the growth of more formal and accountable regulation that creates a more pre-dictable and stable international business environment, in which at least some of the rules of the game are standardized.

This concern with transparency and formalization of the rules of the com-petitive game institutionalizes the separation of the regulator from the regulated. It reproduces at the international level the stereotypical regulatory state whose primary economic role is to provide a stable and standardized environment for private rational actors, rather than to coordinate their investment strategies and share risks. As the cliché about level playing fields suggests, this is a particu-larly Anglo-Saxon conception of the liberal state and of the role of institutions in regulating economic activities.

It is, however, important to note that more varied international regulatory regimes are being developed at the regional level, sometimes in tandem with supranational political entities, especially of course in the European Union. As well as sometimes being largely imposed by the dominant power, as in NAFTA, these regional regimes can be 'negotiated' or 'emergent' (Djelic and Quack in the conclusion to this volume) as in the European case (Midttun et al. or Plehwe with Vescovi this volume). The ASEAN and the states of Northeast Asia may also be developing a negotiated regional economic bloc, but this seems likely to take a considerable time and will involve major geo-political shifts. The developing European regime could check the worldwide extension of the arms' length model of regulatory institutions, given the corporatist tendencies of the European Commission, and of most member states of the EU. The more coor-dinated nature of many continental European economies, and of the EU as a whole, continues to exemplify an alternative form of capitalism. However, the continual negotiations and development of European institutions seem unlikely to provide a model for cross-national regulatory regimes elsewhere, precisely because of their multi-layered European specificity.

Although much of the postwar growth in state-sponsored, arms' length regulatory regimes was achieved through military and economic coercion, as Braithwaite and Drahos (2000) illustrate, much was also achieved through imitating US regulatory institutions and experiences (Djelic 1998). This was partly because the whole idea of an international regulatory agency monitoring national economic behaviour emphasizes the separation of the transnational organization from those it is intended to regulate and the role of systematic and formal procedures in managing their relationships. These sorts of arms' length legalistic governance structures, while not unique to the USA, are probably longest established and most entrenched there, so that the ability of the USA to gain support for its model in constructing international regulatory regimes is not too surprising.

Increasing Significance of Firms, Model Mercenaries and Epistemic Communities

Additionally, though, such modelling reflects the increasing internationalization of private economic actors, both individually and collectively through various roundtables and alliances of firms and business associations. Capital markets especially have become more international in the last few decades of the twentieth century than in the previous 60 or so years (Ventresca et al. in this volume). They have also become dominated by investment and international fund managers demanding standardization and transparency of market procedures and governance forms, as Tainio et al. show is happening in Finland or Kleiner in France. While a global capital market has yet to be established (compare Held et al. 1999; Hirst and Thompson 1996; *Economist* 1997), large firms in many countries are increasingly raising capital on international markets as opposed to relying mostly on house banks.

Even if the amounts raised remain limited compared to internal financing and bank lending for many European and Japanese companies, the decision to issue shares on the New York and London Stock Exchanges increases pressures on multinationals to restructure their financial accounting routines to follow 'international best practice' as understood by the leading accounting firms and the US Securities and Exchange Commission (SEC). In so doing they help to reproduce these standards and norms across the world, although it is not clear how far this will go in establishing the Anglo-Saxon conception as the dominant one (Tainio et al. and McKenna et al. also raise that issue in this volume). The persistence of large shareholding blocks, dual voting rights and pyramiding in many European countries indicates the continued variety of ownership and control patterns (Berglof 1997; La Porta et al. 1998).

This process exemplifies another major shift in regulatory regimes: the increasing importance of privately sponsored international regulation in the late twentieth century, particularly in capital markets. Because investors in large and liquid financial markets typically hold and manage diversified portfolios to reduce risk, relative financial return is the dominant performance criterion for every asset. This requires standardized financial information so that rates of return can readily be calculated and compared. For investors and analysts to operate effectively across borders in unfamiliar environments, such standard accounting practices have to be supplemented by institutional 'comfort factors' such as international regulatory bodies modelled on the most established domestic one – the SEC – or by extending the reach of domestic accounting and legal systems to such environments.

In other words, the internationalization of capital markets depends on the internationalization of governance structures and regulatory regimes that enable portfolio investors and managers to manage risks in a systematic way. This involves ensuring that playing fields are indeed equal across sectors, firms and markets and that information is both standardized and widely available so that remote fund managers can make decisions on the same basis as insiders.

Standardizing financial accounting routines alone, however, is rarely sufficient to ensure the effectiveness of portfolio investment strategies across business environments, as foreign investors found in East Asia and Russia in the late 1990s. Effective regulatory institutions, preferably modelled on the most established and respected ones, are also needed to attract outside capital, and so many peripheral economies and/or newly industrialized ones have established SEC-type agencies as well as following IMF/World Bank prescriptions on a range of regulatory issues. Additionally, global model mercenaries such as the international – but mostly Anglo-Saxon dominated – accounting, law and consultancy firms seek to enlarge the market for their services by propagating the routines and conventions of arms' length business environments (McKenna et al.; Lilja and Moen in this volume).

Combining technical, marketing, financial and strategic advice and knowledge, these business service organizations provide relatively standardized expertise for dealing with business problems. At least in principle, these kinds of international organizations, like the Japanese general trading companies and similar international business service firms, obtain a large amount of knowledge about many industries in many locations and are able to codify that information for clients. Where they differ from earlier business intelligence services is in claiming ownership of high level expertise in dealing with complex problems based on systematic analysis and research.

In addition to the institutionalization of cross-border technical communities sharing engineering knowledge and problem-solving abilities, these business service organizations are helping to create and reproduce international business communities that have a common knowledge base derived from relatively standardized business school curricula and common approaches to conceptualizing business problems (McKenna et al. in this volume). Leading consultancies, business schools and accounting firms together constitute numerous overlapping epistemic communities that develop and promulgate particular norms constituting international best practice and implement these in their client firms.

To the extent that they are effective in diffusing these approaches and recipes throughout national economies, and this is by no means a straightforward task, they will increase the standardization of business routines and practices. Since many of the more strategic consultancies are American in origin and control, and typically recruit new staff from graduate business schools that themselves are often North American in inspiration and orientation, it is not surprising that they promulgate an essentially American model of economic organization and business behaviour (Kipping and Armbruester 1999; Locke 1996). Their rise and expansion across the industrialized world could, then, reinforce the influence of this model on international regulatory regimes, although in practice the homogenizing effects of such firms may have limits, as McKenna et al. indicate.

Another major group of actors involved in developing international regulatory regimes has been non-business NGOs. They have also encouraged the extension of US models to the international arena. This may be partly because many of them originate in Anglo-Saxon civil society. It may also be because the US political system relies on law to regulate the executive thus encouraging social engineering through the legal system. Even if NGOs are opposed to the US form of capitalism, it provides an enticing regulatory model because of the accumulated experience of establishing operating independent regulators at arms' length from firms and national state agencies. Given that many NGOs in, say, the environment arena wish to develop an effective global regime regulating the behaviour of states and private companies, they are more likely to prefer one that is transparent and rule governed than one modelled on corporatist, often opaque, arrangements. Because transparency facilitates external monitoring and influence, NGOs in general seem likely to advocate transparent regimes with strong external accountability norms that in turn are typically associated with arms' length environments.

A similar effect followed the involvement of many developing countries in international arbitration proceedings in the 1970s and afterwards. Even when they distrusted and rejected the whole idea of universalist legal regimes regulating business–state relationships, their participation in such fora helped to legitimize such ideologies. Since they often used US lawyers because these were seen as less likely to be tainted by colonial assumptions, they additionally assisted the development of international law as an important specialism in US legal circles and the generalization of many assumptions current in the US system to international dispute resolution (Dezalay and Garth 1996). As Lehmkuhl suggests in this book, the growth of private arbitration for resolving international trade disputes is itself generating distinctive cross-national norms and conventions for the governance of conflicts, albeit ones that are often contested.

The growth of international arbitration, business service companies and worldwide non-business NGOs extend and intensify a process that became noticeable towards the end of the nineteenth century: the establishment of international technical or 'epistemic communities' (Braithwaite and Drahos 2000, pp. 501–4; Rosenau 1992, 1998; Ruggie 1993). These networks include state bureaucrats, policy advisors, NGOs of various kinds, lawyers, business consultants and employees of private companies who share common cognitive frameworks, often through having experienced similar educational curricula.

While often disagreeing about goals and values, the members of such communities nonetheless communicate with a common discourse that enables them to debate and argue with each other.

In the case of strong technical communities, knowledge and skills become quite standardized across borders such that firms can reduce uncertainty over what is being exchanged and more easily price goods and services across national and regional markets. Such standardization additionally enables companies to focus their innovation strategies on parts of technical systems and so reduces their risks while they reach a much larger market (Whitley 2000). It also, of course, creates profit opportunities for the companies whose standards are accepted as definitive, and so involves much conflict and negotiation between firms, industry associations and states.

It is important not to overemphasize the significance of these international epistemic and technical communities. They are after all neither wholly new nor universal. However the growth of common cognitive frameworks among many of the key collective actors in the international economy has intensified the internationalization of 'benchmarking' practices and routines, both in governance structures and performance standards and in corporate activities. As in earlier instances of social technology transfer (Boyer et al. 1998; Guillèn, 1994; Djelic 1998; Zeitlin and Herrigel 2000) such comparisons involve varied understandings and differ considerably across actors and contexts, but nonetheless encourage cross-national institutional and organizational learning.

Overall, since the end of World War II a number of factors have encouraged the modelling of worldwide regulatory regimes on Anglo-American institutions. These include the dominance of US firms in many industries, the collapse of the Soviet Union, deregulation of many national markets and the common interest of portfolio managers and NGOs in the external monitoring of economic activities. While the EU is clearly an important collective agent in establishing such regimes, and has sometimes prevented US initiatives becoming realized, Braithwaite and Drahos (2000, p. 485) claim that 'most global regulatory agendas are set by the US', not least because of the tradition of legal entrepreneurship in the USA which is difficult for state trained and controlled legal professions to emulate (Casper 2001). Depending, *inter alia*, on the future of the Euro and enlargement of the EU, the coordinated, if not corporatist, European regime may become seen as an attractive alternative to the US model. However, at the turn of the twenty-first century the prevalent form of global business regulation that is being established in a largely top-down, harmonized form with strong regulatory agencies monitoring compliance and policing deviance seems to be more Anglo-Saxon in its principles and procedures than anything else. As such, it is likely to have particular kinds of implications for the management of cross-border transactional uncertainty.

CHANGING REGULATORY REGIMES AND THE MANAGEMENT OF INTERNATIONAL BUSINESS TRANSACTIONS

In broad terms, the growth of more formal models of international business regulation should reduce transaction costs by making the IBE more predictable and providing codified information about business partners and practice in a wide range of countries. If, indeed, the regulation of corporate and state behaviour has become more standardized internationally around the institutions and structures of the leading arms' length economy, we would expect firms to manage international business transactions in different ways as the IBE becomes less particularistic.

Managing Transactional Uncertainty in Different Business Environments

To analyse how these changes might affect firm behaviour in dealing with transactional uncertainty, we need to distinguish between three major areas in which uncertainty arises: search, agreement and control. Search involves finding business partners who are both able to carry out whatever is agreed to the required standards, and willing to do so at the agreed time and price. It therefore requires knowledge of the range and location of potential partners, and the terms upon which they are likely to collaborate. Such knowledge can be largely personal and/or reputational, and may be based mostly on personal networks, or may be available through more formal and impersonal means such as trade associations, bank references and competence certification or auditing agencies.

A second aspect of search and selection processes concerns the extent to which firms rely on collective standards and norms governing membership of an industry and associated groupings. In some countries, entry to and exit from sectors is more difficult and regulated than elsewhere, so that the identity of firms available for particular kinds of transactions at any one time is more clearly bounded than in other institutional frameworks (Herrigel 1994, 1996). While in Italian industrial districts these collective controls may be predominantly informal, elsewhere they are more formally constituted through licensing regulations and certification rules.

Decisions about the sorts of agreements that firms make with each other often turn on the relative costs of opportunism and flexibility. Much of the discussion about agreement costs has focused on how firms can and do use formal contracts to pre-empt opportunism and structure business transactions in a predictable manner, as distinct from more informal and personal agreements that permit greater flexibility. The extent to which business contracts specify performance standards and how to deal with unforeseen contingencies varies quite strongly between countries, reflecting variations in legal systems and prevailing business norms (Deakin and Wilkinson 1998). Agreements also vary in their expected longevity and the range of activities they cover, from single, highly specific transactions between anonymous traders to long-term partnerships dealing with different kinds of collaboration. More generally, business agreements can be distinguished in terms of the degree of mutual commitment and risk sharing between the parties, as opposed to their preference for arms' length contracting and the maintenance of greater freedom of action.

Control over the execution of agreements involves two major activities. First, it requires the monitoring of how agreed commitments are being carried out and assessing whether they comply with the agreement. This is obviously easier when agreements are highly codified and deal with standardized product qualities. Second, it explicitly or implicitly involves the threat and/or use of sanctions against incompetence and opportunism, together with more positive incentives and assistance to ensure compliance, such as continuing collaboration and mutual benefits. In general, monitoring costs increase with the complexity and uncertainty of the activities being carried out, as well as with the inability to rely on third party enforcement of agreements and guaranteeing of incentives.

The more uncertainty there is about what is being exchanged and its value to users, or about how an agreement is to be fulfilled, the more the parties will be concerned to monitor each others' behaviour. Tacit and new knowledge, for example, is difficult to assess and value without using it in cooperation with its developers. Controlling the execution of an agreement to produce it is therefore difficult without extensive interaction. Such monitoring costs will be increased when there are few supporting institutions to encourage cooperation and sanction breaches of trust.

In very broad terms, firms can manage these three areas of transactional uncertainty in different ways that reflect two underlying dimensions. First, the extent to which they rely on more formal procedures and institutions when dealing with search, agreement and control issues, as opposed to more personal, informal and particularistic processes. Second, their reliance on collective norms and associations in selecting partners and policing agreements, as distinct from operating largely in isolation from other firms in an adversarial environment. These two dimensions distinguish 12 contrasting ways of dealing with search, agreement and control issues that are summarized in Table 5.1.

Considering first the different ways in which firms can manage search processes, where search is predominantly personal and/or ascriptive and cannot rely on institutionalized collective standards, it is highly 'idiosyncratic' and ad hoc. Second, higher levels of collective organization that are rarely formalized into written rules and procedures administered by bureaucratically structured agencies, such as those forming distinctive industrial districts, lead to what

Table 5.1 Strategies for managing transactional uncertainty

		Reliance on formal rules and procedures	
		Low	High
Reliance on collective means of standard setting and ensuring compliance	Low	Idiosyncratic search Informal agreements Particularistic controls	Procedural search Formal market agreements Contractual controls
	High	Community search Informal network agreements Partnership controls	Associative rule governed search Codified partnership agreements Formal network controls

might be termed 'community search' strategies. Third, more formalized and bureaucratically organized ways of ensuring competence and reliability when combined with weak collective organization encourage 'procedural' search, while the combination of formalized procedures with strong collective organization generates 'associative rule governed' search.

Agreements similarly can be divided into four kinds. First we find 'informal market agreements' that are limited in scope and time. These range from the exchange of goods in street markets to ad hoc subcontracting arrangements, such as those described by Shieh (1992) in his account of the organization of export industries in Taiwan. They are usually concerned with simple and standardized goods and services where quality can be readily assessed and price is the dominant consideration.

Second, more extensive and continuing relationships can be combined with relatively informal and tacit agreements where the owners and managers involved have close personal ties and/or strong particularistic reasons for presuming a high degree of mutual dependence such that opportunism is improbable and/or dangerous. Kinship ties can provide a basis for such agreements, as can ethnicity more generally, but process-based trust derived from successive dealings is usually needed as well, as Humphrey and Schmitz (1998) point out. These kinds of agreements can be termed 'informal network agreements'. Third, formal and codified agreements covering a single or a limited series of transactions constitute the standard arms' length contracting transaction and so are considered 'formal market' agreements.

Finally, formally structured and detailed contracts covering a range of activities on a continuing basis, such as those common on the European continent (Deakin and Wilkinson 1998; Lane and Bachmann 1996; Lane 1997), can provide a stable basis for pursuing long-term collaboration, information and risk sharing, but also can limit flexibility and radical innovation. When they do function as effective means of regulating economic exchanges, such contracts can restrict the pursuit of short-term self interest and so encourage investment in joint activities and the continuing improvement of collective capabilities. This kind of agreement can be labelled 'codified partnerships'.

Four kinds of control over business partners can be identified. Where both formal rules and reputational control are relatively weak, firms are unable to rely very much on third party guarantees and sanctions (Fafchamps 1996). This means that agreements become highly dependent upon process-based trust for their fulfilment and monitoring costs are quite high. In turn, this limits firms' willingness to invest in complex transactions, and so reduces their ability to cooperate in nonstandardized and innovative activities. Sometimes, of course, ascription-based networks such as ethnic groupings help to increase reputational control sufficiently to encourage owners to engage in more risky agreements, as the overseas Chinese networks in Pacific-Asia illustrate, but these are rarely sufficient in the absence of performance- and process-based trust developed over a series of transactions (Menkhoff 1992). Such weak control systems tend to encourage 'informal, particularistic' means of managing transactions, often relying on market power and/or mutual self-interest.

The combination of strong contractual control and reliance on formal sanctions through the legal systems with weak reputational control represents the sort of arms' length contracting described by Sako (1992) as characteristic of British firms' subcontracting arrangements. Here, sector identities and common interests are weak, with considerable fluidity in the set of leading firms and only a weakly institutionalized 'industrial order' in Herrigel's sense (1994, 1996). As a result, controls over opportunism tend to be limited to the legal system. Given the expense and disruption of legal action, this means that firms are more exposed to short-term opportunism than where reputational control is greater, and so will be relatively reluctant to commit themselves to long-term collaborations. That said, being able to rely on the contractual system in this case does render compliance more predictable than in the previous situation and so enable rational investment calculations to be made about business partners. It is associated, then, with 'formal contractual' control strategies.

Strong reputational control combined with weak reliance on contractual controls enable firms within the boundaries of the reputational community to enter into agreements fairly easily without much concern about short-term opportunism. Furthermore, the lack of reliance on legal sanctions and formal contracts enables considerable flexibility and adaptation to changed circumstances, as acclaimed in the term 'flexible specialization'. This sort of control therefore encourages 'partnership' types of transaction management strategies.

Finally, the combination of strong reputational control with extensive reliance on detailed and standardized formal contracts generates considerable trust in the quality and reliability of business partners within the reputational grouping. It therefore encourages longer-term collaboration and a willingness to share risks in the pursuit of joint opportunities. However, the very strength of these combined control structures can lock firms into a reliance on a limited set of collaborators and restrict new firm entry. In the longer term this may inhibit radical innovation, especially in technologically dynamic industries. Such control strategies can be termed 'formal network' ones.

Firms adopt these contrasting ways of dealing with transactional uncertainty to differing degrees in different institutional frameworks, as summarized in Table 5.2. Particularistic business environments, for example, limit owners' and managers' reliance on formal methods for managing transactional uncertainty so that search for business partners is likely to be highly personal and informal. Equally, agreements in these sorts of business environments are usually informal and uncodifed, as is typical of many transactions between the overseas Chinese within and across borders (Menkhoff 1992; Redding 1990;

Table 5.2 Connections between three types of institutional frameworks and strategies for managing transactional uncertainty

	Type of institutional framework		
	Particularistic	Arms' length	Collaborative
Key Features			
Trust in formal institutions	Low	High	High
State	Predatory	Regulative	Coordinating
Legal system	Weak	Reliable	Reliable
Financial system	Fragmented	Capital market	Bank-based
Strength of intermediary associations	Low	Limited	High
Prevalent management strategies			
Search	Idiosyncratic	Procedural	Associative rule governed
Agreement	Informal market	Formal market	Codified partnerships
Control	Informal	Formal contracting	Formal network
Reliance on formal procedures	Low	High	High
Reliance on collective norms and associations	Low	Low	High

Yeung and Olds 2000). Firms are likely to be reluctant to share risks and enter into long-term commitments with business partners, unless they have strong personal ties to their owners. The pervasive culture emphasizes the lack of supportive, reliable institutions that could resolve disputes and encourage common beliefs in the good faith of other companies. Opportunism is thus presumed, and commitments correspondingly low. Similarly, the weakness of the legal system discourages the use of contractual control, and reputational controls are often also weak because of the fluidity of firm populations and lack of recourse to reliable means of sanctioning opportunism. All these factors inhibit the exchange of complex and novel goods and services in favour of relatively standardized, homogenous objects that are readily priced and transactions that are easily monitored.

Arms' length institutional frameworks in contrast have effective formal institutions for signalling competence and for enforcing agreements through the legal system. They therefore encourage reliance on impersonal and procedural search processes, and firms typically manage transactional uncertainty through legal contracting rather than by more informal processes. However, since institutions generally do not support collaborative relationships, and indeed facilitate 'exit' from long-term commitments and networks through liquid capital markets and deregulated labour markets, agreements tend not to involve major knowledge and risk sharing. This emphasis on fluid and flexible commitments likewise limits the effectiveness of reputational control mechanisms since firms can relatively readily leave industries, and ownership of companies shifts quite frequently.

More collaborative business environments with strong sectoral associations and powerful business peak associations and close business–state linkages have significant lock-ins between capital providers and users. Reliance on collective standards and reputational controls for search strategies and transaction execution is therefore high in such market economies, and business partners are more willing to enter into long-term agreements than in arms' length or particularistic environments. Where the legal organization of labour interests and regulation of labour relations are strong, as in Germany and other continental European countries, this high level of formal regulation encourages firms to rely on codified agreements and contractual controls in addition to reputational ones.

Changing Regulatory Regimes

In the light of these connections we can now suggest how the changing IBE might affect the way firms manage uncertainty in international business transactions. Considering first its impact on search procedures, the greater formalization and transparency of state economic policies and practices in countries that are members of the WTO and similar regimes should reduce the importance of personal networks in selecting business partners. Together with the growth of international technical and business communities, this can be expected to increase reliance on formal search procedures and collectively developed standards of competence. In other words, these changes in the IBE should lead to greater reliability of formal institutions as a means of evaluating firms' capabilities and trustworthiness. They are unlikely to lead to a complete neglect of more personal means of selecting business partners, especially in particularistic business environments, but may, over time, encourage greater trust in impersonal procedures. In the case of the overseas Chinese business community, however, it seems that personal, particularistic search patterns still dominate their internationalisation strategies (Yeung and Olds 2000).

Similarly, the formalization and expansion of international regulatory regimes seems likely to lead to wider use of formal agreements, especially if such regimes institutionalize model contracts and establish dispute settlement machinery, such as the ICC's International Court of Arbitration. If the general IBE is becoming more influenced by legal procedures and institutions, as the increase in arbitration courts and cases suggests (Dezalay and Garth 1996, pp. 6–7, Lehmkuhl in this volume), firms are likely to increase their use of formal agreements. However, it should be emphasized that such contracts do involve costs, both in terms of the actual work required to formalize agreements and in terms of their relative inflexibility. Firms without lawyers and/or the money and knowledge to use them will be reluctant to rely on formal agreements, and are thus excluded from any benefits such formalization may bring. Additionally, in highly dynamic and uncertain industries firms may find contracts too rigid.

The growing reliability of formal institutions governing international business transactions promised by the increasing formalization, standardization and transparency of regulatory rules and procedures is also likely to encourage a greater willingness to share resources and risks with foreign business partners. Strategic alliances, joint ventures and similar cross-national partnership arrangements become more feasible when the rules of the competitive game appear to be standardized and opportunism somewhat constrained by universal norms.

However, these commitments will remain limited in comparison with those encouraged by more collaborative environments because exit strategies are enhanced by arms' length institutional arrangements. The greater reliability of international formal institutions may increase predictability and reduce trans-action costs, but they do not encourage long-term cross-border partnerships in which firms become highly interdependent with one another. Just as domestic institutions in 'exit' economies do not lock firms and other collective actors, such as unions, into each others' destinies, so too internationalizing formal rules of the game, on its own, does not promote interdependence since exit is always feasible once contractual terms have been met. Moving towards a more arms' length institutional environment and away from a particularistic one may, then, encourage greater commitment across borders than the simple exchange of standardized commodities, without leading necessarily to extensive and long-term interdependence.

In terms of managing compliance uncertainty across borders, the institutionalization of more formal regulatory procedures, and of stronger business and technical communities, should enhance the effectiveness of both contractual and reputational processes. Obviously, the growth of harmonized regulation, mutual recognition of foreign procedures and of transparency, national treatment, most favoured nation and reciprocity principles governing international trade and investment (Braithwaite and Drahos 2000, p. 25) should increase confidence in foreign courts policing formal agreements. Even if, in practice, most firms are reluctant to resolve disputes through litigation, the extension and deepening of these principles across territories are likely to encourage reliance on more formal dispute resolution mechanisms, and make threats to do so more credible. Again, this is especially likely to be noticeable in more particularistic environments, although the disjunction between formal commitment to these principles and everyday practices is also likely to be marked in such societies.

Reputational forms of control over opportunistic behaviour is clearly easier when there are strong international business communities exchanging codified information about firms and markets across the globe and risks are systematically monitored by specialized agencies. Such communities and standardized ratings do not, of course, substitute completely for more private and direct knowledge of particular companies and their owners, but they do increase the general transparency of business behaviour and so make the loss of one's reputation a significant factor in strategic decisions. The growing use of public audits and standardization of accounting procedures across a wider range of countries imply more formalized evaluations of corporate performance. They thus complement and enhance more informal means of ensuring reputational control and developing process based trust.

Similarly, even if most capital markets and firms in Asia and other economies beyond the triad of North America, Western Europe and Japan are too small to engage the attention of most investment analysts, the largest companies that seek to raise capital in Europe and the USA do become subject to much more intense and public scrutiny than they were accustomed to in their domestic environment (see Tainio et al. in this volume). This undoubtedly makes them more susceptible to reputational control in the longer term. Again, though, such mechanisms are typically formal and act at arms' length. They are therefore less powerful and constraining than those of strong industry groups and similar collective associations found in collaborative environments. As ways of managing transactional uncertainty across borders they are, then, limited and usually would need to be supplemented by more direct means of ensuring compliance, such as market power, mutual self interest and contracting.

These changes in regulatory regime at the international level are more likely to affect the behaviour of firms that are located in particularistic and collaborative institutional frameworks. As already suggested, the more international regulatory regimes generate trust in formal institutions and procedures generally, the more confidence firms in particularistic environments will have in them, and the less they should need to rely purely on personal knowledge and networks. In principle, then, stronger formal international regulatory regimes and their pressure to increase domestic transparency should reduce transaction costs within such economies.

Insofar as this does indeed happen, firms may become more willing to undertake transactions with a greater variety of business partners, share more risks and information with them, and exchange more complex and novel objects. However, the likelihood of this happening quickly and effectively in countries such as China seems remote, given the continued supremacy of state agencies and their intolerance of large privately owned and controlled concentrations of wealth (Smart and Smart 2000; Tan and Yeung 2000). Joining the WTO may well lead to greater predictability in the Chinese business environment, but it seems unlikely that it will create overnight a reliable and effective legal system for resolving disputes, especially where these involve state agencies. If local enforcement agencies, political and other elites and the norms governing business behaviour in particularistic societies do not change substantially, the basic patterns of economic organization will remain much the same.

The effects of the extension of arms' length institutions and regulatory norms to international transactions on collaborative business environments may even be slower to emerge, especially in large, wealthy and self-sufficient economies with strong and mutually reinforcing institutions such as postwar Japan (Gerlach 1992; Westney 1996; Whitley 1992, 1999). Despite the considerable increase in foreign direct investment since 1997, exemplified by the Renault domination of Nissan, its economic significance in Japan remains small and the bulk of Japanese economy is internally focused. Even in South Korea where trade dependence is greater, FDI has grown since 1997 and Daewoo has been dismembered, the role of the state remains critical to business development in many industries, banks remain weak and/or closely interdependent with their major customers, and prevalent patterns of economic organization have yet to change qualitatively. The effects of joining the OECD and the WTO have not so far transformed dominant institutions or many aspects of business behaviour, as the controversy over corporate governance at Hyundai illustrates.

However, the growth of transnational business communities and their norms of best practice coupled with the pressures of transparency, capital markets and arms' length regulatory regimes could reduce the influence of collaborative institutions on business behaviour in more open, smaller and/or weaker economies. This depends, though, on the development and mobilization of internal pressure groups and other collective actors with strong interests in achieving changes along similar lines (see Tainio et al.; Kleiner; McKenna et al. in this volume for examples). That in turn implies the existence of institutional conflict and contradictions that enable such groups to emerge and organise coalitions for restructuring governance arrangements.

Where, on the other hand, existing frameworks and actors are flexible enough to adapt and reorganize without radically changing the basic ground rules of their constitution, as seems to be the case in the development of biotechnology in Germany for example (Casper 2000), the impact of such changes in the IBE is likely to be limited. In many collaborative economies, then, these developments are more likely to increase the variety and pluralism of institutional arrangements, and so enhance the autonomy of individual firms, their owners and managers, than to result in radical changes.

CONCLUSIONS

The twentieth century has witnessed a considerable expansion of international regulatory agencies and regimes governing economic transactions, especially in its last two or three decades. These have been state-sponsored, privately developed and jointly negotiated. Many of these have followed the norms and frameworks of the primary arms' length business environment as developed in the USA and UK. As such they represent a shift from a varied set of weakly institutionalized international regulatory regimes and have encouraged a greater trust in, and reliance upon, formal institutions and processes for selecting foreign business partners, developing agreements and policing them. By making transactional risks more predictable and controllable through formal and transparent procedures, these developments are likely to encourage the exchange of more complex and novel objects and services across borders, as distinct from highly standardized and widely available commodities.

However, process-based trust and informal networks remain important for firms managing transactional uncertainty across countries, especially in particularistic institutional contexts. Furthermore, such formalization and transparency increase the costs of firms engaging in international exchanges insofar as they raise compliance standards and force them to adopt formalized procedures and routines. They therefore raise international entry barriers and increase the separation between firms that have the cognitive and financial resources to manage transactions in this environment from those that do not.

Whether developed from custom and practice or from inter-state agreements stabilizing formal regimes and agencies to implement and police them, these international regulatory structures and procedures combined with the expansion of international business and technical communities to standardize and codify the norms governing many aspects of transactional behaviour. As yet, though, they have not institutionalized a global set of regulatory institutions and standards that would dominate all national and regional ones. Rather, they represent the generalization of particular kinds of regime across a greater number of economies and industries, in effect making more markets safer for investors and companies who are able and willing to play this kind of economic game.

Transnational governance of economic activities without transnational governments may have grown considerably at the end of the twentieth century when compared with the inter-war period, but scarcely represents a radically new and dominant level of collective organization. As Braithwaite and Drahos (2000) and the chapters in this book make clear, despite the critical role of the USA and its largest corporations in promulgating global standards and particular kinds of regulatory regimes in specific areas they have not been able to impose their model on the rest of the world in all fields. The establishment of formal international regimes is usually a very long drawn out and rather unpredictable process. It is certainly not at all clear that new trade liberalization rounds and international agreements will be easy to conclude, or that the expansion of capital markets will continue indefinitely.

REFERENCES

Arora, Ashish, Ralph Landau and Nathan Rosenberg (1999), 'Dynamics of comparative advantage in the chemical industry', in David Mowery and Richard Nelson (eds), *Sources of Industrial Leadership*, Cambridge: Cambridge University Press, pp. 217–66.

Becht, Marco and Ailsa Röell (1999), 'Blockholdings in Europe: an international comparison', *European Economic Review*, **43**, 1049–56.

Berglof, Erik (1997), 'Reforming corporate governance: Redirecting the European agenda', *Economic Policy*, April, 93–123.

Boyer, Robert, Elsie Charron and Ulrich Jurgens (eds) (1998), *Between Imitation and Innovation*, Oxford: Oxford University Press.

Braithwaite, John and Peter Drahos (2000), *Global Business Regulation*, Cambridge: Cambridge University Press.

Casper, Steven (2000), 'National institutional frameworks and high technology innovation: the case of German biotechnology', *Organization Studies*, **21**, 887–914.

Casper, Steven (2001), 'The legal framework for corporate governance: the influence of contract law on company strategies in Germany and the United States', in Peter Hall and David Soskice (eds), *Varieties of Capitalism*, Oxford: Oxford University Press, pp. 387–416.

Deakin, Simon and Frank Wilkinson (1998), 'Contract law and the economics of interorganizational trust', in Christel Lane and Reinhard Bachmann (eds), *Trust Within and Between Organizations*, Oxford: Oxford University Press.

Dezalay, Yves and Brian Garth (1996), *Dealing in Virtue*, Chicago: Chicago University Press.

Djelic, Marie-Laure (1998), *Exporting the American Model*, Oxford: Oxford University Press.

Djelic, Marie-Laure and Jabril Bensedrine (2001), 'Globalization and its limits: the making of international regulation', in Glenn Morgan, Peer Hull Kristensen and Richard Whitley (eds), *The Multinational Firm*, Oxford: Oxford University Press.

Economist (1997), 'Capital goes global', 25 October, pp. 139–40.

Fafchamps, Marcel (1996), 'The enforcement of commercial contracts in Ghana', *World Development*, **24**, 427–48.

Fligstein, Neil and Iona Mara-Drita (1996), 'How to make a market: reflections on the attempt to create a single market in the European Union', *American Journal of Sociology*, **102**, 1–33.

Gerlach, Michael (1992), *Alliance Capitalism*, Berkeley, CA: University of California Press.

Glimstedt, Henrik (2000), 'Between national and international governance: geopolitics, strategizing actors and sector coordination in electrical engineering in the interwar era', Unpublished paper, Stockholm School of Economics, Institute of International Business.

Guillèn, Mauro (1994), *Models of Management*, Ithaca, NY: Cornell University Press.

Hall, Peter and David Soskice (eds) (2001), *Varieties of Capitalism*, Oxford: Oxford University Press.

Held, David, Anthony McGraw, David Goldblatt and Jonathan Perraton (1999), *Global Transformations*, Cambridge: Polity Press.

Herrigel, Garry (1994), 'Industry as a form of order', in Roger Hollingsworth, Philippe Schmitter and Wolfgang Streeck (eds), *Governing Capitalist Economies*, Oxford: Oxford University Press.

Herrigel, Garry (1996), *Industrial Constructions*, Cambridge: Cambridge University Press.

Hirst, Paul and Grahame Thompson (1996), *Globalisation in Question*, Oxford: Polity Press.

Hollingsworth, Roger and Robert Boyer (eds) (1997), *Contemporary Capitalism*, Cambridge: Cambridge University Press.

Humphrey, John and Hubert Schmitz (1998), 'Trust and inter-firm relations in developing and transition economies', *Journal of Development Studies*, **34**, 32–61.

Kipping, Matthias and Thomas Armbruester (1999), 'The consultancy field in Western Europe', *CEMP Report No 6*, University of Reading: Department of Economics.

Lane, Christel (1997), 'The governance of interfirm relations in Britain and Germany: societal or dominance effects', in Richard Whitley and Peer Hull Kristensen (eds), *Governance at Work*, Oxford: Oxford University Press.

Lane, Christel and Reinhard Bachmann (1996), 'The social constitution of trust: supplier relations in Britain and Germany', *Organization Studies*, **17**, 365–95.

La Porta, Rafael, Florencio Lopez-de-Silanes and Andre Shleifer (1998), 'Corporate ownership around the world', *NBER Working Paper 6625*, Cambridge, MA: NBER.

Locke, Robert (1996), *The Collapse of the American Management Mystique*, Oxford: Oxford University Press.

Menkhoff, Thomas (1992), 'Xinyong or how to trust trust? Chinese non-contractual business relations and social structure: the Singapore case', *Internationales Asienforum*, **23**, 261–88.

Morgan, Glenn (2001), 'The development of transnational standards and regulations and their impacts on firms', in Glenn Morgan, Peer Hull Kristensen and Richard Whitley (eds), *The Multinational Firm*, Oxford: Oxford University Press.

Murphy, Craig (1994), *International Organization and Industrial Change*, Cambridge: Polity Press.

Quack, Sigrid, Glenn Morgan and Richard Whitley (eds) (2000), *National Capitalisms, Global Competition and Economic Performance*, Amsterdam: John Benjamins Publishing.

Redding, S. Gordon (1990), *The Spirit of Chinese Capitalism*, Berlin: De Gruyter.

Rosenau, James (1992), 'Governance, order and change in world politics', in James Rosenau and Ernst-Otto Czempiel (eds), *Governance without Government*, Cambridge: Cambridge University Press, pp. 1–29.

Rosenau, James (1997), *Along the Domestic-foreign Frontier*, Cambridge: Cambridge University Press.

Rosenau, James (1998), 'Governance and democracy in a globalizing world', in Danielle Archibugi, David Held and Martin Koehler (eds), *Re-imagining Political Community*, Cambridge: Polity Press, pp. 28–57.

Ruggie, John Gerard (1993), 'Territoriality and beyond: problematizing modernity in international relations', *International Organization*, **47**, 139–74.

Sako, Mari (1992), *Prices, Quality and Trust*, Cambridge: Cambridge University Press.

Shieh, Gwo-Shyong (1992), *'Boss' Island*, New York: Peter Lang.

Smart, Alan and Josephine Smart (2000), 'Failures and strategies of Hong Kong firms in China: an ethnographic perspective', in Henry Yeung and Kris Olds (eds), *Globalization of Chinese Business Firms*, London: Macmillan, pp. 244–71.

Soskice, David (1997), 'German technology policy, innovation and national institutional frameworks', *Industry and Innovation*, **4**, 75–96.

Tan, Chia-Zhi and Henry Yeung (2000), 'The internationalisation of Singaporean firms into China: entry modes and investment strategies', in Henry Yeung and Kris Olds (eds), *Globalisation of Chinese Business Firms*, London: Macmillan, pp. 220–43.

Teubner, Gunther (1997), '"Global Bukowina": legal pluralism in the world society', in Gunther Teubner (ed.), *Global Law without a State*, Aldershot, Hampshire: Dartmouth.

Westney, Eleanor (1996), 'The Japanese business system: key features and prospects for changes', *Journal of Asian Business*, **12**, 21–50.

Whitley, Richard (1992), *Business Systems in East Asia*, London: Sage.

Whitley, Richard (1999), *Divergent Capitalisms*, Oxford: Oxford University Press.

Whitley, Richard (2000), 'The institutional structuring of innovation strategies: business systems, firm types and patterns of technical change in different market economies', *Organization Studies*, **21**, 855–86.

Yeung, Henry and Kris Olds (eds) (2000), *Globalization of Chinese Business Firms*, London: Macmillan.

Young, Oran (1992), 'The effectiveness of international institutions: hard cases and critical variables', in James Rosenau and Ernst-Otto Czempiel (eds), *Governance without Government*, Cambridge: Cambridge University Press, pp. 160–94.

Zeitlin, Jonathan and Garry Herrigel (eds) (2000), *Americanization and its Limits*, Oxford: Oxford University Press.

PART II

Globalization and Transnational Institution
Building

6. Coordinating transnational competition: changing patterns in the European pulp and paper industry

Kari Lilja and Eli Moen

INTRODUCTION

The strategy and management literature has tended on the whole to ignore issues of coordination of action between competitors, particularly at the transnational level. There is a growing sense however that 'the image of atomistic actors competing for profits against each other in an impersonal marketplace is increasingly inadequate in a world in which firms are embedded in networks of social, professional, and exchange relationships with other organizational actors' (Gulati et al. 2000, p. 203). Such an argument is derived from and builds upon studies that have concentrated on joint ventures, strategic alliances and the pooling of resources for functional activities, as in R&D consortia. But even within these studies the coordination of market behaviour and strategic commitments of competing firms have received little attention.

By contrast, studies in business history and historical sociology have shown that competing firms are able to identify joint interests that constitute the glue for policy networks. Joint interests also form the basis for the founding of interest and trade associations. Within the framework of such associations, competitors have been able to coordinate several aspects of market behaviour as well as underlying strategic commitments. Such associations can also function as platforms for informal coordination of activities including at the transnational level.

In this chapter, we focus on horizontal coordination of markets and firms precisely at the transnational level. Our field of study is the European pulp and paper industry. Like many other sectors, the pulp and paper industry became cartelized in the first decades of the twentieth century, and member firms have continued to coordinate market behaviour horizontally well after 1945. At the very same time, the pulp and paper industry remained highly fragmented with quite a number of actors involved. This system of governance largely came to an end by the early 1990s. Since then, the industry has assumed a more oligopolistic structure. A key objective of this chapter is to explain change in institutionalized rules of the game at the transnational industry level in the pulp and paper industry – from cartels to oligopolistic specialization.

In Europe, cartels proliferated as means of coordination especially during the interwar period (Edwards 1964; Mirow and Maurer 1982; Herrigel 1996; Djelic 1998; Djelic et al. 2001). At that time cartelization was a highly respected approach on the European continent to economic organization and governance. After World War II, cartels became burdened with negative connotations. American influence in the process of European reconstruction explains that in great part (Djelic 1998). In particular, the American antitrust model for competition policies was adopted by a number of European countries and by the emerging European community (Djelic and Bensedrine 2001). This change in regulatory regime made cartels illegal in parts of Europe and tarnished their image in the process. Still, cartels did not disappear everywhere.

Historically and in many industries, cartels have represented a sort of counter-strategy to tariff barriers. From a Nordic perspective, this has especially been the case in the pulp and paper industry. Through various forms of coordination, Nordic producers were able to overcome disadvantages due to tariffs and transport costs, which in fact sheltered the western European market. To achieve this, Nordic-based cartels negotiated a compromise with companies elsewhere in western Europe, and from the early 1950s onward the industrial order in that industry was characterized by the principle of 'live and let live' (Melander 1997; Moen 1998). This meant essentially an elaborate system of rules on and about market shares that were constantly subject to interpretation and renegotiations because new capacity came on stream. Although the industry was exposed to many challenges during that period, the rules of the game remained by and large the same until the early 1990s. The persistence of cartelization can be explained by the role it played as a risk-sharing mechanism in the system of industry governance. Due to high capital costs associated with investments for new generations of technologies and mills the firms periodically faced liquidity squeezes. Some stability in prices was needed to survive those periods of economic strain and the cartels were a way to ensure price stability.

Starting in the 1990s, we find numerous indications of discontinuity in the patterns of strategic action characteristic of dominant firms. The latter move away from investments in greenfield site operations. They noticeably refocus their business portfolios particularly through divestments and they move to create strategic alliances internationally. The most distinctive feature perhaps in the new industrial order is that dominant firms in Europe have been making public and transparent a vision for their own corporate future and that they have started implementing such strategies. Common features behind these corporate visions are specialization in certain products or specific stages of the value chain as well as extension of production operations on a global scale. Lo and behold, this can be seen as just another way to limit or restrict competition

(Moen and Lilja 2001). We argue in this chapter that such a transformation was in the first place conditioned by a progressive integration of Nordic countries into the European Community, the European Union and more generally the European economic area. Secondly, the process was speeded up by the multiplication of mediating actors such as investment funds, investment banks and management consulting firms (for parallel arguments see Tainio et al.; McKenna et al.; Kleiner; Whitley in this volume). The emerging outcome is a new system of strategic groups of firms (Peteraf and Shanley 1997).

The reconstruction of collusive behaviour is a meticulous and difficult process, because participants in cartels do not record unlawful agreements. Participants in clandestine activity will make considerable efforts to conceal it. The regulation of cartels will discourage the taking of notes and there may be a general rule against keeping records and data. This chapter is based on information collected by the authors for previous studies of the pulp and paper industry. These studies have in turn drawn their data from primary sources such as the archives of various associations and the annual reports of companies. In addition, documentary evidence (EUR-Lex 1994) collected by the European Commission has provided important information about the last few decades. In the dominant corporations we have interviewed some of the CEOs, directors of strategic planning and investor relations. We have also interviewed forest industry analysts in two leading investment banks.

The chapter starts by reviewing the literature on strategic options available for industry level horizontal coordination. The review reveals in the first place that the transnational dimension has been ignored, as has interaction between transnational and national levels. After that, we track the genesis of collective action in the industry, that is the origins of transnational cartels in the interwar period, and outline the reproduction and scope of the latter in the postwar period in relation to regulatory regimes. Then we look at a case study of a cartel in the carton board product group of the industry and at the internal organizational changes that have characterized that cartel in the late 1980s. The case study reveals that large corporations started at that time to challenge the principle of 'live and let live' within the cartel. This was part of an offensive occurring on many fronts and that finally led to the dissolution of the old order. In the final section, we analyse the emergence of the new order by considering the role of new actors, in particular transnational institutional investors and investment banks.

HORIZONTAL POLICY NETWORKS AND THE CONSTITUTION OF TRANSNATIONAL INDUSTRIAL ORDERS

Several research traditions have contributed to our understanding of the motives, forms and mechanisms of collaboration between competitors. One important line of research has been the study of cartels with a particular focus on the collaboration of competitors around market and customer issues (Edwards 1964; Mirow and Maurer 1982; Herrigel 1996). A second important research tradition has been concerned with trade and industry associations (Schmitter and Streeck 1981; Streeck and Schmitter 1985). The idea there is to look at how competitors organize and collaborate to handle interactions with societal institutions – such as for example the State or trade unions. The objective of the collaboration is naturally to secure the best possible conditions for the industry or at least to prevent deterioration of existing conditions. Besides these two, mainly historically- and institutionally-oriented research traditions, there is a third one that conceptualizes period-specific industrial orders or shared recipes for survival in an industry. This approach applies cultural and cognitive modes of investigation (Spender 1989; Porac et al. 1989; Nygaard 1999). Within this tradition, researchers have been conceptualizing ways in which specific industrial orders emerge, are maintained, and/or change (Kenis 1992; Fligstein 1996, p. 668; Fligstein and Mara-Drita 1996; Melander 1997). To construct an analytical framework on transnational co-ordination between competitors, this chapter draws on all three traditions.

Our basic unit of analysis is a period-specific industrial order at the transnational level. Although most studies on industrial orders have concentrated on national contexts, there are generic features at all aggregate levels in the ways these orders are constituted, maintained and changed. We will first draw attention to these generic features and then turn to the more historical and institutional aspects when trying to understand the nature of an emerging order in the pulp and paper industry at the European level. For this purpose, we have to take into account multiple levels of analysis. In conceptualizing globalization as a dependent variable we also find it necessary to consider new forms of transnational regulation and collusive behaviour beside the process of concentration and centralization of capital (see Djelic and Quack in the conclusion to this volume).

The study of cartels has revealed extensive collaboration among competitors (see, for example, Edwards 1964; Mirow and Maurer 1982). Mirow and Maurer even maintain that 'unrestricted competition is the exception rather than the rule' (1982, p. 9). These studies also show that competitors are able to negotiate very elaborate sets of rules to regulate relations between themselves and their customers. Herrigel, in his study of German industrialization, identified four types of governance solutions for decentralized industries: price cartels, term-fixing cartels, specialization cartels and communities of interest (Herrigel 1996, pp. 60–68). For the sake of this chapter, the notion of specialization cartels is particularly relevant. It implies that firms divide markets by specializing into certain products and customer segments. In capital-intensive industries, such an evolution implies coordination of competitive strategies at a deep level of managerial action. Indeed, redirecting production to new products, markets and/or customers is quite a challenge in those industries where investments are heavy.

Such deep level coordination of competitive strategies also presupposes a shared understanding of industry fundamentals: what we call an industrial order. There are various types of mechanisms and institutions that facilitate the emergence of such orders. Spender (1989) has shown that industrial orders emerge and are maintained because managers in an industry tend to have similar types of career paths and experiences that shape their view of typical success factors in an industry. Such a perspective is reinforced by Nygaard's (1999) study of small subcontracting firms. He showed that an industrial order emerged due to an industrial and regional subculture. A specific order allowed small regional firms to take into account mutual long-term interests by sacrificing their own short-term profits. This pattern has prevailed over several generations of entrepreneurs through constant renegotiations. Such a pattern was possible despite several structural obstacles: the number of firms was large, they operated in a highly volatile segment of a vertical value chain and they offered relatively similar skill bundles.

In line with Spender and Nygaard, Kenis (1992) has also demonstrated in his comparative study of the British, German and Italian chemical fibre industry that industrial orders can emerge and be maintained through informal mechanisms. This can happen even during periods when industries experience deep restructuring. Industry level conventions can be maintained on an informal basis by signalling behaviour, via explicit rewards and, in case of violation, via punishments. Kenis also found that there were considerable differences depending on the national context. He suggests that if the restructuring of industries is either market- or state-led it is more difficult to maintain horizontal coordination between competitors than in cases where restructuring involves firms, associations and public administrations, none of these being in a dominant position (Kenis 1992, pp. 157–63). Thus the German case contained the most stable mechanism of horizontal coordination. This conclusion was supported by looking at collective action along many dimensions. Examples of such dimensions were, for instance, vertical integration policy, publicity and trademark policy, lobbying, participation in concerted action, the reduction of competition within the national sector through division of labour, the existence of a national cartel, the reduction of competition from foreign producers through price policy and policies for labour force reduction. It is quite obvious that formal interest organizations were also involved in many of these policy issues.

It is widely recognized that trade and industry associations contribute to the emergence and maintenance of industrial orders. Typically they facilitate an intervention when external threats appear in environmental contexts. Schmitter and Streeck (1981) propose that it is useful to separate four types of functions in an industry association. They represent an organized movement that exerts pressure for public goods. They sell compliance to the government and other regulatory bodies, because they exert control over their members' actions. This capacity can be used as a medium of exchange for negotiating advantages from the national or international political system. Interest associations converge with professional service firms by providing a series of expert services but they differ from them by limiting access to services only to members (see McKenna et al. in this volume). An important aspect of trade and industry associations finally is that they, in fact, provide a platform for the creation of a 'club' through the participation of key persons in the industry. This contributes to building up and sustaining the social capital of those individuals that are at the core of the networks.

A recurrent question in the literature has to do with how industrial orders change. Management studies typically offer frameworks where the transformation of an industrial order is driven by a leading firm. This firm has made innovations in technology, organization or products. Such innovations open the way for a transformation of the preexisting industrial order (Tushman and Anderson 1986). Other traditions also emphasise the entrepreneurial factor. New industrial orders emerge typically through the initiative of an 'institutional entrepreneur' (see Kleiner in this volume). This can, for instance, be the CEO of one of the most prominent firms in the industry, building upon his social capital and using the political connections and coercive power that come from the size and significance of his firm (see Fligstein 1996, p. 668; Fligstein and Mara-Drita 1996, pp. 2–4, see also Tainio et al. in this volume). Such an intervention is typically needed in the case of an external threat that may have dramatic effects on the survival of all firms in an industry. Another situation that requires intervention is the emergence of a new, undefined institutional space (see Fligstein and Mara-Drita 1996, p. 6).

Transformation of an industrial order, however, is seldom either endogenous or exogenous. Reference to a new dominant order or to a set of ahistorical success factors behind the breakthrough of a challenger firm often ignore the long historical roots of an innovation or of a corporation, their institutional embeddedness and associated sets of important stakeholders. Furthermore, there are multiple layers in transnational economic and political systems. Beside intergovernmental policymakers, multinational firms and interest organizations there are other kinds of transnational actors involved. Those include management consulting firms (McKenna et al. in this volume), investment banks (Huolman et al. 1999; Tainio et al. in this volume), lawyers, standardization and certification organizations (Morgan 2001) and more generally so-called transnational epistemic communities (Braithwaite and Drahos 2000; Whitley in this volume). Those actors come into the process and play a significant part in it because they are particularly effective in introducing new business models and new ways of managerial thinking and acting.

We propose that to understand the current transformation of the industrial order in the European pulp and paper industry, we have to conceptualize the interaction between the emergence of a new, still partly undefined, institutional space – the European Union – and the role of these mediating types of trans-national actors. The Single Market programme contained the idea that Europe should allow the emergence of European champions. Firms from different national contexts – often considered national champions in an industry – were encouraged via regulatory changes at European and national levels to enter a restructuring and consolidation process with a European scope.

Such a redefinition of the competitive arena also induced new actors – external to the industrial field – to enter the game. Investment funds, investment banks, analysts employed by these institutions and consultants are those new players right now for the pulp and paper industry. Jointly, analysts, investment banks and funds have considerable disciplinary power through their suggestions for placements in stocks, their actual deals with stocks and other types of property rights and through their period-specific models of ideal typical companies and strategies (Huolman et al. 1999). In the implementation of large-scale strategic changes, mergers and acquisitions, the role of transnational management consulting firms is also significant.

To conclude, horizontal coordination of action among competitors is an important and persistent feature in the context of period-specific industrial orders. Historically, competitors have been able to negotiate solutions that support the survival of incumbent actors in the industry. Such solutions can also be transferred to or forced upon the industry by external actors. In the next sections we look at two subsequent industrial orders in the pulp and paper industry at the European level and ask about the mechanisms and conditions triggering transition from cartels to product-based oligopolistic specialization.

HISTORICAL PATTERNS OF COORDINATION

In the pulp and paper industry, formal cartels were established at the transnational level during the interwar period. National trade associations had emerged in the late nineteenth century and up to World War I several attempts were also made to initiate coordination at the transnational level. All these attempts failed, and it was not until the turbulence of the interwar period that comprehensive cooperation was implemented (see Kenis 1992, p. 175). Agreements were made separately for each product group. The most successful and comprehensive cartel was that of kraft paper (a brownish wrapping paper). Its first price convention was agreed upon in 1926, but Scankraft, the lasting and stable cartel organization for that product group, was not founded until 1932 as the first in a series of well-known Scan-organizations. Scankraft served as a prototype for these price-fixing organizations. One reason for its success was the market dominance of Nordic producers in this product group. By the end of the 1930s, they controlled about 90 per cent of total world capacity (Autio and Lodenius 1968, p. 112; Heikkinen 2000, pp. 149–53).

The Ups and Downs of Transnational Cartels

Nordic producers took the initiative and played a leading role, but cooperation was sought with competitors abroad right from the beginning. For example, in 1928, the International Committee on Newsprint (TICON) was established. Gradually producers of newsprint from all countries joined in – Canada, the United States, England, the Netherlands, Germany and the Nordic countries. The first managing director of TICON was Axel Wallenberg from Sweden. This reflects the leading position of Swedish-based firms in Europe at the time (Autio and Lodenius 1968, p. 100; Moen 1998, p. 50; Heikkinen 2000, p. 154).

Characteristically, cartels proliferated during the interwar period (Djelic et al. 2001). In the 1920s, competition had intensified to a high degree, reflecting primarily the growing presence and strength of North American players. The strong imbalance between supply and demand led to a substantial price fall. This was particularly the case in the newsprint market but it was also felt in other parts of the paper industry. Hence, the main concern behind the setting up of cartels was to stabilize markets and price levels. The fact that the price level subsequently stabilized and even improved has been taken as an evidence of the effectiveness of cartels. As a representative of the Finnish industry put it: 'The importance of their contribution can hardly be overestimated' (Autio and Lodenius 1968, pp. 99–112; Heikkinen 2000, p. 153).

During World War II, international cooperation came to a standstill. After the war, cartels in the pulp and paper industry were revived in the early 1950s, as they were in a large number of other industries. When prices fell in 1953 after the Korean boom, Swedish pulp producers supported by producers in both Finland and Norway took the initiative in renewing cooperation. Legislative changes with the aim of restraining collaboration in all Nordic countries during the 1950s led to a reconsideration of cooperation (Melander 1997, p. 115; Moen 1998; Virtanen 1998, pp. 229–306). To comply with regulatory changes, new organizations were set up, now officially called sections. They were independent of industry associations. These sections operated under the aegis of Fides, a fiduciary company located in Zürich, Switzerland. Hence, despite legal measures and strong sanctions to restrain cooperation among producers throughout the postwar period, various documents provide evidence that collusion persisted in a large number of industries (see Mirow and Maurer 1982, p. 9).

A striking feature of transnational coordination in the pulp and paper industry has been the stability of the action system over time. It should also be emphasized that the collective action system emerged and was maintained in a highly decentralized industry. To give an example, the chemical pulp sector on its own counted more than 800 member firms in over 30 countries and this well into the 1980s (EUR-Lex 1994). This finding contradicts previous research that presented informal coordination as a typical mode of interaction between small numbers of large firms (Kenis 1992, p. 165). To explain these two phenomena, this chapter points to two different kinds of forces. The stability of the action system is related to structural problems within the sector, to so-called industry fundamentals. The decentralized nature of the sector can be understood as being in part a consequence of protectionism.

Industry Fundamentals

The production system in the modern pulp and paper industry is defined and structured by the principle of scale economies (Laurila, 1998). In this context, competitive advantage depends upon two conditions. First, a particular company is able to invest periodically into new generations of machines that increase its productive capacity particularly in comparison with that of competitors. Then the company is able at the same time to secure a high usage of this new capacity. However, when new machines come on stream, they tend to create an imbalance between supply and demand; short-term price volatility is a direct consequence. In addition, fluctuations on the demand side can also upset this balance and capacity usage will then suffer. The cyclical nature of the industry means that investments are highly risky and can potentially bring large losses for investors. Hence, one of the main objectives, historically, behind coordination has been to stabilize the balance between supply and demand in order to maintain or even increase prices.

Throughout most of the twentieth century, pulp and paper industrialists have strongly supported self-regulation. As argued above, a precondition for informal collective action is that actors share norms and beliefs of how the industry should be run. Such beliefs are in general not expressed, but tacitly taken as matters of fact. Occasionally, however, we can see traces of those belief systems as in the following quote. This statement by a representative of the Swedish industry in 1977 illustrates the fact that price volatility was then perceived by Nordic players as a key problem for the industry.

> We have to govern the supply and demand and we have to govern the price situation. This is necessary, if we want to maintain a free economy, our free industries and con-sequently our jobs. Nobody in the industry is helped by these wild price fluctuations. Nobody profits from them. Nobody wants them. It is the duty of the industry leaders

to see to it that we achieve price stability, and it is certainly within reach of our capacity. (Melander 1997, p. 297; similar arguments were used by business leaders in France during the interwar period to justify cartels, see Djelic 1998)

In the late 1950s and early 1960s, new generations of machines were introduced in the pulp and paper industry. Volume and capacity expansion was especially significant in chemical pulp, in carton board and in newsprint. Due to these waves of investments the pulp and paper industry in western Europe struggled with overcapacity for the most part of this period, even though paper level consumption was rapidly increasing at the time. The European industry counteracted by cutting down production. However, in some segments, competition from North American producers made these efforts futile. North American producers especially of chemical pulp, carton board and tissue, engaged in dumping to win market shares. To come to grips with the problem European producers attempted to bring North American producers into their system of coordination. These endeavours initially failed, despite numerous rounds of negotiations. It was not until the slump of 1967, 'the worst year since the Second World War', that an agreement was reached with North Americans. At that time the general idea of restricting production was finally gaining ground (Moen 1998; Melander 1997).

With the shift of business cycles in the early 1970s, price-fixing took over as the main preoccupation. In the period of 'prosperity without profit' – gradually increasing costs and thus lower profits – producers were more concerned with prices than with production levels. At the very same time, producers came to share a belief in planning. Statistical improvements and systematic data collection on market trends and production capacities led to relatively homogeneous conceptions at the time on the overall market situation. The idea of coordinating investment plans at the industry level emerged as a potential mechanism to stabilize the future and limit sudden bursts of imbalance between supply and demand.

Such a level of coordination however depended upon getting information from the individual companies. The Finnish industry went quite far in that direction. The national interest organization of the forest industry was the main regulatory agent. Member companies had to submit their proposals for investments to the working committee of the interest organization. To obtain the right to invest, the firm had to demonstrate availability of the raw material necessary to reach the proposed level of production. Such a criterion could be used because the forestry legislation in Finland fostered sustainability and hence set limits to the availability of raw materials. This regulatory system was given great legitimacy – and in fact was partly institutionalized – by the fact that the Bank of Finland was involved in the monitoring process. This procedure was in use from 1970 to 1989 (Kuusela 1999, pp. 137–55). In Sweden, capacity management also had a strong impact on corporate strategies. For example, the industry sponsored a survey in 1973 that reached quite pessimistic conclusions for the period 1973–78. As a direct consequence, a number of major investments were then postponed (Melander 1997, p. 176).

Counter-strategy to Tariff Barriers

Throughout the postwar period, continental European paper producers feared that the Nordic industry would gradually erode their market shares and in the long term force them out of business. This fear was clearly expressed during the Korean boom when pulp and paper prices were skyrocketing. Continental European producers suspected Nordic producers of investing their high profits in paper machinery that would enable them to produce paper at low cost in fully integrated mills. To protect their domestic industries, continental European states hence implemented high import duties. For their part, Nordic producers interpreted the implementation of high custom barriers as a means to force them to supply European markets with raw materials and semi-manufactured goods rather than with high value-added finished goods (Melander 1997, p. 107). One strategy to overcome the disadvantages of tariffs was to maintain a relatively high price level through coordinated action. Simultaneously, this sheltered less efficient local companies.

When Sweden and Norway started negotiations with the EEC in the early 1970s with the aim of joining the community, the resistance from the EEC paper industry proved a clear obstacle in particular to Swedish integration. Repeated reassurances of the 'live and let live' principle were in vain. However, in the renewed negotiations in the early 1970s for a trade agreement between EEC and EFTA, the 'live and let live' policy was successfully used as a facilitator. The aim of this agreement was free trade between the EEC and EFTA. Though the agreement was reached in 1972, tariffs were lowered gradually and in 1984 they were totally abolished for paper products. This was a victory for Nordic producers. Before reaching this point, however, Nordic producers had taken the initiative to strengthen cooperation with the continental European industry. Nonetheless, mutual understanding was hard to achieve, and the Nordic industry was instead accused of price dumping. To soothe European producers, the Nordic industry tried to mobilize support to meet the common threat that North American competitors represented. An attempt to create a cooperative climate was made through the motto 'we have to behave as good Europeans' (Melander 1997, p. 185).

In reality, extended cooperation and concerted actions took place between Nordic, European and even North American producers. However, Community-based producers had a hidden agenda within this cooperative framework. They wanted to stem the increase in market shares of EFTA producers within the

Community (EUR-Lex 1994, p. 19). In 1984, when full free trade was finally a reality, Nordic producers still felt that they should be careful and not challenge continental European producers. This was particularly the case with writing papers. Traditionally produced within the European Community, writing papers were defined by continental European producers as 'commercially and politically sensitive' (Melander 1997, p. 226).

Due to the fears and resistance of continental European players, lip service was still paid for some time to the principle of 'live and let live'. However, deregulation and the end of tariff barriers in Europe paved the way for a radical evolution of the industry. Taking advantage of a new generation of technologies a few firms, particularly within the Nordic area, moved to seize the opportunities that were created by a large open market. Firms grew through mergers and acquisitions and, in the Nordic area, the consolidation of national industries went quite far (Moen and Lilja 2001).

This pattern of growth was legitimated and further strengthened with the signing in 1986 of the Single European Act. This act announced an important step in the process of European integration – the move to a single market that was finally launched at the beginning of 1993. This new competitive environment in the making led EFTA countries to reconsider their relationships with the EEC. At the corporate level, this announcement was met with waves of mergers and acquisitions increasingly this time with a cross-national scope. As EFTA producers themselves acquired production facilities within the Community, the policy of limiting their market shares became less relevant. In other words, a part of the working logic of the international cartel vanished. At the same time, the strategies of key actors in the transnational community challenged incumbent rules of the game (see a parallel argument in the contribution by Kleiner to this volume). In fact, the shift towards an oligopolistic industrial order took place within the framework of the pre-existing coordination system as the carton board case presented below shows.

THE CARTON BOARD CASE

In April 1991, in connection with an informal complaint from the British Printing Industries Federation (BPIF), the European Commission carried out investigations on a number of carton board producers as well as their subsidiaries and selling agents. On the basis of documentary evidence, the Commission opened a proceeding in December 1992 against 19 carton board companies for having committed an infringement of Article 85 of the EEC Treaty. The infringement consisted in setting market shares and fixing prices on the territory of the European Community (EUR-Lex 1994, p. 9).

A Stable Action System

Concerted practice was found to have taken place between mid 1986 and April 1991, but a statement made by one of the companies, Stora from Sweden, showed that the carton board producers had been engaged in regulating the market since 1975 (EUR-Lex 1994, p. 46). Apart from the larger players, most of the producers incriminated did not contest the main allegations. The ringleaders sought to minimize their own position and the decision-making role of the body providing the organizational structure for their meetings – 'Product Group Paperboard' (PG Paperboard). One company claimed that despite all indications to the contrary, it always followed a policy of independence from its competitors. Another company maintained that Stora had acknowledged concertation because it sought to damage its competitors' reputation. This evidence should, therefore, be regarded as tainted (EUR-Lex 1994, p. 39).

There was also an attempt to portray the PG Paperboard as a legitimate trade association that on occasion might have overstepped the line between a legitimate and an illegitimate information channel. The company defending that argument insisted that there was never any question of agreements of the type to be found in a 'classic cartel'. Accordingly, producers did not 'stage-manage' price initiatives by setting in advance the dates on which each would make its announcements. On the contrary, decisions were taken independently. Nor was there any sort of commitment involved with respect to membership. Producers could leave meetings and then do whatever they wanted. Another company emphasized the social aspects of meetings. Its representatives claimed that meetings were merely 'social occasions' and that the conviviality and pleasant location of the meetings had been major attractions.

In spite of this variety of arguments and of the denials of most producers, documentary evidence obtained by the Commission during the investigation proved concerted action beyond doubt. However, no evidence was based on official minutes. The very few existing documents gave the impression that discussions were conducted in general terms and as an exchange of information without individual producers disclosing their own positions or reaching any agreement or decision. Neither Fides, the Switzerland-based agency that provided technical services and acted as a secretariat, nor the key committees kept official minutes. There were no official records of the meetings and there were not even any invitations or attendance lists.

Instead the Commission relied on (1) an institutionalized system of regular meetings in the PG Paperboard that provided the structure for continuing collusion, (2) private notes from different companies, (3) the pattern of virtually exact correspondence in timing and the amounts of the price increases that each producer implemented on various national markets. Furthermore, the lack of official minutes was taken as evidence for concerted action. It was asserted that participants in cartels would not record their unlawful agreements in formal contracts but would rely on oral assurances during secret meetings. The Commission reached its decision against the 19 companies based in 13 different countries in both Western Europe and North America in July 1994 (EUR-Lex 1994, pp. 12–13, 39–41).

PG Paperboard – Objectives and Problems to Solve

Formally, PG Paperboard was a legitimate trade association for information exchange. Although it had certain legitimate activities, the line between legal and illegal activities is difficult to draw. Some of its subcommittees were almost entirely concerned with price fixing and market sharing and PG Paperboard itself had a predominantly unlawful purpose.

Until the early 1980s, few details were available of the activities of the organization. Various attempts were allegedly made to increase prices and deal with overcapacity. Stora claimed that until 1986 such efforts had for the most part been unsuccessful owing to the endemic overcapacity in the industry during the period. After 1986, this state of affairs changed. From 1986 to 1989, wood pulp prices rose by almost 30 per cent on the international market. To a large extent, this was due to a reorganization in 1986 that removed obstacles to effective coordination (EUR-Lex 1994, pp. 7, 11–13).

A major concern was to ensure that concerted price initiatives were not jeopardized by an excess of supply over demand. As the producers realized, the key to success was maintaining a near balance between production and consumption. A decisive step in reaching this goal was taken when all members of the inner group consisting of the large producers agreed to this principle. This agreement was reached in 1987 and was termed the 'price before tonnage' policy (EUR-Lex 1994, pp. 14–18).

In connection with meetings to agree on prices, discussions were also held on market shares in western Europe both of individual producers and of national groups of producers. An outcome of these discussions was a certain 'understanding' between the participants as to their respective market shares. This understanding included the 'freezing' of the west European market shares of major producers at existing levels. It meant that no attempts were to be made to win new customers or extend business through promotional pricing. The shares of the western European market were to be understood as a whole for each of the major producer groups and not as shares in individual national markets. However, the 'freezing' of market shares took account of market growth for the following year. Market share development was analysed on the basis of provisional statistics. Provisions were made to reduce production in difficult times with an effort being asked of all producers. The whole system depended upon 'voluntary restraint' and mutual encouragement. Whether producers complied with the understandings and agreements depended on their perception that it was in their best interests to do so.

Originally, the main concern of some ringleaders was to restrict the expansion of EFTA producers in the Community. Evidently, a key motive was to continue with protectionism despite the fact that free trade was implemented in 1984 between the EC and EFTA. EC producers made it clear to EFTA producers that increasing their market share at the expense of others would upset the balance between production and consumption and undermine the concerted efforts to increase prices. But as EFTA producers started to acquire production facilities in the Community, the policy of limiting the market shares of non-community producers became less relevant. Instead PG Paperboard became concerned with maintaining a balance between major corporate groups in order not to jeopardize price initiatives (EUR-Lex 1994, pp. 14–20). The key point in our context is, however, that the restructuring of the industry affected the rules of the game within the cartel. The introduction of the Single Market and the policy of creating European champions induced a new understanding of competitiveness, which in turn influenced firms' behaviour.

New Rules of the Game

In 1986 and 1987, the PG Paperboard structure went through substantial alterations. First, a new committee was set up, the 'Presidents' Working Group' (PWG) with senior representatives from the eight largest carton board producers. Then the Marketing Committee was restructured and was thereafter called the 'Joint Marketing Committee' (JMC). All producers incriminated by the Commission had participated in this committee. Neither the PWG nor the JMC kept any official record until after the date of the Commission's investigations. However, according to Stora's statement these two committees accounted for a greater efficiency of PG Paperboard during the second half of the 1980s. The key issue is that this reorganization de facto changed the rules of the game, making the 'live and let live' principle increasingly irrelevant.

The key dimension there was the introduction of the PWG. Ostensibly, the function of that committee was to prepare the ground before the Presidents' Conferences. In reality it was the PWG that came to reach agreements and to take broad decisions on both the timing and the level of price increases to be introduced. Earlier, the General Assembly or Presidents' Conference, in which all companies were represented, had made these decisions. Hence, through the creation of the PWG, the largest producers came de facto to dominate the whole carton board industry (EUR-Lex 1994, pp. 2–18). This was the beginning of a new game. At the very same time, those leading players had already started to expand and increase their control span through mergers and acquisitions. The consequence was that those large companies managed to increase their own shares of the market, through negotiations in PG Paperboard, at the expense of smaller companies.

Thus the carton board cartel case demonstrates that a more oligopolistic industrial structure had emerged already before the European Commission started its investigation in 1991. A similar concentration process was also going on in other segments of the pulp and paper sector. This process coincided and converged with changes at the European level – the implementation of the Single Market and the opening of the economic space for European champions. In the new oligopolistic order the key rule was to maintain a balance between a few dominant actors. The principle of this balance was further modified in the 1990s.

FORMS OF COORDINATION IN THE ERA OF GLOBAL PRODUCTION SYSTEMS

While European Union competition authorities were conducting their investigations of the carton board industry, the entire pulp and paper industry was experiencing other calamities as well. In the early 1990s, the competitive environment was radically changing for the pulp and paper industry in western Europe. It all started with a deep recession. Due to a reduction in demand, pulp and paper prices dropped dramatically and the industry experienced overcapacity. An upswing in 1994 prompted firms to announce new greenfield site investments. Simultaneously, share prices dropped because investors sold out shares in large numbers in direct reaction to this announcement. Obviously, the international financial community had reacted negatively to the investment plans. This, clearly, was a new experience for the pulp and paper industry.

New Competitive Rules

From the early 1990s, transnational institutional investors increased their interests in European-based pulp and paper corporations. This form of ownership brought along new expectations to that industry – in particular that of high returns on equity that combined with the principle of a 'maximization of shareholder value' (see Tainio et al. in this volume). New foreign owners had no patience with the prospect of low returns and lack of performance due to over-investment. For this reason, fund managers reduced their stakes in ownership when investments were announced. Rather quickly, CEOs and newly appointed directors of investor relations placed the principle of shareholder value on the agenda. To signal their observance of this principle, pulp and paper firms formulated an explicit dividend policy and started to increase dividends. But more was to come. To avoid potential overcapacity, firms started to abstain from further greenfield site investments, especially in Europe. Investment banks had made thorough analyses of the strength and weaknesses of all the firms in the industry and offered their services for undertaking mergers and acquisitions. Globalized management consulting firms joined in this chorus and formulated models for industrial restructuring (see, for example, Ahlberg et al. 1999).

Within the industry there were several motives that could explain the adoption of new competitive strategies. The leadership of a few large companies had been in the making for some time already and leading corporations had learned that it was not possible to develop a distinctive competitive advantage for a long period just by investing in the latest technology. Suppliers of technology and consulting services had already been globalizing their operations in the 1980s. This meant that after a short lag, the newest technology was available for all firms and consortia that could finance the investment. Consulting firms could even provide managers for rent for extended start-up periods. This made it possible for investors without prior experience of the industry and technology to enter into greenfield site projects. Another reason for pulp and paper corporations to take seriously the principle of shareholder value was their newfound strategy of mergers and acquisitions. European-based corporations had until then not been able to use their shares to pay for acquisitions because in small stock markets the share prices of pulp and paper corporations were undervalued. Foreign ownership was demanding but it tended to have a positive impact on the valuation of a company (see Tainio et al. in this volume). This, however, depended somewhat upon the industry – and in 1999 and 2000 the main priority of foreign institutional investors was not the pulp and paper industry (see Tainio et al. in this volume). Relative undervaluation on the Helsinki Stock Exchange explains why UPM-Kymmene ultimately failed to take over Champion International in the spring of 2000.

Emergence of a New Industrial Order

Hence, together with external actors, leading firms have been active in restructuring the pulp and paper industry. Our argument is that the model for restructuring is based on a shared understanding among actors about the 'best practice' for organizing and governing the industry. In contrast to the traditional order, actors both from within and from outside the industry are active in formulating this new order. Institutional investors, investment banks and customers are among the external actors that are being particularly influential. Within the industry, two types of transnational corporations can be identified. These types could be called consolidator and specialist corporations respectively and some examples are provided in Table 6.1. In a sense they represent the most visible part of a new industrial order that is still very much in the making.

Table 6.1 Growth profiles of consolidators and specialists since 2000

	Consolidators	Specialist firms
Stora Enso Consolidated (since February 2000)	Full line producer in printing and writing papers. Wide product scope in forest industry products.	
UPM-Kymmene	Full line producer in printing and writing papers. Wide product scope in forest industry products.	
M-real (including MoDo since May 2000; and Zanders since 2001)	Largest fine paper and second largest pulp producer in Europe. Third in Europe as a fine paper merchant.	
Norske Skog (including Fletcher Challenge Paper Division since March 2000 and PAPCO alliance)		Second largest newsprint producer in the world; mills on five continents.
SCA (including Mölnlycke since 1975, Danisco packaging, brands from Johnson & Johnson in May 2000, tissue operations in the US from Georgia-Pacific and acquisition of a packaging company Tuscarora in 2001)		Steady growth path towards becoming a leading producer of hygiene and tissue papers and paper-based packaging products.

Transnational consolidators intend to become global forest industry corporations in many branches and product groups and at several stages of the value chain within the forest industry at large. They capitalize on their huge size, global visibility and on their internal resources and competence pools. Transnational specialists, on the other hand, are global in a relatively narrow product range and are present at only one or a few stages of the value chain. Firms of this second type try to establish intimate customer relations, typically at the high end of the product segment. Consolidators try to combine both of these basic strategies by transforming their product divisions into partially autonomous specialist entities. The important point is that these two forms of growth strategies enable a kind of division of labour between leading firms.

By announcing their strategic commitments as to what are their core and non-core businesses, corporations are creating a market for acquisitions and divestments in which consolidators and specialists can complement each other. A consolidator can sell part of an acquisition to a specialist to get rid of non-core production lines, which better fit the product portfolio of a specialist firm. This is also a way to demonstrate that a firm is willing to avoid a dominant market position based on the criteria set by the EU competition authorities. For example, UPM-Kymmene's acquisition of Haindl, a family owned firm in Germany, contained a separate deal in which Norske Skog was to take over two of Haindl's paper mills. Another sort of division of labour is that corporations can position their business portfolios differently along the upstream–downstream dimension. M-real has complemented its own wholesale business with trading business and a sales network alliance. This means that it sells the paper products of other producers. It is the only paper producer in Europe that has a major share of the paper merchant trade across Europe.

The pressure for a new division of labour among pulp and paper firms also comes from customers. The media, publishing and advertisement industries started becoming global well before the pulp and paper industries. Transnational corporations can offer a wide product assortment, consulting services, multiple sourcing opportunities and reliable deliveries. As a consequence, global customers of the pulp and paper firms have welcomed the transnationalization of their suppliers because it generally allowed them to reduce transaction costs.

In facilitating the division of labour, transnational investors have been instrumental in several respects (compare Morin 2000; Tainio et al. 2001). After the series of national and cross-national mergers and acquisitions in Europe, the largest Nordic forest industry corporations have finally reached the size where they can be noticed by large foreign institutional investors. These investors ask for transparent data and a clear communication of figures – results and balance sheets. But they also ask for strategic visions. CEOs in the pulp and paper industries have been working hard on these strategic commitments. And they have been publicizing them in road shows and in private meetings with investors and analysts (see Tainio et al. in this volume). One visible consequence of this practice has been the publication of ratings and the relative positioning of each firm by market share in each of the product groups in which they operate. When the current volume, expectations for growth and the level of profitability are disclosed, it becomes possible for analysts to assess the 'hidden value' of the stock in question.

However, market power cannot be sought without limits. The presence of completely different species of firms and customers in the same markets has made merger and acquisition regulation a highly complex issue. The EU competition authorities have prevented several mergers and acquisitions on the grounds that they would lead to dominant market positions. Hence European regulatory institutions have also been important actors pushing competitors in many industry to coordinate their corporate strategies (Virtanen 1998). A complicating factor, however, is that the European Union's competition policy sometimes runs counter to its industrial policy of supporting the development of European champions. This paradoxical situation has created space for negotiations. The representatives of firms originating from small member countries have questioned the interpretations proposed by the Brussels authorities of dominant market positions. The argument is that such interpretations on the whole tend to prevent firms from smaller countries to become European-wide or global. Due to changing business logics, the relevant geographic market for their strategic visions they argue is the continental or global level.

Taking all these influences into account, we will argue that there is still space for coordinated action in the pulp and paper industry. However, this takes place at the highest tier of the constellation of firms. These firms try to build continental or global product divisions. Corporations that are not able to turn into either a consolidator or a specialist are, on the other hand, vulnerable to takeover bids. This is why the current industrial order can be aptly described by the logic 'eat or be eaten' (see Fligstein 1996, p. 670). The different characteristics of the two industrial orders that have succeeded each other in the pulp and paper industry are summarized in Table 6.2.

CONCLUSION

Transnational coordination of action between competitors has a long history in the pulp and paper industry. A wide range of transnational cartels came into force in the interwar period and several of these persisted into the 1990s despite legislative measures to do away with them. This chapter has emphasized the role of protectionism in European countries as a main reason for their longevity (see, for example, Djelic 1998, p. 48).

Table 6.2   Forms of transnational coordination in the pulp and paper industry

Characteristics	Types of industrial order	
	Live and let live	Eat or be eaten
Timing	1945–1994.	1995–
Geographic context	Europe.	All continents.
Problem definition	Tariffs and sheltered property rights in the EEC countries; periodic overcapacity due to new investments and restrictions on corporate takeovers.	To maintain an acceptable growth rate from the point of view of institutional investors: growth by mergers and acquisitions.
Dominant actors constituting the organizational field	Nordic producers of forest products and Continental producers of paper.	Transnational forest industry corporations, mainly with an origin in the Nordic countries and North America.
Excluded actors in the industry	None.	Small family firms, local producers.
Types of organizational collaborative practice	Trade association for the continental producers, Fides for the Nordic producers, EPI (since 1981, covering both Continental and Nordic producers); European level product group specific organizations.	European level trade association for the pulp and paper industry (CEPI) since 1991; use of strong personalities as figureheads for the industry.
Solutions in the organizational field	Price cartels and market sharing.	Limitation of new investments in Europe, swap of businesses to enhance the focus of business portfolios; specialization at the level of product groups or stages of the value chain.
Significant external actors	National ministries of trade and industry.	Representatives of global financial markets; competition authorities of the EU and the USA.

Protective tariffs were removed between the EEC and the EFTA in the mid 1980s and partly as a result of that, partly under pressure from new transnational actors, the pulp and paper industry experienced a transformation of its internal structure and saw its governing logic evolve radically. The principle of 'live and let live' eroded progressively and more aggressive growth strategies became legitimate in Europe. This evolution was encouraged by European authorities through the implementation of the Single Market and their policy of fostering and supporting European champions. During the 1990s leading firms have become European-wide or even global as to the location of their production systems. The dominant corporations have internalized many value chain steps and functional capabilities, covering not only production, sales and logistics, but also functional capabilities such as finance, marketing and R&D. Divisional headquarters have been relocated to countries where internationally experienced managers can be recruited. The concentration process has transformed pulp and paper mills into multinational corporations that act like 'isolated hierarchies' (Whitley 1999, 2001). At the same time these corporations combine into a new oligopolistic industrial order.

In the contemporary industrial order, pulp and paper corporations position themselves in the value chain with respect to their suppliers and customers in ways that differentiate them from their competitors. In this differentiation game they also make adjustments in their product portfolio with their competitors. The coordination of competition is thus future oriented and occurs at the level of strategic commitments of the firms (see Ghemawat 1991).

To support the differentiation game, investment banks have had a major role. They have acted as architects, messengers and brokers between the firms (see McKenna et al. in this volume for a similar argument on consulting firms). As a result, leading firms have learned to construct strategic projects that appeal to transnational investors and financial analysts. In the new industrial order, financial analysts, consultants and investors compare and evaluate the strategic projects and prospects of different competitors. These external actors play in the process the role of arbiters but they also emerge as mediating mechanisms or channels allowing coordination between a small group of global oligopolistic players.

REFERENCES

Ahlberg, Johan, Antti Pitkänen and Louis Schorsch (1999), 'Forging a new era for steel', *McKinsey Quarterly*, (4), 83–91.

Autio, Matti and Erik Lodenius (1968), *The Finnish Paper Mills' Association*, Helsinki, Finland: Frenckellin Kirjapaino Oy.

Braithwaite, John and Peter Drahos (2000), *Global Business Regulation*, Cambridge: Cambridge University Press.

Djelic, Marie-Laure (1998), *Exporting the American Model*, Oxford: Oxford University Press.

Djelic, Marie-Laure and Jabril Bensedrine (2001), 'Globalization and its limits: the making of international regulation', in Glenn Morgan, Peer Hull Kristensen and Richard Whitley (eds), *The Multinational Firm*, Oxford: Oxford University Press.

Djelic, Marie-Laure, Mitchell Koza and Arie Lewin (2001), 'Are networks new forms of organizations?', *Document de Recherche*, Paris: ESSEC.

Edwards, Corwin D. (1964), *Cartelization in Western Europe*, US Department of State, Washington, DC: Bureau of Intelligence and Research.

EUR-Lex (1994), *Community Legislation in Force*, Document 394D0601, Brussels.

Fligstein, Neil (1996), 'Markets as politics: a political-cultural approach to market institutions', *American Sociological Review*, **61**, 656–673.

Fligstein, Neil and Iona Mara-Drita (1996), 'How to make a market: reflections on the attempt to create a single market in the European Union', *American Journal of Sociology*, **102** (1), 1–33.

Ghemawat, Pankaj (1991), *Commitment: The Dynamic of Strategy*, New York: Free Press.

Gulati, Ranjay, Nitin Nohria and Akbar Zaheer (2000), 'Strategic networks', *Strategic Management Journal*, **21**, 203–15.

Heikkinen, Sakari (2000), *Paper for the World. The Finnish Paper Mills' Association*, Helsinki: Otava.

Herrigel, Gary (1996), *Industrial Constructions*, Cambridge: Cambridge University Press.

Huolman, Mika, Matti Pulkkinen, Mia Rissanen, Risto Tainio and Sampo Tukiainen (1999), *Ulkomaisen omistuksen vaikutus yritysten johtamiseen ja innovaatioihin*, Helsinki, Finland: LTT – Sarja B 157.

Kenis, Patrick (1992), *The Social Construction of an Industry*, Frankfurt am Main/Boulder, Colorado: Campus/Westview.

Kuusela, Kullervo (1999), *Metsän leiviskät*, Jyväskylä, Finland: Atena.

Laurila, Juha (1998), *Managing Technological Discontinuities*, London: Routledge.

Melander, Anders (1997), *Industrial Wisdom and Strategic Change. The Swedish Pulp and Paper Industry 1945–1990*, Jönköping: Jönköping International Business School.

Mirow, Kurt and Harry Maurer (1982), *Webs of Power – International Cartels and the World Economy*, Boston, MA: Houghton Mifflin.

Moen, Eli (1998), *The Decline of the Pulp and Paper Industry in Norway, 1950–1980*, Oslo, Norway: Scandinavian University Press.

Moen, Eli and Kari Lilja (2001), 'Constructing global corporations: contrasting national legacies in the Nordic forest industry', in Glenn Morgan, Peer Hull Kristensen and Richard Whitley (eds), *The Multinational Firm*, Oxford: Oxford University Press, pp. 97–121.

Morgan, Glenn (2001), 'The development of transnational standards and regulations and their impact on firms', in Glenn Morgan, Peer Hull Kristensen and Richard Whitley (eds), *The Multinational Firm*, Oxford: Oxford University Press, pp. 225–52.

Morin, François (2000), 'A transformation in the French model of shareholding and management', *Economy and Society*, **29** (1), 36–53.

Nygaard, Claus (1999), *The Affect of Embeddedness on Strategic Action*, Copenhagen, Denmark: Copenhagen Business School, Ph.D. series 1.99.

Peteraf, Margaret and Mark Shanley (1997), 'Getting to know you: a theory of strategic group identity', *Strategic Management Journal*, **18**, 165–86.

Porac, Joseph, Howard Thomas and Charles Baden-Fuller (1989), 'Competitive groups as cognitive communities: the case of Scottish knitwear manufacturers', *Journal of Management Studies*, **15**, 397–416.

Schmitter, Philip and Wolfgang Streeck (1981), *The Organization of Business Interests*, Labour Market Policy – Discussion Papers, Berlin: Wissenschaftszentrum.

Streeck, Wolfgang and Philip Schmitter (eds) (1985), *Private Interest Government*, Beverly Hills/London: Sage.

Spender, J.C. (1989), *Industry Recipes*, Oxford: Basil Blackwell.

Tainio, Risto, Mika Huolman and Matti Pulkkinen (2001), 'The internationalisation of capital markets: how international institutional investors are restructuring Finnish companies', in Glenn Morgan, Peer Hull Kristensen and Richard Whitley (eds), *The Multinational Firm*, Oxford: Oxford University Press, pp. 152–71.

Tushman, Michael and Philip Anderson (1986), 'Technological discontinuities and organizational environments', *Administrative Science Quarterly*, **31** (3), 439–65.

Virtanen, Martti (1998), *Market Dominance-Related Competition Policy*, Publication Series A 1, Turku, Finland: Turku School of Economics and Business Administration.

Whitley, Richard (1999), *Divergent Capitalisms*, Oxford: Oxford University Press.

Whitley, Richard (2001), 'How and why are international firms different? The consequences of cross-border managerial coordination for firm characteristics and behaviour', in Glenn Morgan, Peer Hull Kristensen and Richard Whitley (eds), *The Multinational Firm*, Oxford: Oxford University Press, pp. 27–68.

7. Path-dependent national systems or European convergence? The case of European electricity markets

Atle Midttun, Augusto Rupérez Micola and Terje Omland

INTRODUCTION

An ongoing debate on the internationalization of modern economy conveys two quite different pictures. On the one hand, international integrationists like Ohmae (1985, 1995) or Doz and Pralahad (1993) argue that the modern economy is moving towards seamless integration. Ohmae goes on to argue that this leads to convergence of firm strategy and behaviour. On the other hand, the national styles argument (Whitley 1992, 1999; Hollingsworth and Boyer 1997; Hall and Soskice 2001) points to national institutions as still exerting a dominant influence over current business practices.

Given the close interplay between economic, political and institutional dimensions (Polanyi 1944, see also Djelic and Quack in the introduction to this volume) this debate may be pursued at two levels: at an economic level and at a political/institutional one. At the economic level the focus is on how international trade, foreign investments, global capital markets and firm internationalization impact on and interact with national markets. At the political level the focus is on international agreements, treaties or institutions and how they impact on national economic behaviour. Of particular interest is the interface between transnational organizations and institutions (for example the World Trade Organization or WTO) or supranational constructions (for example the European Union or EU) and national entities.

Taking the broad institutionalist framework of this book as a point of departure, this chapter specifies a more explicit framework for discussing globalization up against national styles. Drawing on evolutionary theory, and the distinction between variation, selection and retention, this chapter specifies three analytical positions in the globalization/national-styles debate:

- The strong globalization position, arguing for convergence at all three levels: variation, selection and retention.
- The strong national styles position, arguing for diversity at all levels.
- The compromise or soft intermediary position, arguing for considerable functional convergence in selection and retention, but considerable diversity in the institutional forms within which variation and retention take place.

Based on a case study of the internal European market for electricity, this chapter argues for the soft intermediary position and is here in line with the common claim in this volume. As a major European industrial sector currently facing radical policy change in the form of deregulation and internationalization, the electricity industry provides an interesting arena for shedding empirical light on the globalization and national styles debate. The empirical analysis serves both as a critical confrontation of existing theoretical positions and as a basis for further theoretical refinement.

The European electricity deregulation is a particularly interesting case when it comes to the interplay between the political and economic levels. The study finds that, at the present phase in the building up of European governance, the dual process of liberalization and internationalization of the electricity market runs parallel to a process of de facto denationalization and Europeanization. By gradually exposing European industry to European market competition, the European Union may de facto expropriate the interventionist power of the nation-state and erode its control over the electricity sector. We find that the political process of deregulation is reinforced by the economic process that it triggers. Over time, companies operating across European boundaries are bound to foster at least a partial transfer of regulatory power from the national to the European level. These regional rather than national firms aspire to be regulated under a more general European regime which they find more suitable to their international competitive strategies.

However, the chapter also concludes that the increasing Europeanization of electricity companies, that comes with some degree of integration of firms on a European level, may have serious consequences in the long run for the liberalization and deregulation currently at work. The idea that decentralized and 'free' markets will come to characterize Europe may, in other words, hold for a while before we are back again with an oligopolistic order this time at a higher level (see also Lilja and Moen in this volume). In time, stronger market concentration may call for bolder political intervention on behalf of consumers or national interests and in the European context this intervention may easily take on strong national overtones. Internationalization and strategic convergence may hence trigger, in the long run, renewed political intervention including such of a national nature.

The chapter is organized in three parts. We first specify our theoretical framework and the approach. Then we turn to the empirical case – the deregulation of the European electricity market. Finally, we draw insights and conclusions from that case to clarify our position in the globalization versus national styles debate.

THEORETICAL FRAMING

The present study gives support to the idea that globalization is a dynamic process or even more precisely a combination or an aggregation of multiple and partly interrelated dynamic processes (Djelic and Quack in the introduction and conclusion to this volume). This dynamic, processual and complex nature of globalization stems in part from the collision between factors that promote transnational integration on the one hand and the reality of social and institutional variation on the other.

Globalization versus National Styles

Ohmae (1985, 1995) is one of the main champions of the integration and convergence thesis. His basic argument is that goods, capital and money, individuals, knowledge and information flow relatively unimpeded today across national borders. This integration of markets in the large sense of the term comes with an internationalization of firms and a relative convergence of their strategic orientations. In this new global paradigm, Ohmae contends that national diversity will diminish rapidly and that nation-states no longer have a market-making role to play.

For Ohmae, the trend towards internationalization and integration is efficiency-driven and the search for scale and scope advantages is a powerful driver for large multinational companies. The strong globalization position, however, can also be argued from a different perspective that has little to do with efficiency. The idea is that convergence can be brought about through institutional isomorphism where particular structures and practices spread and are rapidly adopted. Mechanisms can be any combination of imitation, search for legitimacy and political pressures or professionalization (DiMaggio and Powell 1991; Scott et al. 1994).

At the other extreme of the strong globalization position, one finds the national styles literature. The argument there focuses on how differences in national, regional and sector institutions generate significant variations in firm and market structures and operations. This general argument is developed under several labels: business systems (Whitley 1992), social systems of production (Campbell et al. 1991), modes of capitalist organization (Orru 1994), societal analysis (Maurice and Sorge 2000) or varieties of capitalism (Hall and Soskice 2001). The essence of this literature is that industrial development proceeds differently in different nations, as national industrial 'milieus' draw on specific legacies and institutions in their national surroundings.

Implicitly, and sometimes also explicitly, the national styles literature draws on a path dependency argument, asserting that industrial systems cannot develop independently of previous events and that local positive loops propagate traditional patterns into future strategic decisions (David 1993). This interpretation implies that small events may play an important role in determining the future course of long-term development. Thus, the path dependency and national styles literatures foresee that institutional, social and organizational factors will continue to produce national differences in strategic orientations, even under international competitive conditions (Whitley 1999; Maurice and Sorge 2000; Zeitlin and Herrigel 2001).

Like the globalization argument, the national style argument could presumably be phrased both in efficiency and non-efficiency terms. The efficiency version is built on assumptions that differences in resources, competencies, organizational practices and institutional structures are based on different and equally competitive economic strategies. A non-efficiency variant of the national diversity argument might be that various organizational and institutional mechanisms specific to each national business style function as filters to cushion international market forces, and shelter national business strategies from their cruel selection.

The globalization versus national styles debate clearly involves both an economic and an institutional level of analysis as economic internationalization is generally intertwined with political and institutional internationalization. Therefore, the discussion of international versus national economic organization must also focus on the relative positioning of national and transnational institutions. The structure of international economic systems can be more or less formal and tight. For instance, the General Agreement on Tariffs and Trade (GATT), later succeeded by the World Trade Organisation (WTO), is a multilateral trade agreement establishing the principles under which the signatories negotiate 'a substantial reduction in customs tariffs and other impediments to trade, and the elimination of discriminatory practices in international trade on a reciprocity and mutual advantage basis'. The GATT/WTO has become a charter governing almost all of the world's trade.

Examples of stronger economic integration are the federal US system, where the Constitution empowers the federal government to regulate international trade and establish common duties. Somewhere in between, we find the European Union (EU). While the European Union is not (yet) a federal state, EU law is stronger than a multilateral treaty, as it provides in particular for the compulsory settlement of disputes by the European Court of Justice, open even to individuals (see, for example, Plehwe with Vescovi or Lehmkuhl in this volume).

Fulfilment of the aims of international treaties like the GATT/WTO and supranational constructions such as the EU represent a major impetus towards internationalization. However, there are often discrepancies between ideals and realities (Djelic and Quack in the conclusion to this volume, see also most contributions to this volume). The existence of formal treaties and other international agreements should not lead us to believe that these contracts have actually materialized. Such international treaties often express common denominator solutions, rather than the strong authoritative fulfilment of ambitious international goals. In order to assess the international integrative capacity of international economic systems, the following must be addressed: decision-making power of central organs versus member countries, the recruitment and discretion of administrative elites as well as the distributive consequences of unified international policies for the members.

An Evolutionary Perspective

The gap between the strong globalization position and the national styles argument seems quite difficult to bridge. There is in fact no debate – much more of a 'dialogue of the deaf'. To go beyond this stark dichotomy, we glean insights from the evolutionary perspective which allows us to reformulate the two positions while focusing on their specific implications for distinct commercial and governance functions. In line with evolutionary theory we consider critical features of sustained commercial performance to include:

- The ability to generate new products and business practices (variation).
- The ability to pick out the most successful among that variety (selection).
- The ability to institutionalize new practices/products in stable and efficient production- and governance systems (retention).

Following Aldrich (1999), variation means the provision of diverse raw material from which selection processes cull those that are most suitable, given some selection criteria. Variation highlights the diversity in economic and business practices and configurations. Selection implies the elimination of certain types of variation. Aldrich points out that selection may be internal or external. In the internal case, selection criteria include managerial discretion, routines and normative orders. In the external case, market forces, competitive pressures, and conformity to institutionalized norms, among others, affect the selection process. Retention denotes selected variations that are preserved, duplicated or reproduced. At the population level, retention preserves and stabilizes collective technological, managerial and regulatory competences. At the organizational level, retention (for example through the establishment of routines) may limit members' discretion and buffer organizations against unauthorized variation from official policies.

Drawing on evolutionary theory and on the distinction between variation, selection and retention, we can now reassess and specify further the globalization versus national styles controversy by addressing it in relation to each specific commercial and governance function. Adding also a distinction between fuctions and the institutional form that is chosen to fill a function, we identify in fact three rather than two different positions. The strong globalization position which sees international convergence on all three counts. Assuming global and internationally regulated markets, it implies that selection is universal throughout the whole market system and that retention takes place at the international level and/or through national bodies adhering strictly to international blueprints. Firms' strategies and practices converge to a globally defined 'most efficient optimum'. Assuming full factor mobility, an ultra strong convergence hypothesis will also eliminate national diversity in generating new products and business practices except for diversity clearly linked to natural resource endowments.

The strong national styles position points instead to differentiation on all three dimensions. It assumes extensive national control over selection, retention mechanisms that function at the national level and autonomy from international decision-making. National variation of business strategies and business practices may be argued both as responses to national selection, cushioning industry against international competition, but also on the basis of a conception of efficiency which includes path dependency and the competitive advantage of specific national resources, competencies and practices.

Finally, we identify a third soft intermediary position that is somewhat of a compromise which seems to gain support from the empirical material which is analysed in this chapter. This intermediary position points to convergence in selection and retention in the context of considerable functional exposure to international competition, but recognizes the national diversity in variation or generation of new products and business practices. Even the tendency towards convergence, implied in the selection and retention functions, is however balanced by institutional diversity that modifies retention and selection towards national style. There may be room in other words for variations in national set ups or solutions as long as they reasonably fulfil converging functional demands. National variation in business strategies and institutions is an option as long as they represent efficient alternatives based on specific national resources, competencies and practices.

The following empirical discussion highlights first, the institutional and technical conditions that serve as major elements of retention of commercial practices. Particular focus is given here to the European deregulation regime.

A second section highlights the selection process and mechanisms in the European electricity markets, particularly as reflected in the electricity prices. A third section focuses on variation in business strategies and internationalization of firms. A final section sums up the implications of the case study for the globalization versus national styles debate.

RETENTION – INSTITUTIONAL AND TECHNICAL FACTORS

Institutions play a key role in the selection and retention of commercial strategies and practices. Hence, in this section, European Union initiatives to deregulate and internationalize the European electricity industry are a major point of focus. If political and institutional retention at the European level remains set to support national sovereignty, then national diversity and specificity will be reproduced and stabilized. The strong national styles argument would in that case be supported. If, on the other hand, the European Union succeeds in harmonizing regulatory, political and institutional arrangements, then it creates retention mechanisms that work in the direction of greater convergence. This would lend some support to the strong globalization or convergence position.

Given the technical complexity characteristic of the electricity sector, processes of institutionalization may interact with technical elements to determine retention. Such technical path dependencies are likely to make retention more stable and long lasting than in cases where the institutional dimension is the only one to operate. For instance, grid access and capacity are critical building blocks in the internationalization of the electricity trade. Hence, the institutional definition of grid access and capacity are bound to have a significant impact on developments in the European electricity market. In this section we shall first look at European regulation of the electricity market. We will then turn to more technical limitations trying to assess their impact on processes of internationalization in the industry.

The Politics of European (de)Regulation

As a point of departure, it is important to remember that electricity markets have traditionally been strictly national in Europe. The dominant model, at the end of World War II, was one where electricity was a strategic utility tightly connected with the process of nation building or rebuilding. Electricity was a key dimension of industrial policy and an important public good that had to be accessible to all consumers. In several countries, like France, this resulted in national monopoly and public provision of electricity. In other countries this led to special agreements between private and public companies and public authorities like in Germany.

The first step towards internationalization of the electricity industry was taken in 1989 when the European Commission (EC) proposed several Directives. The principal targets were price transparency for gas and electricity (COM (89) 332), the transit rights for gas and electricity (COM (89) 334 and 336) and the cooperation on infrastructure and investments in energy projects of common interest (COM (89) 335). These Directives were subsequently adopted by the Council of Ministers, and this in spite of strong resistance from the energy industry and most member states. The consequence of that resistance was that the final texts reflected some degree of compromise and were limited in their scope. Nevertheless, they undeniably represented an important step towards the creation of an integrated European energy market.

Building upon these three Directives, the EC adopted a set of guidelines for completion of the internal market in gas and electricity in 1991. These guidelines set three stages. First came an almost immediate implementation of the three Directives. Then, the progressive elimination of exclusive rights was to follow. Finally, 1996 would see the final completion of the internal gas and electricity markets.

In 1992, two new proposals for Directives went somewhat further. One objective was to fully abolish exclusive rights for the generation of electricity and the construction of power lines and gas conduits. A second objective was to force the separation of management and accounting of generation and distribution activities in vertically integrated companies while allowing 'third party access' (TPA) to the networks for certain distributors and large consumers.

The EC pursued the liberalization process vigorously but was only reluctantly followed by the Council of Ministers and the Parliament. In addition, the break with the traditional closed national-based model led to problems with nations like France, Belgium or Denmark where the electricity industry had been structured by and around a strong public service orientation. In fact, the internationalization policy of the European Union was soon facing strong opposition on many fronts. Decision-making took the character of negotiations under threat of veto from single actors. The EC's efforts to reach majority decisions proved fruitless.

The two 1992 proposals were rejected by the Council of Ministers, and the EC had to modify them in 1993. These new texts differed from the 1992 proposals in four respects. First, they provided for negotiated instead of full TPA to networks. Then, they made clear references to public service obligations. They also brought in the need for harmonization to ensure efficient functioning of the markets. Finally, they pointed to a tender system instead of licensing for new electricity generation and transport capacity.

The negotiated TPA and the public service obligation served to preserve specific national policies in the energy markets. The European Parliament seized upon the controversial nature of a liberalization of energy markets to gain some influence and weaken in turn the policy of internationalization. In 1993, the European Parliament emphasized that environmental and taxation policies should be harmonized before the national electricity markets were integrated. The parliamentary decision stressed the right of member states to oblige their electricity companies to a 'public service' attitude and allowed actors vested with concessionaire rights to protect and maintain monopolies. TPA was proposed under restricted conditions of negotiated agreements, only for large industrial consumers and was not to be introduced for supply companies with a centrally planned electricity model.

When France launched the 'single buyer/supplier principle' (hereafter called the single buyer model) to protect the monopoly position of Electricité de France (EdF), the regulation debate concentrated on the harmonization of this model with the concept of negotiated TPA. Eventually, the Commission had to seek a compromise as the French model was supported by other member nations. In fact, France, Greece and Ireland supported the model, the Dutch, Danish and German electricity industries giving it partial support for different reasons (Arentsen et al. 2000; Midttun et al. 2000).

The June 1996 meeting of the Energy Council of Ministers marked a moderate breakthrough in the stalemate between the TPA and the public-service positions. The Council then found it easier to proceed through a gradualist rather than an in principle position. It reached an agreement to open up 22 per cent of the energy market to competitive international trade by 1999–2000 and 32 per cent by 2003 (European Commission 1996). The very cautious pace of market opening indicated a soft tone *vis-à-vis* national vested interests and made the compromise acceptable even to public service-oriented members. The partial nature of deregulation and the degree of subsidiarity[1] accepted for application of this partial market opening meant that market rules and institutions were shaped to national taste (EU Commission 1996). Member states could limit competition with respect to both generation and supply and had considerable control over the construction of new capacity as well as over the fuel mix.

The result has been a variety of regulatory trajectories and energy policies running in parallel across Europe. In general, most parts of Europe (all nations except the Nordic countries and England and Wales) have taken a gradual 'contestable market' path, where markets are slowly opened and subject to structural constraints. Developments in the European electricity market may be schematically represented in a two-dimensional matrix as in Figure 7.1, with degree of market openness to competition along the horizontal axis and geographic expansion of the market along the vertical axis.

On the whole, developments in Continental Europe point to a trajectory away from a national and monopolistic planned economy (quadrant III) towards a European semi-competitive and semi-integrated market system (between quadrants I and III). There is reason to expect that this peculiar mixture of competition and partial regulation will characterize the strategic context for years to come together with mergers, acquisitions and other forms of strategic integration with a view to limiting competition (see also Lilja and Moen in this volume). Still, in a longer-term perspective, the European liberalization project may lead to full integration, open trade and competitive markets (quadrant II). The drafting of new versions of the gas and electricity Directives and the so called Florence and Lisbon processes indicate ambitions towards a future stronger integrated market policy in Europe.

In contrast to Continental developments, characterized by the attempt to deregulate and internationalize at the same time, British and Norwegian deregulation projects were projects taking place within a single country and where the move was away from monopoly and towards competition within the national space (from quadrant III to IV, Midttun and Thomas 1998).

From an internationalization perspective it might be argued that these developments taken as a whole point to a certain degree of convergence. For continental Europe convergence is pushed by internationalization and institutional harmonization. In the British, Norwegian and more generally Nordic cases, we can show a fair degree of convergence in regulatory styles. However, from a national styles position, it is easy to point out strong national elements both in the institutional interpretation of competition that is made nationally, and in the degree of openness established between the national markets and their environments. After a number of attempts to achieve systematic and radical deregulation that encountered significant resistance in many member nations, the European Union has had to acknowledge national diversity. Instead of a one-size-fits-all strategy, it has had to rely on a mixed and gradualist approach, aiming at moderate market opening in the course of 10 years. In line with the subsidiarity principle, members could choose between three basic models of market opening – regulated-TPA, negotiated-TPA and single buyer.

Multiple Political Economies

The diversity of selection contexts in Europe is illustrated by the fact that across North-Western Europe we still find arrangements in the electricity industry that point to four different political-economy ideal types – oligopolistic capitalism, free trade capitalism (defined as free trade and private ownership), etatism, and municipalism. Figure 7.2 shows that. One dimension of the matrix

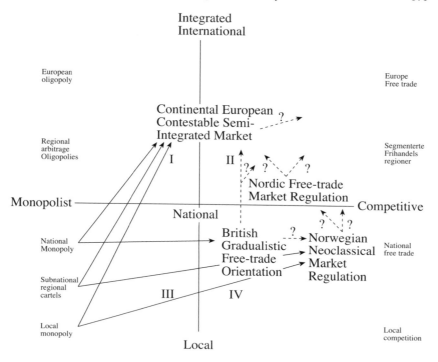

Note: This is a conceptual model and the rankings are partly judgmental.

Figure 7.1   Market opening and competition

has to do with the public versus private nature of ownership, the other indicates market concentration.

Based on aggregate figures for national industries, Belgium is a case of monopolistic capitalism, France illustrates etatism while the German electricity sector is characterized by oligopolistic capitalism.[2] Norway is a case of municipalism and the UK electricity market has features of free trade capitalism. Swedish, Danish and Finnish industries hold more intermediary positions. Sweden stands out as modified etatism and Denmark and Finland really fall in the intersection, between public and private ownership and with a moderate degree of market concentration. It should be noted that private ownership in the Danish electricity sector is decentralized consumer-ownership.

Position in this matrix naturally affects mandates, strategies and conditions for capital accumulation. We have highly differentiated retention contexts with consequences for the selection of firm practices. Municipalistic organization may typically imply a local focus, where companies are oriented at serving local

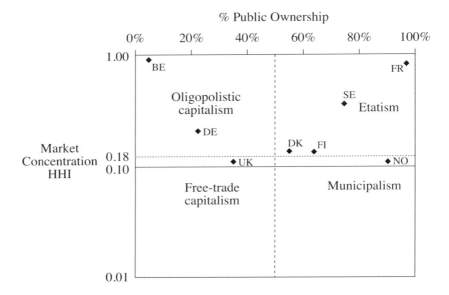

Note: The vertical scale is calculated on the amount of electricity generated on a logarithmic
scale with 0.01 to 0.10 indicating a competitive market, 0.10 to 0.18 indicating moderate concentration, and 0.18 to 1 indicating oligopolistic and monopolistic markets. The ranking of market
concentration, along the vertical axis is based on the Herfindahl-Hirschmann index which is
calculated with the following formula: HHI = $\Sigma(m_i/M^2)$, where (m_i/M) is the market share of
company i in the market.

Source: Midttun et al. (2000).

Figure 7.2   The political economy of national electricity industries in Europe

needs and are influenced by municipal political processes, including local needs
to extract dividends to finance other non-commercial sectors. Etatist organization exposes the company to state policies, where industrial strategy has
traditionally been more developed than at the municipal level. However, general
welfare concerns and political preferences may result in mandates, constraints
and possibilities that are very different from those of privately-owned companies.
The principle of 'specialité', which restrains EdF from pursuing multi-sector
strategies in France, is a good example of such a limitation. However, state
ownership may also imply patient and long-term-oriented capital investments
that enable companies to pursue demanding positioning without facing critical
exposure to short-term investors. Both EdF and Vattenfall's nuclear programmes
and broad positioning in European markets are reflections of this.

Companies in oligopolist or semi-oligopolistic positions do, of course, have
many of the privileges of state companies, without the latter's political con-

straints. The largest German wholesale and generation companies have, accordingly, been in a position to accumulate large capital assets employable for long-term strategic positioning, with few political limitations on their strategic planning. Companies exposed to free trade, such as smaller and medium-sized private companies in the Nordic market, are obviously pressured to develop high static efficiency, but they are also highly exposed to signals from short-term-oriented capital markets, and vulnerable to takeovers.

Interconnection and Grid Regime

In addition to political and institutional factors, some technical features may also impact retention of business forms and practices in European electricity markets. The transmission system is one of those key technical dimensions and it plays a critical role in that respect.

A first segmentation of the West-European electricity market that brings together Great Britain, the Nordic nations and the Iberian Peninsula is fairly obvious for geographical reasons. The British insular and the Nordic peninsular positions are only moderately compensated by inter-linkage through offshore cable capacity. That means that technical limitations on cross-border trade may impose severe restrictions on internationalization of markets. The Iberian links to Southern France are weak and hindered by the mountain chains. Subsequent segmentation of Continental Western Europe is more open to discussion. On the other hand, Austria and Switzerland are so extensively linked up to neighbour nations that we may speak of them as sub-sets of other markets and/or transit nations with a strong potential of integration with other markets.

Whereas the physical limitation of the interconnection system for some regions, such as the Nordic countries and the UK, are significant and can explain in part the persistence of national markets and national styles, persistent diversity in cases such as Germany, France, Austria or Switzerland, can clearly not be accounted for only by interconnection limits and it is also closely dependent upon institutional constraints.

To sum up, in many cases the technical infrastructure remains highly ambiguous with respect to internationalization. This has partly to do with the contested relationship between the EU federal and national decision-making levels, in combination with critical limitations in grid capacity over some essential connections. So far, the European deregulation process has introduced a moderate internationalization through the breakdown of parts of national regimes. However, it also allows considerable scope for retention of national firm strategies and institutional design. Furthermore, for considerable parts of the European electricity markets, limitations in transmission capacity particularly when combined with restrictive regulation of transborder trade, may seriously limit internationalization and work as a protective barrier making it possible to retain national styles and practices. Technology in itself is often not really an operative variable, but often becomes constraining when combined with regulatory practice.

SELECTION – MARKETS AND PRICES

A fundamental element of commercial internationalization is, of course, the strong selective pressure exerted through pricing in the market. If international deregulation and commercial competition work fully on a European scale, we should expect to see strong price convergence only limited by technical constraints. However, one must recognize that the consumer grid systems, that account for more than 50 per cent of price remains a natural monopoly and pricing here, of course, remains in the hands of national regulators. The selective pressure of international market forces may therefore only apply to the electricity generation and supply and to wholesale prices.

Extensive differences in wholesale prices may be registered between zones both in terms of weekly averages over the year and in terms of hourly prices over the day. Figure 7.3 indicates weekly average prices registered in four European trading points: the ESIS or UK spot price, the Nord Pool spot price (Nordic area), the German CEPI index (parts of the German market), the Swiss SWEP index (trade at the Laufenburg central), the APX index (Amsterdam) and the OMEL spot (Spanish Pool). Extensive differences between the high UK spot price and the lowest Nord Pool index reflect limited interconnections between these markets.

The Spanish OMEL spot price is also extensively higher than both the Nord Pool price and the Central European indexes such as the Swiss SWEP and the German CEPI indexes, indicating the relative isolation of the Iberian market from Central Europe. The Amsterdam APEX index also ranks considerably higher than the Central European indexes, indicating considerable barriers to trade even between the neighbouring German and Dutch markets. The argument that the strategic context for Western European competition in electricity remains regionally segmented as far as market selection is concerned, is fairly clearly supported by regional differences in electricity wholesale retail prices.

It might be argued that differences in European electricity prices can be explained by different fuel mixes. The difference between the dominantly thermal-based UK and Dutch electricity generation *vis-à-vis* the lower Nordic and Swiss prices (which are based on hydropower) might be justified by the differences in marginal production costs. In contrast, the difference between the UK price and the intermediary APX price cannot be justified in such terms.

Another striking feature of the British index is the extensive volatility when compared to the rest. Intuitively, one would expect stronger volatility in the hydro-dominated Swiss and Nordic systems, than in thermal systems characterized by less variations in 'fuel' scarcity. It is no surprise, therefore, that the high price level and the extensive volatility has led to claims that the UK market is subject to strategic pricing. In addition to significant price differences when comparing weekly averages, European markets also feature very different prices on a day-by-day basis. First, a striking difference between Nord Pool and the other two indexes is that hourly price variations are on average almost non-existent for the Nordic market. Dutch, Spanish and UK markets on the other hand have very distinct price levels at night and by day. The British variation is the most spectacular, with a variation of up to 1:3. The difference between base and peak load in the German CEPI index also indicates some variation, although lower than in the APX and OMEL cases. These differences are further indications of limitations in European trading resulting from capacity differences and institutional restrictions across trading zones.

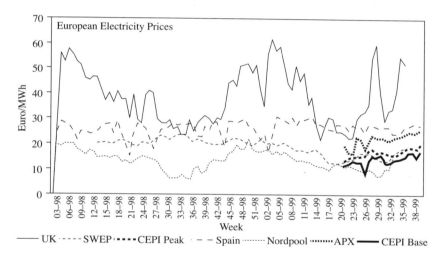

Sources: UK: ESIS (www.ngc.co.uk), CEPI: Dow Jones (www.dowpower.com), SWEP: SWEP (www.egl.ch), APX: APX (system@apx.nl), Nordpool: Nordpool (www.el-ex.fi), Spain: OMEL (www.omel.com/es).

Figure 7.3   Weekly prices in European trading zones, 1998 and 1999

To sum up our empirical investigation of the selection variables, both market prices and the defining features of political economies indicate extensive divergence in selection and selection environment which is hardly compatible with a strong convergence hypothesis.

VARIATION IN BUSINESS STRATEGIES AND INTERNATIONALIZATION

It is difficult to derive implications for the strategic configuration of energy companies either from internationalization theory or from the national styles literature. At first glance, the strategic diversity to which we have pointed above could be taken to support the national styles hypothesis. But then also, this same diversity could be interpreted as revealing specialisation and division of labour under international competition. In this section we review the main patterns of strategic configuration in large European electricity and gas companies. The first part maps variation in strategic configuration. The second part more specifically addresses how some of this variation may be related to internationalization.

Strategic Configurations

As summarized in Figure 7.4, a comparison of the largest national companies indicates highly diverse national patterns with respect to strategy and structure. Some of the larger European companies strive for scale advantages through horizontal and vertical integration. For example, EdF situates itself in the upper left quadrant, with more or less full internalization of the electricity-value chain. On that basis, the company is able to support Europe's most ambitious serial nuclear programme and benefits from important scale advantages. The Italian ENEL and the Spanish ENDESA also have strong vertically integrated and dominant positions in their national markets but without similar nuclear ambitions. In somewhat less dominant positions, EdP and National Power belong however to this group as well (Midttun 2000).

Companies characterized by horizontal and/or vertical integration generally enjoy considerable financial muscle. In addition, they also benefit from a large resource and competence base, which is likely to increase their competitive advantage. However, large organizations run the triple risk of inefficiencies, lack of flexibility and stalled innovation. When exposed to competitive market pressures, they may be vulnerable and lose out to specialist firms if they are unable to push for internal efficiency and reorganization (see also Lilja and Moen in this volume). Specialist firms may be much more competitive in such market conditions and able in particular to leverage their specialized skills in given market segments.

Another group of large national companies is characterized by less vertical integration, but European scope. The group includes the second largest German generator (EON), the Swedish State-owned Vattenfall, two large British generators (Powergen and British Energy) and the Swiss Atel. In the British

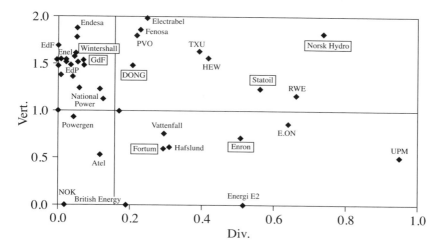

Note: The figure shows vertical and horizontal integration. We have both electricity and gas companies. Where the company is into both sectors, we have placed it in the category where they have generated most revenues. The gas companies are marked with squares.

Vertical integration is somewhat differently calculated for electricity and gas firms, given systematic differences in industrial structure: For electricity firms we have simply calculated the ratio of generation to supply or of supply to generation, depending on which of them is larger. The figure is subsequently corrected by multiplying with 2 in order to make it comparable with the Gas vertical integration measure. For gas firms, the vertical integration ratio is the sum of two measures: First, the ratio of generation to supply as in electricity, however, with a correction of 0.5 to correct for a systematic international location of the resources. Secondly, we have also added control over transport and wholesale to our gas index, under the assumption that this plays a more important strategic role than in the more de-regulated electricity industry. We have thus added 0.25 for the ownership of assets in each of the following steps of the value chain: Upstream transportation, wholesale trading, downstream transportation and storage. As a consequence, the ratio is in a 0–2 scale.

Diversification is calculated as the percentage of total revenues generated in activities other than the primary.

Sources: IEA electricity information 1999. Annual Reports National Companies.

Figure 7.4 Strategic configuration of selected large European companies

cases, weaker vertical integration partially relates to regulatory policy; the reduction of the degree of vertical integration was a major goal of the liberalization policy (Thomas 2000). The German and Swedish cases reflect a traditional division of tasks between municipal city works controlling supply and the large generators. However, some large generators, like the Swedish Vattenfall, have worked to complement their generation portfolio with supply assets, both domestically and internationally. Competition in Germany has moved the large generators in the same direction. In the latter case, however, the companies have used more direct end-user marketing than acquisition of established suppliers (Midttun 2000).

As far as integration into broader energy engagements is concerned, we find that the principle of 'spécialité' in France limits EdF's ability to participate in related businesses. Still, the existence of the twin companies EdF and GdF establishes the conditions for quick and powerful electricity-gas integration if and when the 'spécialité' principle falls (Cauret 2000).

In part through large parent companies, the large German generators (notably EON and RWE energie/RWE but also the smaller VIAG/Bayernwerk) have traditionally held broad energy engagements complementing their electricity portfolios. This reflects the German tradition of industrial clustering, where large groups integrate multi-fuel engagements as part of broader, highly complex industrial strategies. However, the German conglomerates have started to focus on the electricity industry, their traditional cash cow (Mez 2000) at the same time as they scale up and consolidate into larger units. In fact, the new focus may be wide enough to include several other energy activities, notably oil and gas.

In Britain, PowerGen's gas engagement is the result of the liberalized gas market and supply surplus, which together make gas-based electricity generation attractive. Other actors in the British electricity industry have followed the same strategy. The Swedish state-owned Vattenfall appears in the lower end, both in terms of volume and degree of integration. So far, it is engaged in electricity and gas supply to a limited extent, which reflects the reluctance of the Swedish government to promote the use of gas in the country. Electrabel is the company with the largest position in gas, but it is not very vertically integrated in this sector. In addition to gas and electricity, the Belgian generator owns assets in water supply, cable TV and district heating.

A consequence of the German industrial group tradition is the large non-energy engagements of the German firms. Petroleum and chemicals represent almost 35 per cent of RWE's turnover. Other major activities where this firm operates include mechanical, civil and plant engineering, construction, mining and raw materials. In addition, RWE is also engaged in waste management and telecommunications.

To sum up we find extensive variation in strategic configuration along the classical horizontal and vertical dimensions of the business strategy literature, where some of the variety may be seen to follow classical patterns of national business-configuration (Shonfield 1965). However, to what extent this reflects diverse national selection and retention and to what extent it reflects efficient alternative configurations under fully integrated international market economy can only be judged by further exploration of the international dimension of configuration.

Internationalization

As already argued, the differences in strategic configuration may be a function of national style and/or efficient adaptation to internationalization following a specialization principle. However, more direct mapping of international mergers and takeovers may give us some indication of the strength of international influences in the reconfiguration of European electricity industry. We shall here limit ourselves to northwestern Europe.

International involvement in the UK market

Starting in the mid 1990s the UK electricity industry has undergone major changes due to a large movement of takeovers and acquisitions. In the early 1990s UK generation firms had been protected from international takeovers by the Golden Share regulation.

As soon as the restrictions associated with the Golden Share regulation were lifted, British Regional Electricity Companies (RECs) changed ownership rapidly. As indicated by Thomas (2000) and Figure 7.5, US firms took over a majority of the RECs. This takeover wave included Southern's and Scottish

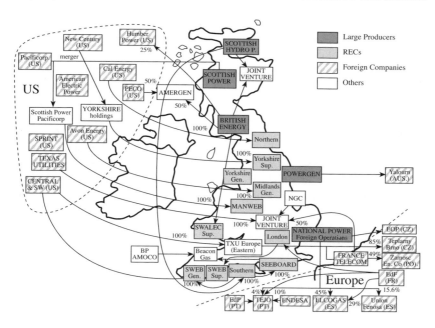

Source: Annual Reports and Internet pages of the respective companies (see literature list).

Figure 7.5   International ownership in the UK electricity industry

Power's joint takeover of SWEB; Central and SW Corp's takeover of SEEBOARD; Pacificorp and Scottish Power's joint takeover of Manweb; Texas Utilities' takeover of Eastern; Avon Energy's takeover of Midlands generation; Dominion Resource's takeover of East Midlands; Cal Energy's takeover of Northern; US Utility Consortium's takeover of Northern and Texas Utilities' takeover of The Energy Group. More recently, EdF has become a major stakeholder in the UK energy industry, through its acquisition of London Electricity and SWEB Supply.

While UK generation firms had been protected by the Golden Share regulation from foreign takeovers, they had also been hampered in their national strategies by government policy. In particular they could not invest, until recently, in British suppliers. As a consequence, all three major British generators had early on invested overseas. National Power is involved in Poland, Spain and the Czech Republic. PowerGen is active in Australia. British Power operates in the US and Canada. In addition, National Grid Company has a joint venture with France Telecom and Sprint to develop electricity grid-based telecommunications.

International takeovers and alliances in the Nordic context

In spite of early deregulation in Nordic countries, public ownership and political protection in Norway and Denmark meant that there were much less international takeovers in those two countries than in the UK. Still, some international engagements within the Nordic boundaries and outside are observed (Midttun and Handeland 1999). Given the large percentage of institutional ownership in the Swedish industry, Swedish firms have been particularly prone to take part in international operations. Figure 7.6 points to some of the major international engagements in the Nordic market. The second largest Nordic firm, Sydkraft, has been the object of rivalry between Preussen-Elektra and EdF. The latter finally pulled out and took a dominant position in the smaller Graningeverken. Eventually the Norwegian Statkraft also bought shares in Sydkraft. The Finnish Fortum acquired the medium-sized company Gullspång and 50 per cent of Stockholm Energy, thereby gaining 'control influence' in Birka Energi, which is close to Sydkraft's volume in Sweden. Fortum also has controlling influence over Birka Kraft, a Nordic-oriented trade and wholesale company.

The Swedish state-owned Vattenfall is actively positioning itself in neighbouring Nordic nations. In Finland, it has control or major influence over three medium-sized suppliers. In Norway, it matched Fortum's strategy by acquiring 49 per cent of Oslo Energy supply, as well as taking up major positions in a medium-sized generator, Hafslund, and a medium-sized supplier, Fredrikstad Energiverk. Vattenfall has also taken a position in the Danish energy market through its 12 per cent acquisition of NESA, which again controls major generation capacities in Sjællandske Kraftværker as well as a trading company, Ström.

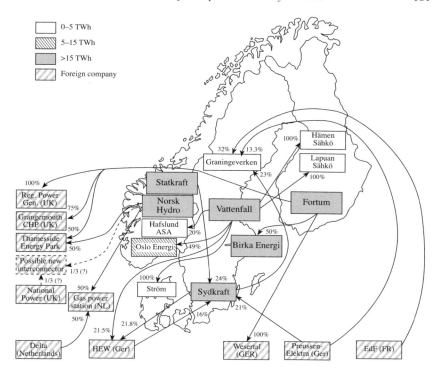

Source: Annual reports and Internet pages of the respective companies and TDN news (see literature list).

Figure 7.6   International takeovers and alliances in the Nordic electricity industry

Fortum and Norsk Hydro are engaged in power generation in Britain. Fortum is involved in Regional Power Generation, Grangemouth CHP, and works together with Norsk Hydro in the Thamesside Energy Park project. Norsk Hydro, Statnett and National Power are discussing the possibility of constructing an inter-connector of 800 MW between Norway and the UK. In addition, Norsk Hydro and the Dutch company Delta are involved in a gas-fired power plant in the Netherlands. The operation of the plant will start in 2003 and Norsk Hydro is to use 100 MW for fertilizer production. The remaining 300 MW will be sold in the open market.

The relative lack of non Nordic players in the Nordic market is probably due to the remaining importance of public ownership and to political restrictions on capital assets and foreign ownership. This seems particularly true in Norway and Denmark (in Finland, changes are recent as shown in Tainio et al. in this volume). In Norway, the so-called concession laws allow the State to take over hydropower generation assets without compensation, after the expiry of the concession period. In Denmark, the State prevented the take-over of NESA by Vattenfall threatening to expropriate its revenue by taxation. As a result, Vattenfall gave up the operation.

International alliances and takeovers in Germany

Given their size and scope, it is not surprising that large German firms are moving into several European energy markets (Figure 7.7). RWE holds major positions in Switzerland through a 20 per cent share in Motor Colombus AG and positions in a number of Hungarian companies. Apart from EON's dominant position in the Swedish Sydkraft, this firm also owned shares in BKW FMB Energie AG in Switzerland as well as in Hungary and the Czech Republic through their partly owned Hamburgische Elektrizitätswerke, which has later been acquired by Vattenfall. The merger between EON (formerly VEBA/Preussen-Elektra) and VIAG/Bayernwerk/HEW reflects the attempt to consolidate the German electricity industry. In the process, EON and RWE are

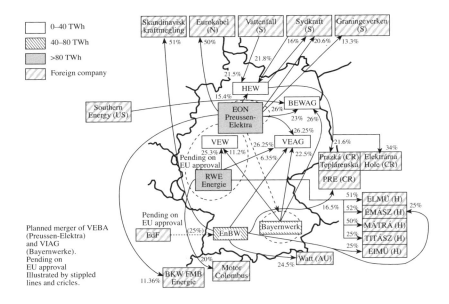

Source: Annual reports and Internet pages of the respective companies and TDN news (see literature list).

Figure 7.7   International clustering in the German electricity industry

emerging as the two highly dominant poles. Hence, RWE's merger with VEW comes as a natural follow-up, although on a much smaller scale. The two polar groups previously met in VEAG, the old East German electricity supplier, collectively 'colonized' by West German firms after the reunification, but later sold to HEW and the emerging Vattenfall-sphere.

Also important in the German market is EdF's 25 per cent acquisition of Energiewerk Baden-Württemberg (EnBW), only an initial move to take control in time of the company.

French engagements in Europe

As shown in Figure 7.8, EdF is moving to acquire key ownership positions in the European electricity market. EdF holds major positions in ESTAG (Austria), Motor Colombus (Switzerland), Graninge (Sweden), London Electricity (UK), ISE (Italy), Tejo Energia (Portugal) and Elcogas (Spain), as well as in the German EnBW, as mentioned above. In Eastern Europe, France is also involved in Edasz and Demasz in Hungary as well as in ECK-SA in Poland.

In France, the two national multifunctional water companies – Suez-Lyonnaise and Vivendi – have cautiously tried to challenge EdF's quasi-monopoly position. These two firms are truly international in scope and

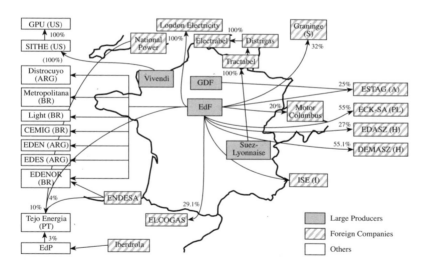

Source: Annual reports and Internet pages of the respective companies and TDN news (see literature list).

Figure 7.8   International takeovers and alliances involving French electricity firms

have broad engagements in many European markets. As described by Cauret (2000), Lyonnaise has traditionally operated local power generation in a few French towns – Strasbourg, Monaco, Grenoble and Bordeaux. The merger of the financial holding company Suez and the technical firm Lyonnaise in June 1996 integrated French operations in the electricity market, with control over the Compagnie de Belgique. Since 1988, Lyonnaise had controlled 50.3 per cent of Tractabel, a position increased to 100 per cent in September 1999. The merger of Electrabel and Distrigas has provided a basis for a complete multi-energy firm. In addition, Suez-Lyonnaise is world leader of water management via its subsidiaries Calgon, Narco and US Filter. The other French water company, Vivendi, moved into electricity through its subsidiaries, Compagnie General de Chauffe (55 GW of thermal) and Esys Montenay, restructured in a new entity, Energy Services. More recently, Vivendi is divesting its energy activities and refocusing on what it sees as its two core activities – communication and environment/water supply.

To sum up, the forms and degrees of internationalization differ greatly across European countries. They range from being open to international takeovers in the UK, to strongly shielded companies in France that are themselves nevertheless highly active in foreign markets. We found evidence indicating strong international commercial pressures and varied responses in the European electricity markets. One may conclude that internationalization is in general leading to a multi-nationalization of firms and concentration, but the degree and form of the process varies extensively from country to country in Europe.

CONCLUDING REMARKS

One important objective in this chapter has been to confront the internationalization/global convergence proposition and the national styles argument. We tried to assess, in particular, their respective adequation to an empirical case – the European electricity industry.

Internationalization, Convergence and National Styles

A main conclusion is that while the strong convergence hypothesis can be rejected fairly clearly on the basis of our empirical material, the distinction between the softer internationalization hypothesis and the national styles hypothesis remains more difficult to pin down.

As already argued, internationalization may, in a path dependency perspective, be compatible with extensive national variation in business configuration. The same would apply to the national style argument. To evaluate the soft intermediary hypothesis up against the strong national style hypothesis, it has therefore been necessary to explore more specific aspects of variation in business strategies such as specific patterns of internationalization as well as the specific mechanisms of selection and retention of firm configuration.

The evidence from our empirical material is here rather mixed. The extensive international takeovers and acquisitions in some countries are obvious indicators of internationalization (see also Lilja and Moen and Plehwe in this volume). However, other countries exhibit little or moderate takeovers in the electricity industry. By this indicator, therefore, internationalization is far from pervasive in the electricity market. The national champion policy of the French public service policy and the Norwegian concession laws that favour domestic public ownership are cases pointing to the pervasive strength of national style.

The same ambiguity is also apparent when we look at selection. While we have seen clear international price-spillovers in the Nordic market as a consequence of the common Nord Pool construct, the EU as a whole exhibits a highly divergent price picture, indicating that nowhere near a universal price selection is taking place in the market.

Furthermore, when it comes to retention, or institutionalization of market organization, the European scene is also characterized by ambiguity. On the one hand, the European Commission has strived for internationalization of common market rules throughout the Union. On the other hand, the principle of subsidiarity has provided each nation state with extensive institutional freedom to mould market rules to national purpose and national taste. We have therefore seen that institutionalization of market rules and grid access come in a number of forms in Europe, where the minimum requirements from the European directives are clearly insufficient to secure full commercialization. The UK, for example, has taken radical steps towards opening its borders whereas other countries like France, have retained a far more restrictive and minimalistic approach.

Fragmentation of markets by institutional framework and national business systems have, in other words, clearly limited the emergence of a common market acting as a uniform contact for selection. Although the EU may succeed in standardizing certain functions, nation-states and firms may retain diversity by designing functional equivalents at the national level outside of the EU's control.

Furthermore, standards to evaluate organizational performance and strategic priorities vary significantly across institutional regimes and cannot be derived from a universal market rationality (Hollingsworth and Boyer 1997). The impact of internationalization on national subsidiaries is also likely to vary depending on the firm's organization. Holding companies are primarily controlled through financial targets. Integrated firms are usually centrally controlled. Therefore, more internationalization may not necessarily imply diminishing national diversity in actual firm behaviour. For instance, Kristensen and Zeitlin (2001) demonstrate that Danish subsidiaries of British multinationals have extensive leverage to pursue Danish style management. Whitley's (1999) argument that multinational companies seem unlikely to change substantially their key national-based attributes and practices unless foreign operations constitute a large percentage of total operations, pulls in the same direction.

However, it remains difficult to conclusively decide whether diversity in business strategies of European energy companies is maintained due to path-dependent multiple efficiencies or due to differences in selection mechanisms. Path dependence implies that different types of firms and technologies may be efficient under the same selection mechanisms, due to different institutional structures and to interaction with different national industrial policies such as technology and innovation policies. Even under similar selection mechanisms, therefore, strategic diversity may be maintained because of the variety of resource bases, firm competencies and national industrial policies and systems of innovation. EdF may have succeeded with efficient management of a large-scale nuclear programme, whilst other companies such as the Danish Elsam and Elkraft may develop advanced combined heat and power strategies and both strategies may be equally efficient. However, we are in a transition situation and some of the differences might wear off after a while (see also Plehwe in this volume who argues that the period is still one of transition when it comes to Europeanization).

Internationalization in the Long Run

Once again, however, it is important to recognize that we may be in a transitory phase. Whereas the early political attempts to establish common market institutions for European electricity markets have only been a partial success, the interplay between economic pressures and new institutional frames may in the longer run make for a stronger push in the liberal direction. The interplay between national systems, the supranational level and commercial strategies may, therefore, lead beyond the limited perspectives embedded in the present partial EU deregulation. By gradually exposing European industry to European market competition, the European Union may expropriate in time the interventionist power of the nation-state and erode its control over the electricity sector while fostering the evolution towards a liberalized and integrated market (see Djelic and Quack in the introduction and conclusion for their definition of incremental but consequential change that could apply here). As argued by Majone (1996) there is an intrinsic liberalist drive in the very EU construction. Lacking the legitimacy of the nation state to pursue interventionist policies, the EU Commission is often restricted to pursue deregulation strategies to assert its power *vis-à-vis* the nation-state.

Companies operating across European boundaries stimulate de facto transfer of regulatory power from the national to the European level. These multiregional firms are regulated under a more general European regime (see also Plehwe with Vescovi in this volume), which by its liberal character may be more suitable to international competitive strategies. In fact, a parallel development is taking place in the USA, where energy companies divest within states and invest across states to come under Federal regulation (Jurewitz 2000).

In spite of institutional subsidiarity, therefore, the European Commission may in the long run succeed in staging a stronger functional convergence of retention mechanisms taking advantage of the multinationalization of industry. The current scaling up of companies through mergers and acquisitions means that electricity firms increasingly transcend national borders of nation-states, which puts them under the purview of European authorities. While institutionalized practices tend to be maintained under national subsidiarity and to be reinforced as part of industrial policy strategies, corporate strategies in the largest European companies may undermine national decision-making, and lift critical regulatory decisions on to the European arena.

However, the increasing integration of electricity companies facing the strategic challenges of European deregulation may, in the long run, have serious consequences for the reform itself. The basic argument for market orientation is that decentralized competition would force companies to provide customer service with maximum efficiency. The argument for maintaining national companies intact even after deregulation has been that they will be competitively exposed in a larger European market. And indeed, this assumption holds if we presuppose open access across national borders for a sufficient amount of countries.

However, with rapid integration and strategic alliances between the larger European actors, firms may face medium- to long-term market concentration problems, which may in fact undermine competitive pressures. In this perspective one may see the European market integration and deregulation of infrastructure industries as opening up a temporary window of opportunity for European competition which is subsequently undermined as companies integrate to develop into larger units. The idea that decentralised markets will govern Europe through free trade competition may, in other words, hold for a transitory period, before we are back again with complexity of regulating oligopolistic competition, but now at a higher level. A similar point is made by Lilja and Moen in their chapter on the Nordic paper and pulp industry (see also Djelic and Bensedrine 2001). A possible scenario is therefore the emergence of a European oligopoly in the electricity industry and a reversal to market regulation by opening up for challenges rather than by direct decentralised competition.

In Central Western Europe, we are already witnessing the first moves in that direction amongst large German companies. The acquisition by EON of Bayernwerk and the acquisition by RWE of VEW are pointing the way. We have also noted EdF's engagement in the UK market, as well as RWE and

EdF's attempts to seek control over Swiss production capacities through the Motor Columbus acquisition. Energy industry in southern Europe is highly concentrated, and unlikely to be split up.

In the long run, strong market concentration may necessitate stronger political intervention on behalf of consumer and national interests, and this intervention may, in the European context, easily have strong national overtones. In the long run, internationalization and strategic convergence may therefore have to be complemented, at least to some extent, by a nationally designed re-politicization.

NOTES

1. The principle of subsidiarity is, as far as we know, borrowed from the Catholic Church and prescribes that tasks should be solved at the lowest possible level of decision-making within the system.
2. Before deregulation German firms enjoyed regional monopolies. The German deregulation in its first stage included distance-based tariffs that undermined competition. Now that distance tariffs have been removed and Germany has been divided into two trading zones, large mergers are shaping an oligopolistic scene.

REFERENCES

Aldrich, Howard (1999), *Organisations Evolving*, New York: Sage.
Arentsen M.J., J.W. Fabius and R.W. Künneke (2000), 'Dutch business strategies under regime transition', in A. Midttun (ed.), *Energy Industry Business Strategies*, London: Elsevier, pp. 151–94.
Campbell, J.L., J.R. Hollingsworth and L.N. Lindberg (eds) (1991), *Governance of the American Economy*, New York: Cambridge University Press.
Cauret, Lionel (2000), 'Wind of change and sustainability of the French power system? new business strategies and interests face to the new *relaxed status quo*', in A. Midttun (ed.), *Energy Industry Business Strategies*, London: Elsevier, pp. 225–78.
David, P.A. (1993), 'Path dependence and predictability in dynamic systems with local network externalities: a paradigm for historical economics', in D. Foray and C. Freeman (eds), *Technology and the Wealth of Nations*, London: Pinter Publishers, pp. 208–231.
DiMaggio, P. and W.W. Powell (1991), 'The Iron Cage Revisited: Institutional Isomorphism and collective Rationality in Organization Fields', in P. DiMaggio and W.W. Powell (eds), *The New Institutionalism in Organisations*, Chicago: University of Chicago Press, pp. 63–82.
Djelic, M.L. and J. Bensedrine (2001), 'Globalisation and its limits: the making of international regulation', in G. Morgan, P.H. Kristensen and R. Whitley (eds), *The Multinational Firm*, Oxford: Oxford University Press, pp. 253–80.
Doz, Y.L. and C.K. Pralahad (1993), 'Managing DMNCs: a search for a new paradigm', in S. Ghoshal and E. Westney (eds), *Organisational Theory and the Multinational Corporation*, London: Macmillan, pp. 24–50.

Hall, P. and D. Soskice (eds) (2001), *Varieties of Capitalism. The Institutional Foundations of Comparative Advantage*, Oxford: Oxford University Press.

Hollingsworth, J.R. and R. Boyer (1997), *Contemporary Capitalism: the Embeddedness of Institutions*, Cambridge: Cambridge University Press.

Jurewitz, J. (2000), 'Business strategies evolving, in response to regulatory changes in the US Electric power industry', in A. Midttun (ed.), *European Energy Industry Business Strategies*, London: Elsevier Science, pp. 279–336.

Kristensen, P.H. and J. Zeitlin (2001), 'The making of a global firm: local pathways to multinational enterprise', in G. Morgan, P.H. Kristensen and R. Whitley (eds), *The Multinational Firm: Organizing Across Institutional and National Divides*, Oxford: Oxford University Press, pp. 172–95.

Majone, G. (1996), *Regulating Europe*, London: Routledge.

Maurice, M. and A. Sorge (2000) (eds), *Embedding Organizations*, Amsterdam/Philadelphia: Benjamins.

Mez, L. (2000), 'Corporate strategies in the German electricity supply industry: from alliance capitalism to diversification', in A. Midttun (ed.), *Energy Industry Business Strategies*, London: Elsevier, pp. 195–224.

Midttun, A. (ed.) (2000), *Energy Industry Business Strategies*, London: Elsevier.

Midttun A. and J. Handeland (1999), *The Nordic Public Ownership Model under Transition to Market Economy: The Case of Electricity*, Norwegian School of Management, Centre for Energy and the Environment, Report 2/1999.

Midttun, A. and S. Thomas (1998), 'Theoretic ambiguity and the weight of historical heritage: a comparative study of the British and Norwegian electricity liberalization', *Energy Policy*, **26** (3).

Midttun A., J.T. Henriksen and A.R. Micola (2000), 'Strategic development and regulatory challenges in West-European electricity markets', in A. Midttun (ed.), *Energy Industry Business Strategies*, London: Elsevier, pp. 375–413.

Ohmae, K. (1985), *Triad Power*, New York: The Free Press/Macmillan.

Ohmae, K. (1995), *The End of the Nation State: The Rise of Regional Economies*, London: Harper Collins Publishers.

Orru, M. (1994), *The Faces of Capitalism*, Paper presented at the Sixth Annual International Conference on Socio-Economics, HEC, Paris.

Polanyi, K. (1944), *The Great Transformation*, Boston/MA: Beacon Press.

Scott, R., J. Meyer et al. (1994), *Institutional Environments and Organizations. Structural complexity and individualism*, Thousand Oaks/CA: Sage.

Shonfield, A. (1965), *Modern Capitalism: The Changing Balance of Public and Private Power*, London: Oxford University Press.

Thomas, S. (2000), 'Corporate strategies in the British electricity supply industry', in A. Midttun (ed.), *Energy Industry Business Strategies*, London: Elsevier, pp. 75–150.

Whitley, R. (1992), *European Business Systems: Firms and Markets in their National Contexts*, London: Sage.

Whitley, R. (1999), *Divergent Capitalisms: The Social Structuring and Change of Business Systems*, London: Oxford University Press.

Zeitlin, J. and G. Herrigel (eds) (2001), *Americanization and its Limits*, Oxford: Oxford University Press.

Other Documentation

EU Commission (1996): Directive 96/92 on common rules for the market for electricity. EU Bulletin L27/20 of 30th January 1997.

International Energy Agency (1998): *IEA Statistics: Electricity Information.*
International Energy Agency (1998): *IEA Statistics: Energy Statistics of OECD Nations.*
UCPTE (1998) Statistical Yearbook 1997, downloaded from http://www.ucpte.org/

Annual Reports

British Energy (1998).
Electrabel (1996, 1997, 1998).
Electricidade de Portugal (1996, 1997, 1998).
Electricité de France (1998) French Version.
ENDESA (1996, 1997).
Enel (1998).
Energie Ouest Suisse (1998).
Iberdrola (1996, 1997, 1998).
London Electricity (1998).
National Power (1998–99).
Omel (1998).
PowerGen (1998).
RWE (1995–96, 1996–97, 1997–98).
Scottish Power (1998–99).
Statkraft (1996, 1997, 1998).
Sydkraft (1996, 1997, 1998).
The Energy Group (1997).
Unión Fenosa (1996, 1997, 1998).
Vattenfall (1996, 1997, 1998).
VEBA (1998) German Version.

Internet Sites

Association of Swiss Electricity Producers: http://www.strom.ch/italiano/
Atel: http://www.atel.ch/
APX: system@apx.nl
Bayernwerk: http://www.bayernwerk.de/
Beacon Gas: http://www.beaconnected.co.uk/
BKW: http://www.bkw.ch/
BP Amoco: http://www.bpamoco.com/
Britain Electricity Association: http://www.electricity.org.uk/
British Electricity Map: http://www.powercheck.demon.co.uk/ele_map.htm
British Energy: http://www.british-energy.com/
CEPI: Dow Jones: http://www.fame.com/products/dowPower.html
CKW: http://www.ckw.ch/
Department of Trade and Industry, UK: http://www.dti.gov.uk/
East Midlands Electricity: http://www.eme.co.uk/
Eastern: http://www.eastern.co.uk/
EGL: http://www.egl.ch/
Electrabel: http://www.electrabel.be/
Electricidade de Portugal: http://www.edp.pt/
Electricite de France: http://www.edf.fr/
EnBW: http://www.enbw.com/

Endesa: http://www.endesa.es/
Energie Ouest Suisse: http://www.eos-gd.ch/
Energis: http://www.energis.co.uk/
EPON: http://www.epon.nl
ESIS: www.nationalgrid.com/uk
European Environmental Agency: http://www.eea.dk/
European Union: http://europa.eu.int/
European Union: http://europa.eu.int/
EZH: http://www.ezh.nl/
Federal Energy Regulatory Commission, US:http://www.ferc.fed.us/
Federal Trade Commission, US: http://www.ftc.gov/index.html
Fortum: http://www.fortum.fi/sahkojalampo/
France Telecom: http://www.francetelecom.fr/vfrance/home/html/indexv4b.html
Gas de France: http://www.gdf.fr/
Gas West: http://www.gaswest.co.uk/
Iberdrola: http://www.iberdrola.es/index.htm
International Energy Agency: http://www.iea.org/
London Electricity: http://www.london-electricity.co.uk/
Lyse Energi: http://www.lyse-energi.no/
Manweb Electricity: http://www.manweb.co.uk/
Midlands Electricity: http://www.meb.co.uk/
National Grid Company: http://www.ngc.co.uk/
National Power: http://www.national-power.com/index_java.htm
NOK: http://www.nok.ch/home.html
Nord pool: http://www.nordpool.no/
Northern Electric: http://www.northern-electric.co.uk/
Nord Pool: http://www.nordpool.no
Norweb Electricity: http://www.norweb.co.uk/
ODIN, Official Information Norway: http://www.odin.dep.no/nou/1998–11/
OMEL: http://www.omel.com/es
Peco Energy: http://www.peco.com/
Powergen: http://www.powergen.co.uk/
Red Electrica Espana: http://www.ree.es/ree-home.htm
Repsol: http://www.repsol.es/webrepsol/esp/home/home.htm
RWE: http://www.rwe.de/
Scottish Power: http://www.scottishpower.plc.uk/
Scottish Southern Electricity: http://www.scottish-southern.co.uk/homeie4.html
Soprolif: http://www.soprolif.fr/
SPE: http://www.spe.be/
Sprint: http://www.sprint.com/
Stadt Zürich: http://www.stadt-zuerich.ch/kap08/elektrizitaetswerk/
Suez Lyonnaise des Eaux: http://www.suez-lyonnaise-eaux.fr/english/index.htm
Swalec Electricity: http://www.swalec.com/
Sweb Electricity: http://www.sweb.co.uk/
SWEP: http://www.egl.ch
Swiss Federal Office of Energy: http://www.admin.ch/bfe/
Swiss Federal Office of Energy: http://www.admin.ch/bfe/e/index.htm
Telefonica: http://www.telefonica.es/home.htm
TIWAG: http://www.tiwag.at/home.html
Transco: http://www.transco-bgplc.com/

Union Fenosa: http://www.uef.es/index.htm
Union for the Co-ordination of Transmission of Electricity: http://www.ucpte.org/
United Utilities: http://www.unitedutilities.co.uk/
Vattenfall: http://swww.vattenfall.se/webb99/index.htm
VEAG: http://veag.de
Veba: http://www.veba.de/
VEOE: http://www.veoe.at/
VIW: http://www.viw.or.at/
Wiennet: http://www.wiennet.at/index_noflash.htm
Yorkshire Electricity: http://www.yeg.co.uk/

8. Europe's special case: the five corners of business–state interactions

Dieter Plehwe with Stefano Vescovi

INTRODUCTION

For students of international relations and business–state interactions, Europe provides a unique puzzle. The European Union is not a supranational state. Nor can Europe be considered merely as another international regime based on sovereign nation-states. No other set of 'combined international organizations' (Rittberger 1995) enjoys institutionalized powers quite on a par with those of the European Court of Justice, the European Central Bank, the European Commission and the European Parliament combined. At the same time, decision-making and controlling powers are shared with national governments represented in the European Council and with national administrative units such as national judiciaries.

This, furthermore, is only part of the picture. Representations of institutionalized power relations tend to be incomplete, giving much less consideration than they should to the role of private interests and in particular private business interests. Aspinwall (1998) observes 'supranational interest group pluralism' juxtaposed to 'national statism' in Europe.

The striking conclusion is that collective action is far more complex than conventional theories allow. In the tug of war with national advocacy systems, EU-level groups are using increasingly sophisticated means to attract allegiance, including group special-isation, diversification of political objectives, and temporary alliances. In addition, both the groups themselves and the EU institutions are socialising private interests to the efficacy of Euro representation. (Aspinwall 1998, p. 198)

Carrying the argument even further and adding a 'neo-corporatist' touch, Kohler-Koch (1999) identifies supranational network governance as an institutional feature peculiar to the European Union.

What indeed is the role in European decision making of supranational network governance – defined as the interplay of public and private influences? Should we consider Europe's supranational arena as negligible space, national systems remaining the main loci of power? Or else should we consider that area as an institutionalized field in the making and an important part of a larger whole? Can we discount the lobbying of supranational authorities by European business interests or should we look at it instead as revealing processes of formation of new transnational industrial orders (see Lilja and Moen in this volume)? Does Europeanization of social forces in other words take us beyond traditional accounts of national statehood and national societies?

We argue that new analytical tools flexible enough to deal with the ambiguities of European power relationships are needed. A simple application of international political economy is far from sufficient to explain the dynamic transformation of Europe's special business–state relationships. We need an institutional account of the European architecture that would position it somewhere in between rigid versions of multi-domestic intergovernmentalism and loose supranational agreements. In line with the approach (Djelic and Quack in the introduction and conclusion) of this volume, Europeanization is seen here as the interplay of supranational institution building and national institutional change – an interplay that involves cooperation and conflict between multiple actors in various arenas, and which through its complexity carries with it a high potential for emergent and unexpected outcomes.

The objective of this chapter is to move some way in understanding that interplay. While pointing to the limits of the literature on the issue of business–state relations, we glean insights from theories on European integration. We then propose our own model of Europe's 'five corner power relationships' that takes into account both the interplay between national and supranational institutions and the interface between public agencies and civil society forces. We test that model by applying it at the sectoral level, focusing on the fields of transport and postal and logistics services.

PUBLIC–PRIVATE INTERFACE IN THE LITERATURE – THE 'MISSING LINKS'

While the International Relations (IR) literature has traditionally paid little attention to private actors, there have been some attempts recently in that literature to get a better grasp of the important interplay between business and states.

From the Triad Relations Model

Stopford and Strange (1991) in particular have pointed to the significance of the 'new diplomacy' in international relations where multinational enterprises (MNE) are seen as independent factors of influence. The simple model they use is presented in Figure 8.1. It reveals triadic relations involving both states and private companies.

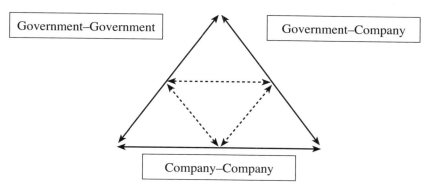

Source: Stopford/Strange (1991, p. 22).

Figure 8.1   Triadic relationships

Stopford and Strange (1991) provide substantial insights into the interplay between public and private strategies for growth and development. Their work has undeniably represented a breakthrough for the study of the impact of MNE in international politics (Underhill 2000). However, they point themselves to two limits of their analysis. First, the theoretical understanding of the impact of states on firms and, conversely, of firms on states remains too superficial. This is essentially due, they claim, to a lack of comparative empirical work. Then, there is a glaring need for 'bringing institutions back in'. The triad model remains essentially a model of disembedded actorhood. 'The "MNE –government" relations rubric may be adequate to analyse a bilateral firm–state relationship which is effectively isolated from other actors and processes; but it is insufficient to capture a concert of plurilateral interaction which embeds both firms and governments in an institutional corpus' (Sally 1994, p. 171).

To the Embeddedness Argument

At the very same time, a rich body of literature was deploying a comparative and historical methodology and an institutional theoretical framework to get at a better understanding of the impact of national states and institutions on firms (Whitley 1992, 1998; Hollingsworth and Boyer 1997; Quack et al. 2000; Hall and Soskice 2001). Those institutional accounts not only identified state-related patterns of organizational reproduction, they also alerted to the larger societal effects of systems of norms and rules that vary more across nations than over time within nations (Sorge 1995). Hence those arguments were pointing to the survival of diverse and competing varieties of capitalism rather than to simple and wholesale convergence.

Common Limits

While extremely different and in fact quite complementary on many counts, both the IR literature and the varieties of capitalism arguments share a common weakness. By and large they have failed to consider the transnational space in its institutional dimension. The triad relations model leaves no room for institutions and processes of institutionalization altogether – including in the international sphere. The varieties of capitalism arguments integrate institutions and processes of institutionalization but only within the boundaries of the nation-state. Hence both literatures are quite inadequate when it comes to taking in the specificities of the European arena. Indeed, the interactions between public and private spheres in that arena are not merely interactions between firms and national states. They also involve other types of public authorities and actors – European ones – that are relatively independent from national institutions and states. The process of European institutionalization started with the European Coal and Steel Community (ECSC) in 1951 and it was both enlarged and deepened with the signing of the Treaty of Rome in 1958. Several rounds of treaty revisions have led to evolutions in the European institutional architecture – in the direction on the whole of stabilization and solidification.

Insights from Theories on European Integration

Scholars working on European integration have differing views on the institutional dimension of the European arena. There are two main lines of thought in that respect that point to different pictures with regard to the interplay between European institutionalization and private interests in general.

Intergovernmentalists understand the European Union mainly as an international regime developed by nation-states and still very much controlled by them. Steps towards deeper integration primarily result from the desire to lower transaction costs in international arrangements but the independent influence of supranational authorities is found to be far less significant than that of national governments of member states (Moravcsik 1993, 1999). Consequently, the impact of supranational institutions on organizations and particularly on private organizations can be regarded as being quasi negligible. Conversely, organized collective action in general and business lobbying are not described as having a great impact on European institutions. In Moravcsik's model, transnational influence is incorporated in domestic preferences and thus remains predominantly filtered by national governments (compare Caporaso 1998, pp. 346–9).

Supranational institutionalists on the other hand claim a rising influence of supranational institutions to which domestic institutions increasingly are having to adapt (Sandholtz and Stone Sweet 1998). Europe's federalists support such a movement toward an integrated supranational state whereas opponents are wary about the loss of national autonomy and its impact on the democratic scene (see the interesting debate between Mancini 1998 and Weiler 1998, compare also with von Bogdandy 1999). We are not just talking here of limited 'horizontal federalism' but really of a new type of federalism with stronger and more varied elements of both horizontal and vertical divisions of labour and power. With regard to business–state relations, the consequence is an acknowledgement of greater direct impact of supranational institutions unto firms and private organizations in general. Reciprocally, scholars fear or applaud the rising influence of private interests within the Euro-Polity, but rarely discuss this ambiguity systematically. The focus is more often in fact on the public authority side of the equation, though scholars studying private business interests are increasingly shifting attention to a wider governance perspective (Kohler-Koch and Eising 1999; Greenwood and Aspinwall 1998).

Both groups of scholars do agree that Europe is not a centralized hierarchy of the German or US type, given in particular its extremely limited fiscal powers and many other weaknesses characteristic of supranational authorities. Both groups also acknowledge on the other hand the strong dynamics of integration processes (oscillating between enlargement and deepening). We propose that the crucial difference between Europe and other transnational arrangements is precisely its character of 'institutionalized transformative design'. No other supra- or transnational institutional arrangement has a density, spread and degree of (delegated) supranational authority that comes close to that of the European Union (Rittberger 1995). Europe is 'special' amongst 'combined international organizations' in delegating substantial powers to supranational authorities (European Commission, European Court of Justice or more recently the European Central Bank for example). European institutions also stand out against other powerful international organizations such as the World Bank due to their broad scope of activities and responsibilities encompassing virtually all aspects of social life (compare Rittberger 1995, p. 33).

That said, however, one cannot fully close the debate between intergovernmentalists and supranational institutionalists. Different integration regimes in fact persist and coexist within the European space. In the realm of single market politics (European Community referred to as 'pillar one') features of supranational authority have grown stronger over time than in the realms of security or foreign policy for example. The latter realms are referred as, respectively, 'pillar two' and 'pillar three' and, there, intergovernmental modes of decision making still remain quite predominant. Each line of thought thus can easily point to rich empirical evidence to buttress its wider argument without addressing, alas, systemic contradictions.

Europe and the Five Corner Model

'Comprehensiveness' and 'depth' of European integration were and continue to be matters of protracted battles within and between member states as well as within and certainly between supranational authorities and member states. Most of the time, furthermore, the practical workings of European decision making contribute to the segmentation and fragmentation of supranational authorities. To be convincing, a theoretical model of the European Union thus needs to incorporate the multidimensional nature of relations between public and private actors. The 'five-corner model' of European institutionalized power relations that we propose in Figure 8.2 defines a structural framework that can be used to identify and analyse actor relations and institutional hierarchies on a case-by-case basis. It is foremost an analytical tool designed to capture each angle of European institutional power relations as represented by the five tangents.

Each tangent can, and we argue should, be scrutinized carefully to draw a complete picture that would not be misrepresenting either supranational or

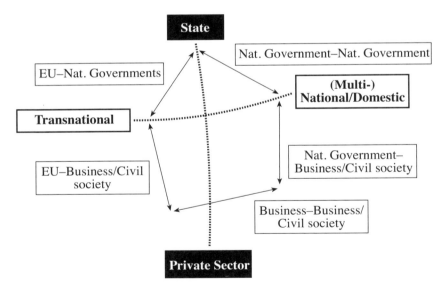

Source: Own composition based on 'triad relationships' conceptualized by Stopford and Strange (1991, p. 22). EU: for example Commission, EP, ECJ, Council.

Figure 8.2   Europe's five-corner relations

national influence and that would not misconstrue either public or private influence. If multi-domestic governance prevails by design or irrespective of formal transfers of authority in a particular instance, then the supranational angles of relationships would be of no or relatively low importance to decision making (dominance of government–government relations, and government–business/civil society relations in each society). If instead supranational governance comes more fully into play, the supranational angles (EU authorities–national governments, EU–business/civil society) should strongly impact on each of the respective domestic orders, and transnational private interest groups should qualify and combine with more traditional national forms of interest aggregation. We now proceed by turning to evidence from notoriously resilient fields of European integration – namely transportation, postal and logistics services. We want to test for those fields the appropriateness and explanatory power of the five-corner model.

EUROPE'S COMMON TRANSPORT POLICY REVISITED

Supranational by Design but Intergovernmental in Practice ...

Transport belonged to the few areas originally considered in the Treaty of Rome for a common European policy together with agriculture and international trade (see articles 3b, d, e in Treaty of Rome). The commitment for those areas was to reach the highest possible degree of integration. Within a 12-year period that was to end in 1969, the Treaty mandated the elaboration of common rules for international transport services within Europe and common rules for allowing non-resident firms to operate services in member countries (article 75). It was specified that the European Council of Transport Ministers would have to reach unanimous decisions until 1969 but that subsequently majority voting would be sufficient.

The real-life process, however, proved less smooth. The creation of a single European transport market (certainly conceived of as a regulated single market at the time) was quite a task and the emergence of a truly common transport policy would take longer than the 12 years originally planned. This political stagnation was revealing of the continuing exclusive control exerted by nation-states. In fact, national governments quite simply chose to ignore the Treaty that their predecessors had signed. Pressures from European industrial and commercial interest groups in favour of European deregulation of transports, but also notably from US airlines and express carriers such as Federal Express, DHL and UPS, had been steadily growing in the period. But the few European governments in favour at the time of cross-border liberalization (most notably the UK) found their efforts thwarted simply by the prevailing regime of veto powers and resulting lowest common denominator bargaining. This would all seem to be quite in line indeed with neorealist and intergovernmentalist assumptions and accounts. The latter have a hard time explaining, however, the radical unfolding characteristic of the 1980s when supranational champions finally managed to take centre stage. In 1983, some members of the European Parliament supported by the European Commission brought a case to the European Court of Justice (ECJ) against the European Council for lack of action on treaty obligations. This eventually got things moving in the direction of the institutionalization of a supranational transport policy authority (for a parallel timing–protracted persistence of the previous order and then rapid acceleration triggered in part by a court case, see Lilja and Moen in this volume).

The 1985 ECJ judgement rejected demands made by the EP on the Council to act on a number of Directives that had been initiated jointly by members of the European Parliament and the Commission. This judgement, however, also instructed the Council to finally comply with original treaty obligations. The initiative of members of Parliament thus did not lead at that time to more weight for Parliament in the regulation of European transport (to come later with expanded co-decision rights in the Maastricht and Amsterdam treaties). But the Council was forced to deal with some of the entrenched obstacles preventing deeper integration of transport markets (Plehwe 1997). At the Milan Council summit in 1985, a unanimous decision was reached to give mandate to the Commission to complete the internal market. To get around national resistance, qualified majority voting on single market matters was adopted after the passage of the Single European Act in 1997. Later on (codified in the Maastricht and Amsterdam treaties), qualified majority voting was expanded to cover social and environmental issues associated with the transportation field.

... and More Deeply Integrated at Last!

The inclusion of transport and subsequently of related postal services into the single market programme effectively acted as an 'external shock' (Fligstein 1991) which set into motion new 'path dependent processes of change' (Mahoney 2000) spreading cross-border liberalization as well as reinforcing commercialization, deregulation and privatization at the national level in due course. Demands stemming from customer industries and non-European competitors started to be taken much more seriously in the ranks of government officials both at supranational and national levels. Nevertheless, after a full decade of growing commitment to single transport market politics, the record remains mixed. While road transport and forwarding deregulation has been completed by and large, early success in rail transport to separate infrastructure and operations was stifled with regard to effective cross-border liberalization in the course of the 1990s. It was only towards the end of the decade that new legislation was passed that finally secured the common rail market agenda. Conversely, the process to gradually open up postal services for competition was stalled towards the end of the 1990s after an initial successful step in 1997. Severe obstacles continue to mitigate against deeper European integration in apparent contradiction to idealist versions of rising influence of supranational institutions.

In fact, a number of obstacles continue to be deliberately designed and integrated in the treaty. Title IV of the treaty of Rome with articles 74–84 contains a quite ambiguous language on many aspects of transport politics that leaves lots of space for a diversity of national practices (for example related to subsidies). This reflects the great significance of transport services in general for social, regional and other domestic policy priorities. Furthermore, obligations in article 75 relate only to road, rail and inland shipping transport while article 84 explicitly reserved domestic authority in the fields of air and ocean transport. Certain policy issue areas also continue to be more strongly controlled by national governments than others. Thus the multi-domestic character of European policy, while significantly attenuated for inland transport remains strong for air and ocean transport.

With the Trans European Networks programme that was codified in the Maastricht treaty, the Commission gained new competencies in infrastructure development, this attesting to the agenda-setting power of the European Roundtable of Industrialists (Holman 2000). And since the late 1980s, the Commission rediscovered its treaty-based antitrust authority to make inroads even in air and ocean transport governance. Although the Council maintained that treaty articles 85 (cartels) and 86 (abuse of dominant position) did not apply to airlines and ocean shipping, a European Court of Justice ruling (the famous Nouvelles Frontières case) affirmed the relevance of European competition law to the aviation sector (Schmidt 1997, p. 15).

Towards Supranational Governance?

Transport politics that had been in theory common but in practice truly multi-domestic before that were transformed after the 1985 single transport market decision and undeniably came to exhibit intensified supranational elements of governance.

The Council decision to rely on majority voting to complete the single market was undeniably a landmark (Garrett 1993). Starting with the Single European Act, all subsequent treaties have expanded the policy and issue areas in which unanimity is not required anymore. Unanimous decision making that ensured maximum control for national governments has become an exception in many fields. The 'new inter-governmentalism' translates into attempts at changing integration dynamics rather than putting obstacles to supranational decision making (Felder et al. 2001; Wessels 2001).

The European Parliament had fought for more influence in European policy making throughout the 1980s and it did finally secure expanded powers in the 1990s. Co-decision procedures have been extended in line with the switch to Council majority voting. '*In fact, the changes eliminate the procedural imbalances between the two major players, i.e. the Council and Parliament, to a very large extent*' (Nentwich and Falkner, 1997, p. 2, emphasis original). These changing procedures have led to a role of parliamentarians in supranational decision making far more similar to the role of national parliamentarians in national decision making. Though there is a long way to go before matching constitutional rights characteristic of national democracies, the EP is an increasingly recognized player in European decision making (American Chamber of Commerce 2001).

The European Court of Justice has continuously increased its weight as a supranational authority adding strongly to the production of European secondary law. To an unexpected extent, the Court increased its capacity as an institutional actor by establishing the 'direct and indirect effect' doctrines forcing national governments to actually comply with supranational legislation. This supranational enforcement mechanism establishes a direct link with the individual citizen (or corporate actor) thus circumventing national authorities and increasingly integrating national courts into a European hierarchy (Stone Sweet and Caporaso 1998, pp. 102–4). Member states have been acutely aware of this mechanism and have for the first time in its history mandated a restriction of the role of the court in the (Maastricht and Amsterdam) proceedings (Alter 2000). However, this cannot be regarded as evidence for a reduction of the weight of the court, since it is merely a limitation to further expansion.

The European Commission increasingly relies on longstanding residual treaty powers (for example antitrust authority and other rights providing means to exert supranational authority, and to effectively pressure both member states and organizations into agreements, Schmidt 2001) in addition to singular rights of agenda setting and treaty enforcement. The Maastricht treaty further enhanced Commission transport policy authority in infrastructure planning related to Trans European Networks (TEN).

With the newly established Committee of Regions, an additional lightweight arena (no veto powers) has been added to the supranational level of the EU polity where the Social and Economic Committee of organized interests has been established and consulted on a regular basis since a long time. Despite clearly limited influence at this stage it remains to be seen to what extent the stronger link between the supranational and the sub-national level will matter in multi-level deliberations.

Finally, the European Monetary Union has established in the form of the European Central Bank yet another supranational authority which is hardly to be overestimated regarding broad transnational impact and control in monetary (and indirectly fiscal) matters.

> The decision to assign responsibility for defining and implementing monetary policy within a group of member-states to a single central bank, and to cede all responsibility in the domain of exchange-rate policy to the institutions of the EU, undoubtedly represents one of the most significant extensions of supranational authority in the four decades since the Treaty of Rome. (Cameron 1998, p. 189)

For transportation politics then, the final implementation of the single market agenda from 1985 onwards led to what can be regarded as a European federal pre-emption clause similar to historical US developments at the national level (federal authorities versus state authorities, see Plehwe 2000). Subsequent expansions of supranational authority in regulatory fields important to transport (social policy, environmental policy, technology policy and so on) complement the protracted efforts to firmly establish single and common transport politics at the supranational level (Hey 1998). While the 'federal creation clauses' (requiring positive integration efforts) are certainly weaker than the 'federal pre-emption clause' (promoting negative integration and the removal of domestic obstacles to competition), harmonization and liberalization are certainly linked again, albeit in reverse order.

Residual powers of the Commission, rulings of the European Court of Justice, initiatives and activities of the EP and the increasing commitment of the Council to majority voting eventually all contributed to what may be regarded as a substantial loss of domestic control over European transport politics. The inbuilt 'transformative design' of European institutional relations was clearly effective, and not restricted to intended changes by member state governments. The institutional transformation process, and supranational institutionalization in particular, is rarely radical, frequently piecemeal in character, and certainly uneven if we look at the outcome. Supranational authority is still more restricted in air or ocean transport than in land-based transport and single market-making encounters far stronger difficulties in rail transport compared to road transport. Segmentation certainly prevails, but today's fragmented impact of supranational authorities is fundamentally different from what it was in the 1980s.

European five-corner relations thus certainly shifted from the multi-domestic side (state–state, state–business relations within a weak supranational framework) to the supranational side (EU authorities–member states, EU authorities–business/other civil society). After 1985, the transport sector has more truly become a part of the European Community – pillar one of the EU. This shift should reflect on the output of legislation at the supranational level which we discuss next before we finally turn our attention to the business (association) side of European governance.

THE PROLIFERATION OF 'HARD' TRANSPORT LAW IN EUROPE

Changes after 1985 and the overall move from a mostly multi-domestic logic to a more transnational one lead us to anticipate an evolution with respect to the legislative output. More precisely, we expect a substantial increase of legislative output in the later period when a supranationalized transport authority has been institutionalized (see Fligstein and McNichol 1998 for a general analysis of European secondary law). Compared to previous analyses, however, we go one step further and differentiate between binding 'hard law' (Regulations, Directives and Decisions) and non-binding 'soft law' (Communications, Opinions). In particular, we expect the rise in supranational authority to lead to an increase in supranational law of the hard kind.

We have focused on legislation related to general transport policy and land-based transport.[1] As Figure 8.3 indicates, the expectation of an overall growth of legislative output is not fully matched by the data. Whereas legislation on transport issues clearly increased from the 1960s to the 1970s, the following two decades saw a small decline in the overall number of laws issued. Closer examination reveals that an extraordinarily high number of soft law activities of the Commission during the 1970s (for example assessing parts of each national code) was responsible for this pattern. More importantly, however, Figure 8.3 shows a considerable increase of 'hard' Community transport legislation between 1960 and today and more particularly from the 1980s. The 1970s show a remarkable effort on soft laws – Commission opinions on various countries in particular – reflecting attempts by the Commission to overcome the deadlocks of intergovernmental decision-making at that time. The bulk of the increase in hard law clearly took place during the 1980s, and the 1990s essentially show stability. Thus, the last two decades that were characterized by a shift of decision making on transport issues from a multi-domestic to a transnational logic went hand in hand with an increase in binding European hard law.

A fine-grained differentiation of legislative activism, this time according to issue areas, does lend further support to the claim of an intensification and broadening of the supranational logic. Figure 8.4 identifies policy areas and shows the evolution through time of legislative activity in those areas – for both hard and soft law together.

Legislative output on common and statistical issues remains steady throughout. Efforts in the field of market regulation increased in the 1970s and

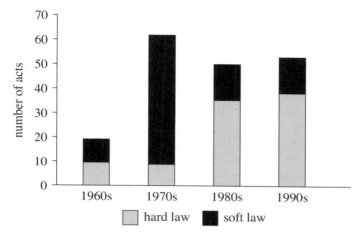

Figure 8.3   European legislation acts in the field of transport policy

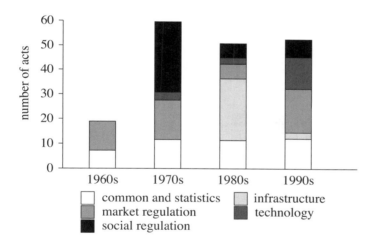

Figure 8.4   European legislation acts in different policy areas of transport

decreased in the 1980s to strongly increase again in the 1990s. Infrastructure-related output was very high in the 1980s and it was then a new policy area. It went down radically in the 1990s essentially because this issue area was moved to another legislative arena outside of transport. Technology-related output was steady in the 1970s and 1980s with a strong increase during the 1990s. Legislative activity related to social issues was very strong in the 1970s and shrank in the 1980s to rise again in the 1990s.

Once again, however, it is interesting to assess the share of soft and hard laws for each individual policy area to qualify this general evaluation of legislative activism. Figure 8.5 provides data on the evolution of European legislative acts in four policy fields, differentiating between hard and soft law. In the area of common and statistics regulation, soft law output increased considerably in the 1970s and 1980s as compared to the 1960s. This was followed in the 1990s by a strong increase in hard law output. Legislative output on market making also confirms the growth pattern of hard law during the 1990s back from a low level in the 1970s and 1980s. The 1960s had been marked by a relatively high level of hard law activity. This period corresponded to the initial efforts at establishing 'common rules for international transport' (part of the title of Council Directive 62/2005) as required by the treaty of Rome. Subsequently, and particularly during the 1970s, the activities of the Commission concentrated on commenting on legislation in individual countries. The period of low level activity ended in 1989 with Council Regulation 4058/89/EEC on the fixing of rates for the carriage of goods by road between member states. Subsequently, the programme to establish a single European market spurred strong legislative output, mainly until 1993 (Erdmenger 1994). After that, leg-

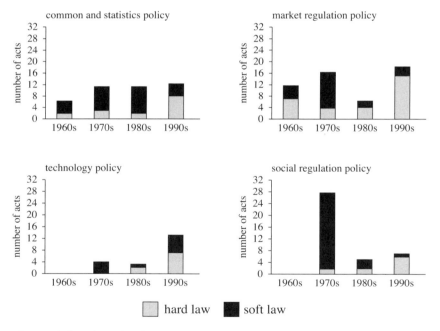

Figure 8.5   The role of hard and soft law in different policy areas of European transport

islative output on the issue of market making consisted in further defining the common market framework that had been set up in broad terms by 1994.

Figure 8.5 shows, furthermore, that the impact of hard law on the issue of technology and social regulation (mostly working time regulation) went up very significantly in the 1990s. In the technology field (mostly satellite navigation, telematics and recording equipment in road transport) hard law emerged in the 1980s and increased in the 1990s. In the meantime the intensity of soft law activity was also growing. On the other hand, in the social regulation field, strong soft law efforts during the 1970s similar to those observed in market regulation abated in the 1980s. Commission opinions and recommendations – that indicate essentially conflicts between national laws and European directives – gave way in the 1990s to universal supranational legislation.

Considerable hard law dynamics in market, technology and social regulation are not nearly matched so far for environmental and public-service issues. This is partly because legal activities that are statistically recorded as technology-related (for example vehicle emission standards), fall outside the generic field of transport law altogether (for example obligations resulting from binding international treaties to reduce energy consumption and emissions contributing to the greenhouse effect). In the field of ecological issues, a high level of soft-law activities has yet to turn into supranational hard-law activity (see Hey 1998). In the field of public service issues, early efforts towards supranational clarification of common rules for public service obligations (1960s) were taken up again in the 1990s in legislation related to market making and by the introduction of the public service concept into primary EU law through the Amsterdam Treaty.

A further qualification needs to be made regarding the potential impact of hard and soft law. Whereas European hard law in the form of binding regulations can be expected to have a strong immediate impact on actors at the national level, this is not the case to the same extent for hard law in the form of directives. The latter require strong engagement by national actors in order to be implemented into national legal orders. Furthermore, soft law activities are likely to involve companies and associations in a search for agreement about rules and thus can also mean strong impact in fact in a medium-term perspective.

In sum, the analysis suggests that the shift of transport policy authority and decision making to the supranational level observed in the 1980s and 1990s coincides with a substantial increase in hard law issued at the supranational level, frequently though not always at the expense of previous soft law activities. We also find a certain widening of scope of transport-related hard law (in particular towards social and technology issues). Regarding public service and environmental issues, development has been slower but a future expansion of transport law in these directions is likely.

We now turn to examine the second tangent of the European five-corner relationships: the public–private interface. If the weight of supranational authorities and decision-making has indeed increased, further evidence beyond the growth in European hard law should be provided. We should be able to point, in particular, to a rising level of activity of interest groups and business associations within supranational European arenas. A closer look at business associations in the transport sector will make it possible to ponder on the transformation of private sector influence in Europe.

THE CHANGING LANDSCAPE OF BUSINESS ASSOCIATIONS IN EUROPEAN TRANSPORT[2]

Since the foundation of the European Community, but particularly during the last two decades, business associations in the transport sector have faced pressures for change from two sides. The increasing weight of supranational institutions has shifted 'logics of influence' (Schmitter and Streeck 1999) from the national to the transnational level. If business associations want to participate in and to exert influence on European transport policy, they need to build up a representation and webs of influence both in Brussels and across different EU member countries. In parallel, the proliferation of European transport regulation as well as increasing cross-border competition within Europe have generated a previously unknown dynamic of company reorganization, cross-border mergers and acquisitions (see Lilja and Moen and Midttun et al. in this volume for similar corporate dynamics in other Europeanizing industries). Developments at the corporate level have led to an increasing fragmentation and polarization of the transport sector in terms of organizational structures and policy interests that are reflected by rapidly changing 'logics of membership' in previously existing national business associations as well as in newly created European business associations. What we find as a result of these double pressures is a rapid proliferation of European business associations combined with considerable fragmentation and polarization of interest representation at the transnational level.

From State-Administered (inter)National Regimes of Transport ...

Up until the late 1970s, European transport inter-governmentalism was associated with diverse, though limited, roles for associations representing private interests. In those fields of transport most closely tied to national administrations, namely railway and postal companies, interest representation fell for a long time into the exclusive realm of respective national ministries of transport and postal affairs. International coordination was achieved from the late nineteenth century onwards through the establishment of international regimes, such as the World Postal Union (founded in 1874) and the European Rail Union (founded in 1890, later renamed the International Rail Union) (Murphy 1994). The work of these international regimes was to rationalize international exchange and it involved a limited participation of organized private interests (frequently providing expertise) in what was essentially a state-administered bargaining field (Bjelicic 1990). In both the railway and the postal sector a separate role for independent business associations – at the national and European level – did arise only in the late 1980s and early 1990s when regulatory state functions and commercial operator functions have been more strongly separated in most European countries. For example, the Community of European Railways (CER) was founded in 1988 and PostEurop in 1992. In both cases, the establishment of European associations preceded cross-national liberalization efforts by only a few years.

In other, mostly privately organized, fields of transport, such as road transport and forwarding, private business associations emerged much earlier at the national level. In both areas, supranational federations and umbrella organizations of national associations were created in the decades following World War II. But again, the role of these associations consisted predominantly in assisting state agencies in the international coordination of transport systems. The International Road Union (IRU, founded in 1948) and the forwarding federation Comité de Liaison Européen des Commissionaires et Auxiliaires de Transport (CLECAT, founded at the inception of the EC in 1958 and subsequently extended to new member countries) seconded national ministries in the multilateral co-ordination of strictly international transport affairs such as customs issues. The IRU was also endowed with state functions in running the international freight insurance system TIR.

... to Organized Business Interest in European Transport

From the end of the 1980s throughout the 1990s, the combined effects of privatization and reorganization of transport companies and the liberalization of European transport markets led to the proliferation of a great variety of private business associations at the national and European level. Regarding the latter, a first impression can be gained by looking at associations related to all kinds of transport interests establishing offices in Brussels.

The findings presented in Figure 8.6 clearly underline the rise in importance of supranational arenas and authorities in the transportation field. While a number of business associations were founded throughout the earlier decades of the development of the European Communities, more associations than ever decided to invest resources to be present in supranational arenas of decision

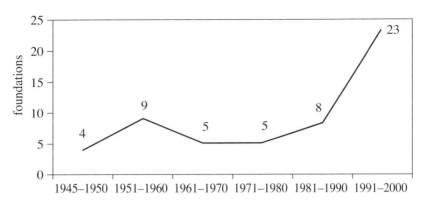

Source: EC Commission Interest Group Directory, http://europa.eu.int/comm/civil_society/ coneccs/index_en.htm, download November 15, 2001.

Figure 8.6   Development of European transport associations

making in the aftermath of the Single European Act of 1987. Altogether, we counted at least 40 more full-time officials walking the halls of power in Brussels on behalf of their national and, increasingly, transnational constituencies since the early 1990s. That figure is conservative and does not include human resources devoted to the negotiations with Brussels business in HQs of large companies, which frequently outnumber the officials directly employed in Brussels. These activities can be interpreted as an attempt by business actors to create associational channels for interest coordination and representation within an emerging transnational transport order (see Lilja and Moen in this volume for similar developments in the pulp and paper industry).

Across different fields of transport, however, the timing and dynamics of business interest organization at the European level varied considerably. This revealed distinct history and internationalization trajectories. In railways and postal services, the initial formation of national private interest associations was closely connected with the organization of business associations at European level. The Community of European Railways, for example, was created in 1988 with the explicit aim to fill the void of railway interests representation *vis-à-vis* European political institutions. PostEurop was founded in 1992 by a number of postal companies, then still publicly-owned, to meet the challenges of increasing competition between companies. National ministers (and the state administrations behind them) which hitherto used to coordinate regulatory oversight through the European Council of Ministers are now confronted by and have to coordinate with separate associations of rail and postal companies both at the domestic and at the supranational level.

In road transport and forwarding, in contrast, European market integration has brought about severe challenges for existing federations of national associations resulting from conflicting member interests. This has eventually led competing interest groups to open separate offices in Brussels. In this field, supranational and national public authorities are confronted and cooperate with a growing number of competing business associations. In road transport, for example, small and medium-sized truckers from various countries founded a new European lobby group named Union Européenne des Transporteurs Routiers (UETR) in 1997. Various national associations furthermore found it necessary to directly set up offices and influence channels at the supranational level. Whereas the national association of trucking firms from the Netherlands did so to maintain the momentum towards open markets, French and German associations joined the small and medium-sized truckers' federation in their efforts to give priority to harmonization. The latter was seen as necessary to prevent a further spiral downward with regard to earnings and working conditions.

While in road transport the foundation of competing business associations was initiated by smaller firms, in forwarding the largest firms were those that became dissatisfied with the cumbersome performance of the federation of national forwarding associations CLECAT. CLECAT in fact almost disintegrated when several member associations left the federation. A major conflict had arisen between Southern European and Northern European members due to the more rapid move to advanced logistics services in northern countries whereas many forwarding companies in Southern Europe continued to focus on broker and customs services. In 1994, nine giant forwarding companies created by successive waves of mergers and acquisitions founded a competing business association named Freight Forward Europe (FFE) with the aim of addressing a broader range of transport policy issues and building more direct links between the top management of companies and political decision makers in Brussels.

Special Interest Pluralism in European Transport

One of the key issues that we aimed to tackle with our concept of the five-corner relations was whether a shift from a multi-domestic to a transnational logic of transport policy was likely to go hand in hand with a redefinition of the relative influence of state and business actors. The tensions and conflicts of interest described above cast some doubts on whether the increasing number of business representations in Brussels translates into a strengthening of business *vis-à-vis* public actors.

The difficulties which large European transport associations, for example in the railway and postal sector, face in formulating coherent interest policies point in a similar direction. Within these associations, cross-border cooperation of national monopolies has turned within a short period into cross-border competition. The case of PostEurop, in particular, shows how corporate restructuring across borders and sectors leads to 'changing logics of membership' in business associations. The privatization of the Dutch and German postal operators have allowed the two companies to rapidly expand their operations across borders and beyond traditional postal supply chains. By way of mergers and acquisitions, the two companies transformed themselves into leading European and indeed global transport and logistics service companies, blurring sectoral border lines between postal and express companies (see Plehwe 2001a). Within PostEurop the former Dutch Post office now leads a determined single postal market campaign while the German postal company maintains an intermediate position partly due to the strength of the postal workers' union in Germany (Plehwe 2001b). Both are opposed by a third group of still mainly domestic postal companies that are in favour of a gradual and rather slow process of cross-border liberalization of reserved markets. As a result of the blurring of sector borders between postal and express companies, competing agendas have been introduced within postal and express business associations leading to new tensions within and between them.

Coherent association action is further challenged by direct lobbying of the postal and express operators: each single large company has opened offices in Brussels to influence European decision makers. Each of the two opposing camps in the postal field, however, has reached out to other public and private forces to forge cross-country alliances pro and contra liberalization. The French and the British postal operators, for example, have managed to build a formidable public service alliance involving consumer groups, trade unions and regional interests which managed to effectively slow down the deregulation process in 2000.

The railway industry provides a further example of the complex interactions between supranational regulation, company strategies and the articulation of business interests in associations. In compliance with the 1991 railroad directive (mandating separation of infrastructure management and service operations), different solutions have been promoted by various member states of the EU. While the UK chose to privatize Railtrack (without positive results), several countries maintained infrastructure management companies as public corporations yet completely severed the organizational ties between infrastructures and services. Germany instead chose to formally separate the two sides of railway organization, but keep the infrastructure managing unit under the roof of the overall holding company (Dörrenbächer and Vescovi 2000; Dörrenbächer 2002). The uneven implementation of the 1991 Directive led to growing conflicts, not only between the European Commission and member states, but also within the Community of European Railways (CER). Attempts by the CER to maintain coherence overall and exclusive representation in the rail sector failed when the infrastructure companies decided that their interests would be better represented by a separate association. The creation in 1994 of European Rail Infrastructure Managers (EIM) was at least indirectly promoted by European transport authorities (Commission 2001, p. 34).

Increasing numbers of business associations and business lobbyists thus appear to represent a greater variety of business interests in Brussels. What this means in terms of potential shifts of power at the business–state interface is still difficult to assess. A diversification of business interests could mitigate undue corporate power since public officials can more easily pit one group of business or other private interests against the other. In fact, the European Commission has given support to the European Transport Workers' Federation, for instance, when the International Road Union attempted to avoid serious bargaining on working time regulation within the Social Dialogue framework. At the same time, the large transport groups now often have two or three major voices in several associations apart from maintaining direct lobbying efforts, and thereby have multiplied their influence channels on transnational policy making.

The analysis of the changing landscape of business associations in European transport thus leads to a rather ambiguous outcome. The increasing number and diversification of European business associations, the growing amount of resources which they invest into lobbying as well as the sheer number of business representatives found in Brussels lend support to a growing weight of supranational authorities and decision-making arenas. So far, however, this shift has not been accompanied by the development of fully-fledged associational coordination functions necessary for the emergence of supranational network governance. Transnational transport associations assume, if at all, a coordinating function between competitors regarding their special interest representation and lobbying activities.They do not yet provide, however, a more elaborate coordination of market behaviour and strategic commitments of major companies (for contrasting results in the European pulp and paper industry, see Lilja and Moen in this volume). Overall, the representation of business interests in the transportation field remains rather fragmented with regard to suppliers of transport, postal and logistics services. This in fact leaves the various branches rather feeble *vis-à-vis* major customer industries represented in a more unified manner by the European shippers' council or by particular target groups such as the European Council of Transport Users, the Supply Chain Council Europe or the European Rail Circle, all founded since the early 1990s. Large freight forwarding and logistics companies are frequently considered crucial with regard to a deeper integrated governance structure. Currently, however, the forwarders appear to play a double game. On the one hand, large forwarders band together (in Freight Forwarder Europe) in an effort to improve their bargaining effectiveness with regard to Community officials and powerful customers. On the other hand, they join customer industries opposing rail and other carrier interests (for example they join the European Rail Circle).

CONCLUSION

European integration, as understood in this chapter, is still an open-ended process and not at an end stage. It is a complex process of distinct, and sometimes opposing, developments in different economic sectors, various member states and at multiple levels of decision making ranging from the local over to the national or to the supranational. Taking into account the openness and the multi-directionality of the process, however, we can observe that many decisions have become consolidated through time in structures, rules and practices that are enduring (see also the contributions of Lilja and Moen, and Midttun et al. in this volume). The co-evolution of institution building at the European level and institutional change at the national level involves intensive mutual interactions and influences (see McNichol and Bensedrine in this volume for a similar observation regarding the formation of multilateral rules at the global level). The density and range of 'trickle-up' and 'trickle-down' mechanisms linking different areas of rule-making (see Djelic and Quack in the conclusion) make the European Union a likely candidate for the most advanced and coherent attempt of transnational institution building in modern times.

More specifically, we have argued in this chapter that the process of European institution building is no longer explicable in terms of simple intergovern-mentalist bargaining but emerges from a much more complex and pluralistic political process. The five-corner model of institutionalized power relations was suggested as an analytical framework which has the potential of providing a broader picture by pointing to various axes of power relations – bridging the national and supranational – as well as private and public actors. In other words, we advocated that various types of interactions should be looked at between firms; between firms, national governments and supranational institutions; and between national governments and supranational institutions.

In the transport sector, which we studied in detail, clear indications were found for a transformative logic strengthening supranational governance in the late 1980s and 1990s. This was reflected by the intensification of European transport policy following the single market programme and the subsequent proliferation of hard transport law in the fields of common and statistical issues, market regulation, technology and social regulation. This trend was also confirmed by the parallel rise in number and activity of European business associations operating in Brussels. Our results, thus, point further towards supra-national integration than the conclusions drawn by Aspinwall (1999, p. 121) who saw European transport policy, except for market regulation, still strongly controlled by national actors. Changing as well as diverging domestic business state relations have translated into new dynamics along the axis of relations between businesses and supranational institutions. While the Commission reinforced the emergence of independent rail infrastructure companies at a European level, transnational public service alliances successfully challenged the priorities of Commissioner Bolkestein in charge of postal liberalization. It is no longer possible to draw a clear-cut line between 'negative' and 'positive' integration, furthermore, due to the expansion of supranational social and environmental policymaking. Many and increasingly diverse forces take part in the social struggles triggered by the process of supranational centralization of regulatory policy making.

European institutional impact at the same time certainly remains uneven and fragmented for reasons discussed above: not all member countries subscribe to all aspects of the European Union, supranational legislation is stronger in some policy areas than in others and different types of decision making leave more or less room for national adaptation. In transport, we found a prevailing dominance of special interest lobbying on the side of private business interests. This fragmentation of business interests, if continued in the future, is likely to maintain the currently dominant pattern of supranational governance in which most of the decision making is done by European and national public authorities.

The relative weakness of business actors, however, clearly connects to the specific sectoral logics of interest representation in transport with its strong state legacy in some and a strong private focus in other subsectors, the current overturn of 'membership logics' due to the recent wave of privatizations, reorganizations and mergers across sectors and borders, and the coexistence of giant firms with rather small transport and logistic providers. Firms and business associations in other service sectors, in communications and multi-media for example, have been much more cooperative and successful in creating 'interface actor associations' which translate their interests more coherently into a stronger power position and influence in supranational policy-making processes in Europe (Knill 2001; Blank 2001).

The results of our analysis highlight the need for sectoral comparisons of the co-evolution of developments at the level of corporate action, industrial cooperation and competition, and national and European regulation. The studies of Lilja and Moen (in this volume) on the European pulp and paper industry and of Midttun et al. (in this volume) on the European electricity industry provide interesting comparisons to our study. As in our chapter, they find rather gradual, often emergent processes of co-evolution at work between European and national level actors, both within the polity and economy, which through 'key events', such as the single market programme, generate new path dependencies (Mahoney 2000). At the same time, these studies point to the diversity of industry-specific trajectories towards European industrial orders. A transition towards oligopolistic competition regimes, as hinted at by the abovementioned authors for the European pulp and paper and European electricity industry, is a rather unlikely scenario for the transport sector as a whole – although such tendencies are visible in postal and express services which are at the forefront of privatization and liberalization. Other fields of transport, however, are much more likely to remain under strong public influence (for example railways) or to develop a rather fragmented industrial order (for example road transport) in between national and European authority.

The European five-corners relationships model presented in this chapter hopes to encourage more empirical research of this kind, and to provide a framework for more systematic comparison of company, branch and sector level trajectories. Such empirical investigations could help to understand the unevenness, multidirectionality and contradictions in the European integration process (Sandholz and Stone Sweet 1998; Djelic and Quack in the introduction and conclusion of this volume). In this way, the five-corner model of institutionalized power relations could contribute to a joint academic effort to assemble parts of the fascinating puzzle named European integration.

NOTES

1. The database for the tables consists of all documents of EUR-Lex Directory of Community Legislation in Force – analytical structure transport policy 7.05 to 7.20.60 except ocean and air transport, passenger transport, and legislation related to external relations (http://europa.eu.int/eur-lex/en/lif/ind/en_analytical_index_07.html). Research results presented here were primarily generated by the work of Stefano Vescovi and Marc Kaulisch.
2. The following section is based on extensive interviews with company and business association representatives conducted in 2001 (Plehwe and Dörrenbächer 2001).

REFERENCES

Alter, K.J. (2000), 'The European Union's legal system and domestic politics', *International Organization*, **54** (3), Summer, 489–518.
American Chamber of Commerce (2001), 'The EU committee: from Amsterdam to Nice: the growing role of the European Parliament', Workshop Brussels, February 20.
Aspinwall, M. (1998), 'Collective attraction – the new political game in Brussels', in J. Greenwood and M. Aspinwall (eds), pp. 196–213.
Aspinwall, M. (1999), 'Planes, trains and automobiles. Transport governance in the European Union', in B. Kohler-Koch and R. Eising (eds), *The Transformation of Governance in the European Union*, London and New York: Routledge, pp. 119–34.
Bjelicic, B. (1990), 'Die Träger nationaler und internationaler Verkehrspolitik und ihr Zusammenspiel in verkehrspolitischen Entscheidungsprozessen', *Zeitschrift für die Verkehrswissenschaft*, pp. 85–121 (Part I, #2) and 177–96 (Part II, #3).

Blank, Oliver (2001), 'The impact of changing sectoral definition upon associability: the convergence of business interests in the information and communication technology sector in Europe', Conference Paper 'The Effectiveness of EU Business Associations', http://www.ey.be/EYBE?Site.nsf/Pages/ENCConfBlank, download November 1, 2001.

Cameron, D.R. (1998), 'Creating supranational authority in monetary and exchange-rate policy: the sources and effects of EMU', in W. Sandholtz and Alec Stone Sweet (eds), *European Integration and Supranational Governance*, Oxford: Oxford University Press, pp. 188–216.

Caporaso, James A. (1998), 'Regional integration theory: understanding our past and anticipating our future', in W. Sandholtz and A. Stone Sweet (eds), *European Integration and Supranational Governance*, Oxford: Oxford University Press, pp. 334–51.

Commission of the European Communities (2001), *White Paper. European Transport Policy for 2010: Time to Decide*, Brussels (Com(2001)370).

Dörrenbächer, C. (2002), 'Corporate Reorganisation in the European Transport and Logistic Sector in the 1990s', Discussion Paper, Social Science Research Centre, Berlin.

Dörrenbächer, C. and S. Vescovi (2000), 'Logistik aus politischer Sicht: Zum Zusammenhang von verlagerten Entscheidungskompetenzen, veränderten Unternehmensstrukturen und Interessenpolitik im europäischen (Schienen-) Güterverkehr', in K. Inderfurth, M. Schenk and D. Ziems (eds), *Logistik 2000plus. Herausforderungen, Trends, Perspektiven*, Kongressband zur 6. Magdeburger Logistiktagung, Magdeburg, pp. 194–209.

Erdmenger, J. (1994), 'Verkehrspolitik', in W. Weidenfeld and W. Wessels (eds), *Jahrbuch der Europäischen Integration*, Bonn: Europa Union Verlag, pp. 197–202.

Felder, M., A. Statz and S. Tidow (2001), 'Alter und neuer Intergouvernementalismus', in H.-J. Bieling, K. Dörre, J. Steinhilber and H.-J. Urban (eds), *Flexibler Kapitalismus. Analysen-Kritik-politische Praxis*, Hamburg: VSA-Verlag, pp. 161–76.

Fligstein, N. (1991), 'The structural transformation of American industry: an institutional account of the causes of diversification in the largest firms, 1919–1979', in W. Powell and P. DiMaggio (eds), *The New Institutionalism in Organizational Analysis*, Chicago: University of Chicago Press, pp. 311–36.

Fligstein, N. and J. McNichol (1998), 'The institutional terrain of the European Union', in W. Sandholtz and A. Stone Sweet (eds), *European Integration and Supranational Governance*, Oxford: Oxford University Press, pp. 59–91.

Garrett, G. (1993), 'International cooperation and institutional choice: the European community's internal market', in G. Ruggie (ed.), *Multilateralism Matters*, New York: Columbia University Press, pp. 365–98.

Greenwood, J. and M. Aspinwall (eds) (1998), *Collective Action in the European Union. Interests and the New Politics of Associability*, London: Routledge.

Hall, P. and D. Soskice (eds) (2001), *Varieties of Capitalism*, Oxford: Oxford University Press.

Hey, C. (1998), *Nachhaltige Mobilität in Europa. Akteure, Institutionen und politische Strategien*, Opladen: Westdeutscher Verlag.

Hollingsworth, J. and R. Boyer (eds) (1997), *Contemporary Capitalism. The Embeddedness of Institutions*, Cambridge: Cambridge University Press.

Holman, O. (2000): 'Transnationale Wirtschaft und europäische Integration: Die Rolle des European Roundtable of Industrialists', in C. Dörrenbächer and D. Plehwe (eds), *Grenzenlose Kontrolle?* Berlin: Sigma, pp. 254–68.

Knill, C. (2001), 'Private governance across multiple arenas: European interest associations as interface actors', *Journal of European Public Policy*, **8** (2), April, 227–46.

Kohler-Koch, B. (1999), 'The evolution and transformation of European governance', in B. Kohler-Koch and R. Eising (eds), *The Transformation of Governance in the European Union*, London and New York: Routledge, pp. 14–36.

Kohler-Koch, B. and R. Eising (eds) (1999), *The Transformation of Governance in the European Union*, London and New York: Routledge.

Mahoney, J. (2000), 'Path dependence in historical sociology', *Theory and Society*, **29** (4), 507–48.

Mancini, F. (1998), 'Europa: Gründe für einen Gesamtstaat', *Kritische Vierteljahreszeitschrift* (KritV), **81**, 386.

Moravcsik, A. (1993), 'Preferences and power in the European Community: a liberal intergovernmentalist approach', *Journal of Common Market Studies*, **31** (4), December, 473–524.

Moravcsik, A. (1999), 'A new statecraft? Supranational entrepreneurs and international cooperation', *International Organization*, **53** (2), 267–306.

Murphy, C.N. (1994), *International Organization and Industrial Change*, Cambridge: Polity Press.

Nentwich, M. and G. Falkner (1997), 'The Treaty of Amsterdam: Towards a New Institutional Balance', European Integration online Papers (EIoP), 1 (15), http://eiop.or.at/eiop/texte/1997-015a.htm.

Plehwe, D. (1997), 'Eurologistik, Europäische Verkehrspolitik und die Entwicklung eines transnationalen (Güter-)Transportsystems', *Prokla*, **27** (2), 217–43.

Plehwe, D. (2000), *Deregulierung und Transnationale Integration der Transportwirtschaft in Nordamerika*, Münster: Westfälisches Dampfboot.

Plehwe, D. (2001a), 'National trajectories, international competition, and transnational governance in Europe', in G. Morgan, P.H. Kristensen and R. Whitley (eds), *The Multinational Firm*, Oxford: Oxford University Press, pp. 281–305.

Plehwe, D. (2001b), 'Arbeitspolitische Probleme ungleicher Reorganisation. Zur veränderung der Arbeit in Logistiknetzwerken', *Industrielle Beziehungen*, **8** (1), 55–82.

Plehwe, D. and C. Dörrenbächer (with S. Vescovi) (2001), 'The transformation of European logistics governance', (unpublished research report) Social Science Research Centre Berlin.

Quack, S., G. Morgan and R. Whitley (eds) (2000), *National Capitalisms, Global Competition and Economic Performance*, Amsterdam and Philadelphia: Benjamins.

Rittberger, V. (1995), *Internationale Organisationen – Politik und Geschichte*, Opladen: Leske + Budrich.

Sally, R. (1994), 'Multinational enterprises, political economy and institutional theory: domestic embeddedness in the context of internationalisation', *Review of International Political Economy*, **1** (1), 161–92.

Sandholtz, W. and A. Stone Sweet (eds) (1998), *European Integration and Supranational Governance*, Oxford: Oxford University Press.

Schmidt, S.K. (1997), 'Behind the Council Agenda: The Commission's impact on decisions', MPFIG discussion paper 97/4, Köln.

Schmidt, S.K. (2001), 'Die Einflussmöglichkeiten der Europäischen Kommission auf die europäische Politik', *Politische Vierteljahresschrift*, **42** (2), 173–92.

Schmitter, P.C. and W. Streeck (1999), 'The Organization of Business Interests: Studying the Associative Action of Business in Advanced Industrial Societies', MPFIG Discussion Paper 99/1, Köln.

Sorge, A. (1995), 'Personnel and organisation from a comparative perspective', in A.-W. Harzing and J. van Ruysseveldt (eds), *International Human Resource Management: An Integrated Approach*, London: Sage, pp. 99–123.

Stone Sweet, A. and J.A. Caporaso (1998), 'From free trade to supranational polity: the European Court and integration', in W. Sandholtz and A. Stone Sweet (eds), *European Integration and Supranational Governance*, Oxford: Oxford University Press, pp. 92–133.

Stopford, J.M. and S. Strange (with John S. Henley) (1991), *Rival States, Rival Firms. Competition for World Market Shares*, Cambridge: Cambridge University Press.

Underhill, G.R.D. (2000), 'From ships passing in the night to a dialogue of the deaf: the contribution of international relations theory to understanding organised business', in J. Greenwood and H. Jacek (eds), *Organised Business and the New Global Order*, New York: Palgrave, pp. 20–38.

Von Bogdandy, A. (1999), *Supranationaler Föderalismus als Wirklichkeit und Idee einer neuen Herrschaftsform. Zur Gestaltung der Europäischen Union nach Amsterdam*, Baden-Baden: Nomos.

Weiler, J. (1998), 'Europe: The Case Against the Case for Statehood', Havard Jean Monnet Working Papers, http://www.law.harvard.edu./Programs/JeanMonnet/papers/98/98-6-.html.

Wessels, W. (2001), 'Nice results: the millennium IGC in the EU's evolution', *Journal of Common Market Studies*, **39** (2), June, 197–220.

Whitley, R. (ed.) (1992), *European Business Systems*, London: Sage.

Whitley, R. (1998), *Divergent Capitalisms. The Social Structuring and Change of Business Systems*, Oxford: Oxford University Press.

9. Multilateral rulemaking: transatlantic struggles around genetically modified food

Jason McNichol and Jabril Bensedrine

INTRODUCTION

Until recently, decision making over environmental, health and safety regulations remained the purview of national governments and was largely excluded from multilateral trade negotiations. But in recent years such issues have become increasingly common sources of conflict in international trade. Debates over issues ranging from hormone-treated beef to genetically-modified crops have become the locus of major multilateral disputes, especially between the European Union (EU) and the United States (US). The nature and outcomes of these disputes are not just of significance to policy makers – they also offer valuable insights into the mechanisms through which emerging 'global' norms, rules and structures are both forged and contested over time by actors grounded in particular national institutional spaces. The manner in which these conflicts unfold demands that scholars of international politics develop new tools to understand how domestic and transnational regulatory areas are co-constituted and influence one another over time.

The present chapter seeks to shed light on current conflicts over multilateral governance by bringing a sociological perspective to bear on recent disputes over the regulation of a particular type of environmental, health and safety standard. We look at labelling of genetically modified (GM) food, and more specifically, GM soy. The case of soy is interesting for several reasons. Soy derivatives are common in a variety of foodstuffs (from chocolate to cereals to prepared meals) and are a widely traded global commodity. As the US (the world's largest soy exporter) began actively exporting GM varieties in 1996, the soy trade became a lightning rod of controversy symbolizing disagreement about the environmental and health implications of biotechnology and the public's 'right to know' when consuming GM products. Within months of the introduction of GM soy to the global marketplace, a battle erupted between EU and US interests over whether it should be labelled. The multilateral conflict and recent partial compromise that ensued stand as one of the most dramatic and telling cases of transnational wrangling over regulatory questions.

Drawing upon publicly available data,[1] we use a sociological institutional perspective to examine the genesis, trajectory, and early outcomes of US–EU struggles to establish new regulatory norms over the labelling of GM soy and other genetically engineered crops. We find that national differences in relative power and influence of consumer-oriented versus agro-industrial groups, pre-existing norms and rules for regulating agricultural processes, and distinctive political–cultural frames all contributed to the divergent positions originally taken by the EU and US. Using the same framework, we suggest how interactions between these variables at the domestic and transnational levels also help explain recent moves toward compromise witnessed in late 1999 and 2000 that culminated in a *de facto* acknowledgement of a new international standard for labelling. Finally, drawing upon broader empirical and theoretical insights, we speculate on how continuing conflict and uncertainty in the transnational regulatory field embody broader trends in institution-building and institution-alization typical of the recent 'globalization' of regulatory debates over environmental, health and safety issues.

CONCEPTUAL FRAMEWORK

In the recent past, researchers, governments and journalists have tried to account for the difficulties of developing a common international regulatory framework for GM crops. Observers have pointed to differences in power between key interest groups as one explanation, noting in particular that US exporters dominate markets for GM products and enjoy strong state support (Arthur 1996). Observers have also underscored differences in national styles of regulation (Levidow 1994; Vogel 1986). Yet another set of writers has focused on cultural differences in how debates over GMOs are framed (*Nature*, 22 April 1999). While these *ad hoc* assessments have been useful, each is by itself only partial. Researchers have yet to explore in a comprehensive way how political–economic, institutional and cultural variables interact over time at both the domestic and international levels in any process of negotiation over international governance rules.

This chapter builds upon recent work in economic sociology to look at how debates over trade in GMOs unfold within overlapping fields of strategic action at both domestic and supranational levels (for recent reviews, see Swedberg 1997; Fligstein 1996, 2001). A 'field' (or policy domain) is constituted by the set of actors (such as government bodies, business groups and NGOs) who seek to influence a shared outcome (such as regulation) and pay attention to one another in the process (Laumann and Knoke 1989). A regulatory field or policy domain is thus composed of all groups who have an interest in the outcome (for example labelling rules) and see one another as relevant 'actors' in the debate. A stable field or domain is characterized by a common set of rules (both formal and informal) and conditions of membership that usually serve the interests of the most dominant firms or groups. However, during times of crisis when external shocks cast doubt on the legitimacy of the existing order, entrepreneurial challengers can mobilize new coalitions to change the balance of power and forge new shared meanings and rules (Fligstein and McAdam 1995; Fligstein 2001, see also Kleiner in this volume).

From a sociological institutional perspective, then, recent multilateral disputes over the regulation of GMOs are best seen as struggles to mobilize, define and enforce shared understandings over what the regulatory rules should be, who should define them and how they should be enforced. Successful resolution of such conflicts would provide a set of mutually-agreed upon, legitimate and stable rules – normative–cognitive as well as structural–institutional (see Djelic and Quack in the conclusion, see also Tainio et al., Kleiner or Lilja and Moen in this volume). Under those rules, various actors could engage in the production, trade and marketing of products across national borders (an essential component of all institutionalized trade regimes – see, for example, Lehmkuhl this volume or Murphy 1994).

However, when representatives from industry, citizens groups and governments come together to struggle over multilateral regulatory issues in a field of strategic action, they do so with cognitive frameworks and resources that are generally drawn from the political–economic, regulatory–institutional and cultural environments of their respective nations. Without discounting the increasing salience of 'global' structures and social forces, we start from the observation that national institutional environments constitute the primary spaces within which most stakeholders in multilateral negotiations normally operate and understand their preferences (McNichol 2000; Bensedrine and Kobayashi 1999). We identify furthermore three major dimensions that characterize a national institutional environment (McNichol 2000, 2002).

Pre-existing relations of power: Different actors do not come to the table with equal abilities to influence an outcome. To understand the character of a conflict over regulation, we must see such debates as occurring within an existing distribution of resources, power and control. An examination of the distribution of power and influence along the commodity chain (for example, which groups tend to control which aspects of production, trade and marketing within particular countries and at the international level) helps us understand why the interests of some groups prevail over others.

Regulatory style: In matters of regulation, different nations often demonstrate distinctive patterns regarding how interest groups organize, lobby for and implement new regulatory rules (Vogel 1986). The role of state regulatory agencies, the mechanisms by which new regulations are negotiated and the definition of what public goods should and should not be regulated are all components of a national 'regulatory style' (Storper and Salais 1997). We hypothesize that these pre-existing national patterns also shape the attitudes and strategies of actors in transnational interactions.

Cultural frames and perceptions: At the core of a sociological institutional analysis of market governance lies a focus on how markets are constituted by shared meanings and common understandings of the rules that govern them. But shared meanings or cultures also constitute the building blocks that help actors frame their options, their interests or preferences. In debates over GMOs, variations in how different groups understand and appraise the meanings of major sources of contention (such as 'risk', 'barrier to trade', and so on) are substantial. In order to fully understand the dynamics of such debates, then, one must be careful to identify and examine how distinctive meanings, often rooted in national or regional political–cultural histories and public attitudes, help shape the trajectory of events.

As a model of action, our focus on power, regulatory style and culture within national institutional contexts and the emergent transnational arena does not lead us to argue that these factors are static. Rather, when crises or other external disturbances to the status quo emerge, entrepreneurial groups and individuals ('institutional entrepreneurs') may take advantage of opportunities and build alliances to change the balance of power and alter 'rules' about how a market should work (see also Kleiner in this volume). The descriptive analysis that we undertake here focuses on such a moment of disturbance – a pointed conflict between EU-level and US perspectives on how a multilateral governance system for GM soy and other GM products should be constructed.

OVERVIEW: EVOLUTION OF THE DEBATE AND ACTORS

In 1996, American farmers began growing Monsanto's genetically modified (GM) soybeans – *Glycine max* L (Feder 1996). While the new seed repre- sented only 2 per cent of the total US soybean harvest that year (which totalled 61 million tons), it was forecasted to reach 40 per cent by the year 2000 (Arthur 1996). The transgenic seeds had been easily authorized in the US, and the European Commission followed suit by approving them in April of 1996 (*Agence Europe*, 25 September 1997). Imports of Monsanto's soybeans were authorized in the EU under Directive 90/220 without any segregation or labelling requirement. Furthermore, a nascent but optimistic European biotechnology industry had by the mid 1990s invested in a number of edu- cational initiatives to strengthen public support for biotechnological advances (Smith 1996).

Early Disagreements

Reactions, however, were not long in coming, and European civil society rose in insurrection against Monsanto's crops. European Greens found it intolerable that the European Commission had authorized the import of these soybeans without labelling requirements. The Greens were all the more incensed that a draft regulation on 'novel foods' originally introduced in 1992 was still being considered at the European level. Moreover, a recent draft regulation had been rejected at the European Council of Ministers in October of 1995 because of its loose labelling requirements (rejected by Austria, Germany, Denmark and Sweden).

In fact, labelling 'proved to be one of the most contentious issues' (Smith 1996, p. 162). Working through organizations such as Eurocommerce and Eurocoop, retailers strongly called for GMO labelling. Before Europe was to import 200 000 tons of genetically modified soybeans in September 1996, Eurocommerce and Greens in the European Parliament joined forces to urge European consumers 'to boycott American genetically modified soy bean products until they are adequately labelled' (*Agence Europe*, 27 September 1996). The boycott was relayed in member states by national trade associations, such as the British Retail Consortium in the UK (Williams 1998).

Americans seemed surprised at the level of resistance in Europe to what they considered a safe and innocuous technology. Aside from isolated protests by well-known groups such as Greenpeace, the new seeds had been embraced by many farmers in the US and elsewhere with little public concern (*Financial Times*, 1 November 1996). American producers responded to EU consumer and retailer labelling requests by arguing that they were unrealistic and unnecessary since there were no scientific proofs of health or environmental dangers. Supported by the US Department of Agriculture, several American trade associations directly attacked EU boycott and segregation schemes as unfair barriers to trade.

A Chorus of EU Dissent

Nonetheless, European dissent persisted. Eurocommerce asserted that it was determined 'to fight to obtain open and transparent systems that offer consumers a choice', adding that 'the mere lack of traceability from the farmer to the European market, passing through the warehouse, represents a threat for the use of biotechnology in the food sector' (*Agence Europe*, 21 May 1997). In doing so, the retailer organization was keeping in step with the preferences of consumers. All along, the European Consumers' Organization (BEUC) was asking European authorities to impose strong labelling requirements for genetically modified food (*Agence Europe*, 2 June 1995, 14 January 1998). In parallel, Greenpeace had repeatedly denounced the fact that 'thousands of products' had yet to be labelled.

Demand from EU consumer and retailer groups to segregate and label GMO inputs quickly filtered down the supply chain. While major importers and processors of soy in Europe did not initially oppose the introduction of GM soy, some of them responded to increasing public and governmental opposition by freezing their purchases. All over Europe, large firms such as Unilever, Nestle, Kraft-Jacobs-Suchard, Ferrero or Danone, announced they would not use products derived from transgenic soybeans until a separated supply chain became effective (Boulton 1996). These firms also took official positions regarding the labelling of food derived from GM, for example through the Con-federation of Food and Drink Industries of the EU (CIAA) or the European Seed Crushers' and Oil Producers' Federation (FEDIOL) (*Agence Europe*, 6 January 1998, 12 January 1998). Although they made clear that herbicide-resistant soy was equivalent to conventional soy, these organizations supported the labelling of products containing GM soy.

Domestic agricultural producers in the European Union also championed segregation and labelling, working through groups such as the Committee of Agricultural Organizations in the EU (COPA), the General Committee for Agri-cultural Cooperation (COGECA), and the European Farmers' Coordination (CPE) (*Agence Europe*, 30 December 1996, 1 April 1997). As early as 1996, the European Farmers' Coordination had been supporting strong and extensive labelling requirements and had been denouncing the priority 'given by the Union to the interests of industry rather than to the principle of consumer precaution' (*Agence Europe*, 30 December 1996). In parallel, some national farmers' associations proved even more violent in their opposition to GMOs than their European counterparts (Le Dréaut 1998).

Mounting US Resistance

As European constituencies came together to pressure US exporters, American business groups continued to strongly oppose labelling requirements, arguing that they were not in the best interests of farmers, processors or consumers. Major business interests argued that segregation and labelling would signifi-cantly increase production costs of foods and compromise economies of scale (Steyer 1996b). American firms also feared that regulatory stringency would give the wrong signals to consumers, implying that GM food was dangerous (Miller 1999). Since, according to US industry and government-sponsored scientific studies, existing GMO crops were safe for consumers and the envi-ronment, the industry argued that no productive purpose would be served by 'alarming' consumers through labelling.

American farmer groups and their major buyers also initially opposed requests to ensure separate harvests for GM and GM-free grains. Even as late as 1999, only about 10 per cent of Midwestern grain elevators had separated harvests (*Knight-Ridder*, 6 February 2000). In the US, Monsanto and other major seed companies had aggressively marketed GM soy and other crops to American farmers, arguing that converting to GM crops would improve productivity and profitability. As US acreage planted in GM soy grew from zero in 1995 to approximately one-third of the total in 1998, the American Soy Association, grain purchasers and traders (such as Archer–Daniels–Midland – ADM) were alarmed to see prospective buyers threatening to reject their crops. ADM, the American Soybean Association and other agricultural producer and processor interest groups aggressively sought to challenge prospective labelling and segregation requirements among their European customers, soliciting in the process the help of the American government (Marks 1999, archival sources).

EU Governments Begin to Act, the US Reacts

As US resistance mounted, most EU member states enacted a number of measures – including France, the Netherlands and all of Scandinavia (*Agence Europe*, 3 February 1997). Furthermore, on 18 June 1997, the European Commission (EC) modified Directive 90/220's Annex III by defining new labelling requirements for genetically modified beans starting 31 July 1997. As far as the use of GMOs in consumer products was concerned, the Directive 258/97 on 'novel foods' had just been adopted in January 1997 and enacted on 15 May 1997. Article 8 defined labelling requirements, but most products derived from GMOs were not covered. In September 1997, the EC went further and adopted a retroactive regulation (1813/97) requiring mandatory labelling for products containing GM soy and corn that had been produced before the Directive 258/97 on 'novel food' (*Agence Europe*, 16 January 1997).

The US government and American agro-industrial interests expressly hoped the proposals would be dropped on grounds that they constituted trade barriers. Through the US Agriculture Secretary Dan Glickman, they announced that they 'strongly oppose[d] efforts to have mandatory labelling and/or segregation of genetically engineered products'. The USDA made it clear that proposed European labelling regulations had 'a questionable scientific basis and (were) ambiguous and impractical' (Williams 1998). A representative of the US Department of Agriculture's (USDA) foreign service informed the British House of Lords in July 1998 that the American industry had 'expressed considerable frustration at the cumbersome and unpredictable procedures in the [EU] and at the length of time it takes for the EU to review and approve products for commercialization'. According to this same spokesman, 'unless Europe can sort out its review processes, we could see a trade war developing' (Williams

1998). At around the same time, Monsanto founded the 'soybeans/biotechnology' information bureau within Burson-Marsteller, a leading public relations firm part of the Young & Rubicam PR conglomerate (Fuchs 1998).

Towards a First Compromise

But a full-blown trade war was never waged. At the same time that US government and industry representatives were preparing for the worst, about 600 delegates from 170 countries met in Cartagena (Colombia) in February 1999 to negotiate a global Protocol on Biosafety under sponsorship of the United Nations (UN). For a number of countries and environmental NGOs such as Greenpeace and Friends of the Earth, the aim was to shape a global regulation for the international trade of genetically modified organisms according to the precautionary principle. They lobbied for separate international supplies of GM and GM-free products, to impose the principle of 'informed consent' of the importing nation prior to the delivery of any GM food and to give the right to individual countries to impose compulsory labelling (*Agence Europe*, 24 February 1999, Lambrecht 1999). American industry groups were also present, represented by around 20 'observers' who were lobbying for, among other issues, unimpeded trade in agro-biotechnological products (Lennard 1999).

While most European representatives supported a new labelling protocol, the US delegation and delegates from a handful of other countries including Canada, Australia and Argentina, combined into what came to be known as 'the Miami Group' (Lennard 1999). This group struggled to have agricultural commodities such as GM grains and processed foods derived from these grains dropped from the Biosafety Protocol. Its members claimed that these products should be dealt with under World Trade Organization (WTO) negotiations. But other negotiators knew that if labelling and segregation were not included in the Biosafety Protocol, even European regulation on labelling or segregation would be overruled by the WTO, which would likely consider them as unnecessary barriers to international trade (*Financial Express*, 22 February 1999). This led to very intense discussions (*Financial Express*, 22 February 1999), parts of which were denounced as not transparent (*Interpress*, 24 February 1999). This ended up with a suspension of negotiations for 18 months. Many European labelling advocates blamed the US for sabotaging the talks (Lennard 1999).

Following these global discussions and while the debate was still going on in Europe, the European Council of Ministers reached a strong decision in June 1999. It imposed a *de facto* moratorium on any new authorization of GMOs in food until more stringent rules were enacted, especially regarding traceability and labelling (2194th Council meeting, Luxembourg, 24/25 June 1999). According to the agreement reached by the Council, labelling should become mandatory at all stages of production and processing. Labelling requirements were complemented by provisions on the traceability, enabling public authorities to keep track of GM inputs through the various stages of the supply chain. These decisions were strongly denounced by US trade officials. One US representative went so far as to claim that 'the disagreement over biotechnology could dwarf recent trade disputes over beef and bananas' (Hess 1999).

Meanwhile, the UN negotiations on Biosafety had resumed in Montreal in January of 2000. Disagreements remained important between countries in favour of strong control of GMOs on one hand, and the 'Miami group', on the other. Nevertheless, in a surprising move toward compromise on the part of the US and other 'Miami' nations, discussions led to the first ever agreement on labelling of GM foods. After what was described as 'a hell of a battle' by the British Environment Minister (Vulliamy et al. 2000), the agreement finally signed by about 130 countries required labelling of genetically modified raw materials but not of ingredients such as oil or processed food products (*Knight-Ridder*, 6 February 2000).

The American delegation, however, did not sign the agreement because its government was not a party to the Convention on Biological Diversity (Rio de Janeiro 1992). Still, federal officials did announce that the US would honour the treaty (Pollack 2000). In Europe the Environmental Commissioner stated that it was 'a victory for consumers and importers' (Brodie 2000). Although there was some discontent in the US and Secretary of State Madeleine Albright asserted that it was 'a less than perfect agreement' (Lambrecht 2000a, 2000b), the American secretary of State for oceans, environment and science presented it as 'an agreement that protects the environment without disrupting world food trade' (Farley 2000). Industry representatives also welcomed the outcome. According to Monsanto the agreement established 'a framework for standardized rules around the world' that would 'open markets for crops and foods with altered genetic codes' (Lambrecht 2000b). The Global Industry Coalition, representing 2,200 biotech companies, was also supportive of the agreement, while Greenpeace described it as a 'very positive step forward in protecting the environment and consumers' (Farley 2000).

In the 18 months that followed, the EU continued to debate and enact further measures specifying labelling and traceability requirements (Mann 1999). At the same time, several major US biotechnology and governmental interests continued to lobby against EU efforts to institutionalize stricter labelling requirements. In particular, they threatened action under the Dispute Settlement Mechanism of the WTO for non-tariff barriers to trade. Nonetheless, the modest but sustained shifts in position on the part of US regulatory, consumer and industry positions suggest that the January 2000 compromise agreement was a key step towards a multilateral governance system.

TOWARDS AN ANALYSIS OF THE US–EU STRUGGLE OVER LABELLING RULES

The chronology of events before the Montreal compromise indicates two major periods. The first period lasted from 1996 until mid 1999. During this time US representatives from industry and government maintained a strong and powerful stand against European demands for mandatory labelling. But by late summer of 1999, the formerly unified American front broke down with some constituencies reconsidering their positions. The result was a compromise in the form of the labelling agreement negotiated at Montreal in January 2000 under the auspices of the Biosafety Protocol. We begin our analysis with a focus on the first period.

Strong Opposition from 1995 to Summer 1999

Structure of industry and power
On the American side, key actors combined in a powerful agro-industrial alliance. The US produces more than half of the world's soybeans and ships over 35 per cent of its harvest to Europe, while the EU heavily depends on these shipments for processing food and animal feed (Johnson 2000; Chase 2000). In 1995, the US agricultural biotechnology industry saw itself as a world leader with a strong competitive advantage (Ibrahim 1996). Moreover, US 'life sciences' firms were dedicating huge budgets for the development of GM crops and thus needed a quick development of international sales in order to recover their investments. In the case of soy, stakes were high for US agricultural exporters – and thus for their providers of seeds such as Monsanto. Exports of soybeans to Europe in 1996 were valued at approximately 1.3 billion Euros (ECUs – equivalent to 5.6 million metric tons). These figures should be compared to the 345 million Euros for corn exports (Schleicher 1998). Then the share of GM soybeans in American harvests grew from 1.6 per cent in 1996 to approximately 51 per cent in 1999 and it was expected to grow further (Commission of the European Communities 2000; Chase 2000). Hence, the European rejection of GM soybeans was indeed of great concern for the American agro-industrial alliance (Williams 1998). The significance of economic stakes involved helps explain why the American government was very willing to support lobbying in Europe and to strong-arm the EU under multilateral trade rules to reject labelling and segregation requirements.

In sharp contrast with the US, the domestic European biotech lobby was not strong enough to effectively dismantle a powerful pro-labelling coalition of consumer and environmental organizations, large retailers and active groups of farmers who dominated the political scene. Our archival research reveals that European NGOs played an important early role in alerting the media and influencing public opinion, which in turn strongly influenced large retailers' strategies and led policymakers to seek more restrictive regulatory oversight of GM foods. Already in the late 1980s, German environmentalists had voiced public alarm over GM products, relaying their concerns to sister NGOs across Europe. Consequently, while American consumers had started eating food derived from GMOs without knowing it, European consumers had been alerted about GMOs before they had reached their plates.

European farmers' groups also voiced strong and active opposition to GM crops. Their opposition could partly be explained by the structure of the farm sector, composed predominantly of small and family-run farms that would benefit less from agricultural biotechnology than their larger American counterparts (Williams 1998). Some farmer groups also denounced the distortion of competition that the authorization of importing GM crops from the US would create when they themselves were prevented from growing such plants. Furthermore, most European farmers did not see any advantage in a technology that increased yields and thus resulted in further price declines in a context of overproduction (Williams 1998).

On the other end of the European debate, the biotech lobby was not able to mobilize a strong anti-regulatory alliance. Its weak influence was partly due to its small size, but it also stood as testament to the heterogeneity of business interests along the supply chain. Indeed, large retailers themselves were early champions of GMO labelling, and they put significant pressure on their suppliers – farmers, food processors or biotech firms.

Differences in domestic regulatory styles
The US was initially able to present a powerful front of opposition to labelling in part because such a position was a natural extension of the domestic regulatory situation. According to US regulatory agencies, genetically modified crops and food products would not be treated differently from conventional crops and foods as long as they did not demonstrate significant differences in nutritional content or potential allergens. Both the Bush and Reagan administrations actively sought to reduce the 'regulatory burden' on the fledgling and potentially lucrative biotech industry by minimizing 'unnecessary and burdensome' new rules (Miller 1992). Even after the incoming Clinton administration responded in 1992 to non-governmental activist group pressure to reconsider rules on GM crops, regulatory agencies responded by issuing a clarification statement that fundamentally retained the anti-regulatory stance and the laissez faire philosophy (FDA Statement of Policy #92N-0139).

Meanwhile, American biotech firms argued that their new products were not substantially different from non-genetically modified varieties. Despite a few well-publicized studies that suggested GM crops could have adverse environmental or health consequences, the industry maintained a unified stance on labelling: it was an unnecessary and alarmist tactic that was not grounded in 'facts' (Cordtz 1994). The American government and industry thus upheld an 'innocent until proven guilty' model for regulating new GM products, and the US Secretary of Agriculture solidly supported the position of its national industry through mid 1999.

On the European side, an intriguing question was the rapid change of heart. Why did the EU reconsider its position after initially authorizing GMOs without labelling requirements? First, the European regulatory process has long been characterized by a need to reach a compromise among a number of countries with different cultural, economic and political characteristics. Moreover, EU-level institutions are themselves composed of multiple agencies with divergent priorities on the issue of GMOs (*Agence Europe*, 16 January 1997). In particular, positions varied widely between the European Parliament (EP), the European Commission (EC) and its committees of experts and the Council of Ministers (CM). Even within the EP and EC, subcommittees often disagreed in their assessments and recommendations on segregation and labelling requirements.

The EC's Directorate General for the Internal Market underlined the need to harmonize member states' regulations in order to avoid barriers to trade in the internal market, while some member states and the EP's Greens claimed the European right to protect national markets from potentially dangerous products (*Agence Europe*, 26 November 1997). The recently-established Directorate General for External Relations focused on the need to avoid trade conflicts with the US while others, such as the Directorates General for the Environment and for Health and Consumer Protection, stressed the duty to meet consumers' demand for labelling. The Directorate General for Industry on the other hand feared that restrictive labelling could raise costs, stigmatize biotechnology and create confusion about the safety of products (EU Press Release, 51/97). Thus, the fragmented and multi-stakeholder character of the EU system made it easier for a variety of organizations to provide input, including active NGOs that were strongly opposed to GMOs. All categories of actors had thus to negotiate with others, which made it difficult to reach any clear-cut political decision regarding GMOs and accounts for changes in direction.

Differences in cultural contexts and dominant frames

From the historical narrative presented above, it is clear that dominant public perceptions and frames about GM foods substantially differed between the EU and the US through the mid 1990s. In the US, GM products entered the marketplace without great commotion. In the case of soy, our review of press coverage found that 'Roundup Ready' soy derivatives entered the US food supply virtually unnoticed. Furthermore, the industry was very careful not to call attention to the growing percentage of food supply containing GM products.

In those early years, when a few radical environmental groups attempted to raise public awareness, their arguments were aggressively criticized and discounted by government, industry lobbying groups and many journalists (Steyer 1996a).

Why did the American public and Congress care so little in the early years? Some observers pointed to a relatively low level of public concern over food safety issues in general, coupled with a high level of trust that regulatory authorities would not permit dangerous substances to enter the food chain (*Economist*, 1 May 1999). In addition to the obvious fact that Americans have not had to face in recent years the same onslaught of food scares as the Europeans, Americans have also historically not invested food consumption with the same broader concerns over justice and environmental well being as Europeans. In the US, the mainstreaming of markets for 'fair trade' coffee, 'certified' wood from well-managed forests and other products that incorporate social and environmental values has proceeded less quickly than in Europe (McNichol 2002). Simply put, food consumption in the US has historically been much less politicized than in Europe.

In marked contrast to the US, a longstanding distrust of the food industry and official regulators followed numerous alarms in Europe, from salmonella to BSE – or 'mad cow disease' (Williams 1998). This undeniably predisposed EU citizens to be wary of GM foods. Other scandals, over issues ranging from asbestos to contaminated blood – though not related to agricultural biotechnology – had also contributed to a general distrust in science, experts and public authorities. Furthermore, European consumers did not perceive any advantage in eating genetically modified food (Williams 1998). Surveys carried out for the European Commission in 1991 and 1993 on the opinions about biotechnology in Member States, for instance, found the level of support for the use of biotechnology in the production and processing of food to be much lower than in the healthcare area. In all countries there was willingness for stronger governmental control. Consumers in Europe regarded genetic modification as a serious risk in food products – 65 per cent in Sweden, 60 per cent in Austria, 50 per cent in Germany, and 39 per cent in the United Kingdom. The equivalent figure for the US was 14 per cent (*Science Magazine* 1998).

While it is difficult to compare survey data between the EU and the US on public attitudes towards biotechnology and GM foods in particular, our review of US press data indicates that through the mid 1990s, American consumers paid less attention to, and showed less fear of, biotechnological advances in the agro-food sector than did their European counterparts. Interestingly, we found almost no survey data on American attitudes toward GM foods until the European debates spilled over into the US in 1998 and 1999.

Moving Toward Compromise

The first part of the analysis helps us explain the initial failure of US and EU representatives to reach a common agreement on labelling. But how can we explain the slow but unmistakable shift that culminated in US observers supporting a limited international labelling agreement at the beginning of 2000? Our review of the evidence suggests that the shift primarily reflected the need for major US export interests to take in continuing European resistance. The shift also revealed an evolution of American public opinion and the growing strength of pro-labelling NGOs in the US.

Changing interests and balance of power

As European governments and the EU enacted new regulations requiring the labelling of GM imports, American grain processors and exporters increasingly suffered from cancelled orders for mixed shipments. Major customers were beginning to look elsewhere for supply contracts. The second largest global grocery chain, Carrefour, for example, sought to establish a GM-free supply chain with Brazilian farmers (LeHenaff 2000). In January 1998, the Confederation of Food and Drink Industries of the EU called on its national federations to urge their members to voluntarily label their food products containing genetically modified ingredients. The Dutch industry had already done so in April 1997, while the French, British, German and Belgian industries were expected to follow rapidly (*Agence Europe*, 6 January 1998). Japan, the second largest buyer of US soybeans after Europe, began restricting purchases of mixed GM imports. In July 2000, after a heated three-year debate, the joint Australia-New Zealand Food Standards Council decided to enact strict new rules on the labelling of almost all food containing genetically engineered DNA or protein. Upon implementation one year later, these new rules were expected to be the toughest in the world (Hall and Marsh 2000).

These developments, naturally, were disturbing for American interests. In 1999, furthermore, the debate spilled over on the domestic scene. Several American supermarket chains reacted rapidly, promising to avoid GMOs wherever possible (Cox 2000). The position of grain processors and exporters was in the meantime also changing (Moore and Scott 1999). These groups held direct business relationships with major industrial buyers in Europe. Hence they were the first to fully appreciate the tangible market implications of continued European opposition. By harvest year 1999, Archer–Daniels–Midland – the largest grain processor in North America and a formerly strong supporter of GM exports – announced that it would segregate its GM crops and offer a significant price premium for GM free deliveries (Nuttall 1999).

American Farmers, too, reacted to EU pressures. In 1998 and 1999, growing numbers of US farmers, who made planting decisions several months in advance by anticipating market trends, either held off from planting GM soy or reduced their acreage in order to hedge against possible boycotts and prepare for possible premiums offered by major buyers for GM-free harvests (Steyer 1999). A survey of farmers by the American Farm Bureau released in January of 2000 found that farmers on average planned to reduce their acreage of GM soy by 15 per cent over 1999 levels. The growing market share of organic farmers, who were concerned about cross-contamination jeopardizing their organic certification status, also reduced enthusiasm for planting GM seeds (*Knight-Ridder*, 6 February 2000).

American biotech giants responded accordingly. In a number of conferences and documents on the future of the industry, Monsanto and other firms began to look strategically at how to assuage public concerns over the long term (Feder 1999; Moore and Scott 1999). Our evidence suggests that Monsanto and other leaders began to reconsider labelling more positively as a means to help regain public trust. In fact, already in March of 1998, Monsanto executives were quoted as saying that some sort of labelling protocol would be necessary to assuage public fears (Koenig 1998). Monsanto accordingly initiated a large communication strategy, well illustrated by an extensive newspaper advertising campaign in Britain and France in 1998, where the firm announced its acceptance of GM food labelling while underlining that GM food was safe (*Le Monde*, 20 Juin 1998). In an effort to appease Japanese worries, Monsanto hosted a Japanese delegation at its St. Louis headquarters to show its renewed commitment to transparency and accessibility (*St. Louis Dispatch*, 5 September 1999).

Major firms also supported a uniform labelling code to reduce uncertainties in the regulatory and legislative arenas. A less-than-ideal segregation and labelling system, one might argue, is preferable to major uncertainties about a marketplace potentially riddled with boycotts and reactionary legislation around the world (Lambrecht 2000b). A uniform code would also reduce the costs and complexities of attempting to meet a number of overlapping and perhaps contradictory regulatory policies in different countries (see Ventresca et al. this volume). In fact, in European negotiations major industrial groups lobbied forcefully for a uniform labelling system as a strategy to reduce costs and improve the viability of GM markets more generally (Koenig 1999).

Changes in American perceptions of GM foods
Hence what we see is that highly negative reactions to GMOs in Europe created pressure for US exporters well into the late 1990s (Graham 2000). Our analysis also suggests that this process led in time to a significant shift in American public perception and discourse, which helped strengthen the legitimacy of the pro-labelling lobby on American soil.

While public and political concern around biotech products remained minimal in the US through most of the 1990s, by mid 1999 scholarly and press coverage of the industry had adopted an increasingly critical stance (for example Buzalka 2000). In late 1999, a Cornell University study on potential risks of GM corn to Monarch Butterfly larvae received widespread attention, as did re-telling of earlier findings of potential allergens in new GM varieties. Stories about growing public resistance to GM crops in Brazil, Japan and of course in Europe, were also widely told. American consumers as a consequence grew wary. During the late 1990s, surveys found the American public increasingly concerned about the safety of their food supply. According to a 1997 study, two-thirds of Americans polled were more concerned about food safety issues at that time than 'a few years ago' (Martin 1997). In early 2000, a *Time Magazine* poll found that 81 per cent of Americans surveyed wanted labelling of products that contained GMOs (Buzalka 2000).

American pro-labelling NGOs and citizens groups both drove and capitalized on this domestic shift in attitudes. Inspired and supported by their Western European counterparts, anti-biotech NGOs and citizens groups in the US exploited new coverage of potential risks by issuing petitions, bringing lawsuits and staging a number of highly visible demonstrations in 1998 and 1999. In January of 1999, the major pro-labelling lobbying group, the Center for Food Safety, charged the FDA with ignoring potential hazards of GMOs (*Chemical Market Reporter*, 4 January 1999). Supported by Friends of the Earth, in June of 1999 a coalition of groups submitted a petition of 500 000 signatures from the 'Mothers of Natural Law' to Congress asking for a federal overhaul to strengthen regulation of GM products (Allen 1999; Christie 1999). At about the same time, the *Los Angeles Times* reported that Greenpeace had detected GMOs in domestic baby food supplies. The State of Maine banned GMO crops, and the *Washington Post* ran a prominent editorial that the US should honour fickle European consumers and label its GM exports (Fulmer 1999; *Washington Post*, 17 July 1999). Thus, taking over the lead from their European counterparts, US activists were able to get renewed attention from regulatory authorities and industry.

Shifts in domestic regulatory environments: boomerang and 'trickle-up' effects

Taken together, these threats and evolutions put significant pressure on American authorities. In light of European resistance and stronger domestic voices criticizing misinformation, the US Department of Agriculture (USDA) announced in July of 1999 that it was 'beefing up' regulation of GM crops to help increase scientific legitimacy and ensure customer acceptance (Hileman 1999). In August of 1999, the American Secretary of Agriculture Dan Glickman announced that the USDA was 'reconsidering' the labelling issue. In late September of 1999, after a US Congressman introduced the first GMO labelling bill, Glickman acknowledged that European consumers might have reason to be sceptical. A consultant to the USDA also commented that allowing for labels might help consumers feel more comfortable with GMOs by giving them a choice (Eaton 1999). Later in the year, the Food and Drug Administration (FDA) launched a series of public meetings around the country for input into the issue of biotech regulation. As the FDA went into 'listening mode', several prominent pro-biotech organizations, including the Union of Concerned Scientists and the Rockefeller Foundation, made public statements supporting a more cautious regulatory stance (Jacobs 1999; Conway 1999; Marks 1999). Even though the FDA did not issue mandatory labelling guidelines at the domestic level, the shift in attitudes of domestic regulatory agencies suggested an increased flexibility of the US government's position regarding this issue, which contributed to the begrudging acceptance of the outcomes of the Montreal negotiations in January of 2000.

IMPLICATIONS FOR AN UNDERSTANDING OF TRANSNATIONAL INSTITUTION BUILDING

Table 9.1 summarizes the findings of our analysis thus far. We found that a strong and well-organized biotechnology and grain export sector in the US, supported by a pro-export federal government, was able in the face of little mobilized public opposition to maintain a strong stand against EU requests for labelling between 1996 and 1999. The EU, while not a consistent and unified actor in its own right, nevertheless maintained a pro-labelling position as a result of stronger and better mobilized consumer and green groups, domestic agricultural sectors with different economic interests, a federal regulatory approach modelled on the 'precautionary principle' and a more sceptical and risk-averse public.

By late 1999, continued moves toward mandatory labelling in the EU, high-lighted by decisions on the part of major grain processors and retailers to require segregation of soy and other products, began to seriously influence domestic US industrial and governmental actors. American opponents to labelling were also suffering from increasing negative publicity and growing lobbying pressure from newly strengthened domestic NGOs. By early 2000 the balance of power had begun to shift, and US government and export representatives begrudg-ingly agreed to a partial multilateral labelling agreement.

As we noted at the outset, the significance of the Montreal compromise to the future of GM transnational regulation is still uncertain. The agreement reached in Montreal does not cover all products and only acknowledges limited labelling requirements (Secretariat of the Convention on Biological Diversity 2000). At the time this chapter was completed, the US had still not ratified the

Table 9.1 *Stability and change in EU–US relations over labelling of GMOs, 1995–2000*

	Institutional elements	Europe	US	Multilateral governance system
1995 to 1999	Structure of industry and power	In favour of Greens and consumer pressure groups	In favour of American biotech firms and farmers	Dispute No multilateral governance system for the labelling of GM soy
	Domestic regulatory style	Extensive precautionary principle	Innocent until proven guilty approach	
	Cultural context and dominant frames	Distrust of public experts. Substantial media coverage.	Trust of regulatory agencies. Little media coverage	
1999 and after	Structure of industry and power	Even more in favour of Green and consumer pressure groups.	Stronger international and domestic pressure for labelling. Stronger pressure from major clients	Limited compromise First negotiaton of multilateral governance rules for the labelling of GM crops
	Domestic regulatory style	Strong regulatory decisions in spite of American pressure	A more sympathetic federal response	
	Cultural context and dominant frames	Growing public concern	Growing but uneven public concern	

Convention on Biological Diversity that sponsored the agreement. At the EU level, despite a Parliament agreement on several regulatory points in February 2001, several member countries maintained a moratorium on planting of GM crops pending a stronger EU legislation regarding traceability, labelling and corporate environmental liability – France, Austria, Italy, Denmark, Greece and Luxembourg (Mann 2001a, 2001b). To complicate matters further, the Biosafety Protocol is only one of several multilateral rule-making authorities relevant to negotiations over regulatory oversight. Others are the FAO and Codex Alimentarius, the WTO and intergovernmental agencies such as the OECD (Buckingham and Philips 2001). Most tellingly, the continued rhetoric of opposition voiced by several US agricultural biotechnology interests (along with some EU-based ones) against recent EU efforts to pass strict new labelling and traceability legislation suggests that the broader debate over whether mandatory labelling is legal or desirable is far from over.

While these uncertainties caution against ascribing too much significance to the Biosafety Protocol compromise, they nonetheless provide additional analytical insights into the contested process of global institution-building we have explored. Based on our analysis, the evolution of new transnational institutional forms seeking to regulate trade in novel foods may best be understood as a multimodal, multi-stakeholder and uneven process of co-evolution of national and multilateral regulatory norms, rules and structures (Whitley; Ventresca et al.; Plehwe; Lehmkuhl in this volume all reach parallel conclusions). First, international controversies over the labelling and regulation of genetically modified foods are typical of broader negotiations around environmental, health and safety issues in that they fall under the jurisdiction and policy domains of several overlapping institutional frameworks. The EU itself continues to wrestle with questions of regulatory sovereignty *vis-à-vis* individual member states. This multiplicity of regulatory points of reference for transnational debates over GMO regulation suggests that the process of global rule-making will proceed along multiple paths, with actors pursuing alternate strategies in a number of regulatory fora.

Second, in this multimodal arena interested stakeholders extend well beyond traditional 'state' representatives to include a number of non-state actors, as well (Lilja and Moen; Plehwe; Ventresca et al.; Lehmkuhl but also Tainio et al. and Whitley come to parallel conclusions in this volume). In fact, in the case study at hand non-state actors appear to have played a larger role in explaining outcomes than formal state institutions. These actors, who comprise business associations, environmental and public health NGOs, consumer groups, farmer unions, and so on, as well as major firms are central players in the fields of strategic action concerned with multilateral trade rules (see also Lehmkuhl in this volume).

Among these non-state actors, challengers or 'outsiders' can alter the 'rules of the game' during crises of legitimacy in the multilateral arena by mobilizing transnational pressure on incumbents or 'insiders' (Djelic and Quack in the conclusion to this volume) where they are most vulnerable – in their pocket-books. In the present case, pro-labelling European NGOs and their American counterparts were successful in convincing major grain processors and retailers to demand segregated GMO inputs or avoid them altogether, thereby leveraging far more power over the US export industry and government. They offer us real-world examples of 'institutional entrepreneurs' identified as agents of change in the conceptual framework we use here (see Kleiner in this volume for other kinds of 'institutional entrepreneurs').

This multimodal and multi-stakeholder process leads us to be cautious on the other hand about the solidity of emergent regulatory frameworks. We find quite a few signs in fact that the institutionalization of new multilateral norms, rules and structures is uneven and fragile. The successful negotiation of the Biosafety Protocol compromise, while certainly a significant instance of early rule-making, has not put to rest the underlying political–economic, regulatory, and discursive–cultural contrasts that gave birth to the first major disagreements over labelling of GM inputs. Most notably, dominant US agricultural biotechnology companies and trade representatives have continued to pursue alternative institutional channels – including, most recently, threats to enlist the adjudication of the WTO – to resist the broadening of EU labelling and traceability demands as new GM crops come to market (Drozdiak 2001). Furthermore, recent domestic US trends around labelling practices, while suggestive of a continuing new flexibility to consider voluntary labelling protocols domestically and in export markets, also show signs of robust resilience against now taken-for-granted EU requirements for mandatory labelling.

Taken together, these findings suggest that the relationship between national institutional environments and new multilateral rules and norms may best be understood as a process of co-evolution, where domestic and transnational actors within and across national policy domains engage one another to both reproduce and (albeit slowly) shift the normative and structural characteristics of overlapping fields of regulatory oversight. Such an observation, of course, is at the heart of a number of contributions to this volume (for example Midttun et al.; Lehmkuhl; Lilja and Moen).

While domestic institutional environments (relations of power, regulatory style and cultural context) largely explain the stated 'interest' of national trade representatives, the transnational arena itself can and does alter constituent elements of national environments over time. In the present case, a loose coalition of major buyers, NGOs and government representatives in Europe tangibly altered understandings of self-interest and the options available to major American actors at the domestic level in the late 1990s. This process exemplifies empirically a mixture of 'trickle-up' and 'trickle-down' mechanisms theorized by Djelic and Quack in the conclusion to this volume. In this sense, firms and other functionally equivalent structures or organizations can themselves sometimes alter the institutional environments (national or transnational) within which they or their peers operate. At the same time as the US regulatory environment has begun to shift, however, it still retains many of the same characteristics that explained its earlier resistance to labelling. The 'stickiness' of some of these characteristics – political economic, regulatory and cultural – has continued to influence and affect regulatory debates in a variety of other institutional venues at the transnational level – for example WTO or OECD (for similar arguments on resilience see Tainio et al.; McKenna et al.; Whitley in this volume).

While the future of multilateral rule-making over the oversight of GM food flows remains murky, we believe that the current exercise illustrates how a sociological institutional perspective sheds light on both the character of such processes and the mechanisms by which they contribute to the co-evolution of institutional change and institution-building at the domestic and transnational levels. The present study suggests that only models which can explore how political–economic, regulatory and discursive–cultural characteristics surrounding an international commodity chain articulate over time are adequate for describing and explaining the evolution of multilateral institutions. Furthermore, only frameworks that can entertain both structural constraints (that is power) and moments of opportunity that introduce agency (that is institutional entrepreneurship) are capable of explaining outcomes that differ from the self-interest of the most powerful actors at the outset. In the realm of struggles over the regulation of GM foods, the uneven, multimodal, multi-stakeholder nature of the emerging transnational institutional arena suggests that the possibility of a stable, legitimate new global governance system is still remote, indeed. Instead, consistent with the findings of other contributors to this volume and of broader historical surveys (for example Murphy 1994), it is more likely that such a system will emerge slowly over time (see Djelic and Quack in the conclusion to this volume) as dominant actors increasingly come to see its successful institutionalization as in their long-term best interest. In the meantime, emergent global rules over GM foods may continue to be characterized by marked heterogeneity across industries and products.

NOTE

1. The study that follows is based on an extensive analysis of publicly available documents covering the period from 1995 to 2001. Drawing from industry and governmental sources, bib-

liographic databases, academic research, and major press coverage in the EU and US, we collected and analysed over 700 documents, triangulating our findings from multiple sources whenever possible. Because of space restrictions, in this chapter we only cite sources directly referred to in the text.

REFERENCES

Agence Europe
(2 June 1995), 'BEUC criticisms on the "Ethical Committee" report on labelling foods derived from biotechnology.'
(27 September 1996), 'Eurocommerce and the EP Greens urge EU Consumers to boycott American genetically modified soya bean products until they are adequately labelled.'
(30 December 1996), 'European Farmers' coordination is very critical of Council/Parliament compromise on labelling of genetically modified foodstuffs.'
(16 January 1997), 'Parliament approves compromise reached with the council on novel foods – for the greens, who voted against, this is a "black day" for consumer protection.'
(3 February 1997), 'Commission confirms that member states may impose national labelling laws for genetically modified food.'
(1 April 1997), 'Copa and Cogeca urge the Union to develop a coherent, transparent and reliable system for market release of genetically modified organisms, both European and imported.'
(21 May 1997), 'European commerce calls on American farmers to separate genetically modified food from other products at source.'
(25 September 1997), 'Commission adopts regulation to retroactively apply novel food regulation labelling rules to food produced from genetically modified soy beans or maize.'
(26 November 1997), 'The Commission adopted the principles it will propose for the long-awaited modification of Directive 90/220/EEC on the voluntary release of genetically modified organisms (GMOs) into the environment.'
(6 January 1998), 'The Confederation of Food and Drink Industries urges its affiliates to voluntarily label their products containing transgenic ingredients.'
(12 January 1998), 'For Fediol, the labelling rules proposed by the commission for transgenic soya and maize based foods are a source of confusion for the consumer.'
(14 January 1998), 'BEUC initiative encourages the EU standing food committee to reject the draft regulation on foods containing transgenic soya or maize.'
(24 February 1999), 'International negotiations on "Biosafety" Protocol.'

Allen, Scott (1999), 'Group lobbies for labelling genetically altered foods', *Boston Globe*, 18 June, p. A3.
Arthur, Charles (1996), 'Trade war threat over genetically altered soya', *The Independent*, 30 September, p. 7.
Bensedrine, Jabril and Helena Kobayashi (1999), 'Firms' strategies and national institutional environments', in Michael Hitt, Joan Ricart and Robert Nixon (eds), *Managing Strategically in an Interconnected World*, John Wiley & Sons, pp. 39–54.
Boulton, Leyla (1996), 'US pressed on soya beans', *Financial Times*, 26 October, p. 2.
Brodie, Ian (2000), 'Global deal agreed on GM food', *Times*, 31 January.

Buckingham, Donald and Peter Philips (2001), 'Hot potato, hot potato: regulating products of biotechnology by the international community', *Journal of World Trade*, **35** (1), 1–31.

Buzalka, Mike (2000), 'Does GE bring good things to life?', *Food Management*, **35** (3), March, 10–79.

Chase, Brett (2000), 'Biocrops aren't an easy sell', *Chicago Sun-Times*, February 13, p. 39.

Chemical Market Reporter (4 January 1999), 'FDA charged with ignoring BGH hazards', *Chemical Market Reporter*, **255** (1), 6–40.

Christie, Rebecca (1999), 'FDA under pressure on gene-modified food', *Financial Times*, 18 June, p. 7.

Commission of the European Communities (2000), 'Economic impact of genetically modified crops on the agri-food sector – a first review', Working document Rev. 2, Brussels: Directorate-General for Agriculture.

Conway, Gordon (1999), 'GM foods can save lives, if we use them sensibly', *Independent*, 15 November, p. 5.

Cordtz, Dan (1994), 'Fruit that swim?', *Financial Word*, **163** (12), 7 June, p. 32–4.

Cox, James (2000), 'Retailers dropping bio-foods', *USA Today*, 4 January, p. 1a.

Drozdiak, William (2001), 'EU plans tight biotech food controls', *Washington Post*, 11 April, p. E01.

Eaton, Sabrina (1999), 'Inspired by butterflies, Kucinich seeks labels for altered foods', *Plain Dealer*, 29 September, p. 1A.

Economist (1 May 1999), 'Science and technology: sticky labels', **351** (8117), p. 75–6.

EU Press Release 51/97 (25 July 1997), 'The College of Commissioners of the EC's guidelines for the regulatory process.'

Farley, Maggie (2000), 'Deal struck to regulate genetically altered food', *Los Angeles Times*, 30 January.

Feder, Barnaby (1996), 'Out of the lab, a revolution on the farm', *New York Times*, 3 March, p. 3.

Feder, Barnaby (1999), 'Plotting corporate futures, biotechnology examines what could go wrong', *New York Times*, 24 June, p. C1.

Financial Express – India (22 February 1999), 'Agriculture: protocol on biosafety being hammered into shape'.

Financial Times – London (1996), 'Monsanto reaps benefit of genetic engineering', 1st November, p. 26.

Fligstein, Neil (1996), 'Markets as politics: a political–cultural approach to market institutions', *American Sociological Review*, **61**, 656–73.

Fligstein, Neil (2001), *The Architecture of Markets*, Princeton and Oxford: Princeton University Press.

Fligstein, Neil and Doug McAdam (1995), 'A Political–Cultural Approach to the Problem of Strategic Action', Unpublished manuscript: University of California.

Fuchs, Ursel (1998), 'Propaganda strategy of gen-multis leaked out', *Raum und Zeit*, **91**, January, translated by Franz Beck.

Fulmer, Melinda (1999), 'Technology; activists push for labelling of genetically altered foods', *Los Angeles Times*, June 18, p. C3.

Graham, Robert (2000), 'Concern is mounting: greater public awareness has led to a pause on further GM experiments while British beef remains a meaty issue', *Financial Times*, June 14.

Hall, Terry and Virginia Marsh (2000), 'Tough line on GM food labels', *Financial Times*, 29 July.

Hess, Glen (1999), 'Consumer group urges modified food labelling', *Chemical Market Reporter*, **256** (9), August 30, 5–11.

Hileman, Bette (1999), 'USDA beefs up biotech regulatory process', *Chemical and Engineering News*, **77** (29), July 19, p. 12.

Ibrahim, Youssef (1996), 'Genetic soybeans alarm Europeans', *New York Times*, November 7, p. D1

Inter Press (24 February 1999), 'Official complaints from delegations of Brazil, India, Switzerland and Venezuela. Environment: debate over transgenics heats up.'

Jacobs, Paul (1999), 'Protest may mow down trend to alter crops', *Los Angeles Times*, October 5, p. A1.

Johnson, Jessica (2000), 'Eat your veggies: used in everything from Diesel to dogs, soybeans are hot', *Financial Post – Canada*, May 1, p. 32.

Knight-Ridder (6 February 2000), 'With focus on bio-engineering, food goes under the microscope', *Knight-Ridder Tribune Business News*.

Koenig, Robert (1998), 'EU confronts the genetics of trade', *Journal of Commerce*, March 30, p. 1A.

Koenig, Robert (1999), 'Complex array of label rules gives US exporters headaches', *Journal of Commerce*, January 11, p. 7A.

Lambrecht, Bill (1999), 'Compromise proposed for pact on genetically altered products', *St. Louis Post-Dispatch*, February 22, p. A5.

Lambrecht, Bill (2000a), 'In a hearing, Ashcroft assails new accord on gene-altered food', *St Louis Post Dispatch*, February 9.

Lambrecht, Bill (2000b), 'Monsanto vows to be open about altered food', *St Louis Post Dispatch*, November 28, p. A1.

Laumann, Edward and David Knoke (1989), *The Organizational State*, Chicago: University of Chicago Press.

Le Dréaut, Jean-Yves (1998), *L'utilisation des organismes génétiquement modifiés dans l'agriculture et dans l'alimentation*, Rapport 545, Paris: Office Parlementaire d'Evaluation des Choix Scientifiques et Technologiques.

Le Henaff, Stéphane (2000), 'Carrefour lance sa filière sans OGM', *Points de Vente*, **797**, 23 février, p. 27.

Le Monde (20 juin 1998), 'Les messages des industriels.'

Lennard, Jeremy (1999), 'Washington kills global pact to govern GM trade', *The Guardian*, 24 February, p. 14.

Levidow, Les (1994), 'Biotechnology regulation as symoblic normalization', *Technology Analysis and Strategic Management*, **6** (2), 273–88.

Mann, Michael (1999), 'Luxembourg: EU close to temporary GMO moratorium', *Reuters*, 24 June.

Mann, Michael (2001a), 'Europe passes tough GMO laws', *Financial Times*, FT.com site, 14 February.

Mann, Michael (2001b), 'Countries refuse to lift crops ban', *Financial Times*, FT.com site, 15 February.

Marks, Alexandra (1999), 'US poised for a biotech food fight', *Christian Science Monitor*, November 17, p. 1.

Martin, Michele (1997), 'A taste of the future', *Campaign London – Good Houskeeping Supplement*, September 5, pp. 26–7.

McNichol, Jason (2000), 'Contesting governance in the global marketplace: a sociological assessment of British efforts to build new markets for NGO-certified sustainable wood products', Center for Culture, Organization, and Politics Working Paper #2000–06, Berkeley, CA: University of California.

McNichol, Jason (2002), *Contesting Governance in the Global Marketplace: A Socio-logical Assessment of Non-Governmental Partnerships to Build Markets for Certified Wood Products*, Ph.D. Dissertation, Berkeley, CA: University of California.

Miller, Cyndee (1992), 'Midwest will be test market in '93 for genetically engineered tomatoes', *Marketing News*, **26** (19), 14 September, pp. 1, 20–21.

Miller, Henry (1999), 'Genetic engineering: a rational approach to labelling biotech-derived foods', *Science*, **284** (5419), 28 May, 1471–2.

Moore, Samuel K. and Alex Scott (1999), 'Biotech battle: waging a war for public approval', *Chemical Week*, **161** (48), December 15, pp. 23–6.

Murphy, Craig (1994), *International Organization and Industrial Change*, Cambridge: Polity Press.

Nature (22 April 1999), 'Europe and US in confrontation over GM labelling food criteria', *Nature*, **398**, p. 641.

Nuttall, Nick (1999), 'GM soya firm yields to pressure', *Times*, 3 September.

Pollack, Andrew (2000), '130 nations agree on safety rules for biotech food', *New York Times*, January 30.

Ruggie, John (1993), *Multilateralism Matters*, New York: Columbia University Press.

Schleicher, Ursula (1998), Written question No E-4222/97 to the Commission (21 January), *European Official Journal*, C310, p. 15.

Science Magazine (1998), 'A tomato by any other name? US and EC grapple with labelling', **281**, 30 July, p. 714.

Secretariat of the Convention on Biological Diversity (2000), Cartagena Protocol on Biosafety to the Convention on Biological Diversity: Text and Annexes, Montreal: Secretariat of the Convention on Biological Diversity.

Smith, Jacqueline (1996), *The Future of Biotechnologies in Europe*, Club de Bruxelles Report for its conference on 26–27 September 1996, with the support of the European Commission (DG XII).

St. Louis Dispatch (5 September 1999), 'Sunday tipsheet', p. E2.

Steyer, Robert (1996a), 'Biotech boycott', *St. Louis Post-Dispatch*, October 8, p. 6C.

Steyer, Robert (1996b), 'Euro debate over new crops', *St. Louis Post-Dispatch*, October 27, p. E1.

Steyer, Robert (1999), 'Biotech crops gain favour on the farm; controversy abroad hasn't slowed planting', *St. Louis Post-Dispatch*, May 23, p. E1.

Storper, M. and Robert Salais (1997), *Worlds of Production*, Cambridge, MA: Harvard University Press.

Swedberg, Richard (1997), 'New economic sociology: what has been accomplished, what is ahead?' *Acta Sociologica*, **40**, 161–82.

Vogel, David (1986), *National Styles of Regulation*, Ithaca, NY: Cornell University Press.

Vulliamy, Ed, John Madeley and Anthony Browne (2000), 'America backs down with deal on GM food', *The Observer*, 30 January.

Washington Post (17 July 1999), 'Wars of the plate', p. A18.

Williams, Nigel (1998), 'Plant genetics: agricultural biotech faces backlash in Europe', *Science*, **281** (5378), 7 August, 768–71.

10. Innovations in governance: global structuring and the field of public exchange-traded markets[1]

Marc J. Ventresca, Dara Szyliowicz and M. Tina Dacin

INTRODUCTION

In January 2002, ArchEX came online as a fully-authorized equities exchange, the outcome of several years of negotiations between regulators, the Pacific Exchange in the US, and Archipelago. This electronic communications network (ECN) was among the first to petition for SEC recognition. In that same month, a dozen other strategic innovations in governance and organizational forms occurred among stock exchanges around the world. Euronext, a four-way alliance among the Brussels, Paris, Amsterdam and Lisbon Stock Exchanges, launched NextEconomy, a technology market segment. The New Zealand Stock Exchange confirmed plans to demutualize, that is, to become a publicly-traded firm and list its own shares. The Taiwan Stock Exchange's TIGER market was joined by the Emerging Stock Market in Taipei, virt-X, a new business model venture between the Swiss Stock Exchange, Tradepoint (itself a London-based electronics communications network, authorized as an official exchange by the British FSI), and a consortium of global investment banks announced new alliance relations. The Stockholmsbörsen became a fully operational entity under the OM Gruppen organization, a securities and technology firm.

These governance innovations, novel for the field of exchange-traded markets, provide an empirical context through which we investigate the mechanisms of global field structuration. In the background is the enormous rise of world structuration and discourse in the scientific domain. Structuration refers to the creation and elaboration, within and among social actors, of organizational structures with increased capabilities, rights, duties and obligations. Actors become more elaborately organized in a domain and enter in more differentiated and more elaborate formal and informal relations with one another. These governance innovations provide evidence of a dramatic shift in core institutional features of the financial markets, for both specific exchanges and for the industry overall (Porter 1993). The result is evident in new kinds of struggles and conflicts over basic questions about 'What is an exchange?' (Lee 1998) and 'What are the best institutional forms for a securities market in a global industry?' (Van Zandt 1991).

Exchange-traded markets take shape under national and other professional, political and regulatory forces. In the modern period, institutional actors and processes play an increased role. The terms on which they do this are imprinted by the broader social context within which nation-states and economies are constructed (Dobbin 1994; Granovetter 1985, 1992; Meyer 1997; Radice 2000; Whitley, 1992 and 1999). Current research questions in institutional and regime theories of governance highlight how overall changes in the interaction between states, transnational actors and new technologies affect organizational forms and the institutional features of markets. We focus on processes that generate more institutional structuring at the global level (formal organizations, expert discourse and new 'vertical' institutional arrangements), relative to prior nation-state based regimes of governance. This shift in the degree of global social structure is under-specified in much work on the contemporary globalization of finance. Global activity on such a scale is a new development. It is evident in both formal organizations and expert discourse and it contributes to a global competitive regime for the equities markets.

Our approach highlights the contribution of organizational analysis: to develop and test arguments that ground broad terms like 'globalization', 'convergence', and 'integration' in more proximate organizational and institutional processes (Guillén 2001). We look beyond standard accounts of 'globalization' understood as imperative or unruly flows of capital, to consider emerging transnational social structures. Here, we describe the emergence and thickening of global social structures in the exchange-traded markets field, as an alternative to the accounts of globalization that document capital mobility but under-specify how political and other institutional mechanisms inflect that mobility across sectors, space and borders (Verdier 2001).

We develop the idea of 'vertical' institutional structuring processes to emphasize both the increase of social structure at the global level and the introduction of new elements of social structure (Coleman 1974; Drori et al. 2003; Ventresca 1995). We argue that this field of financial markets has become a global rather than a national field through distinctively institutional and organizational mechanisms (Morgan and Sturdy 2000; Knorr-Cetina and Bruegger, 2002; Verdier 2001). We also treat the spread of contemporary conceptions of neoliberal economic policies as an important development that has provoked much public discussion and action amongst experts (Dezalay and Garth 1996). These twin developments – more global structuring and the renewal of a strong cultural model of market forces – drive activity in the field of exchange-traded markets in specific ways. In particular, we focus on the period after 1980 when new forms of linkages change the basic terms of competition and regulation among exchange-traded markets – implementing and provoking new technologies, common state initiatives to regulate them, novel business models and, increasingly, struggles over which authorities will be able to regulate the markets and other actors in the field.

We argue that the increased institutional complexity and density of global social structure creates opportunities for new jurisdictional claims by actors themselves or by what Meyer (1994) calls 'others'. It promotes and makes possible novel linkages among industry actors and infrastructural others that drive the theorization and editing of governance innovations such as demutualization,[2] alliances or mergers (see also Lilja and Moen this volume). These innovations are the artifacts of fundamental changes in the institutional features of the standard nation-state model of an exchange-traded financial market. The particular structuring of this field is marked by institutional processes – the proximate conflict and power dynamics among potential actors, the construction of new actors and the erosion of earlier actors (see also Kleiner; McNichol and Bensedrine, this volume), as well as by more general institutional processes of increased global formal organization and expert discourse (Weber 1928, 2000). We highlight the cultural and organizational components that underpin the specificity of the rationalization of organizational actors, models of governance and regulation and modules of activity, ideologies and logics that organize and make activity accountable and available to market forces.

The growth of global social structure as both a cultural and organizational activity is the case we develop here. We identify logics and governance arrangements. We also identify key actors who enter the field, their purposes and interests and the eventual outcomes; our focus is on the post 1970s period and on European activities.[3] We also try to develop the tension of challenger and incumbent rules as reflected for example in struggles over technology, but push focus back to the infrastructures that support these local skirmishes.

We report evidence from three kinds of structuring processes that are remaking venues for strategic action in the exchange-traded markets industry: (1) the growth and role of international organizations; (2) the initiatives of existing, often dominant exchange-traded markets; and (3) the activities of institutional 'others' that provide technical (and ontological) expertise. We provide a theoretical account of the redefinition and structuration at the global level and the subsequent shifts in governance arrangements that are imaginable and that become standard and available. We treat governance infrastructure as the constitutive and enabling legal, regulatory and administrative arrangements that order the field. The contemporary dynamics among exchange-traded markets are historically distinctive: direct challenges to long-established core trading technologies, the proliferation of exchanges, both in developed market economies but also in the emerging economies of Asia, Latin America and

Africa; major increases in volume, and distinctive patterns of merger, consolidation, and strategic alliance formation indicating increased interaction among exchange and other industry participants. These new developments in governance typically are treated as outcomes. We suggest that in the aggregate they provide cultural evidence that 'tracks' the presence of new venues for knowledge, expertise and solution-provision in ambiguous, unsettled, or contested global domains (Morgan and Sturdy 2000).

This chapter contributes to the overall arguments of this volume in three ways. First, our data and findings reinforce the arguments that suggest transnational processes of institution building depart in important ways from institutionalization at the local and national level and are potentially having 'trickle-down' effects (Djelic and Quack in the conclusion to this volume). These processes of collective ordering and institutional construction establish infrastructure at the global level. Further, it is in the jurisdictional conflicts and struggles that occur between and among claimant orders and actors that the de facto texture of the field gets worked out. The result is (1) conflicts and (2) quick adoption and exploitation of models of governance. But these models remain quite heterogeneous in practice. Second, we provide an account of 'globalization' that presents its plural, often contradictory and heterogenous dimension. We focus on globalization as in part formal organization and in part discourse and meaning produced at the global level (see Djelic and Quack in the introduction and conclusion to this volume). We provide analytic descriptions of the key structuring mechanisms, as well as evidence about the origins of actors and activities involved in constituting this infrastructure. Third, we highlight important outcomes from this process, in particular the development of new forms of organization and governance. Much work in finance presents the new trading technologies as the drivers of dramatic change and the explanation for all manner of innovation. We put 'technology' back into organizational strategies and practices, and we argue for attention to the institutional restructuring that makes possible and channels the effects of technological change. We step back from standard arguments about the diffusion of forms and models, to highlight the institutional conditions at time $t-1$ when struggles among actors and heterogeneity of options prevail, tracking the particular resolutions of these such that one or another innovation comes to be seen as obvious or a necessary competitive or strategic solution – for example, the case of alliances among exchange-traded markets.

THEORY AND ARGUMENT

The vast expansion of global financial activity since the 1980s is a central fact of international economic life.[4] The outlines of this are well-documented –

increased volumes of capital flows, increased speed of transactions and changes in financial centres. The distinctive institutional conditions and features of this field since the early 1980s are much agreed upon, though less well-specified (Khoury 1990; Van Zandt 1991, esp. footnotes 1–5; Verdier 2001).

Political scientists in both the more neoliberal regime traditions (Simmons 2001) and political institutional approaches (Posner 2002; Weber and Posner 2000; Woodruff 2000) highlight the contested rules of game that shape financial market development, especially with regard to changes in the kinds of actors pursuing interests through market development processes. Studies of regulation and law have puzzled over the conditions that would make possible an 'international' securities market (Van Zandt 1991). More generally, the standard finance scholarship on the emergence and development of equities markets and innovation in equities markets emphasizes firm performance considerations, though some recent studies expand this to include both actor motives for market participation (Leleux and Muzyka 2000) and the politics of financial market development (Rajan and Zingales 2001). Standard arguments in finance present the drivers of these trends as technology, the action of traditional nation-state regulatory agencies, exchange demutualization and other governance innovations, as well as changing measurements of stock exchange outcomes. These accounts all neglect a fundamental shift in the institutional infrastructure of the global field of exchange-traded markets; they do not attend to the changing organizational and institutional features of this system of activity.

Institutional organizational accounts of the evolution of large-scale global fields of activity (Boli and Thomas 1999; Dezalay and Garth 1996; Drori 1997; Haas 1990; Ventresca 1995) highlight structuring processes that are left underspecified in other orthodox approaches. These empirical studies emphasize the cultural and organizational aspects of global industry fields. In contrast to the internationalization of finance literature, studies of the global industry fields examine global structures and processes as more than the aggregate of networks. They see them as revealing an emergent and distinctive level of social reality, a system of economic and political interactions and exchanges.

Our concern with field structuration makes central the idea that new types of actors and new forms of action often precede new governance forms (see also Kleiner in this volume). Sometimes these are consensually and cooperatively defined; other times they are mandated or imposed by authorities and rulemakers, or even inherited from prior historical activity. Similarly, we conceptualize the institutional sources of governance to include initiatives that codify and consolidate the rules and arena of competition, that is work that occurs in defining new competitive spaces whether in the early moments of industry emergence or in the midst of market evolution (see Kleiner; McNichol and Bensedrine in this volume).

Stinchcombe (1965) highlighted mechanisms by which social structures affect social organization. DiMaggio and Powell (1983) motivated classic concerns in cultural and political sociology to contrast competitive and institutional processes of change in organization form, structure and activity; this and later papers develop *organizational fields* as a useful level of analysis and focus on field-level structures, elements and mechanisms as critical to understanding the links between social structures and social organization. Organizational field approaches have substantial analytic value in making sense of changes in the global financial system (Fligstein 2001; Morgan 1997; Morgan and Sturdy 2000, chs 2, 8, 9). This concept of a field extends the notion of sector or industry as used by both sociologists and economists to highlight a distinct view of interorganizational relations that includes state and other collective political actors, consumers and constituencies, and regulatory actors. An organizational field approach emphasizes the importance of collective rationalities – origins, process, uses – and makes central the activity of organizational and other actors. Developments in a field take form in the context of an embedding business system (Quack et al. 2000). The social organization of fields – flows of information, boundary processes and the resulting stratification and segmentation, the development of dominant actors and modes of valuation, the presence and deployment of rhetorics of common identity and purpose, the definition and incorporation of new actors, and the interplay of rules and resources that spur change are all empirical questions (Morgan and Sturdy 2000, pp. 47–9; DiMaggio and Powell 1983; Scott 1995; Ventresca and Lacey 2001; Kleiner; McNichol and Bensedrine; Lehmkuhl this volume).

Hence exchanges are not only 'markets'. They are also elements of a field and hence take on form at the intersection of potentially contradictory institutional logics that may reflect different cultural logics. Dominant and challenger logics are expressed in governance arrangements – structures of policy and decision making that embody these wider cultural institutions and constructs, rather than being built up from aggregate activity or the immediate interactions among current social networks. Such patterns of regularized activity are crucial for the maintenance of governance arrangements and may also contribute to innovation, but the core argument gives primacy to external and collectively-ordered institutional rules ordering forms and governance arrangements. Institutional change in fields occurs with the respecification of central elements – the constitution of new actors, the emergence of alternative organizational forms or shifts in the regulatory authority that provides stability. New actors enter fields, bringing potentially disruptive or reinforcing logics and resources, as challengers for recognition and authorization (Fligstein 1996). This entry is not mere physical presence, but rather recognition in the institutional terms of the field. The processes of incorporating these new actors and editing their new logics are important boundary processes, and underscore the role of authority to field structuration and redefinition processes.

Studies of markets and by extension industries often begin with already well-structured and established arenas of economic and social activity. Field structuration, however, is a relatively underspecified outcome in the empirical literature, but it is central to our concerns.[5] The field structuration focus keeps our attention on processes of institutional definition and change – of emerging economic arenas, shifts in boundaries, and the authorization of actors and activity. The field structuration approach represents an alternative to more standard efficiency arguments, that simply presume 'better' arrangements will triumph. We argue that no technology or new actor is inherently superior, better, or more efficient, but rather these features are outcomes of complex, dense social embedding and conflict processes. Empirical studies of field structuration reflect the early studies by DiMaggio and colleagues (DiMaggio and Powell 1983; DiMaggio 1983, 1986) which emphasize the role of state and professional actors. More recent studies look more directly at governance associations in industries and sectors (Galvin 2002; Schneiberg 1999; see also Lilja and Moen this volume) and focus on social movement and mobilization processes. The mechanisms of field structuration derive from the interplay of activity – varied processes of formalization, rationalization, and cultural editing and redefinition. These processes establish boundaries, provide and allocate identity elements and authorize particular classes of actors and activity. The key processes are: (1) Increased flows of information and the sources that produce this information. This refers to increased production of self-defining and self-constituting information. The growth of trade associations and such is one indicator; (2) Emergence of stratification with dominant and less central players. This process of ordering and segmenting a field of activity is seldom studied directly. (3) Rhetorics of common identity and fate, and the production of specialized agencies and categories that confirm these identities. The pervasive language of globalization is central to contemporary public discussions about and between exchanges.

Accordingly, we turn to research in the world polity tradition (Boli and Thomas 1999; Schneiberg and Clemens 2002; Thomas et al. 1987) to highlight how changes in the social structures of meanings and resources at the global level matter for innovations in governance arrangements in the exchange-traded markets field. The world polity approach points to the institutional and cultural aspects of transnational structures (Meyer et al. 1997; Thomas et al. 1987), at the transnational level of 'cultural and organizational formation that operates as a constitutive and directive context for states, business enterprise, groups, and individuals' (Boli and Thomas 1999, p. 3).

This approach stands in contrast to the standard economic arguments on the internationalization of finance that focus on stylized facts emphasizing capital flows, profit-making and efficiency and typically neglect the process aspects. A concern with the institutional mechanisms and process of field structuration is at the analytic heart of organizational field approaches in institutional analysis. Because markets are constructed within an organizational field, institutional and organizational analysis of the normative and practical construction of products, consumers and competition processes are a crucial component of enriching standard economic conceptions of exchange or social networks perspectives that predominate in economic sociology (Morgan and Sturdy 2000). These scholars argue that organizational fields comprise empirically

> transnational, national, and local states and self-regulatory organizations (which set rules and regulations about types of products), commercial organizations (which sell or distribute products), consumer organizations (which articulate and construct the 'needs of the consumer' or 'society' or 'future generations') and a range of other organizations which have interests in the field that may or may not be significant in particular exchange processes (for example, mass media, trade unions). (Morgan and Sturdy 2000, pp. 48–9)

We instead develop analytic descriptions of core structuring processes. Our argument draws on institutional organizational accounts of the evolution of large-scale global fields of activity (Boli and Thomas 1999; Dezalay and Garth 1996; Drori 1997; Haas 1990; Meyer et al. 1997; Ventresca 1995).

We identify five analytic elements common in this process:[6]

1. The shift from local and often horizontal social organization among proximate, individual actors, to collective and reflexive organization at the global or international level, enacted by corporate actors and supporting institutional others (Meyer 1994). This is an argument around the emergence of new types of action (and organizations and actors). This is a shift not from the nation-state to international action but rather to viewing that state as part of an overall global system where other actors (MNCs, IGOs, NGOs) play a large role in the activity in a given field (see also McNichol and Bensedrine this volume). A shift in the locus of a field occurs from the nation-state to the international level. In terms of the global stock exchange industry, the pattern we document is a shift from local and federal connections within a national economy to linkages throughout the wider global economy. This change may be seen through the transformation to wider, more vertically-structured linkages as well as more heterogeneous connections and a more extensive range of partners. Consequently, in the global stock exchange industry, the number of alliances between exchanges increase, while at the same time there is an expansion of alliance activity with other organizations such as international trade associations.

2. The spawning of a more solidary intermediate social structure, usually in emulation of central collective initiatives, no matter how tenuously achieved

these collective structures of meaning and sources. Structure in this case is not just formal organizations or institutions but the actual effects of inter-actions between players. Overall, this manifests itself as processes of erosion and replacement. For example, as regionalization occurs in Europe, central banks and specific national constituencies become less important and are replaced by linkages between organizations. These linkages may be similar in nature but with different partners or actually new forms of relationships – for example, alliances between exchanges. Whatever the form that emerges, these relationships reflect the changes in these wider environments.

3. The emergence of new, usually collective-level venues for organized activity, which typically form crucibles for innovation in governance models and provide bases for the development and promotion of novel identities, interests, and repertoires of action. These informal agreements may lead to the creation of actual formal organizations and institutions as well as (or alternatively to) different forms of governance for both individual organ-izations and the field as a whole. This can have far-reaching implications for organizational activity and change as well as field identity and how actors conceptualize interests. Since action is often the result of pursuing interests this will impact how firms behave.

4. Over time struggles for jurisdiction and the (re)definition and division of organizational labour, in which a settled regime of one era is contested as new actors and activity make incursions on these established organizational venues, and the field restructures. This is a commentary on how change occurs in a field. Struggles over interests, the emergence of new actors or changes in field activity can all lead to restructuring and the emergence of new governance arrangements throughout the field (Kleiner; Lilja and Moen; Plehwe with Vescovi; McNichol and Bensedrine in this volume).

5. Sectoral variation in the degree and kind of dominant central organization and the presence of more or less well-defined intermediate social structure, with expert-saturated domains and activities have the earliest and most dense forms of central, collective organization. Therefore epistemic communities play an important role in centralizing and creating agreement early on in a field. Obviously the amount of variation and strength of existing actors will influence the structuring of a field, in particular, how centralized it is.

METHODS, DATA AND SOURCES

Our core argument focuses on the linkage between increased amounts and kinds of global social structures and changes in a series of industry and competitive outcomes. In terms of outcomes, we sketch developments in three relevant areas: (1) changes over historical time in the pattern of foundings of new exchanges; (2) experimentation and innovation in models of governance; (3) the emergence of new, hybrid, and contested forms of exchanges.

To track changes in global social structure, we focus on evidence in changes in organizational actors and organized talk at the global level. This evidence includes several kinds of indicators: (1) over-time levels and sources of 'public talk' (publications, conferences, handbooks) about the global industry that provide evidence of field-level identity and rhetorics of common purpose; (2) the activity of intergovernmental organizations and others such as consulting and accounting firms, for example, the creation of 'practice areas' that deal with financial markets and that provide sources of expertise, legal and technical; (3) participation and network interactions among established exchanges and exchange-in-formation as evidence of field stratification and segmentation; and (4) foundings of new organizations at the global level with explicit missions to foster, promote, rationalize and support the activities of exchanges.

We used secondary and archival sources to compile a 'chronology' of actors and activities that points to more global social structure in the exchange-traded markets field. This includes materials from web sites of many international organizations such as the IFC, USAID, the industry trade associations WFSE, IOSCO, IOMA, and many individual exchanges. We also reviewed evidence from searches through AIB of all articles dealing with exchange-traded markets and developments in the industry from 1985 to the present.

We draw from primary documents including the current publications of many of the industry associations, especially the FIBV *Focus*, a monthly publication that chronicles developments in the industry. A set of directories provided enormously useful summary information regarding the history and current conditions of all the exchange-traded markets. Notable among these is the Salomon Smith Barney annual directory, *Global Stock Exchanges*. Secondary histories also proved useful (Spray 1964; Ayling 1986).

THE SHIFTING GLOBAL TERRAIN OF EXCHANGE-TRADED EQUITIES MARKETS

Simmons points to the regulatory challenges posed by the internationalization of global capital markets: 'Overall, financial markets are swiftly moving targets [the] supervision and regulation [of which] require streamlined decision making and a tremendous amount of technical expertise' (2001, p. 592). Regulation across country borders is difficult as there is no common enforcement mechanism. So how does integration of this field occur? Especially when 'global equity markets are not as deeply integrated as other types of capital markets' (Lavelle 2001, p. 717).[7]

This was not a problem until the end of the nineteenth century because the dominant organizational form was a nation-state model of an exchange-traded market for equities. At this time, relatively few and specific forms of exchange-traded markets existed. The modal governance form was dominated by state institutions of the national economy such as central banks. Regulatory arrangements were shaped by national polity forms, often with a combination of state agency and self-regulatory industry arrangements. Altogether there was relative national separation and typically single exchange listing practices (Szyliowicz et al. 1999). These are only a few types of stock exchanges that are familiar to us. In the Anglo-American tradition, stock exchanges were collective member organizations that provided a physical site in which exchange and a market-place were one and the same, and which was supported by varied clearing and settlement systems, all overseen by a public agency such as the SEC. In the continental European tradition and elsewhere, quasi-public organizations provided a similar venue, again with clearing and settlement systems, but closely coupled to a central bank and with regulatory functions built into the same organization. The actors were known and stable with standard technology, some version of open outcry or listing, liquidity depending on the volume of market participants. Network ties among actors in the field were dense within nation-states, with relatively few linkages across national boundaries and even fewer formal organizations that spanned national boundaries. The traditional actors in exchange-traded markets were firstly the exchanges themselves – in the Anglo-American tradition, often membership organizations in complex regulatory relationships with either states or professional associations; in more banking-centred systems, central banks, ministries of finance and economic planning commissions.

A great barrier to constructing a world securities regime was an absence of an organizational frame in which these issues could enter a global agenda since neither a central authoritative world actor nor any organizational structures existed (Schofer 1999; Djelic and Quack in the introduction to this volume, see also Whitley in this volume).

GROWTH OF FORMAL INDUSTRY ORGANIZATION AT THE GLOBAL LEVEL

A standard chronology of the internationalization of stock exchanges tracks little activity in the late nineteenth century, despite substantial increases in volume and variety of international capital flows. The late nineteenth century saw a high point in international initiatives and political support for international agreements on financial matters, peaking in 1897 when the major powers agreed to fix the values of their currencies to gold.

This lack of historical interaction reflects the limitations of a field dominated at the time by nation-state actors and agencies. Before the 1970s, little in the way of a formal or systematic global field of exchange-traded markets existed; the nation-state model of exchange was dominant. The exchanges were reflective of national interests and concerns and often controlled directly by agencies of the state (via national ministries of finance or central banks), often with legislation prohibiting cross-border listings. Variation occurred in particular relation to the state, trading technology, repertoire of products, and links with broader financial services, investment banks, and so on, including notable variation in form and degree of regulation. Policy and action, however, were imprinted by a nation-centric logic.

Nonetheless, the early years of the twentieth century witnessed a revolution in the technologies of modern finance, which had an impact on the field, with the international focus shifting from London to New York, and the growth in capital markets' capacity to finance innovative industries around the globe. After World War I, London regained some primacy as an international finance centre. But, in 1931 the world's economy collapsed. When international investment did pick up, much of the funds were directed into the US, which had reregulated its markets through the SEC Act of 1934.

Historically, there was no 'field' in our terms, since there was little interaction, few direct connections between exchanges, and the individual actors were moored in local activity. Obviously some exchanges were more important and larger and this reflected a wider dominance order among exchanges. The early discourse about securities markets occurred in private and informal conversations within the existing exchanges, among global bankers, and between the exchanges and relevant government ministries. The first venues for explicit industry discussions among business leaders were initiatives by the International Chamber of Commerce (ICC), which promoted a set of conferences from the early 1910s on world economic conditions and policies. The first formal effort to create a forum about exchanged-traded markets were initiatives by the ICC to set up an International Bureau for Stock Exchanges in the early 1930s.

From its founding in 1905, the ICC was one of the first attempts to deal with financial markets across countries (Ridgeway 1938). Representatives to the early sessions were often from national central banks. This organization sponsored a series of conferences after World War I, part of the international efforts in the reconstruction of global commerce: 1919 Atlantic City International Trade Conference (focused on postwar debts and global financial and exchange crisis, and reparations or League-coordinated cooperation and reconstruction); the 1920 meeting of the International Economic Union (by the bypassed German states), the 1920 Organizational Conference in Paris of the ICC as a formal body, the 1920 International Financial Conference at Brussels sponsored by the newly-formed League of Nations. The first Congress of the ICC was held in May, 1921 with 36 countries represented. It considered a wide range of international business issues – statistics, standardization control and regulation of business by the state, foreign banks, and bills of exchange (ICC 1921).

Additionally this was also the beginning for the systematic collection of data not only about markets around the world but also about the industry itself as the League of Nations initiated systemic collection and dissemination of data on exchanges from the 1920s in annual yearbooks. They collected data on the capital appreciation of market indices from 1929 to1942. This collection effort was continued by the United Nations (Goetzmann and Jorion 1999, p. 8). By the early 1930s, the International Chamber of Commerce was involved in efforts to coordinate cooperation among the stock exchanges of the world. These activities laid the framework for the first intentional 'global' infrastructure that came with efforts and discussion by the International Chamber of Commerce to develop standard practices and linkages among exchanges in 1930. As a result of these activities we see the beginnings of standardization across the field.

The development of the global industry field of exchange-traded markets follows one common path in such global structuring processes (Ventresca 1995). Early informal and idiosyncratic interactions come to be formalized through the auspices of a key interest-based organization, here the International Chamber of Commerce. Stock exchanges in particular were the focus in the early 1930s when the International Chamber of Commerce created the International Bureau of Stock Exchanges to promote standards and the development of exchanges. However World War II interrupted the workings of this non-governmental organization.

In the mid 1950s, informal cooperation began again among the major European stock exchanges, in a spirit of international coordination. Interactions took a more stable form in 1961 with the creation of a trade association, the Fédération Internationale des Bourses de Valeurs (FIBV). Concerns around regulation of markets have always been central to this organization. The FIBV services to exchanges worldwide, providing systematic, public data about exchanges. This organization presently comprises 55 exchanges worldwide and accounts for over 97 per cent of world stock market capitalization. Additionally, in an attempt to respond to the changing global environment, the FIBV is now affiliated with 10 other exchanges and to 40 more that correspond to emerging markets (www.fibv.org).

From the1950s on, major changes occured in the field. The growth in capital markets and risk came with an increase in interactions and the creation of collective organizations (see Spray 1964, p. ix). This shift to a more solidary social structure also led to redefinition of the field and dominant actors or technologies. For example, these processes of change have led to the incorporation of US/Anglo exchange models by European exchanges (see Djelic 1998; Tainio et al.; Kleiner; McKenna et al. in this volume). These changes were hastened not just by field specific activity but by the more general deployment of neo-liberal conceptions of markets and corporate governance, in part by the institutional frameworks promoted in the Single European Market Program and the institutional remaking of European financial capital (Fligstein and Mara-Dritta 1996; Leyshon and Thrift 1997, ch. 3; Morgan and Sturdy 2000).

Through the 1970s, the formation of specialty units in professional associations began at the international level, keyed on defining expertise relevant to the workings of the exchanges and providing venues and nodes for professional dialogue across rule systems (for example, securities legislation, accounting standards, and the like). In this period, a regime both in the Krasner usage of core precepts and norms, decisional rules and venues around which actor expectations converge (Krasner 1983) and in the extended sense Meyer and colleagues propose[8] took shape – an elaborated field of discourse and formal organizations at the world level.

In contrast, since the 1970s in emerging markets around the globe, a distinct institutional constellation of international actors, agencies, and professional services firms have promoted the development of exchanges and associated regulatory agencies, enabling legislation, and institutions like investment banks as part of a project to build modern capital markets. These two processes differ in substantive content, but overlap in terms of institutional mechanisms and the growth of global social structures of interest in this chapter. We argue that the emergence of these new collective venues for activity plays a large role in the structuring of the field and eventual governance arrangements.

INSTITUTIONAL OTHERS AND GLOBAL INFRASTRUCTURE

The contemporary developments support the notion that the primacy of national business systems in shaping exchanges is no longer operative in the field, and this leads us to refocus on the embeddedness of national exchange systems into wider business systems and an international financial services context which influences forms of structure and action in the national context (Morgan 1997; Djelic and Quack in the introduction and conclusion to this volume). Today, traditional exchanges are joined and changed by the presence of a wide array of international agencies and organizations from the IFC to USAID and their contractors including consultancies both in strategy and accounting (for the role of this type of actors see also Tainio et al.; McKenna et al.; Lilja and Moen in this volume) as well as independent groups like the Financial Markets Group; family conglomerates such as Tata which often 'own' new markets, trading technology firms like OM Gruppen and Townsend Analytics; and trade associations at the global level such as WFSE (formerly FIBV), IOSCO, IOMA, and all the regional versions of these.

Recent transformations in financial markets challenge the conventional view that stock exchanges engage only in the listing and trading of securities within a single domestic economy. Four trends are evidence of basic transformations: (1) the multiplication of alliances (which affect broker allegiance, trading volume and liquidity, reduce the natural experiments of trading technologies because of linked systems with implications for the software development industry, and challenge regulatory frameworks); (2) electronic trading is now the rule; (3) financial regulation now allows for competition between stock exchanges and other exchange forms or electronic networks under liberalized regimes; and (4) location has changed meaning and value (Galper 1999). At the level of the state, these changes were part of general loosening of the power that states had over their national economic and social policies. The uncertainties and ambiguities in these processes of globalization of financial markets spurred firms to undertake strategic ventures such as experiments in governance (for example, demutualization, alliances, mergers) that have precipitated further changes in the social structure of competition in this now transnational field.

These developments translated into the European trend in the early to mid 1980s away from the traditional state-centric model of exchange activity and control towards the US/Anglo model of self-governance within an industry. Exchanges then lost their quasi-public status and became more like 'private' organizations that were self-regulating with governmental oversight. This is not just a shift in logics of the industry or the triumph of one series of actors over another but a change that has profound influence on governance arrangements that are and will be possible. As a result of this shift, certain activities will tend to prevail.

ENTRY OF OTHER GLOBAL ACTORS, REDEFINITION OF THEIR AGENDA AND ZONE OF EXPERTISE

Hence, after World War II movement toward intergovernmental agreements on finance issues increased. The new prosperity fostered renewed strength among financial institutions coping with the provision and control of large volumes of government loans and private equity capital financing new industries. Industrial countries recognized the capital needs of developing countries and the need for a stable international monetary system. In 1944

Bretton Woods established a new international monetary regime, a fixed exchange rate system for the currency markets that tied currency values to the dollar. It also set up the IMF and the IBRD. Within Europe, the Marshall Plan funds led to the setting up of the EPU in 1950, the ECSC in 1951 and their successor EEC in 1958 (Djelic 1998). By the early 1960s, international capital movements were increasing faster than the volume of world trade. In characteristic fashion (Strang and Meyer 1993; Tainio et al.; Kleiner; McKenna et al. in this volume), the US stock exchange system was promoted as a model for the new stock exchanges being inaugurated in many countries.

We see a shift in the field at this time away from a logic of national control to international activity through a variety of collective level venues. These international agencies and institutions (Ayling 1986, ch. 5) such as the IMF and the World Bank support the creation of this field.

The immediate postwar period marked the initiation of systematic global economic and financial institutions, including those remaking capital markets. These agencies also began to produce specialized expert knowledge about the global financial markets, creating a new form of domination and competition, and challenging the prominence of the US SEC that through the 1960s had concentrated and dominated such expertise (Moran 1994). The OECD begins to report data on exchanges on its member states in the 1970s and the IFC begins to monitor and report data on exchanges in emerging economies at about the same time, formally defining 'emerging markets' in 1981 (Goetzmann and Jorion 1999). In the 1980s, regional associations of stock exchanges form, with the support and encouragement of the global federation. In the interim, many types of organizational actors and institutional others begin to define exchange-traded markets, consulting and advising exchanges and other interested parties, in setting standards and doing the technical coordination among professional and expert constituencies who become important in confirming standard exchange forms (International Bar Association, Accounting Standards, growth of Basel Committee on Banking for example).

These developments point to one of the key arguments of this chapter: the role of new actors in the creation of governance of the field. This process is seen clearly through the founding of organizations with the express purpose of creating standards, generating expertise and information, providing venues for multilateral consultation and the development of common policies (see also Standifird et al. 2001). One is the International Accounting Standards Committee (IASC, later IASB) which was created in 1973 to promote the integration and harmonization of accounting principles worldwide. This organization is a private organization that works for convergence among accounting principles used by firms throughout the world. In 1979 collaborations with OECD began, resulting in the 1985 OECD Forum on Harmonization. Since the 1980s, IASC has worked towards the goal of regularized global financial reporting; in concert with IOSCO, international accounting standards and guidelines were created in the 1990s. Similarly, the International Bar Association (IBA) was founded in 1947 to provide an international forum for lawyers to exchange information and ideas on legal subjects. The IBA established in 1970 a section dealing with business law (IBA/SBL), then specialty interest groups on 'issues and trading securities'. Many of these topics pertained directly to financial services with the lawyers discussing how to deal with matters of arbitration, banking law and particularly capital markets.

At the same time we see alternative practices: trading equity on several domestic exchanges, the rise of consortia arrangements in global investment banking, underwriting and security distribution; the creation of new types of markets such as the IMM in Chicago in 1972 to provide a wider range of speculation and hedging alternatives. The late 1970s were a period of broad liberalization, basically the opening of national markets. These field changes were occurring in a tumultuous environment. Developments in the 1980s took place in the context of world recession, technical revolutions in the financial markets, and general movement towards deregulation of financial markets and institutions. International dialogue and agreements proliferated in this period – international capital movements now dwarfed the economic activities of most individual nations. Only consortium activity could produce the required capital. This represents a major shift towards collective organization and signalled the end to the national, parochial logic that had dominated the field.

The International Finance Corporation was founded in the early 1950s as a lending agency for emerging markets within the World Bank agencies. The commitment to lending and the need to be able to harvest those loans led to the creation of the Capital Markets Group in 1971. This unit of the IFC has for over 30 years provided expertise and consultation, often with subcontracts to transnational consulting and accounting firms, to develop capital markets in countries around the globe (author interviews with IFC senior staffers, 2002). This includes the provision of legal infrastructure, regulation, the establishment of regulatory agencies and the direct promotion of exchange-traded markets, as well as ongoing technical assistance. When do exchanges become the focus of attention? How does the kind of attention shift – from technical assistance to 'promoting' exchanges in emerging markets? One way has been through the growth in the language of rationalization – so new actors and new agendas. In addition, since 1988, USAID has a wide-ranging programme to support the development of exchange-traded markets (www.USAID.org). Professional services firms such as Deloitte and Touche, PriceWaterhouseCoopers and others establish practices in supporting and advising financial markets and specifically providing technical support to establish exchange-based markets worldwide (author interviews with USAID staff and with current and former consultants, 2002).

Table 10.1   *Publications issued by global exchange-traded markets agencies, 1980–2000*

Year	IOSCO[*]	IFCI[**]	BIS[***]
1980			4
1981			1
1982			2
1983			1
1984			3
1985			0
1986			0
1987			1
1988			0
1989	2	1	0
1990	12	2	3
1991	4	4	2
1992	9	3	1
1993	7	5	1
1994	8	6	4
1995	7	8	9
1996	17	21	6
1997	11	12	13
1998	11	28	10
1999	15	13	21
2000	12		15
2001	To June 6		to Sept 7

Sources: [*] IOSCO: 'Public documents' from www.iosco.org/library_docs-public.html
[**] IFCI: 'Core documents' on 13 key risk concepts assembled from key global Organizations: BIS – Basle Committee on Banking, BIS (Committee on Payment) and settlement systems; Eurocurrency standing committee, now the Committee on the global financial system); IOSCO (Technical Committee), SEC, International Chamber of Commerce, G30-Global Derivatives Study Group, G10, CFTC, IAIS, [***]BIS working papers www.bis.org.publ/work.html: central banking supervision

The International Organization of Securities Commissions (IOSCO), founded in 1974, is the global association of government agencies and regulators involved with the supervision of financial markets (Porter 1993). IOSCO is central in discussions about regulatory standards, investigating challenges confronting the exchanges, and in harmonization of regulatory policies around the world. In 1984, the International Financial Risk Institute (IFCI) was established under supervision of the Swiss Federal Authorities. Founders included leading derivatives exchanges, large OTC providers, auditing companies, information service providers, market regulators, end-users, and the Swiss Futures and Options Association. From the mid-1980s, there has been increasing collaboration among these agencies, for example, Joint Exchange Task Forces between FIBV members and the International Options Market Association (IOMA) and the FIBV and the World Bank/IFC in development of capital markets in emerging countries, with a permanent linkage to the IFC. The FIBV is a member of the Consultative Group of the International Accounting Standards Committee; FIBV also maintains close contact with regional exchanges organizations, as well as business relations with regulatory agencies, central banks and ministries of economics or finance (Grasso 1999). These collaborations and consultations increased from the mid-1980s. Table 10.1 presents data on counts of the number of official documents, reports, and public studies or working papers issued by several of these agencies.

INITIATIVES BY DOMINANT AND CONTENDER EXCHANGES

Fligstein (1996, 2001) argues for a view of 'markets as politics', in which contenders challenge dominant firms for access and primacy in markets, as well as constructing new markets. He presents a market as an institutional regime complete with broad precepts and conceptions of control, specific governance arrangements, and the possibility of struggles between incumbents and new entrants over technologies, products and even core conceptions of the enterprise. Szyliowicz (1998) develops these arguments in the idiom of regime arguments that feature the study of how changes in regimes reshape the terms and content of competition. Her research identifies a key shift in the US securities regime in the early 1980s, ushering in an era of broadly international attention and activity among dominant US exchanges. Leading and challenger exchanges in the US begin to focus on global markets and to implement strategies to internationalize their activities. They joust for primacy and dominance across the globe. In doing so, their strategies and initiatives further structure global activity and attention. The NASDAQ strategies and initiatives since the late 1980s demonstrate the role leading exchanges play in the global structuring process. The New York Stock Exchange rests on its pre-eminent status, continuing a decades-long set of international consultations without the direct promotion characteristic of the NASDAQ strategy. The NYSE in early 2000 does mount a substantial effort to build a 'global' market through alliance and merger strategies. This remains in process.

The case of the NASDAQ illlustrates the wide variety of strategies and the varied motives that support the increased formal activity at the global level. Our analysis points to four main ways in which NASDAQ initiatives drive the changes. We report on these initiatives since the mid-1990s.

First, NASDAQ established consulting and development efforts to promote its technology (NASDAQ-style screen-based trading systems) throughout the world, particularly in emerging market economies. NASDAQ worked diligently to advance its technical system of screen-based trading among exchanges worldwide. This technology competition is with the NYSE and a few other exchanges that continue to use traditional open outcry auction-based trading systems. But it is also a competition with other electronic exchanges and new actors – technology firms and consultancies, electronic communication networks (ECNs) and other hybrid trading platform enterprises such as virt-X. This promotion of technology and efforts to set global standards is an under-explored aspect of the deep politics of strategy. OM Gruppen has pursued a similar set of initiatives, and the efforts of several regional bourses such as Barcelona Stock Exchange show common features (BSE author interviews, 2000). NASDAQ efforts to promote its technology concurrently creates a working technology standard but also generates many direct and indirect linkages among the sister exchanges. This is not only a story about the advancement of a technology – an account of the screen vs. open-outcry in which screen-based technologies become pre-eminent. Rather, we interpret the events as a story of actors and interests that are represented by these competing technologies and influence the restructuring of the field. The redefinition of a field gets played out in the advancement of and struggles over ideologies, technologies and dominant logics.

Second, NASDAQ worked on directly building markets by promoting formal organization, alliances, and regulatory styles. NASDAQ established NASDAQ International to provide services to both US and foreign companies seeking to attract foreign investors as well as to assist foreign companies in accessing US domestic financial markets. This organization promoted the US model of self-regulatory organizations (SROs) and technological systems through the creation of overseas investor seminars. The NASDAQ International Market Initiative (NIMI), another programme, offered consulting services to help established as well as emerging securities markets with technical applications and regulations. NIMI opened offices in London and Tokyo as a formal attempt to influence the eventual outcomes for the industry. NIMI engaged in a wide range of activities with exchanges around the world: it helped to create the Australian small cap market (AUSDAQ), licensed NASDAQ to the Société des Bourses Françaises (SBF) to establish an automated confirmation transaction system (ACT). The NIMI worked with the Russian Federation to create the first national self-regulatory organization among the post-Soviet states. This organization,

PAUFOR, was modelled on the NASD, the American regulatory agency. NIMI worked with interested European Community actors to have exchanges and regulatory organizations reflect this regionalization – it also worked with European venture capitalists, issuers, dealers and regulators to establish a European NASDAQ-like dealer-driven electronic stock market, the EASDAQ (Weber and Posner 2000). The technology and consultation initiatives were two key mechanisms by which NASDAQ strategies shaped the collective structure of the field.

Third, NASDAQ initiated a direct strategy to construct a 'borderless' market with a global network of screen-based securities markets through international coordination and cooperation. In 1997, NASDAQ increased its international presence by setting up overseas investor relations offices in China, Russia, and Sao Paulo. The NIMI continued to provide consulting and advisory services and technological developmental assistance to market operations, regulatory systems and technology. Moreover, the NASDAQ devised the International Market Advisory Board (IMAB), an organization that would meet twice a year to give the NASDAQ board updates on major international developments. The influence of these organizations in promoting a new technological platform was directly visible; a 1996 FIBV study showed that of the 45 developed economy stock exchanges only three relied on trading floors, 28 were screen-based and 14 were a combination of a trading floor and screen-based technology. The trend to screen-based and all-electronic trading have continued apace (WFE 2002).

The goal continued to be to provide the development and improve infrastructure of securities markets. The NASD maintained its efforts in advancing international cooperation among securities regulators worldwide by considerable participation in global venues such as trade association and technical working committees. As a member of the FIBV, the NASD actively participated in the international regulation subcommittee. In particular, they were working on promoting international cooperation regarding trading halts. As an affiliate member of the IOSCO's SRO consultative committee they maintained a dialogue with other members in the international field. Besides trying to influence conventions on worldwide trading halts, they participated in the working committee responsible for disclosure and accounting standards. This concern with coordinated regulation was also key in developing an affiliation with the Intermarket Surveillance Group (ISG) where the NASD promoted intermarket regulation investigations. The NASD also assisted directly with regulatory changes and growth of the Cairo, Bombay, Calcutta and New Dehli stock exchanges. In the process of working with these collective level organizations, NASDAQ promoted certain issues and identities critical to their strategies. However, other exchanges and organizations also provide available governance models. NASDAQ, though influential, is one of several voices in this discussion. NASDAQ strategies and actions both reflect existing arrangements and options and influence them.

Coordinated action occurs not only through promoting a technological system or through consultative activity, but through direct action. In 1998, the NASDAQ and AMEX exchanges formally allied. The success of this alliance prompted an increased desire to explore the possibility of both acquisitions and alliances with other stock exchanges worldwide. The strategy was to create NASDAQ-style markets that would initially allow the dual-listing of companies on NASDAQ-AMEX and overseas markets, and lead to the eventual creation of a 'transparent, seamless, electronic, well-regulated market where global investors would be able to buy and sell global securities anytime, anywhere' (NASD 1998). As an initial step, a cross-listing programme with the Hong Kong Stock Exchange was established involving a joint website that enabled US investors to trade non-US securities and vice versa. This was part of a larger pilot programme that allowed Hong Kong companies to trade on NASDAQ and vice versa. By December 1999, seven US companies were traded on the Hong Kong Stock Exchange. The restructuring of the field is evident as companies are able to list on a variety of exchanges without the legal, policy and operational obstacles to cross-national listing.

NASDAQ strategy gave primacy to the Asian market and so work began on cross-border operations with the Shanghai Stock Exchange and the Singapore Stock Exchange. NASDAQ opened an office in Shanghai in 1999. NASDAQ-Japan was launched in 1999 in partnership with Softbank Corporation of Tokyo and in cooperation with the Osaka Stock Exchange. Once again these activities can be seen as an effort by NASDAQ to extend its reach within the field. The activities of field structuring included the European market as well, where NASDAQ commenced several joint programmes: the launch of a web-based stock screening investment service, in addition to creating a UK NASDAQ-AMEX website. The Deutsche Börse approached NASDAQ, interested in cross-border options. In November 1999, NASDAQ-Europe was opened as a joint venture between NASDAQ, Softbank Corporation of Tokyo, Vivendi and News Corporation Group, replacing the failed EASDAQ. The joint ventures created regional exchange-traded markets, but there were also technology platforms like Indigo Markets, a joint venture with SSI technology of India that links NASDAQ, NASDAQ-Europe and NASDAQ-Japan, into seamless trading activity. This joint venture along with the dual listing agreement between NASDAQ and Hong Kong are operational steps in field integration and the creation of a fully global trading field.

These were clearly entrepreneurial efforts by NASDAQ; the outcomes included a changing set of alliances and formal and informal interactions. It is instructive that the EASDAQ quietly became NASDAQ-Europe in 2001.

Similarly, NASDAQ-Japan, competes with MOTHERS, another screen-based growth market in Japan.

INNOVATIONS IN GOVERNANCE AND FORM

Innovations in governance and form provide primary evidence of the impact of changes in global social structure and new conceptions of control and competition. Here we report two. One is the introduction of new markets into the field (Table 10.2). This historical data on the creation of stock exchanges by geographic market shows an increase in foundings in the contemporary period. Additionally these patterns are broken out by geographic region. As the data shows, there are sectoral variations in founding patterns.

Table 10.2   *Exchange-traded market foundings by historical period and region, 1700–2000 (by percentage of period total)*

Region	Europe	Americas	Asia/Pac	Africa	Mid/East	Total N =
< 1800	82	18	0	0	0	11
1801–1850	74	21	5	0	0	19
1851–1875	29	47	24	0	0	17
1876–1900	36	32	23	5	5	22
1901–1925	41	18	29	0	12	17
1926–1950	17	33	50	0	0	6
1951–1975	7	23	50	10	10	30
1976–1985	35	12	29	12	12	17
1986–1995	38	3	24	17	17	29
1996–2000	60	20	20	0	0	5
N =	66	37	46	11	13	173

The second and perhaps most important shift is toward alliance formation. The effects of the field restructuring can be seen in the patterns of alliance and mergers activity that were unimaginable even ten years ago and now dominate the financial headlines as well as the time and activity of a very wide range of professionals, government staff, and specialist industry folks associated with the financial markets. Moreover, these shifts are accompanied by new rhetorics of accountability and the entry of new kinds of constituencies which are reshaping the role of stock exchanges in firm governance (Tainio et al. this volume). As such these new governance patterns are representative of the struggles for juris-

Table 10.3 Governance innovations in global exchange-traded markets – total counts, and alliances as a percentage of all, 1985–2001

Year	1985	1986	1987	1988	1989	1990	1991	1992	1993	1994	1995	1996	1997	1998	1999	2000	01
All innovations	3	6	4	5	3	6	2	1	12	6	23	31	28	53	19	10	27
Alliances	3	0	0	1	1	5	0	0	3	1	7	18	13	20	12	4	16
Alliances as %	100	0	0	20	33	83	0	0	25	17	30	58	46	38	63	40	59

Source: Author data collection from ABI Inform, FIBV archives, *Financial Times*, *Wall Street Journal*, field interviews, and other industry sources.

diction and the competition between exchanges. These processes highlight the issue that interests are neither fixed nor established for this industry.

The global exchange industry is a particularly interesting setting to observe alliance behaviour because only recently are the conditions supporting alliances as strategic solutions to competition pressures among exchanges becoming common in this industry. A second strategy is the creation of joint ventures. Here too this represents an opportunity for firms to create a new organization. Table 10.3 reports simple annual counts of public reports of such governance innovations: alliances and joint ventures of several kinds, as well as mergers among stock exchanges and demutualization (IOSCO 2001), with the proportion of alliances broken out.

These counts represent cases reported in the industry media where one or more exchange-traded market agreed to some change in governance. The larger type of alliances are agreements about common technology platforms. A wider category of activities include joint ventures in the establishment of new exchanges, market segments, or indexes, as well as MOUs. Mergers include consolidation within country exchanges, as well as cross-border mergers such as the regional arrangements among Nordic exchanges, throughout Africa, and in Asia (IOSCO 2001; FIBV 1997–2002). The trends are clear. Prior to the mid-1980s, there were virtually no governance innovations among the exchange-traded markets. The trends changed in 1985, with between three and six such innovations reported annually for the rest of the decade. After a brief hiatus, reports of governance innovations rose quickly to over 20 a year worldwide, peaking in 1998 at 53 events, then declining somewhat to the 10s and 20s. Alliances account for over 50 per cent of these overall. How and why alliances become so common, such a 'standard' solution to novel challenges of competition in an industry with virtually no history of such activity remains a useful question.

CONCLUSION

We provide the history of the industry as evidence that markets don't just happen. This history illustrates how a collective system emerges. We can see the shift from a localized, nation-state system of stock exchanges to an integrated system across states with actors engaging in both local and international actions – an important element in the formation of a field. As organizations shift to a more global level, the creation of collective initiatives between them becomes possible. These collective initiatives influence the field through increases in agencies, regulatory organizations and exchanges. It is not just the creation of organizations that matters here, but rather that all of this activity creates a new social structure within which organizations must now work. We have demonstrated how this process occurs by showing change in the number of new exchanges as well as in the number of alliances formed between them. This data, when analyzed within the historical context, demonstrates how the creation of collective initiatives leads to new organizations and how new organizations cause the thickening of social structures and transform the industry.

Collective initiatives lead to stronger ties between the organizations and collections of actors who then organize to create standards and agreements. However this does not lead to the emergence of a completely hegemonic field. Rather alternative practices arise and different practices, organizations and technologies compete for prominence. The NASDAQ case demonstrates how this process occurs with one organization in this field, how it promoted specific technologies (i.e. screen-based trading), and specific markets – NASDAQ vs. NYSE or other markets. The industry as a whole was interested in promoting equity markets as the best arena for access to capital as well as investment activity. Other ideologies were also promoted, aided by the efforts of a wide range of actors to create a regulatory structure, such as the importance of free markets and equivalence in practices between exchanges. Informal agreements became codified and organized over time. And new governance arrangements emerged as a result of ongoing relationships between organizations, in this case, alliance activity. These alliances may also lead to restructuring of the field as actors come together to work towards specific goals. In this case we see efforts to make one type of market system dominant, worldwide.

In short, we have focused on the structuration of the industry field that *de facto* establishes a global competitive regime for the equities markets embodied in international principles (liberalization, democratization), a redefinition of relevant actors and their interactions, technological innovation, and changes in governance forms. Recent structuration processes have redefined the sources of governance forms, structures, and strategies among exchange-traded equities markets such as stock exchanges, evident in recent flurries of alliance and merger activity, demutualization, and innovations in trading technologies. Global regimes of meanings and mechanisms increasingly comprise the formative conditions of such industry governance and competition. Current research questions in institutional and regimes theories of governance highlight how overall changes in the interaction between states, transnational actors and new technologies affect organizational forms and the institutional features of markets. Alliance dynamics are important as the empirical site in which these new governance forms are taking shape. Such regimes provide sources of authorization and models for alliance activity – they are the infrastructure that embeds strategic activity.

Institutionalists in organizational analysis have argued that market processes and other 'efficiency' accounts are inadequate or incomplete explanations for much organizational structure and activity (Clemens and Cook 1999; March and Olsen 1984). Non-functionalist explanations of the structuring of large-scale economic and political spaces confront two challenges and provide two opportunities. Strang and Meyer (1993) present arguments for theorizing 'institutional conditions for diffusion', evident in their insight that the ritual experts of modern, developed economies – lawyers, accountants, economists and management theorists, consultants, along with scientists and others – are central actors in the institutional shaping of economic institutions and activity. This is in contrast to the more stylized conceptions of impersonal, aggregate forces prevalent in neoclassical accounts or to the (important) attention to political interests and historical process common to institutional economics in the early part of the century and again today (Stinchcombe 1997; North 1990).

First, standard accounts report outcomes as if they were linked inevitably to the proximate economic drivers. At the heart of structuration accounts is the intent to generate explanations that incorporate contingency, conflict and a potential empirical role for activity. Accepting the premises of smoothed efficiency arguments replaced assumed/theorized process for observed/empirical process. March and colleagues warned against this putative functionalism with their precept 'history is not efficient' to recall the importance of studying process and politics (March and Olsen 1984).

Economic and organizational sociologists contend that institutions 'work' by mechanisms other than simple efficiency processes, and have provided evidence of variety of social market microstructures central in the dynamics of financial markets (Baker 1986; Carruthers 1996; Knorr-Cetina and Bruegger 2002). Fligstein (2001) provides a fully sociological and organizational account of dynamics in capitalist markets, focusing recent sociological theory and empirical studies of the making of financial markets that present political and cultural dynamics among state and other collective actors as drivers in creating local market forms (Carruthers 1996) and, more generally, in shaping the institutional features of markets (Fligstein 1996; Swedberg 1994) and industries (McGuire and Granovetter 2002; Ventresca and Porac 2002). This stream of research emphasizes the dual processes of state- and market-making, often in geographically and administratively bounded jurisdictions.

Second, institutional accounts in the sociological idiom emphasize the generative and constitutive aspects of institutions, in contrast to more narrowly-drawn 'constraint-within-choice' approaches to institutional analysis (Ingram and Cook 2000). This is distinctive to the sociological and cultural frame institutionalisms and their intellectual grounding in phenomenology, and contrasts to other 'new' institutionalisms in political science and economics which assume more materialist foundations. In our approach, social structure connotes both systems of meaning and the institutional arrangements of governance, with emphasis on the *constitutive rules* that define the meaningfulness of activity, in contrast to *regulative* rules that evoke preferred outcomes (Ruggie 1998, pp. 23–39; Searle 1995, pp. 26–8; Thomas et al. 1987).

This chapter has developed organizational field approaches with the empirical case of the structuration of the global exchange-traded markets industry field. We have argued that the mechanisms and content of global structuring of exchange-traded markets fields have developed in ways that shape expertise and global discourse and formal organization, that these, in turn, affect the development and governance of exchanges. The historical and empirical evidence supports a process model of structuration whereby global structuration occurs prior to and informs intermediate social structures, both formal organization at the regional level and new forms of social structures among the exchanges themselves. We have highlighted the institutional and cultural aspects of this growth of social structure, arguing that these global mechanisms bring expertise directly into the exchanges in ways alternative to the standard sources of national policy expertise. This is a preliminary case, but one that is vivid in contemporary media and consequential for policy and practice. As next steps, we will develop the interplay between field arguments and regime arguments, and continue the work on political and institutional mechanisms at work in the study of changed global infrastructures and changed governance forms, strategies, and means.

NOTES

1. We thank Marie-Laure Djelic and Sigrid Quack for comments on earlier versions, Lynn Prince Cooke, Katlyn Gao, Peter Levin, Komala Ramachandra, Geraldine Schneider, and Yu Zhuge for expert research assistance. We thank Kent Daniels, Jerry Davis, Ian Domowitz, Michael Fishman, Kathleen Hagerty, Peter Levin, Bob Korajczyk, Mitchell Peterson, Huggy Rao, Brian Uzzi, and Klaus Weber for discussions that introduced us to issues in financial markets. The chapter is better because of comments from session participants at Purdue University Strategy Colloquium, EGOS 2001, SMS 2000, and the Comparative Workshop at Stanford University. We acknowledge generous research support from the Department of Management and Organizations and from the Dean's Research Fund at the Kellogg School of Management, Northwestern University. In addition, Dean Dipak Jain and Professor Judy Messick supported fieldwork among European exchanges for this project through a Global Initiatives in Management faculty appointment for Ventresca.
2. 'Novel' is at least temporally relative – see Goetzmann et al. (2001) for the account of how the Shanghai Exchange demutualized and listed its own shares in 1891.
3. We do not discuss in detail outcomes such as specific changes in membership and listing rules for companies on particular exchanges, new development in valuation, cross-listings of equities, or the implications of stock exchange activity for ownership, liquidity, and variation in ownership patterns (see for this, Rao et al. 2000; Szyliowicz et al. 1999; Tainio et al. this volume; Useem 1998).
4. Thoughtful analysts point to the historical case of the 1870s–World War I as a comparable period of high internationalism, economic and political – evident in increased trade volumes, growth of capital markets, the rise of international political activity and efforts at global governance (Herren 2001; Murphy 1994).

5. Research in the organizations literature on fields has emphasized three key issues: (1) the dimensions along which field structuration proceeds, (2) the role of authoritative public and corporate actors (states and professions) in the development of fields, often as incidental outcomes to other 'professionalization' projects, and (3) a suggestive imagery of orders of domination and stratification, which they refer to as the presence of core/periphery. These studies often treat organizational fields as stable and already stratified – in the parlance, structurated.

6. Meyer et al. present three propositions: (1) worldwide expansion of scientific discourse and associations facilitated the rise of world environmental organization; (2) the rise of a world regime with an agenda broad enough to include facilitated expansion of organization around these issues; (3) the formation of official world organizations and structures, slowing rates at which new nongovernmental and multilaterial activity increase but consolidating existing activity; in sum – from informal to more official structures. International associations grow and arise prior to treaties or IGOs. Temporal order is substantively meaningful – in sum, the development of world social discourse and activity creates the grounding for more official multilateral and international structuration.

7. Lavelle argues that as world financial markets integrate, where equity transactions occurs still matters, if we understand 'globalization' to represent capital flows across borders, and 'integration' to mean the ability to buy and sell share of stock interchangeably across borders.

8. Meyer and colleagues (1997) propose an enriched conception of world 'regime' to include the discourse and organizational arrangements that comprise a global field of activity. 'A partially integrated collection of world-level organizations, understandings, and assumptions that specify the relationship of human society to nature ... codify rules and practices in exchange-traded markets.' They argue that a world regime comprises both discourse and organization. Discourse includes 'worldwide discussion and communication, universalistic, rationalized, and authoritative in character, occurring in international public arenas among policy professionals, scientists, and representatives of nation-states, in intergovernmental organizations, and in international nongovernmental associations' (1997, pp. 623–5).

REFERENCES

Ayling, David (1986), *The Internationalisation of Stockmarkets*, Vermont: Gower.
Baker, Wayne (1986), 'The social structure of a national securities market', *American Journal of Sociology*, **89** (4),775–811.
Boli, John and George M. Thomas (eds) (1999), *Constructing World Culture*, Stanford, CA: Stanford University Press.
Carruthers, Bruce (1996), *City of Capital*, Princeton, NJ: Princeton University Press.
Clemens, Elisabeth and James Cook (1999), 'Politics and institutionalism: explaining durability and change', *Annual Review of Sociology*, **25**, 441–66.
Coleman, James (1974), *Power and the Structure of Society*, New York: W.W. Norton.
Dezalay, Yves and Bryant Garth (1996), *Dealing in Virtue: International Commercial Arbitration and the Construction of a Transnational Legal Order*, Chicago, IL: University of Chicago Press.
DiMaggio, Paul (1983), 'State expansion and organizational fields', in R.H. Hall and R.E. Quinn, *Organizational Theory and Public Policy*, Beverly Hills, CA: Sage.
DiMaggio, Paul (1986), 'Support for the arts from private foundations', in Paul DiMaggio (ed.), *Nonprofit Enterprise in the Arts*, New York: Oxford University Press.
DiMaggio, Paul and Walter W. Powell (1983), 'The iron cage revisited: institutional isomorphism and collective rationality in organizational fields', *American Sociological Review*, **48**, 147–60.

Djelic, Marie-Laure (1998), *Exporting the American Model*, Oxford, UK: Oxford University Press.

Dobbin, Frank (1994), *Forging Industrial Policy: The United States, Britain, and France in the Railway Age*, New York: Cambridge University Press.

Domowitz, Ian (1994), 'Mergers and market power in the global financial exchange services industry', working paper 94-28, Institute for Policy Research, Northwestern University.

Drori, Gili S. (1997), *The National Science Agenda as a Ritual of Modern Nation-Statehood: The Consequences of National 'Science for National Development' Projects*, unpublished doctoral dissertation, Stanford University.

Drori, Gili S., John W. Meyer, Francisco O. Ramirez and Evan Schofer (2003), *Science in the Modern World Polity: Institutionalization and Globalization*, Stanford, CA: Stanford University Press.

Federation of Euro-Asian Stock Exchanges (FEAS) (2002), http://www.feas.com.

Fligstein, Neil (1996), 'Markets as politics: a political–cultural approach to market institutions', *American Sociological Review*, **61**, 656–73.

Fligstein, Neil (2001), *The Architecture of Markets*, Princeton, NJ: Princeton University Press.

Fligstein, Neil and Iona Mara-Drita (1996), 'How to make a market: reflections on the attempt to create a single market in the European Union', *American Journal of Sociology*, **102** (2), 1–33.

Galper, Joshua (1999), 'Three business models for the stock exchange industry', working paper, Paris: International Federation of Stock Exchanges (FIBV).

Galvin, Tiffany (2002), 'Organized interests and governance in the health care field: institutional perspectives on field-level dynamics',[1] *Academy of Management Journal*, **46**.

Goetzmann, William N. and Philippe Jorion (1999), 'Re-emerging markets', *Journal of Financial and Quantitative Analysis*, **34**, 1–32.

Goetzmann, William N., Andrey Ukhov and Ning Zhu (2001), 'China and the world financial markets, 1870–1930: modern lessons from historical globalization' (English version), October, working paper, The International Center for Finance, Yale School of Management.

Granovetter, Mark (1985), 'Economic action and social structure: the problem of embeddedness', *American Journal of Sociology*, **91** (3), 481–510.

Granovetter, Mark (1992), 'Economic institutions as social constructions: a framework for analysis', *Acta Sociologica*, **35**, 3–11.

Grasso, Richard (1999), 'Building a global equities marketplace', presentation at the Economic Club of New York, 14 December.

Guillén, Mauro (2001), *The Limits of Convergence: Globalization and Organizational Change in Argentina, South Korea, and Spain*, Princeton, NJ: Princeton University Press.

Haas, Ernst (1990), *When Knowledge is Power*, Berkeley, CA: University of California Press.

Haas, Ernst (1991), 'Why collaborate? Issue linkage and international regimes', *World Politics*, **45**, 357–405.

Hamilton, Gary and Nicole Biggart (1988), 'Market, culture and authority: a comparative analysis of management and organization in the Far East', *American Journal of Sociology*, **94**, S52–S94.

Herren, Madeline (2001), 'Governmental internationalism and the beginning of a new world order in the late nineteenth century', in Martin H. Geyer and Johannes

Paulmann (eds), *The Mechanics of Internationalism: Culture, Society, and Politics from the 1840s to the First World War*, Oxford: Oxford University Press, pp. 121–44.

Hollingsworth, Rogers (2000), 'Doing institutional analysis: implications for the study of innovations', *Review of International Political Economy*, 7 (4), 595–644.

ICC (1921), 'Proceedings of the First Congress', London, brochure no. 18.

Ingram, Paul and Lee Cook (2000), 'The new institutionalism in sociology', *Annual Review of Sociology*, 26.

International Federation of Stock Exchanges (FIBV), *Annual Reports*, various years, http://www.fibv.com

IOSCO (2001), 'Issue paper on exchange demutualization', Report of the Technical Committee of the International Organization of Securities Commissions, OICV-IOSCO, June, www.iosco.org.

Khoury, Sarkis (1990), *The Deregulation of the World Financial Markets: Myths, Realities, and Impact*, Westport, CT: Quorum Books.

Knorr-Cetina, Karin and Urs Bruegger (2002), 'Global microstructures: the virtual societies of financial markets', *American Journal of Sociology*, 107 (4), 905–50.

Krasner, Stephen D. (ed.) (1983), *International Regimes*, Ithaca, NY: Cornell University Press.

Lavelle, Kathryn (2001), 'Architecture of equity markets: the Abidjan regional bourse', *International Organization*, 55 (3), 717–42.

Lee, Reuben (1998), *What is an Exchange?*, Oxford: Oxford University Press.

Leleux, Benoit and Daniel Muzyka (2000), 'Courting the European growth firms: a survey of attitudes towards listing alternatives', *Venture Capital*, 2 (1), 41–59.

Leyshon, Andrew and Nigel Thrift (1997), *Money/Space: Geographies of Monetary Transformation*, New York, NY: Routledge.

March, James G. and Johan Olsen (1984), 'The new institutionalism: organizational factors in political life', *American Political Science Review*, 78.

McGuire, Patrick and Mark Granovetter (2002), 'The social construction of the electric utility industry, 1878–1919', in Marc Ventresca and Joseph Porac (eds), *Constructing Industries and Markets*, New York: Elsevier Science, Ltd.

Meyer, John W. (1994), 'Rationalized environments', in W. Richard Scott and John W. Meyer (eds), *Institutional Environments and Organizations*, Thousand Oaks, CA: Sage Publications, pp. 29–54.

Meyer, John W. (1997), 'The changing cultural content of the nation-state: a world society perspective', in George Steinmetz (ed.), *New Approaches to the State in the Social Sciences*, Ithaca, NY: Cornell University Press.

Meyer, John W., John Boli, George M. Thomas and Francisco O. Ramirez (1997), 'World society and the nation-state', *American Journal of Sociology*, 103 (1), 144–81.

Moran, Michael (1994), 'The state and the financial services revolution: a comparative analysis', in *The State in Western Europe: Retreat or Redefinition*, Newbury Park, Essex, UK: Frank Cass & Co., Ltd.

Morgan, Glenn (1997), 'The global context of financial services: national systems and the international political economy', in Glenn Morgan and David Knights (eds), *Regulation and Deregulation in European Financial Services*, London: Macmillan, pp. 14–41.

Morgan, Glenn and Andrew Sturdy (2000), *Beyond Organizational Change: Structure, Discourse and Power in UK Financial Services*, New York, NY: St. Martin's Press.

Murphy, Craig (1994), *International Organization and Industrial Change: Global Governance Since 1850*, Cambridge, UK: Polity Press.

North, Douglass (1990), *Structure and Change in Economic History*, New York: W.W. Norton & Co.

NASD (1960–1998), *NASD Annual Reports*, National Association of Securities Dealers, Gaithersburg, MD.

Porter, Tony (1993), *States, Markets, and Regimes in Global Finance*, London: St. Martin's Press.

Posner, Elliot (2002), *Financial Change and European Union Politics: The Origins of Europe's Market of Nasdaq Marketplaces*, unpublished doctoral dissertation, Department of Political Science, University of California Berkeley.

Powell, Walter W. and Paul DiMaggio (eds) (1991), *The New Institutionalism in Organizational Analysis*, Chicago, IL: University of Chicago Press.

Quack, Sigrid (2000), 'Transnational governance through global markets', paper presented at the European Group on Organization Studies (EGOS), 17th Colloquium, Helsinki.

Quack, Sigrid, Glenn Morgan and Richard Whitley (eds) (2000), *National Capitalisms, Global Competition, and Economic Performance*, Amsterdam: John Benjamin Publishing.

Radice, Hugo (2000), 'Globalization and national capitalisms: theorizing convergence and differentiation', *Review of International Political Economy*, **7** (4), 719–42.

Rajan, Raghuram G. and Luigi Zingales (2000), 'The great reversals: the politics of financial development in the 20th century', working paper, GSB, University of Chicago.

Rao, Hayagreeva, Gerald Davis and Andrew Ward (2000), 'Embeddedness, social identity and mobility: why firms leave NASDAQ and join NYSE', *Administrative Science Quarterly*, **45** (2), 268–92.

Ridgeway, George (1938), *Merchants of Peace*, New York, NY: Columbia University Press.

Ruggie, John Gerard (1998). *Constructing the World Polity: Essays on International Institutionalization*, New York, NY: Routledge.

Schofer, Evan (1999), 'Science associations in the international sphere, 1875–1990: the rationalization of science and scientization of society', in John Boli and George M. Thomas (eds) *Constructing World Culture*, Stanford, CA: Stanford University Press.

Schneiberg, Marc (1999), 'Political and institutional conditions for governance by association: private order and price controls in American fire insurance', *Politics and Society*, **27**, 67–103.

Schneiberg, Marc and Elisabeth Clemens (2002), 'The typical tools for the job: research strategies in institutional analysis', in Walter W. Powell and Daniel Jones (eds), *How Institutions Change*, Chicago: University of Chicago Press.

Scott, W. Richard (1995), *Institutions and Organizations*, Thousand Oaks, CA: Sage Publications.

Searle, John R. (1995), *The Construction of Social Reality*, New York, NY: Free Press.

Simmons, Beth (2001), 'The international politics of harmonization: the case of capital market regulation', *International Organization*, **55** (3), 589–620.

Spray, David E. (ed.) (1964), *The Principal Stock Exchanges of the World; Their Operation, Structure, and Development*, Washington, DC: International Economic Publishers.

Standifird, Stephen S., Marc Weinstein and Alan Meyer (2001), 'Establishing reputation on the Warsaw Stock Exchange: international brokers as legitimating agents', Working paper, Western Washington University.

Stinchcombe, Arthur (1965), 'Social structure and organizations', in James G. March (ed.), *Handbook of Organizations*, Chicago, IL: Rand McNally, pp. 142–93.

Stinchcombe, Arthur (1997), 'On the virtues of the old institutionalism', *Annual Review of Sociology*, **23**, 1–18.

Strang, David and John W. Meyer (1993), 'Institutional conditions for diffusion', *Theory and Society*, **22**, 487–511.

Swedberg, Richard (1994), 'Markets as social structures', in Neil J. Smelser and Richard Swedberg (eds), *Handbook of Economic Sociology*, Princeton, NJ: Princeton University Press, pp. 255–82.

Szyliowicz, Dara (1998), *Competitive Regimes and Entrepreneurial Activity: The Case of the United States Brokerage House Industry, 1965–1996*, unpublished doctoral dissertation, University of Illinois, Champaign, IL.

Szyliowicz, Dara, Teresa Nelson and Kevin Kennedy (1999), 'Shaping of strategic behaviour: global practices of listing on the NASDAQ Stock Exchange', working paper, Texas Tech University.

Thomas, George M., John W. Meyer, Francisco O. Ramirez and John Boli (1987), *Institutional Structure: Constituting State, Society and the Individual*, Beverly Hills, CA: Sage.

USAID http.www.usaid.org

Useem, Michael (1998), 'Corporate leadership in a globalizing equity market', *Academy of Management Executive*, **12** (4), 43–68.

Van Zandt, David E. (1991), 'The regulatory and institutional conditions far an international securities market', *Virginia Journal of International Law*, 32–47.

Ventresca, Marc J. (1995), *When States Count: Institutional and Political Dynamics in Modern Census Formation, 1800–1995*, unpublished doctoral dissertation, Stanford University.

Ventresca, Marc J. and Rodney Lacey (2001), 'Industry entrepreneur origins and activities in the emergence of US online database services, 1969–1982', working paper, Kellogg School of Management, Northwestern University.

Ventresca, Marc J. and Joseph Porac (eds) (2002), *Constructing Industries and Markets*, New York: Elsevier Publishing.

Verdier, Daniel (2001), 'Capital mobility and the origins of stock markets', *International Organization*, **55** (2), (Spring), 327–56.

Weber, Max (2000 [1924]), 'Stock and commodity exchanges', translated by Steven Lestition, Princeton University, *Theory and Society*, **29**, 305–38.

Weber, Max (1928), *General Economic History*, New York, NY: Greenberg.

Weber, Steven and Elliot Posner (2000), 'Creating a pan-European equity market: the origins of EASDAQ', *Review of International Political Economy*, **7** (4), 529–73.

WFE (2002), *Annual Report and Statistics 2001*, World Federation of Exchanges, www.world-exchanges.org.

Whitley, Richard (1992), *European Business Systems*, London, Sage.

Whitley, Richard (1999), *Divergent Capitalisms*, Oxford, UK: Oxford University Press.

Woodruff, David M. (2000), 'Rules for followers: institutional theory and the new politics of economic backwardness in Russia', *Politics and Society*, **2** (4), 437–82.

11. Structuring dispute resolution in transnational trade: competition and coevolution of public and private institutions

Dirk Lehmkuhl

INTRODUCTION[1]

Social life is replete with controversies, grievances and conflicts. One is actually tempted to say that the more people interact, the higher the probability that conflict will emerge and, as a consequence, the more important the existence of institutions for the settlement of disputes becomes. Generally, economic interactions are no exception to this general rule. Yet, insofar as economic exchanges are transnational interactions, they face peculiar challenges. In contrast to intra-national economic exchanges, which take place within a national framework with well-defined legal norms and rules, at the international level such a framework is largely missing. Although states have committed themselves to the liberal framework of the World Trade Organisation, cross-border transactions are still largely subject to national laws. These laws often vary significantly, thus conflicts between laws inevitably arise in transnational contracts.

The claim that territorially restricted laws inevitably lead to constitutional uncertainty in transnational[2] trade is anything but new (Schmidtchen and Schmidt-Trenz 1995). However, today as in the past, the absence of an international regulatory framework that guarantees rights as they are guaranteed in the national legal framework has not prevented economic actors from crossing borders. A long-range view shows that throughout 'recorded history new forms of trade have disturbed the established political order' (Condliffe 1951, p. 832). And '[i]t would be wrong to believe that trade awaited the restoration of law and order' (Condliffe 1951, p. 42) to flourish and develop.

The historical explanation lies in a two-dimensional solution to the problems of transnational contracting and disputes. On the one hand, trade codes (such as the *lex mercatoria moderna* or new law merchant) acquired strong normative power and proved capable of governing the behaviour of individuals in economic transactions, both at local and translocal levels. On the other hand, private commercial arbitration, as a mechanism for solving disputes in translocal and later transnational trade, grew in significance. Some scholars even claim that the contemporary evolution of a worldwide culture of transnational arbitration links the two dimensions: it implies the definition of shared beliefs and norms that become generally accepted principles and practices and provide the basis of action (Holtzmann 1999, p. 303).

One interesting aspect of this two-dimensional solution is that it represents a form of self-regulation within particular transnational communities (see the parallel with 'self-disciplining transnational communities' defined by Djelic and Quack in the conclusion to this volume). As a solution for handling translocal disputes, furthermore, it existed before national and international legislation on cross-border transactions and may be in the process of supplanting it again (Carbonneau 1990). Over time, the early forms of privately created sets of norms and structures were taken over and absorbed by public entities or bodies – be they city-states, city-leagues, sovereign states or international organizations. There are signs and increasing evidence, however – to which we will get below – that a reverse process may be in the making today, at least in part (for example Dezalay and Garth 1996).

These considerations can be read as a warning not to overstate the novelty of contemporary social, political and economic developments (Whitley in this volume). At the same time, they point to a complex interaction through time between different actors and multiple rationalities that function in different social and/or geographical territories. The institutionalization of mechanisms for handling dispute resolution in the transnational context reveals the competition between and coevolution of various logics, actors and interests – some originating from the public or semi-public realm, others belonging to the private sphere. This process reveals as well the 'rubbing against each other' of multiple national rationalities together with the role of more emergent actors and communities with less clear national identities (Djelic and Quack in the conclusion to this volume).

The approach to this study rests on three general assumptions. First, the institutions that function today to facilitate trade and to provide legal certainty are embedded in the social, political and economic fabric characteristic of our contemporary period. Second, those institutions also reveal and reflect a long history of preexisting solutions as well as the evolution through time of that fabric. Third, actors who live in and function within those institutional frameworks are not merely constrained by them. They also contribute to making them evolve through time. Actors or networks of actors are key mechanisms for bringing along institutional change (see Djelic and Quack in the introduction to this volume). In our contemporary world, those actors or networks of actors are still very much set within national spaces and rationalities. The dynamic process of 'institution building' at the transnational level is thus bound to reflect the 'rubbing against each other' of these multiple national rationalities. An interesting question is how far this process will reverberate and have an impact in turn upon national institutions and rationalities. Hence a central focus in this chapter will be the point of intersection and interaction between national and transnational levels.

In the first section of this chapter, we spend some time identifying and describing the major issues associated with cross-border trade. We also look at the solutions that have been found to cope with these problems, both historically and today, and trace the evolutions in particular of the new law merchant. In the second section, we look at the contemporary process of institution building, particularly with respect to transnational arbitration. We focus on two defining dimensions of that process – a constitutive competition between and coevolution of public and private actors and logics and a constant interplay between transnational and national levels.

PRIVATE NORMS AND THE GOVERNANCE OF TRANSNATIONAL TRADE

The contemporary international system is made up of sovereign nation-states, each with their own socio-political institutions, legal order and cultural identities. The heterogeneity of this constellation forms the backdrop for cross-border transactions and economic exchange. In this context, naturally, 'Collisions of norms and gaps between different norm systems' are standard fares, 'an accord in decisions is often coincidental, and the assistance of the judicial and penal institutions in foreign countries is not at all a matter of course' (Schmidtchen and Schmidt-Trenz 1995, p. 16). Whereas the territoriality of law represents the foundation for the 'protective state' (Buchanan 1975, p. 95) such an unequivocal legal basis is largely absent at the international level. In the face of specific political and economic uncertainties, the development of a number of self-regulated private business institutions is credited with guaranteeing the extension of cross-border trade and transactional security. Amongst these institutionalized private safeguards that reduce risk in international trade, the so-called *lex mercatoria moderna* or new law merchant, on the one hand, and the various arbitrational organizations, on the other, are of key importance. The rest of this section focuses on the new law merchant – on its origins and evolution in light particularly of the interplay between public and private norm-setting capacities. We turn to transnational arbitration in the next section.

Norms in Cross-border Trade – an Historical Perspective

An historical take on the issue of cross-border trade shows that the development of private norms and rules is anything but new. Merchants have always, historically, devised their own practices and rules to ensure adequate protection for themselves and their interests (Stoecker 1990). Already the *ius gentium* of ancient Rome was tailored with the ambitious objective of governing disputes with and between non-Romans (Juenger 2000, p. 172). In the twelfth and thirteenth centuries, the needs of an increasingly mobile sea-borne trade community led to the creation of the cosmopolitan *lex mercatoria*. 'Out of his own needs and his own views the merchant of the Middle Ages created the Merchant Law' (Trakman 1980, p. 5f). From the outset the fulcrum of commerce was custom rather than law. The merchant law was distinct from local, feudal, royal and ecclesiastical law, and its primary seat and source – both in terms of origins and legitimacy – were mercantile customs. Another specificity of merchant law was that it was monitored and administered not by professional judges but by the merchants themselves (Berman and Kaufman 1978, p. 225). The official and actual law, enacted by public authorities, did little more than echo the existing customs of the merchant community. Its specific link to the Western legal tradition was expressed in the qualities it shared with other legal systems of the time – objectivity, universality, reciprocity, participatory adjudication, integration and growth (Berman 1983, p. 341).

In the middle ages, trans-local trade generally had precedence over local trade and it tended to require more business acumen and sophistication. The risks and challenges associated with it were also greater. Hence the setting up of norms, regular practices and rules was originally associated with non-local trade. Trans-local mercantile law provided a model for commercial transactions and their regulations in general including at the local level (Berman 1983, p. 342). In other words, between the eleventh and sixteenth centuries, merchant practice was the primary source of regulation, while law functioned as a secondary control over commerce. By increasingly gaining a universal character, this cosmopolitan system of regulation transcended the local diversity of the socio-political environment in which economic transactions were embedded.

This socio-political environment would soon change however with the rise in particular of nation-states in the post-medieval period (Berman 1983; Greif et al. 1994; Spruyt 1994). The emergence of the nation-state came together with a structuring of national jurisdictions and a progressive expansion of their reach. The principles and the rules defining the *lex mercatoria* were after a while embodied in national domestic legal systems, which were in line with and serving state policies and national interests (Trakman 1981). This 'nationalization' took place from the seventeenth century onwards and meant that private mechanisms were partly relegated to a place of secondary importance.

In the twentieth century, it seems that the pendulum has again been swinging in the reverse direction. The innovative and flexible nature of private mechanisms has emerged as a striking asset of mercantile norms. Older rules and customs have been adapted to fit changing circumstances. An increase in cross-border trading and new types of problems has also led to the setting-up of new norms and procedures.

What is the New Law Merchant?

In discussing the nature of the new law merchant, one can easily be trapped in a stalemate or 'dialogue of the deaf' (Fortier 2001, p. 122). Transnationalists argue on the one hand that only the evolution of an autonomous set of transnational norms is apposite to overcome the deficiencies of a system characterized by a multiplicity of highly diverse national regulations – that system creating many obstacles to cross-border trade. Traditionalists, on the other hand, believe that there can be no such beast as a non-national or an 'anational' system of rules and norms for the governance of economic transactions. In the present context, however, we will not enter that debate. Rather, we will dwell on the origins and nature of the new law merchant. Doing so gives us interesting insights into underlying processes of transnationalization and their dynamics, pointing in particular towards the actors involved in those processes.

The new law merchant has traditionally not consisted in a comprehensive body of provisions, nor does it do so today. Rather, it is associated with a large number of sectoral and regional differences. What is referred to today as *lex mercatoria moderna*[3] may be defined as an 'institutional arrangement consisting of trade usages, model contracts, standard clauses, general legal principles and international commercial arbitration' (Volckart and Mangels 1996, p. 7). The new law merchant provides much more than mere informal guidelines. The label 'institutional arrangement' is right because the new law merchant is a set of norms and workable tools structuring and governing relationships in cross-border economic transactions (see Djelic and Quack in this volume for a parallel definition). The rules and principles of the new law merchant extirpate contractual provisions from embedding national contexts. As such they contribute to overcoming a situation described as the constitutional uncertainty of transnational trade. Basically, there are three different mechanisms for getting there.

The first and most important such mechanism is the standardization of contractual provisions. Contractual provisions are being standardized into full-fledged systems of provisions that may come to replace national law. There are two variants – either model contracts or standardized clauses for specific transactions. These standardized contractual provisions mean that different economic actors and different economic sectors share and follow encompassing, transnational and uniform systems of rules. Standardized contracts govern almost the entire market for bulk products and play an important role in international transport by sea and air, as well as in the construction industry or in finance.

The standardization of commercial clauses, or even the codification of transnational rules, occurs in a wide array of different fora. One the one hand, standardization takes place within private organizations. Transnational branch organizations and interest associations frequently establish codes of conduct that combine general contractual principles with sector-specific or sub-sector-specific clauses. In addition to such sectoral codification of trade customs, one finds transnational private organizations with more general approaches. The International Chamber of Commerce in Paris is one example and its International Commercial Terms (Incoterms) provide a good illustration of how a private organization can manage to create influential although legally non-binding norms with universal reach independently of public influence. Incoterms codify contractual standards and aspire to harmonize the common practices of various countries. Incoterms are regularly updated and, if necessary, revised. Once agreed to by the contracting parties, both national courts and arbitral tribunals recognize their contractual nature.

Private organizations are not the only active 'formulating agencies' (Schmitthoff 1987; Stein 1995) that contribute to overcoming national regulatory diversity. Other important actors are public or semi-public international organizations that work to harmonize and unify law in international trade. One example is the 'United Nations Commission on International Trade Law' (UNCITRAL), established by the United Nations General Assembly in 1966 to progressively harmonize and unify law bearing on international trade. Its most successful efforts resulted in the 1980 Convention on Contracts for the Sale of Goods. This was a model contract law that could and should be transferred and transposed, it was suggested, into national legislation. Still another example is the International Institute for the Unification of Private Law that defined in 1994 Principles of International Commercial Contracts (UNIDROIT Principles). One thinks also of the Principles of European Contract Law (Lando Principles, named in honour of the commission chair Ole Lando). This particular set of principles was published by the Commission on European Contract Law in 1995 and expanded in 1999. Those last two sets of principles reveal an attempt to incorporate into domestic regulations homogeneous and transnational commercial practices or customs that will grant merchants a maximum amount of autonomy and flexibility. Both sets of principles are designed to function as model laws for national legislation. Hence, in a very direct sense, they are clear and concrete examples of how privately emerging transnational norms and rules can penetrate national laws.

It should be mentioned, finally, that the Center for Transnational Law published in 1996 a list of principles, rules and standards for the *Lex Mercatoria* (CENTRAL Principles). In contrast to the formalized approaches of the

UNIDROIT and Lando Principles, the CENTRAL list is characterized by an open technique. This is more likely to provide the adaptability and flexibility that are needed to follow and take into account the rapid development of transnational trade.

We now turn to a second type of mechanism that contributes to removing and decoupling cross-border activities from diverging national regulations – the displacement of state regulation by broad contractual agreements. Such self-regulatory or self-executing agreements are not restricted to substantial contract matters. They also include provisions of procedural concern, including with respect to conflict resolution. All these provisions aim at maintaining the parties' interests throughout the contractual relationship. As self-executing contracting is quite demanding in terms of pre-contract negotiations, these forms of agreement are more likely in long-term business relationships bearing, for example, on the exploitation of raw materials or on the transfer of technical know-how (Stein 1995, pp. 41ff).

The third mechanism, finally, refers to the institutionalization of cross-border activities within transnational organizations or transnational spaces (Stein 1995, pp. 41ff). Such transnational schemes take the shape, for example, of multi-national firms, transnational cartels or transnational interest associations (Kronstein 1963; Muchlinski 1997; Knill and Lehmkuhl 1998, see also Lilja and Moen in this volume), but also of more unstructured negotiation spaces or arenas (McNichol and Bensedrine in this volume). The tendency in that context is to internalize juridical issues within the organizational system or field, par-ticularly through inter-firm contracts and the setting-up of voluntary codes of conduct (Muchlinski 1997; Robé 1997).

Competition and Co-evolution in the Process of Norm Setting

The information presented thus far shows much more than the significance and practical involvement of private actors in the process of norm setting and elab-oration. It also points to important evolutions in and around the law merchant. Historically, a standard argument against the viability of the law merchant has been that its constituent principles and rules were vague and ambiguous. This standard argument has been losing ground recently and acceptance is getting more widespread of a self-organized and self-disciplined process as a means to elaborate and formulate 'rules of law' (Art. 17 (1) ICC Arbitration Rules of 1998). Insofar as international formulating agencies have tended to reproduce, formalize and standardize the norms that were formerly created by private parties involved in cross-border economic exchange or by private arbitral tribunals, we are confronted with a 'reversal of the traditional legal process' with an 'advancement of the law from below' (Berger 2000a, p. 97) or from the periphery (Teubner 2000). These norms originate in the interactions between private individuals in the first place, and they are only subsequently explicitly codified and standardized. When codification indeed takes place, it does so either at the global or European level, and actors, as we have seen, can be either mostly private, mostly public or even a motley combination of both.

The consequence is that decentralized forms of self-organization and codified rule or norm systems, self-enforcing contracts and other private strategies for conflict avoidance tend to substitute in time for public regulation and national laws. And they do so at a transnational level, thus contributing to the structuration of an authentically transnational institutional frame or set of rules of the game. Some even talk of an 'authentically global law' (Teubner 1997, pp. 3–28). At the end of the day, this process of explicit or creeping codification at a transnational level may lead to a partial erosion of national diversities. Indeed the contemporary movement does share common features, as we argued above, with the pre-nation-states situation, where the regulation of trans-local commercial interactions transcended the 'local diversities of socio-political environments' (Berman 1983, p. 42).

The type of privately created norms presented here differs from other forms of private norms such as those we find emerging, for instance, in standard setting organizations (Mattli 2001; Brunsson and Jacobsson 2000; Schmidt and Werle 1998). In the case of standard setting organizations, the authority to generate norms reflects a delegation of responsibility by public actors. In the cases described here, private norm generation is rather the consequence of an absence of public actors. Instead of public actors delegating *ex ante* norm generating responsibilities to private actors, autonomous private action is only sanctioned and legitimated *ex post* through public and state regulation. This was true in pre-nation-states times and remains so today, in the context of the development of the modern version of transnational mercantile regulation.

In the contemporary world, national states make an effort to catch up with the regulatory capacity of private actors. They do so either unilaterally, by determining the spatial reach of substantive rules, including the exterritorial application of national law, or by multilateral efforts aimed at reducing conflicts and incompatibilities between laws. In this respect it might be interesting to ask whether processes of legalization[4] have any impact on private self-regulatory capacities (for that concept see Knill and Lehmkuhl 2002). The European integration process, with its far-reaching purpose of legal integration and harmonization, makes Europe an interesting case in point. What can be observed, in that instance, is that public actors are guiding efforts aimed at incorporating the dual structure of 'freedom and coercion' into contract law – aimed in other words at accommodating private autonomy with court supervision (Joerges 1995).

TRANSNATIONAL COMMERCIAL ARBITRATION

> In these [arbitration] cases as well as in many other cases, I did invoke in my briefs, memorials or oral arguments ... rules of transnational law or the lex mercatoria, but, on practically all occasions, although all these cases were won, the arbitrators, if I remember correctly, preferred in general to avoid any specific reference to transnational law or the lex mercatoria. ... On a number of occasions, the arbitrators have indeed resorted to these new legal concepts but left them nameless.

This quotation, from an 'eminent European arbitration specialist' (Berger et al. 2001, p. 106), provides some interesting insights into the ways in which transnational disputes are settled. To avoid the difficulties of a debate on the character of the law merchant, arbitrators in fact prefer to be secretive about the norms that guide their decisions. At the same time, however, there is no doubt that the law merchant plays a role in the private resolution of transnational conflicts. Self-regulation or self-governance through contract has been a 'critically important doctrinal and practical factor in liberating the international arbitral process from the regimes of national law' (Pechota 1998, p. 260). At the heart of this process lies not only the autonomy of contracting parties to choose the rules of law they deem appropriate for their exchange relationship, but also their autonomy to delegate the authority to resolve their potential conflicts to a transnational arbitral tribunal. In this respect, transnational commercial arbitration is part and parcel of the emergence and evolution of transnational governance, 'conceived as the process through which the rules of the system in place in a social setting are adapted to the needs of those who live under them' (Stone Sweet 1999, p. 147).

Commercial Arbitration in Historical Perspective[5]

The expansion of commerce not only led to the formulation of merchant law, it also fostered the emergence and stimulated the use of merchant or commercial judges. Adjudicators were generally selected from the ranks of the merchants on the basis of their commercial experience, their objectivity and their seniority. It was expected that a merchant judge be able to assess mercantile custom, to appreciate the needs of merchants and, in particular, to assess the relevance of the facts surrounding a transaction and to perceive changing trade dynamics (Trakman 1981, p. 15).

Examples of such commercial courts include market and fair courts or guild courts, all of which were non-professional community tribunals. One also finds local maritime courts in seaport towns – 'admiralty courts' – with jurisdiction over both commercial and maritime transactions involving transport of goods by sea. Other examples were so-called courts of staples in England, Wales and Ireland, that handled trade disputes in certain 'staple' products such as wool, leather or lead. One can think as well of urban mercantile courts in Northern Italy, which were gradually granted jurisdiction over all mercantile cases within Northern Italian cities (Trakman 1981, pp. 16f; Berman 1983, p. 346).

These commercial tribunals devised their own *modus operandi* to deal with the cases that came before them. As they gathered together a vast body of commercial experience, commercial judges increasingly managed both to govern trade conflicts with reasonable standards and to ensure local and foreign merchants of just treatment (Trakman 1981; Berman 1983). Over time, however, as these forms of private adjudication developed and were institutionalized, they encountered a fate quite similar to that of the law merchant. In post-medieval times, they went through a period of relative decline and subordination. Although merchant guilds did not disappear, emerging nation-states undeniably set limits and constraints. Then, in the twentieth century and in particular after World War II, there has been a significant revival of private adjudication that parallels the revival of the law merchant (North and Thomas 1973; Landes and Posner 1979).

During the second half of the twentieth century, along with the development of transnational trade, the number of disputes has increased. Commercial arbitration has come back to the fore in that context as a widely accepted method for settling transnational commercial disputes (Mentschikoff 1961; Berger 2000a). A recent statistical survey of the International Chamber of Commerce (ICC) gives a sense of the increasing role played by private commercial arbitration in recent years. By 1976, only 3000 requests for arbitration had been filed with the ICC, while in 1998, the ICC Secretariat received its 10 000th case. Thus, more than two-thirds of all cases of arbitration brought to the ICC arose in the last 20 years of its 75-year existence (Craig et al. 2000, p. 2).

Commercial activities are embedded in a number of national provisions and multilateral agreements that also provide the regulatory framework within which arbitrational institutions have evolved and private dispute settlement now takes place. Over the second half of the twentieth century, the extension of arbitration has accompanied the extension of the liberal regulatory framework, which for its part has allowed for an increase in cross-border economic activities. In that context, arbitration complements public litigation at the international level, as public and private conflicts address different actors. Whereas the dispute settlement procedure of the World Trade Organisation addresses disputes between states, and the Washington Convention of 1965 settles disputes in which one party is a state or a state entity, private commercial arbitration handles disputes deriving from private cross-border economic exchange.

It is estimated today that about 90 per cent of all cross-border contracts contain an arbitration clause (Bernstein et al. 1998; Guzman 2000, p. 128). This gives some indication of the comparative dominance of private transnational dispute settlement over state-centred forms of litigation (Dezalay and Garth

1996). While a large number of international trade associations have their own conflict resolution procedures (Bernstein 1996; Benson 1999, p. 93), old institutions administrating dispute resolution have expanded, and we have witnessed the rapid appearance of new institutions the world over. Amongst these, the International Court of Arbitration of the International Chamber of Commerce (Paris), the London Court of International Arbitration, the Chartered Institute of Arbitrators, the American Arbitration Association (New York), the Vienna Arbitration Centre, and the Arbitration Institute of the Stockholm Chamber of Commerce are the most prominent providers of institutionalized arbitration in the Western World. The reform of arbitration laws in many countries in recent years demonstrates the increased importance of arbitral procedures at both the international and national level.[6] Many of those national reforms of arbitration laws have been inspired by the 1985 arbitration model law of the United Nations Commission on International Trade.

Private commercial arbitration offers a number of advantages over litigation in state courts – and these advantages resemble those of its medieval ancestor. Foremost among these advantages is the high degree of procedural flexibility in the choice of the location and arbitrators. Both parties can influence the choice of the three arbitrators generally required, since each may name at least one of them. Major multi-million dollar arbitration cases even imply so-called 'beauty contests' in which each party conducts interviews with possible candidates prior to nominating its arbitrator. The third arbitrator is then chosen by the first two arbitrators, or in some other manner (Bernstein et al. 1998, p. 204; Berger 2000b, p. 25). Arbitrators are normally experts in the issue at stake.

On the whole, arbitration is less time-consuming and more cost-effective, due in part to the fact that it often only involves one procedure. Arbitration also guarantees secrecy. Neither the procedures nor the awards are open to the public. This allows for better protection of commercially important information. Unlike public litigation, private arbitration has less effect on the general commercial relationship between the parties. If only a limited aspect of their long-term or complex commercial interaction is touched upon, and these relations are highly valued by both partners, then they will both prefer arbitration in order to avoid that controversies over one issue cast a shadow over their entire interaction.

Contemporary Transnational Commercial Arbitration: Pushing Back the Boundaries

Privacy and confidentiality, as just mentioned, are important aspects of private commercial arbitration. This holds not only for the procedure before the arbitral tribunal itself but also for the arbitral award. Hence, parties only reluctantly agree to have an award published and, if so, only anonymously. Nevertheless, the 'veil has been lifted' and several institutions have started to publish awards.[7] By doing so, they have contributed to a more consistent development in the field of arbitration, as more recent awards could be based on earlier decisions. This has not only increased the importance of arbitration as part of the process of creating transnational rules, it has also provided important examples that illustrate the relationship between mandatory national provisions and the scope and autonomy of private transnational arbitration.

That said, it is important to specify that transnational commercial arbitration takes place at the crossing of four different systems of law. First, we find the law that governs the recognition and enforcement of the agreement to arbitrate. Then there is the law that governs the actual arbitration proceedings. Third, we have the set of rules that the arbitral tribunal must apply to the substantive matters in dispute before it. And to that we have to add the law that governs the recognition and enforcement of the award. Most of the time, these systems are not linked to the same jurisdiction and they often differ significantly. For instance, the law governing substantive matters may differ from the law of the seat of arbitration, which may well differ from the law of the place where enforcement is sought, which, in turn, may differ from the law in force where the parties reside.

Going through the various publications of arbitral awards, one can find ample evidence that, in all four dimensions, the autonomy of private transnational dispute settlement has increased significantly in the past two decades. This increase of autonomy implies that, with respect to all dimensions in which the settlement of transnational disputes potentially touches national provisions, this self-regulatory mechanism has become increasingly detached from national law and from the control of national institutions. Let me briefly present some evidence to back up this assertion.

The *first* dimension to be considered has to do with what can be legitimately submitted to an arbitral tribunal. To restrict the matters that may lawfully be submitted to arbitration means limiting the parties' autonomy to engage in arbitration and the arbitrators' authority to rule. Traditionally, national laws determined that a number of areas were non-arbitrable. These areas, which are frequently characterized as entailing issues of national interest or belonging to the public policy realm, generally include antitrust law, security law, intellectual property law or bankruptcy law. In recent years, however, there are clear signs of a broader interpretation of the notion of arbitrability. Not only is non-judicial dispute settlement found in international financial transactions, there are also areas within competition law that have become subject to arbitration. The *Mitsubishi* decision of the US Supreme Court of 1985 and the *Eco Swiss China Time v. Benetton* decision of the European Court of Justice of 1999[8] are outstanding examples of this. In both cases it has been acknowledged that, although the disputes came under the purview of national or European competition provisions, they were still arbitrable.

The *second* dimension refers to the procedural law governing the process of transnational dispute settlement. Frequently, the principle of party autonomy is interpreted as allowing the parties to customize the arbitral process to the needs of their transactions. They can even eliminate trial techniques that might prove inconvenient or unsuitable. The actual reach of this freedom, however, repeatedly raises controversies. It is, for instance, questionable whether the choice of a place of arbitration implies the choice of the procedural law governing arbitration.[9]

However, neither the delocalization theory nor the claim that parties have the right to choose to detach themselves from systems of national law has yet become generally accepted (Redfern and Hunter 1991, p. 81ff; Collier and Lowe 1999, pp. 232f; Gaillard and Savage 1999, no. 1205ff). Whereas Article 15 of the 1998 arbitration rules of the International Chamber of Commerce in Paris supports the so-called delocalization theory by stating that parties may choose not to have any municipal procedural law applied to the arbitration, a counter position is expressed by an English court stating that 'our jurisprudence does not recognise the concept of arbitral procedures floating in the transnational firmament, unconnected with any municipal system of law' (Collier and Lowe 1999, p. 249).

The most controversial discussion on the autonomy of transnational arbitration revolves around the *third* dimension, that is, the question regarding which rules govern the substance of the dispute, as this is the dimension in which the doctrinal controversies about the character of the law merchant and the autonomy of the arbitral tribunal culminate. On the one hand, an arbitral tribunal may apply mandatory national law. Both the *Mitsubishi* and *Eco Swiss China Time v. Benetton* cases are examples of this first pattern. What makes these cases even more intriguing is that a transnational arbitral tribunal not only rendered an award that applied mandatory national provisions, but also that it did so in both cases in an area that has not traditionally been considered arbitrable. The fact that national courts have recognized both arbitral awards as enforceable has been interpreted as a final step in the transformation of transnational arbitration – from a consensual exercise of contractual autonomy into an exercise of state adjudicatory power (McConnaughay 1999, p. 456).

A second pattern is that where an arbitral award applies non-state rules, thus displacing mandatory law. This displacement may either be implied in the parties' contractual agreement or be enforced by an arbitrator who is granted the freedom to choose the applicable law without concern for otherwise mandatory provisions. The arbitrator may base his decision on customs and trade usages. For instance, in the case of *Compania Valenciana de Cementos Portland v. Primary Coal Inc.* of 1989/1991, the French *Court de Cassation* recognized an arbitrator's right to refer to the *lex mercatoria* in settling the dispute before him. In accordance with the new French arbitration provision, the court has authorized arbitrators to look beyond the application of a particular national law and to apply rules of various types and origins. The French system is only one among numerous legal systems that allows arbitrators to apply transnational rules when the parties are silent about which law is to govern the substance of disputes.

The fact that the decision of the French court carefully avoided taking a position on whether general principles of law and trade usages, including the *lex mercatoria*, constitute a distinct legal order can be interpreted as another example illustrating the introductory quotation of this section. This indicates in other words the discrepancy between the practical importance of commercial rules and the secretiveness surrounding their use.

The *fourth* interface between transnational arbitration and national law happens around the recognition and enforcement of the arbitral award. Neither cross-border commercial transactions nor the resolution of their disputes and the implementation of resolutions float freely in the transnational firmament. Rather all those stages are physically located (for parallel arguments see McNichol and Bensedrine; Ventresca et al. in this volume). As Sassen (1998, p. 96) puts it 'to a large extent the global economy materializes in concrete processes situated in specific places'. Moreover, it is sometimes being claimed that the entire system of private commercial arbitration ultimately depends on the compulsory power of the state to induce enforcement against assets in its territorial jurisdiction.

Nevertheless, even at the level of this fourth interface we can observe a significant increase in the autonomy of commercial arbitration. Most contemporary national arbitral laws narrow the scope of the review at this final stage. They contain a general regulation favouring the enforcement of foreign arbitrational awards and limiting the grounds on which enforcement of those awards may be refused (Stewart 1994, p. 164; Carbonneau 1998). Thus, the main international conventions[10] on the recognition of arbitral awards prevent national courts from reviewing the arbitrators' decision on the core issues of the dispute, accordingly strengthening the principle of party autonomy. Yet, despite the clear trend towards extending arbitrational adjudicatory authority and harmonizing basic notions and perceptions, which the internationalization of arbitration has brought about, this development has been uneven. Even today, there are still significant differences in national regulations with respect to the degree of autonomy from courts' judicial review. Portugal and Belgium, for instance, do not allow the judicial review of transnational awards. The French and Swiss statutory frameworks have even further narrowed the scope of review (Drobnig 1990; Blessing 1992; Gottwald 1997; Bernstein et al. 1998; Carbonneau 1998). By contrast, British law is still reluctant to extend the autonomy of arbitration, despite several amendments in both theory and practice (Landes and Posner 1979).

Dynamics of Transnational Commercial Arbitration and their Evolution

The interpretation which has been presented thus far describes the settlement of cross-border disputes as a process that has become increasingly detached from national restrictions. To explain this development we can refer to a range of aspects that are located both inside and outside the arbitration process itself.

Detaching transnational arbitration from national review

One important aspect is that, parallel to the continuing increase in foreign trade, private commercial arbitration has become a growth industry and a distinct market, which follows rules of supply and demand (Dezalay and Garth 1996). As such, international commercial arbitration is not only subject to economic policies that spur transnationalization and liberalization, but also to the dynamics of regulatory competition among states (Héritier et al. 1996). In other words, a favourable framework for the arbitration process is expected to be positive for the domestic industry. To create such favourable conditions, nation-states have steadily amended their domestic regulations by expanding party autonomy and by restricting the scope of the judicial review of arbitrational agreements and awards (Carbonneau 2000, p. 23). This 'scramble among Western European nations' (Mustill 1989; Park 1989) in competition for the arbitration business has in the end significantly contributed to the waning role of the state in the resolution of private cross-border disputes (for the story of a parallel process of competition this time across American states and around corporate legisla- tion at the turn of the twentieth century with as a consequence less power to the states and more to the corporations see Roy 1997).

A second important aspect contributing to the self-sustaining character of transnational commercial arbitration is the high degree of voluntary compliance with arbitral awards. Although the confidentiality of arbitration proceedings makes exact statistical surveys difficult, it is assumed that awards are settled vol- untarily in an overwhelming number of cases, with the losing party abiding freely (Stoecker 1990, p. 105; Berger 1992, p. 17; Nienhaber 2000, p. 100). This is especially surprising since this voluntary compliance occurs in the absence of straightforward legal sanctions.

This finding qualifies the frequently heard claim that the autonomy of arbi- tration comes to an end with enforcement (McConnaughay 1999). In fact, what we find is a *reputation-based* compliance mechanism that resonates with Axelrod's 'shadow of the future' (1990, p. 174). At the heart of reputation- based explanations of the voluntary acceptance of arbitral awards is a purely commercial mechanism designed to increase the transparency of the post-contractual behaviours of firms.[11] It has to do with the common practice, characteristic of numerous associations, of blacklisting and publishing the names of recalcitrant members who fail to comply with the decision of an arbitral tribunal. This rather draconian method of public shaming does not benefit the injured party, but it may cause substantial economic harm to the non-compliant party, and it is thus a powerful incentive for compliance.[12]

At this stage, it is necessary to take a step back. The movement towards greater autonomy of arbitration is real but it is not a smooth or one-sided process. There are developments that tend to counter the progressive emancipation of arbitration from national constraints. Those countervailing forces come from inside as well as outside the arbitration process.

Limits to autonomy: bureaucratization and political appropriation

A first development has to do with changing rules of the (arbitration) game. This change reflects both increasing competition between different arbitral organizations and an evolution in the composition of actors and in their attitudes towards arbitration. The rapid expansion of the arbitration market has awakened new appetites. Together with the multiplication and diversification of arbitration places and institutions came competition and a proliferation of arbitral rules (Dezalay and Garth 1996, p. 44; Holtzmann 1999, p. 305). As such, this proliferation seems to be an ironic development. After all, the primary goal of arbitral organizations should be to facilitate and not to complicate the arbitral procedure. In fact, organizations that offer arbitral services have used those differences in rules as competitive assets.

Arbitral organizations have thus proliferated and entered into acute competition. Hence, the arbitration court of the International Chamber of Commerce in Paris (ICC) has lost its position as a quasi-monopoly. Still, the ICC remains the main and central organization for the private settlement of cross-border disputes (Dezalay and Garth 1996, p. 45). In recent years, the internal dynamics of the ICC reveal changes in structure but also in the identity of actors. The key role both real and symbolic of the ICC means that this may have important implications for the arbitral process in general.

The story is one of transformation in only two generations. For the pioneers of arbitration – for the most part honoured European law professors – arbitration was considered a 'duty and not a career', and it was argued that arbitrators 'should render an occasional service, provided on the basis of long experience and wisdom acquired in law, business, or public service' (Dezalay and Garth 1996, pp. 34f). However, the boom in cases deriving from the success of transnational arbitration challenged the structure of the ICC and made it necessary to recruit a new generation of arbitrators. While the authority of the old generation was based upon an aura of experience and charisma, the new generation defined itself as a professional group (Larson 1979). They presented themselves as 'entrepreneurs selling their services to business practitioners, contrasting their qualities to the "amateurism" or "idealism" of their predecessors' (Dezalay and Garth 1996, pp. 36f). As a consequence of this change – both real and symbolic – in the identity of actors, the structure of the arbitral organization has also evolved. The technical side of arbitration has been strengthened and the ICC has become a more bureaucratic organization (for a parallel evolution in the French asset management industry, see Kleiner in this volume).

The increasing importance of Anglo-American law firms in transnational arbitration has added further momentum to the change of rules in the arbitration game (see also Tainio et al.; McKenna et al.; Kleiner; Whitley in this volume for the importance of Anglo-Saxon players in parallel developments). Most important in that respect has been the disappearance of the long-lasting consensus that arbitration ought to take place in an amicable manner. By contrast, the adversarial dimension known from US-style litigation has increasingly been emphasized. American law firms consider transnational arbitration to be but one kind of litigation or dispute resolution among others (Dezalay and Garth 1996, p. 55). Forum shopping activities and recourse to any legal means available – including the purposeful use of national courts to prevent the recognition and enforcement of arbitral awards – characterize this new tactical approach towards the resolution of transnational commercial disputes.

What follows from these developments is the juridification of transnational arbitration (Dezalay and Garth 1996, p. 57; Flood and Caiger 1993). Arbitration has become more complex, more time-consuming and more expensive. In addition to all these factors, which tend to chip away the advantages of arbitration when compared to litigation, there is also a tendency towards re-localization. These developments undeniably set limits to the autonomy of transnational arbitration.

A second factor at work threatening autonomy is the political appropriation of arbitration (Stein 1995, pp. 247ff; Teubner 1997, pp. 21f). While arbitration is generally alleged to be apolitical (but see Kronstein 1963 and Cutler 1995), it is exposed to political interference for a number of reasons. A first and very basic point concerns whether or not arbitration is able to warrant fundamental requirements of justice. Given that protecting the weak is certainly one of these fundamental requirements, it has been proposed that arbitration based on the *lex mercatoria* could find its Waterloo in and around the issue of consumer protection (Karnell 1985). In addition, it has been pointed out that in the final phase in which judicial interference is possible, court decisions based on the national public policy argument have further reaching implications, since they bear a strain of parochialism and protectionism (Donahey 1997). These decisions indicate that the 'hands off' policy of the courts cannot be taken for granted and, at the end of the day, it is the national courts that have the final say regarding whether or not an award has violated national mandatory law.

CONCLUSION

The basic function of institutions is to stabilize expectations and provide a framework for action. Because trade over long distances and across borders is complex, risky and involves high stakes, it calls for the emergence of institutions that will decrease the need for each agent to know a lot about the behaviour of other agents and about the complex interdependencies generated by their interactions (Heiner 1983). More generally, institutions have to emerge that lower transaction costs in cross-border trade. However, the tasks these institutions have to fulfil are quite demanding, as they have to guarantee stability *and* flexibility at the same time, the former referring to the need for predictability and reliability in turbulent and anonymous environments, the latter referring to the need for open and elastic adjustments to the changing commercial realities of modern business practices.

As the recourse to history has shown, neither public nor private institutions have been able to permanently fulfil these demanding tasks. Rather, the analysis of the institutionalization of authority for the settlement of economic disputes at the transnational level has presented us with a story in which the competition and co-evolution of private and public institutions is seen to spur change and transformation. The interpretation of contemporary developments offered here has revealed that some generalizations drawn from the historical findings are basically still valid. Major differences are that the organizational density has significantly increased (see also Whitley; Djelic and Quack in the introduction and conclusion to this volume) and that patterns of interaction between public and private institutions and between national and transnational institutions have become increasingly complex. Nevertheless viewing the institutionalization of authority in transnational economic exchange in terms of continuous interactions between institutions and the (individual and collective) actors living in these institutions has been worthwhile (see also Tainio et al.; Kleiner; McNichol and Bensedrine in this volume). From this perspective, actors are, on the one hand, states – or more precisely their legislative and judicial entities – and international organizations and, on the other hand, a wide range of private actors including, for example, organizations that offer arbitral services or assistance in arbitration, firms that contract and seek to settle their disputes, and academics who contribute to the codification of norms.

In the course of interaction between these institutions and actors, the institutional matrix itself has changed since the 1970s. The outcome of this change is highly ambiguous, as it points simultaneously in contradictory directions.

For instance, both the unilateral efforts of states to expand the reach of their domestic law beyond their territory and the multilateral efforts of states to improve the interface-management between jurisdictions by co-ordinating their domestic international private laws aim at localizing transnational disputes. These efforts can be interpreted as exemplifying the fact that states do not fade away in the course of internationalization or transnationalization, but rather adapt and transform themselves (Weiss 1998; Djelic and Quack in the introduction and conclusion to this volume).

At the very same time, states were extending both the contracting parties' autonomy and the arbitrators' competence to make choices about the rules that govern contracts and the resolution of disputes. This undeniably has contributed to increasing the autonomy of arbitration relative to national constraints. What makes this even more intriguing is that the increase in autonomy of private modes of dispute settlement has not been restricted to the transnational level. Rather, it has also spread into the domestic domain. This 'trickle-down' effect (Djelic and Quack in the conclusion to this volume) is perceptible in recent reforms in the arbitration laws in many countries, which have extended party autonomy and restricted judicial review to national arbitration. Finally, and to puzzle the reader some more, the complex dynamics of competition between and co-evolution of public and private institutions and actors brings about a third result, which also contributes to an overall ambiguous impression. As has been described in the discussion of norm-setting, both the rule creation and norm innovation of the contracting parties and the arbitral tribunals occur in decentralized patterns. Once these rules and norms have gained a certain currency, they find their way into codified transnational codes, principles and lists or model clauses established by private, public and hybrid organizations. Thus codified, decentralized and privately developed transnational norms contribute to eroding national diversity either by being applied in transnational or national contracts or by being transposed into national law.

To conclude, *ambiguity* might be the most general finding we reach. Put differently, we document in this chapter a double process. On the one hand, we find an increasing structuration, formalization and standardization of the arbitration field and activity in the space between nations but with an undeniable trickle-down and homogenizing impact on national rules of the game. A gradual process of codification, harmonization and standardization of trade practices and divergent national provisions contributes in time to the erosion of national diversity. This, however, does not seem to reduce ambiguity. Instead, the process comes with a proliferation of actors and with an intensification of competition between those actors and between the codes and practices they champion. Ultimately, growing ambiguity around the seat of regulatory authority for transnational trade appears to be an integral aspect of the reconfiguration of political authority in the process of transnationalization (Cutler 1999, p. 316).

NOTES

1. Special thanks for highly helpful comments go to the editors of this volume and to the participants of the 2000 ESRI Workshop in Lisbon.
2. The term *trans*national here goes beyond the traditional concept of *inter*national relations as state-created regulatory activities, rather it refers to more complex patterns of interaction involving various economic and societal actors and institutions.
3. The German term is *autonomes Recht des Welthandels* (Großmann-Doerth 1923; Bonell 1978).
4. See special issue of *International Organization* (2000), **54** (3).
5. Parts of this section draw on Lehmkuhl (2001).
6. For example, in the UK 1979, France 1981, Belgium 1985, Canada 1986, The Netherlands 1986, Switzerland 1987, Spain 1988, Austria 1989, Hong Kong 1989, Russian Federation 1993, Hungary 1994, China 1994, Germany 1997. Many of these reforms of national arbitration law have largely been inspired by the 1985 arbitration model law of the United Nations Commission on International Trade Law.
7. For instance, the ICC Bulletin, The Yearbook of Commercial Arbitration, the Revue de l'Arbitrage, the Journal of International Arbitration or the Bulletin de l'ASA.
8. *Mitsubishi Motors Corp. vs Soler Chrysler-Plymouth Inc.* 473 U.S. of 1985. *Eco Swiss China Time Ltd (Hong Kong) v Benetton International NV*, Court of Justice of the European Union, 1 June 1999, C-126/97 [1999] All ER (Comm) 44.
9. The practical relevance of a particular choice finds expression in aspects relating to (1) the support of local courts in the arbitrational procedure, (2) the nationality of the award, (3) the possibility to challenge an award in the country where it is made and, (4) the forum-shopping activities of parties employed to assist them in choosing the most favourable location.
10. At the global level: The New York Convention of 1958 on the Recognition and Enforcement of Foreign Arbitral Awards. At the regional level, for instance: the Brussels Convention of 1968 on Jurisdiction and Enforcement of Judgements in Civil and Commercial Matters (European Union) or the Lugano Convention of 1988 (extending the Brussels Convention to the Members of the European Free Trade Area).
11. For other mechanisms designed to increase control of post-contractual opportunistic behaviour, for example 'hostage-taking' or self-enforcing contracts, see Williamson 1979, 1983.
12. In historical terms, founding a private mechanism of adjudication and centring it in merchant courts not only made it possible to gather information on the creditworthiness of trading partners, it also functioned as a valuable reputation system (Milgrom et al. 1990; Greif 1992; Greif et al. 1994).

REFERENCES

Axelrod, Robert (1990), *The Evolution of Co-operation*, London: Penguin.

Benson, Bruce L. (1999), 'To arbitrate or to litigate: that is the question', *European Journal of Law and Economics*, **8**, 91–151.

Berger, Klaus Peter (1992), *Internationale Wirtschaftsschiedsgerichtsbarkeit*, Berlin and New York: De Gruyter.

Berger, Klaus Peter (2000a), 'The new law merchant and the global market place: a 21st century view of transnational commercial law', *International Arbitration Law Review*, **4**, 91–102.

Berger, Klaus Peter (2000b), *Understanding International Commercial Arbitration. Understanding Transnational Commercial Arbitration*, Center of Transnational Law, Münster: Quadis, pp. 5–41.

Berger, Klaus Peter, H. Dubberstein et al. (2001), 'The CENTRAL enquiry on the use of transnational law in international contract law and arbitration', in Klaus Peter Berger (ed.), *The Pratice of Transnational Law*, The Hague/London/Boston: Kluwer Law International, pp. 91–114.

Berman, Harold (1983), *Law and Revolution*, Cambridge, MA: Harvard University Press.

Berman, Harold and Colin Kaufman (1978), 'The law of international commercial transactions (lex mercatoria)', *Harvard International Law Journal*, **19** (1), 221–77.

Bernstein, Lisa (1996), 'Merchant law in merchant court: rethinking the code's search for immanent business norms', *The University of Pennsylvania Law Review*, **144**, 1756–821.

Bernstein, Ronald, John Tackaberry et al. (eds) (1998), *Handbook of Commercial Arbitration*, London: Sweet & Maxwell.

Blessing, Marc (1992), 'Globalization (and harmonization?) of arbitration', *Journal of International Arbitration*, **9**, 79–89.

Bonell, Michael J. (1978), 'Das autonome Recht des Welthandels – Rechtsdogmatische und rechtspolitische Aspekte', *RabelsZ*, **42**, 485–506.

Brunsson, Nils and Bengt Jacobsson (2000), *A World of Standards*, Oxford: Oxford University Press.

Buchanan, James (1975), *The Limits of Liberty*, Chicago: University of Chicago Press.

Carbonneau, Thomas (ed.) (1990), *Lex Mercatoria and Arbitration*, Dobbs Ferry, NY: Transnational Publisher.

Carbonneau, Thomas (1998), 'A definition of and perspective upon the lex mercatoria', in Carbonneau, Thomas (ed.), *Lex Mercatoria and Arbitration*, New York: Juris Publishing/Kluwer Law International, pp. 11–22.

Carbonneau, Thomas (2000), *Cases and Materials on the Law and Practice of Arbitration*, New York: Juris Publishing/Kluwer Law International.

Collier, John and Vaughan Lowe (1999), *The Settlement of Disputes in International Law*, Oxford: Oxford University Press.

Condliffe, John B. (1951), *The Commerce of Nations*, London: Allen & Unwin.

Craig, Laurence, William Park and Jan Paulsson (2000), *International Chamber of Commerce Arbitration*, Dobbs Ferry, NY: Oceana Publications.

Cutler, Claire (1995), 'Global capitalism and liberal myths: dispute settlement in private international trade relations', *Millennium*, **24** (3), 377–97.

Cutler, Claire (1999), 'Private authority in international trade relations: the case of maritime transport', in Claire Cutler, Virginia Haufler and Tony Porter (eds), *Private Authority and International Affairs*, Albany, NY: State University of New York Press, pp. 283–329

Dezalay, Yves and Brian Garth (1996), *Dealing in Virtue*, Chicago and London: The University of Chicago Press.

Donahey, M. Scott (1997), 'From The Bremen to Mitsubishi (and beyond): international arbitration adrift in the U.S. waters', *The American Review of International Arbitration*, **7**, 149–61.

Drobnig, Ulrich (1990), 'Assessing arbitral autonomy in European statutory law', in Thomas Carbonneau (ed.), *Lex Mercatoria and Arbitration*, Dobbs Ferry, NY: Transnational Juris Publications, pp. 161–6.

Flood, John and Andrew Caiger (1993), 'Lawyers and arbitration: the juridification of construction disputes', *The Modern Law Review*, **56**, 412–40.

Fortier, L. Yves (2001), 'The new, new lex mercatoria or back to the future', *Arbitration International*, **17** (2), 121–8.

Gaillard, Emmanuel and John Savage (1999), *Fouchard, Gaillard, Goldman on International Commercial Arbitration*, The Hague: Kluwer Law International.

Gottwald, Peter (ed.) (1997), *Internationale Schiedsgerichtbarkeit*, Bielefeld: Gieseking.

Greif, Avner (1992), 'Institutions and international trade: lessons from the commercial revolution', *The American Economic Review*, **82** (2), 128–33.

Greif, Avner, Paul Milgrom and Barry Weingast (1994), 'Coordination, commitment, and enforcement: the case of the merchant guild', *Journal of Political Economy*, **102** (4), 745–76.

Großmann-Doerth, Hans (1923), 'Der Jurist und das autonome Recht des Welthandels', *Juristische Wochenzeitschrift*, **3447**.

Guzman, Andrew (2000), 'Arbitrator liability: reconciling arbitration and mandatory rules', *Duke Law Journal*, **49** (5), 1279–1334.

Heiner, Ronald (1983), 'On the origins of predictable behavior', *The American Economic Review*, **73**, 560–95.

Héritier, Adrienne, Christoph Knill and Suzanne Mingers (1996), *Ringing the Changes in Europe*, Berlin: de Gruyter.

Holtzmann, Howard M. (1999), 'Centripetal and centrifugal forces in modern arbitration', *Arbitration*, **65**, 302–7.

Joerges, Christian (1995), 'The Europeanisation of private law as a rationalisation process as a contest of disciplines', *European Review of Private Law*, **3**, 175–91.

Juenger, Friedrich (2000), 'The lex mercatoria and private international law', *Uniform Law Review*, **2**, 171–87.

Karnell, Gunnar (1985), 'Will the consumer law field be the Waterloo of the new lex mercatoria?', *Svensk Juristtidning*, 427–37.

Knill, Christoph and Dirk Lehmkuhl (1998), 'Integration by globalization: the European interest representation of the consumer electronics industry', *Current Politics and Economics in Europe*, **8** (2), 131–53.

Knill, Christoph and Dirk Lehmkuhl (2002), 'Private actors and the state: internationalization and changing patterns of governance', *Governance*, **15** (1), 41–63.

Kronstein, Heinrich (1963), 'Arbitration is power', *New York University Law Review*, **38**, 661–700.

Landes, William and Richard Posner (1979), 'Adjudication as a private good', *The Journal of Legal Studies*, **8**, 235–84.

Larson, Magali (1979), *The Rise of Professionalism*, Berkeley, CA: University of California Press.

Lehmkuhl, Dirk (2001), 'Multiple providers of governance services: settling transnational commercial disputes', Bonn: manuscript available upon request.

Mattli, Walter (2001), 'Governance and international standard setting', *Journal of European Public Policy*, **8** (3), 328–44.

McConnaughay, Philip (1999), 'The risks and virtues of lawlessness: a "second look" at international commercial arbitration', *Northwestern University Law Review*, **93** (2), 453–523.

Mentschikoff, Soia (1961), 'Commercial arbitration', *Columbia Law Review*, **61**, 846–69.

Milgrom, Paul, Douglass North and Barry Weingast (1990), 'The role of institutions in the revival of trade: the law merchant, private judges, and the champagne fairs', *Economics and Politics*, **2** (1), 1–21.

Muchlinski, Peter (1997), '"Global Bukowina" examined: viewing the multinational enterprise as a transnational-law-making community', in Gunther Teubner (ed.), *Global Law Without a State*, Dartmouth: Aldershot, pp. 45–77.

Mustill, Michael (1989), 'Arbitration: history and background', *Journal of International Arbitration*, **6**, 43–56.

Nienhaber, Volker (2000), 'The Recognition and Enforcement of Foreign Arbitral Awards', *Understanding Transnational Commercial Arbitration*, Center of Transnational Law, Münster: Quadis, pp. 99–124.

North, Douglass and Robert Thomas (1973), *The Rise of the Western World*, Cambridge: Cambridge University Press.

Park, William (1989), 'National law and commercial justice: safeguarding procedural integrity in international arbitration', *Tulane Law Review*, **63**, 647–709.

Pechota, Vratislav (1998), 'The future of the law governing the international arbitral process', in Thomas Carbonneau (ed.), *Lex Mercatoria and Arbitration*, The Hague: Juris Publishing/Kluwer, pp. 257–63.

Redfern, Alan and Martin Hunter (1991), *Law and Practice of International Commercial Arbitration*, London: Sweet & Maxwell.

Robé, Jean-Pierre (1997), 'Multinational enterprises: the constitution of a pluralistic order', in Gunther Teubner (ed.), *Global Law Without a State*, Dartmouth: Aldershot, pp. 45–78.

Roy, William (1997), *Socializing Capital*, Princeton, NJ: Princeton University Press.

Sassen, Saskia (1998), *Globalization and Its Discontents*, New York: The New Press.

Schmidt, Susanne K. and Raymund Werle (1998), *Coordinating Technology*, Cambridge, MA and London: The MIT Press.

Schmidtchen, Dieter and Hans-Jörg Schmidt-Trenz (1995), 'New institutional economics of international transactions. Constitutional uncertainty and the creation of institutions in foreign trade as exemplified by the multinational firm', *Jahrbuch für Politische Ökonomie*, **10**, 3–34.

Schmitthoff, Clive (1987), *International Trade Usages*, Paris: International Chamber of Commerce.

Spruyt, Hendrik (1994), *The Sovereign State and Its Competitors*, Princeton, NJ: Princeton University Press.

Stein, Ursula (1995), *Lex Mercatoria: Realität und Theorie*, Frankfurt: Klostermann.

Stewart, David (1994), 'National enforcement of arbitral awards under treaties and conventions', in Richard Lillich and Charles Bower (eds), *International Arbitration in the 21st Century*, Irvington, NY: Transnational Publishers.

Stoecker, Christoph (1990), 'The lex mercatoria: to what extent does it exist?', *Journal of International Arbitration*, 101–25.

Stone Sweet, Alec (1999), 'Judicialization and the construction of governance', *Comparative Political Studies*, **32** (2), 147–84.

Teubner, Gunther (1997), '"Global Bukowina": legal pluralism in the world society', in Gunther Teubner, *Global Law without a State*, Dartmouth: Aldershot, pp. 3–28.

Teubner, Gunther (2000), 'Privat regimes: Neo-spontanes Recht und Duale Sozialverfassungen in der Weltgesellschaft?' in Dieter Simon and Manfred Weiss (eds), *Zur*

Autonomie des Individuums, Liber Amicorum Spiros Simitis, Baden-Baden: Nomos, pp. 437–53.
Trakman, Leon (1980), 'The evolution of the law merchant: our common heritage. Part I: ancient and medieval law merchant', *Journal of Maritime Law and Commerce*, **12** (1), 1–24.
Trakman, Leon (1981), 'The evolution of the law merchant: our commercial heritage. Part II: the modern law merchant', *Journal of Maritime Law and Commerce*, **12** (2), 153–182.
Volckart, Oliver and Antje Mangels (1996), *Has the Modern Lex Mercatoria Really Medieval Roots?*, Jena: Max-Planck-Institute for Research into Economic Systems.
Weiss, Linda (1998), *The Myth of the Powerless State*, Cambridge: Polity Press.
Williamson, Oliver (1979), 'Transaction-costs economics: the governance of contractual relations', *Journal of Law and Economics*, **22**, 233–61.
Williamson, Oliver (1983), 'Credible commitments: using hostages to support exchange', *The American Economic Review*, **73**, 519–40.

Conclusion: Globalization as a double process of institutional change and institution building

Marie-Laure Djelic and Sigrid Quack

Globalization is a word that suffers from overuse. Still, behind the overstretched concept lies the reality of an economic world that is neither fully contained nor constrained by national boundaries. Economic organization and coordination increasingly reach across national borders and the impact is being felt both within the transnational sphere and, through rebound and indirect impact, at the national level as well. We started this book by acknowledging the need to take into account this transnational reality and its potentially quite significant impact. We now want to point, however, to its full complexity.

The focus in previous chapters has been on globalization as a dependent variable, an 'object' to be explained rather than an independent variable or an explanatory factor. Globalization can be taken as a given, a context and reality with a significant impact on economic behaviour and coordination – but also potentially on cultural repertoires, political processes and human interactions. This is indeed the approach that dominates in journalistic contributions as well as in most academic work. Questions tend to bear on how globalization is changing our lives, or in Giddens' words how it is 'reshaping our lives' (2000). Generally, the picture that emerges from that kind of approach is one where globalization is a neutral, impersonal, inevitable and ahistorical force (Guillén 2001).

Our collective understanding and project in this book has been both different and complementary. We have treated globalization as a phenomenon in the making, to be described, explained and understood. This phenomenon is worthy of being studied in itself and not only for the consequences it may have. Our objective was to take the first steps in that direction. Chapter after chapter, we have engaged in this book in the problematization and deconstruction of the phenomenon of globalization. Naturally there have been quite a few episodes in world history of internationalization of economic activities (see, for example, Wallerstein 1974; Robertson 1992; Murphy 1994; Williamson 1996, 1997 or Moore and Lewis 2000). Our focus, however, has been on the latest of such episodes, to which we reserve the term globalization. We see it starting after the end of World War II (McKenna et al.; Whitley and Lehmkuhl in this volume) and accelerating significantly from the 1980s (all other contributions to this volume).

DECONSTRUCTING GLOBALIZATION

Deconstructing the phenomenon of globalization requires a contextualization of the multiple layers and empirical forms that make up and reveal that phenomenon. The empirical chapters above delineate three main paths to contextualization, which contributors have combined in different ways and to different degrees.

The first path has been the reintroduction of history and the attempt to take a long view on any particular layer or dimension of the globalization story. This path appears particularly salient in the chapters by McKenna et al., Whitley, Lilja and Moen or Plehwe with Vescovi. The main points of focus there have been the question of origins, the identification of moments of bifurcation and the description of the process of emergence of new logics. A second path has been the emphasis on actors and the identification of their multiple and sometimes conflicting motivations, interests and strategies. This comes out quite clearly in the contributions by Tainio et al.; Kleiner or McNichol and Bensedrine. The third path, finally, has been a systematic focus on the interplay or articulation between the global or transnational on the one hand, and the local or national on the other. Without any exception, this path has been followed by all contributors.

At this stage of our collective road, the picture of globalization that emerges is far from glossy or unitary. Rather than an end, naturally, this chapter is probably the conclusion of a first step and hopefully a solid beginning. Nevertheless, we can already start making a number of observations. From the combination of contributions to this book, globalization clearly does not seem to be a smooth, unitary and neutral reality. Rather, it very much appears to be a multilevel and multilayered historical process, which is socially constructed and locally contested and reveals coexisting, competing and conflicting actors and logics. Globalization, we find, is a process or even more precisely a combination of multiple and partly interrelated processes, meaning that it is still very much open ended and in construction. Rather than a given reality or inevitable force bringing along and triggering significant transformations, we propose that globalization might be seen in fact as the sum and combination of transformations, an emergent and emerging multilayered construction.

This understanding of globalization as an aggregation of multilayered and multilevel open-ended processes, as a sedimenting and dynamic construction does resonate with recent calls in the academic debate to move away from static, homogeneous and unitary conceptualizations of globalization and towards understandings that take in complexity (Held et al. 1999; Guidry et al. 2001; Guillén 2001). The step we take in this volume makes it possible to point to some of the key mechanisms of complexity and hence contributes to reducing it, at least to some degree. The set of empirical chapters in this volume reveals that interactions, competitions or conflicts between different actors, different institutions and different rationalities, are constitutive of the globalization phenomenon. The latest episode of globalization is the aggregated result of those multiple interactions, conflicts and contestations. Interactions, conflicts and contestations are taking place within national spaces, at the borders of the national space as well as in the transnational arenas. And they are not the same everywhere. Taken collectively, the contributions to this book show that these interactions and conflicts are contingent and contextual, which accounts for the multiplicity and variety of layers in the phenomenon of globalization.

GLOBALIZATION AND INSTITUTIONAL RULES OF THE GAME

Behind a glossy word, we find therefore a collection of contested and discontinuous processes. The chapters in this book collectively also seem to show that the tensions, discontinuities and contestations that fall under the label 'globalization' are fundamental and profound ones. The contemporary episode of globalization has been naturally about the internationalization of exchanges, about flows of goods, money, technology, organizations and people across national borders (for example Ohmae 1990; Sassen 1998; Giddens 2000; Guillén 2001). It has indeed been about the 'widening, deepening and speeding up of global interconnectedness' (Held et al. 1999, p. 14). In that sense, globalization shares quite a few similarities with earlier episodes of internationalization of economic activity (Murphy 1994; Moore and Lewis 2000; James 2001). The conclusion we reach, however, looking at the empirical contributions to this volume, is that the internationalization of exchanges or increasing interconnectedness are probably only the tip of the iceberg, mere epiphenomena, in contemporary globalization.

The most striking thing about globalization, we argue, is that it seems to be principally and deeply about institutional logics and systems, about conflicting contextual or 'bounded rationalities' (Kristensen 2000), about what we call here 'rules of the game'. We focus in this volume on the economic dimension of the episode of globalization that started after 1945 to accelerate in the 1980s. Hence our interest lies in the rules of the economic game although the argument is likely to be valid in a much more general way, well beyond the economic sphere. As illustrated by the contributions to this volume, globalization means contested negotiations and renegotiations of those 'rules of the economic game'. And those negotiations and renegotiations mean conflicts between preexisting sets of rules, possibly translate in re-combinations using preexisting bits and pieces or even lead to the emergence of entirely new rules or sets of rules.

In the way we use it, the term 'rules of the economic game' is wide and encompassing. It resonates with the idea of an institutional backbone for economic activity. The institutional frame in which economic activity takes place is in part structural – laws and regulations, political institutions and structured channels of interaction, education and financial systems amongst others (Whitley 1992, 1999; Lane 1995; Maurice and Sorge 2000). We find examples and illustrations of the defining role of those structural rules in most if not all contributions to this volume. At the same time, structural frames often reveal or combine with normative, cognitive or ideological rules (Meyer and Rowan 1977; Campbell 1998; Campbell and Pedersen 2001). Quite a number of contributions to this volume empirically document that (Tainio et al.; Kleiner; Lilja and Moen; McNichol and Bensedrine; Ventresca et al.). We propose the term 'rules of the economic game' to encompass both the structural and normative institutions that frame economic activity in any particular context. Collectively, we thus break the firewall that tends to separate those who define institutions as structures from those who see them as normative and cognitive frames (this firewall has been one of the main problems with neoinstitutional theory, see for example Campbell 1998; Clemens and Cook 1999; Djelic 2001). Rather than opposing structural or material and ideological analyses, we contend that both are necessary.

Globalization is at the very same time a material and an ideational phenomenon. An important contribution of this volume, we believe, is to show that globalization is about these institutional rules of the game, both the structural and the normative/cognitive ones and their transformation particularly in the recent past. Our collective results point in two different directions.

At a first level, globalization is about the redefinition of economic rules of the game and institutional systems within national spaces, for the most part through a slow and incremental process. Globalization is about institutional change and the evolution and transformation of national business systems (Whitley 1992) and 'national business rationalities' (using and transforming a term coined by Dobbin who talked in 1994 of 'national industrial rationalities'). This comes out particularly clearly in the contributions by Tainio et al.; Kleiner; McKenna et al. or Whitley, which were grouped together under Part I of this book.

Then, at a second level, globalization is also about the elaboration of new rules for the economic game, about the building of new institutional frames particularly within the space between and across nations. This we have found to be illustrated and documented quite clearly in the contributions by Lilja and Moen; Plehwe with Vescovi; Midttun et al; McNichol and Bensedrine; Ventresca et al. or Lehmkuhl. This second group of contributions constitutes Part II of this volume.

We have separated contributions in two groups in this manner mostly for analytical purposes. The first set of chapters does have as a common focus the transformation of national institutional systems. The second set is clearly better defined by an interest in the building and emergence of new institutional frames at a transnational level. Nevertheless, all contributors see and acknowledge the interactions between these two types of processes – institutional change at the national level and institution building at the transnational level. Those interactions play themselves out in a way that is schematically illustrated in Figure C.1.

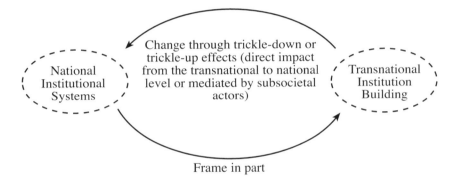

*Figure C.1   National institutional change and transnational institution
               building: the interplay*

We have collectively argued in this book that transnational institution (or rule) building may be one of the most striking features of the current period of internationalisation. As Part II shows, this process of institution building at the cross-national or transnational level cannot be conceived in total isolation and abstraction from national rules of the game. Even in cases of multilateral negotiations such as the one described by McNichol and Bensedrine the objectives, projects, resources and logics of participants – be they individuals or organizations – are shaped and framed to some, and sometimes to a great, extent by the national institutional systems those participants are originally or primarily connected with.

In turn, however, we have shown also that new transnational frames are likely to challenge, to confront and to change – even though slowly and incrementally – national institutional systems. They can do so through direct impact – what we call here 'trickle-down' effects or mechanisms. When European Union institutions or any other kind of transnational institution (for example the WTO, the IMF or the World Bank or the Biosafety Protocol) exert pressure directly at the national level on member governments to rewrite national laws or in more general terms to redefine national rules of the game, then we have what we call 'trickle-down' effects or mechanisms. Illustrations of that type of mechanism can be found in a number of contributions to this volume, particularly in Part II. The impact can also be more indirect as documented in most chapters of Part I and in some chapters of Part II. Through cross-national interactions at subsocietal or meso levels – sectors, industries, professions or even from region to region – actors are being drawn into social spaces that extend well beyond their national context of origin. In that process, those actors are likely to be confronted with and to have to function within sets of rules that may be quite different from those of their country of origin. Subsocietal actors (firms and/or groups of individuals in Tainio et al.; Kleiner; McKenna et al. or Midttun et al., firms and networks or associations in Lilja and Moen or McNichol and Bensedrine, stock exchanges in Ventresca et al.) become the vectors and transmission belts through which those new rules are brought into a given national space. In certain circumstances, those subsocietal actors may be more than mere messengers. They may become real mediators. They may contribute indeed to pushing those new rules up towards the national institutional level, fostering in the process a transformation of the national business system or of the national business rationality. This path or pattern we associate with 'trickle-up' effects or mechanisms.

GLOBALIZATION AS A PROCESS OF INSTITUTIONAL CHANGE

After confronting and combining the empirical contributions to this book, we are able to make the following claim. The latest period of economic internationalization has created several paths and opportunities for the transformation of national institutional systems and rules of the economic game. National institutional systems are robust but in contrast to recent books that emphasize stability and self-reinforcing path-dependencies (Whitley 1999; Maurice and Sorge 2000; Zeitlin and Herrigel 2000; Hall and Soskice 2001) all contributions in this volume point towards change. The change we document can be quite significant but it appears to take place in more of an incremental than an abrupt or radical way. This book complements – and does not necessarily contradict – a literature on radical and abrupt changes following large-scale ruptures and crises most of which bears on Eastern Europe after 1989 (Stark and Bruszt 1998; Elster et al. 1998; Kitschelt 1999; Jones-Luong 2001; Aslund 2001 but see also Djelic 1998 on Western Europe after 1945). Even though it focuses on radical turning points in the life of a particular country, this literature indeed also points to much less than clear-cut revolutions and to a fair degree instead of step-by-step adaptation, backlash or boomerang effects and partial hybridization.

The globalization story we tell in this book is thus a story of national institutional change – resistance and partial persistence being natural correlates (Djelic 1998). This story is one of incremental rather than abrupt and radical change, with nevertheless, we argue, quite consequential effects. A particular aim of this volume has been to provide evidence of and contribute to a better conceptualization of the trickle-up and trickle-down trajectories through which national institutional systems are being transformed in co-evolution with a globalizing world economy.

Incumbent versus Challenger Rules

All contributions to this volume start from the recognition that economic activity is embedded within a larger institutional frame (Weber 1978; Polanyi 1944; Granovetter 1985). The economic sociology literature that builds upon this idea of embeddedness has tended to underscore the historical significance of the national level in defining and shaping this institutional frame (for example D'Iribarne 1989; Fligstein 1990; Dobbin 1994; Lane 1995; Whitley 1999; Maurice and Sorge 2000; Hall and Soskice 2001). The argument in that literature is that, at least in the modern age, rules of the economic game have been essentially defined and shaped at the national level. Nation-states and political institutions have traditionally played a key role in that process. And that process has often been intimately linked and correlated with state and nation building.

Those historically dominant national frames or rules of the game we propose to call 'incumbent rules', at least when they are considered from within their national system of origin. Most contributions to this volume document a still quite significant role and place in today's economic world for incumbent rules of the game. However, the presence and increasing role and significance of competing or 'challenger rules' is also one of our main collective findings. Globalization, we find, is about challenger rules of the economic game, challenger institutional frames colliding within a particular arena or space with nationally defined, incumbent rules.

The contributions to this volume point to two main categories of challenger rules. Challenger rules can be the rules of the economic game from another national space – those challenger rules are themselves incumbent rules in their geographical context of origin. The chapters by Tainio et al.; Kleiner or McKenna et al. look at the impact of this particular type of challenger rules. In all three cases, the challenger logic is the Anglo-Saxon if not the American one. Another category of challenger rules, particularly salient in Part II of the volume, are these rules with no particular or clear national origin that come to structure the transnational economic space. We look in greater details, in the section below, at the process through which those rules are being constituted, at what we call the process of institution building at the transnational level. The contributions by Lilja and Moen; Plehwe with Vescovi; Midttun et al; McNichol and Bensedrine; Ventresca et al. or Lehmkuhl all show that this particular category of challenger rules has come to play an increasingly significant role over the past 50 years, colliding regularly and sometimes violently with incumbent national institutional frames.

A 'Stalactite' Model of Change – Incremental but Consequential

Work on national institutional systems or national business systems (D'Iribarne 1989; Dobbin 1994; Hollingsworth and Boyer 1997; Lane 1995; Whitley 1999; Maurice and Sorge 2000; Hall and Soskice 2001) generally underscores the interdependence and close integration of institutional elements within any single one of those national systems. A common argument in that tradition is that national systems are self-reinforcing and hence quite stable equilibria. The idea is that pressures at the level of certain institutional dimensions are likely to be neutralized and absorbed by the system as a whole, leaving little or no traces behind. The possibility of change is not ruled out but it appears quite unlikely in this framework since, in fact, for it to happen most if not all constitutive elements of the system would have to evolve or be transformed simultaneously. This indeed will be rare if not totally unlikely, including in situations of extreme shock or crisis or in the most acute of revolutionary episodes. As the experience of Germany after 1945 (Berghahn 1986; Schwartz 1991; Djelic 1998) or the more recent fate of Eastern European and Post Soviet countries (Stark and Bruszt 1998; Kitschelt 1999; Jones-Luong 2001) show, blitz-type interventions, shock therapies or radical institutional reengineering are bound to encounter significant resistance and obstacles that are created in part by robust and enduring institutional configurations. They will generally have much less impact than anticipated and the persistence of preexisting patterns will be stronger than expected. Hence if change is defined as a radical and time-bound overhaul of the system as a whole, we are indeed quite unlikely to see change.

Taken together, the contributions to this volume offer a somewhat different perspective on the issue of change. Our proposition is that the succession and combination, over a long period, of a series of incremental transformations could lead in the end to consequential and significant change. Each single one of these incremental transformations may appear quite marginal and even transparent – mitigated and partially absorbed as it is likely to be by the national institutional system as a whole. However, the succession and combination of multiple and multilevel transformations ultimately and with a longer term view of the process adds to the significance and heightens the impact of each single transformation. The image is that of a minuscule drop of water falling from the vault of a cave. In itself, it seems totally insignificant with no impact whatsoever on the cave as a whole. However, under given conditions of temperature, the succession and combination of large numbers of droplets falling upon each other may lead to an aggregation of the calcite contained in those drops. After a (long) while the result will be the emergence of a thick landscape of innova- tively shaped stalactites and stalagmites and a radical transformation, one could say, of the cave as a whole.

This image, we argue, is probably closer than the image of the 'Big Bang' to the way most national institutional systems change. National institutional configurations cannot dissolve and be replaced by others at the snap of fingers. Building on the empirical evidence collected for this book, we propose that under repeated, multidirectional and multilevel attacks from challenger rules, both through trickle-up and trickle-down trajectories, national configurations may erode and be reshaped progressively through time. Instead of all consti- tutive elements changing together at the very same time, the chapters collectively point to a process where one constitutive element after another might be weakened or transformed. The destabilization or change of each con- stitutive element feeds on that of the others, leading in time to an overall system erosion or system change, all elements 'giving way' or being transformed at least in part after a while. This, the chapters show, can be a very slow process where change is always associated with resistance and persistence. The chapters also show that this may be happening at least as much in an indirect way as through direct assault on national institutional frames.

It is through this type of stalactite change that national business systems are most likely to switch tracks and to enter a different logic of path dependency (Mahoney 2000; Thelen 2000; Pierson 2000a, 2000b; Crouch and Farell 2002). In most cases this

> new path does not represent a radical break from the past, yet neither is it simply rapid evolution or innovation within the old path. Rather it is a new path character- ized by an hybridization process (not convergence) in which many of the institutions of the old path continue as before, some old institutions are transformed to new purposes, and new institutions are introduced (Deeg 2001, p. 7).

One of the contributions of this volume is to identify, keeping to railway imagery, the factors and mechanisms that generate potential switching points or junctions. There, national business systems, or at least some of their subparts, may engage on new path dependencies that will involve logics of action and contextual rationalities quite different from what had been the case before.

Trickle-up Trajectories

Threats and challenges, we have argued above, may come from below, from subsocietal or subnational levels. The contributions to this volume point to two main scenarios for what we have called 'trickle-up' trajectories.

Scenarios and actors

First, national actors crossing national borders may find that the rules of the game with which they are familiar come into collision with, and sometimes even are in contradiction with, rules of the game dominant elsewhere. Those national actors could be individuals, groups of individuals, firms, associations or networks of firms as documented in Tainio et al.; Kleiner; McKenna et al. or Lilja and Moen in this volume. This type of scenario will be all the more widespread that the internationalization of economic activities and of exchanges in general is becoming increasingly dense and intense.

The open nature of the economy may stimulate a second scenario that is parallel but goes in the other direction. Foreign actors move into a given national space with rules of the game that are quite different from those of local actors (Tainio et al.; Kleiner; McKenna et al. in this volume). A variant of that scenario is when the champions of challenger rules on the local or national scene are themselves locals or nationals who are pushing for new rules of the game in order to carve a space for themselves (Kleiner). What this is all about is the attempt by new or emerging actors, whether local outsiders or foreign entrants, to redefine rules of the game in an industry or impose 'new' ones in order to enter the field and the game and to reshape it to their advantage (Djelic and Ainamo 1999).

The contributions in Part I and a few contributions in Part II show how this encounter between incumbent and challenger rules plays out at subsocietal levels, whether at the level of the firm (Tainio et al.), at the level of an industry (Lilja and Moen), an organizational field (Kleiner) or at the level of a profession (McKenna et al.). But those chapters also indicate that this interplay at the subsocietal level is not neutral for national institutions. Rules of the game may change at the subsocietal level well before this is institutionalized at the national level. But transformations at the subsocietal level may also reverberate in time at the national level. The decision by the German government in 2001 to create a Kodex-Kommission in charge of 'modernizing the rules and practices of German capitalism' is a clear case of such a process of post hoc 'regularization' (*Le Monde*, 7 November 2001). The object of this commission was to take stock of changes that had already redefined the German economic game and to institutionalize them at the national level. For some, this may be formally ringing the knell of Rhenan capitalism (Institut de l'Entreprise 2001). Drawing from and comparing the evidence presented in the empirical contributions to this volume,

it is possible to identify the conditions in which contestation and transformation of incumbent rules of the game at the subsocietal level are likely to reflect
and impact on the national level.

Conditions for trickle-up trajectories

One such condition seems to be the central position and overall leverage of the
subsocietal actors concerned by or involved in the collision of rules. Changes
within core and strategic firms or industries are more likely, ultimately, to have
some impact on national level institutions. This appears to be particularly true
in smaller countries as shown by the cases of Nokia in Finland (Tainio et al.)
or of the forest industry in Norway and Finland (Lilja and Moen). In smaller
countries, core firms or industries have proportionally more clout, strategic
importance but also leverage which could explain their more direct impact.

Other important conditions are the strength and legitimacy of those outsiders
championing and pushing for challenger rules. In that respect, Anglo-Saxon
players benefit from something akin to a 'trademark' advantage in professional
fields such as corporate law or management consulting (McKenna et al.) as
well as in other activities related to banking or financing (for example asset
management, see Kleiner, or stock exchange related activities, see for example,
Tainio et al. and Ventresca et al.). This allows them to be more forceful and
convincing in the promotion of their own sets of rules of the game.

Naturally, the strength and legitimacy of those outsiders and challengers will
be more or less filtered and mitigated by the existence and embeddedness of local
incumbent rules. Local appropriation will likely be more complex and contested
in situations where incumbent rules already exist and are deeply embedded – to
get back to the terms used in the introduction, when local institutional rules have
already entered the phase of sedimentation. The case of the consulting profession,
for example, shows that American actors had less trouble imposing their rules
of the game in Finland than in France (McKenna et al. in this volume). Part of
the explanation lies in the fact that the Finnish consulting space had barely been
structured before they arrived and that it was still hovering between level 1 and
level 2 of institutionalization – between habitualization and objectification. A
similar type of conclusion can be drawn from the description by Kleiner of the
emergence of an asset management organizational field in France.

Another condition seems important that is not unrelated to those identified
above. The greater the shock or the more intense the collision, the more likely
that it will reverberate at the national level. The collision will be more intense
if subsocietal actors – firms, industries, professions or even possibly regions –
lack protective buffers or else are in a situation of perceived and self-acknowledged crisis. The lack of protection can be due to the immaturity of the local
field, as argued above for the consulting profession. It can be strategically
engineered, either by political authorities or by the actors themselves, through

deregulation, for example, or a lowering of trade or other protective barriers (Djelic and Ainamo 1999). It will also be related, naturally, to the strength of the push coming from outsiders and challenger rules. A perceived and self-acknowledged situation of crisis will tend to correspond, on the other hand, to a high degree of dissatisfaction with incumbent rules, either because these rules do not seem to coevolve with environmental conditions and/or because they narrow the opportunities of local and incumbent actors in a changing world.

Trickle-up trajectories and mechanisms

We argue that under these conditions – or a subset thereof – transformations in rules of the game that were initially happening at a subsocietal level are likely to have an impact and reverberate, after a while, at the national level. Building on the empirical contributions to this volume, particularly in Part I, we now turn to the mechanisms allowing reverberation or 'trickle-up' trajectories. The chapters in Part I point to three main categories of mechanisms and we use here DiMaggio and Powell's (1983) terminology.

The first category of mechanisms we label 'coercive'. They correspond to the situation where the subsocietal actors concerned have enough clout and power in the local space to push for a more widespread adoption of those changes initially happening at their level. Amongst coercive mechanisms, one finds direct political action and lobbying through existing institutional channels or social networks. Another path, somewhat more indirect, is through the pressure put by key actors, initially in the cyclone's eye, on their local interlocutors – competitors, clients, suppliers, trade unions, providers of education or financial institutions – to appropriate some if not all the changes they have themselves gone through. Such pressure is possible when those key actors have economic or social leverage over their interlocutors reflecting either situations of dependence and/or tight networking arrangements. A building up and aggregation of multiple micro changes through such a process is likely to lead to a de facto situation where preexisting incumbent rules of the game have been changed or replaced even before the legislator or political institutions get involved. The contributions by Tainio et al.; Lilja and Moen or Kleiner point to the role of such coercive mechanisms along the trickle-up trajectories.

A second category of mechanisms we label 'mimetic', following once again DiMaggio and Powell's (1983) terminology. What takes place in this case is essentially a process of spread and diffusion through imitation. The combination of multiple acts of imitation at the subsocietal level can here again create a de facto situation where the rules of the game have changed well before this is being acknowledged, officialized and institutionalized at the national level. Mimetic mechanisms can be identified in the contributions by Tainio et al.; McKenna et al. or Lilja and Moen. At the same time, those chapters show that it is often difficult to decouple coercive from mimetic types of mechanisms, the two being closely tied up and interconnected and shaping in interaction trickle-up trajectories.

Finally, evidence from Part I points to a third category of mechanisms, the impact of which is probably slower and more difficult to trace. This category we label 'normative'. It covers and encompasses processes by which outsiders are able to socialize a number of local actors into their own 'challenger' rules of the game – the cognitive or ideational dimension here becoming key. This is clearly illustrated in contributions by Tainio et al.; McKenna et al. or Kleiner. The 'maximization of shareholder value', the 'boardroom professional counsel' or the 'independent asset management firm' become appropriated through time as cognitive frames by local actors and are neutralized in the process. Appropriation means that their origins and initial context of embeddedness are all but forgotten – hence a neutralization. These cognitive frames may even in fact become transparent to the actors who have appropriated them. In time, the organizations and institutions supporting those cognitive frames emerge and are being structured locally – either ex nihilo or through transformation of the preexisting structuring field. This process of normative integration or normalization can be greatly furthered in any particular national context if challenger rules find a relay in local institutions of socialization such as professional schools or universities. This clearly was the case in both the consulting and 'maximization of shareholder value' stories where local business education systems proved to be powerful relays (Tainio et al.; McKenna et al.).

To sum up, we bring together in Table C.1 the defining features of what we called trickle-up trajectories. Thus, national institutional systems may come

Table C.1   Trickle-up trajectories

Scenarios and Actors	Conditions	Mechanisms
• Local actors extending abroad • Foreign actors coming in • Local outsiders trying to redefine the game in order to enter it	• Power and centrality of those national actors who are first movers in adopting challenger rules • Power and legitimacy of foreign actors bearing challenger rules • Intensity of collision between incumbent and challenger rules	• Coercive: political lobbying, different types of constraints on local interlocutors • Mimetic: multiple imitations of role model actors • Normative: Socialization of key actors relayed by local institutions of socialization– education system …

under pressure from below and be affected by transformations of the rules of the game at the subnational or subsocietal level. Challenge it seems may, however, also come from above, from the transnational level. We will get back in the next section to the process of construction and stabilization of transnational rules of the game. But we will now look at how those transnational rules are bound to create challenges for incumbent national institutional systems.

Trickle-down Trajectories

With respect to the influence of transnational rules on national systems, contributions in Part II of this book point to two main scenarios.

Scenarios and actors

First, the challenge may come from transnational organizations or supranational constructions. A characteristic of our world since the end of World War II has been the emergence, multiplication and stabilization of such organizations and constructions in the transnational space (Whitley this volume; Meyer et al. 1997a). Those organizations and constructions quite often turn out to be rule-making bodies and some of them have gained significant and direct influence over national polities. This is clearly and particularly the case with the European Union as illustrated in the contributions by Lilja and Moen; Plehwe with Vescovi; or Midttun et al. With respect to the economic realm, other supranational organizations such as the International Monetary Fund (IMF), the World Bank, the European Bank for Reconstruction and Development (EBRD) or the World Trade Organization (WTO) should be mentioned. These organizations nurture and contribute to the diffusion of particular rules of the game, which are likely to collide with incumbent rules or practices in any given national space. The collision can be particularly violent and intense in weaker countries or in countries going through an acute internal crisis such as in the Eastern part of the European continent (for example, Stiglitz and Muet 2001; Stiglitz 2002; Rodrick 2002). The challenge created by those transnational organizations and supranational institutions for national rules of the game has started to be studied over the recent years. The impact of the European Union, in particular, has been the object of an increasing number of studies (Marks et al. 1996; Sandholtz and Stone Sweet 1998; Fligstein and Mara-Drita 1996; Streeck 2001).

There is less attention being paid to a second type of scenario where challenger rules emerge from a less structured and hence less visible transnational space. The contributions by McNichol and Bensedrine; Ventresca et al. or Lehmkuhl all show that rule setting and rule making also take place in transnational fields or arenas lacking structuration in relative terms. Actors – all kinds of actors, from private firms to consumers, lobbies, nongovernmental organizations (NGOs) or state representatives – come together to negotiate and agree on rules of the game. This is illustrated by McNichol and Bensedrine for environmental issues, by Ventresca et al. for financial markets and by Lehmkuhl for the arbitration of conflicts in transnational trade. Those rules of the game are institutions, in the sense we have used in this volume, to the extent that they structure action and economic activity. A comparison between those chapters seems to show furthermore that, for the most part, those are cognitive and normative institutions (Meyer and Rowan 1977). The rules that emerge or are negotiated in that context are essentially norms that are enacted, appropriated and enforced by the actors themselves. The structural apparatus – formal organization, legislation or coercive machinery – comes, if at all, in support of those norms.

Conditions for trickle-down trajectories

Beyond this difference in scenario, all contributions in Part II point to trickle-down trajectories where the construction and stabilization of transnational rules is not neutral for national institutions. From a comparison of these contributions, we draw a number of conclusions as to the conditions in which transnational challenger rules may indeed come to trickle-down to the national level with a potentially significant impact upon incumbent national rules of the game. One important variable appears to be the degree of centrality of a particular country, through its private and public representatives, in the process of construction and stabilization of transnational rules. Building on contributions in Part II of this book, it seems fair to differentiate between at least three main groups of countries in that respect.

The first group is a little peculiar; it is a one unit sample. In the genetically modified foods (McNichol and Bensedrine), financial markets (Ventresca et al.) or commercial arbitration (Lehmkuhl) stories, the United States plays a unique role. An explanation to that special place and role lies in the unique position of geopolitical dominance that characterizes the US after 1945 (Djelic 1998 and Whitley in this volume). Through its private and public representatives, that country is guiding and structuring the process of construction and stabilization of transnational rules in a more or less direct and visible manner. The US does not always manage to impose the solution that will best serve its interests as McNichol and Bensedrine show in their contribution, but the role of that country in the process of transnational rule building has no equivalent. A second group is made up of a few core (and rather rich) countries, which are proactive and quite involved in trying to shape the process. The third group finally is the larger one, and brings together those countries with a more passive connection to the process.

From comparing the contributions in Part II, we come to the following observations, some of which should be further tested. Most of the time, the US is highly central to the process of transnational institution building. Ultimately, however, it seems that the level of compliance of that country to the transnational rules that emerge is irregular and changing (McNichol and Bensedrine this volume, see also Djelic and Bensedrine 2001). The profound geopolitical imbalance in favour of the US increases the degrees of freedom of that country regarding compliance with transnational rules although it may have played a significant role in the process of construction and elaboration of those rules. The recent change of heart of the US on the Kyoto Protocol is in that respect an interesting case. In 1997, 39 industrialized countries including the US had agreed in Kyoto, Japan, to cut emissions of six greenhouse gases to 5.2 per cent below the 1990 level and this by 2008–2012. On March 28, 2001, the US announced that it was pulling out of the Kyoto Protocol. Christie Todd Whitman, head of the US Environment Protection Agency, announced: 'We have no interest in implementing that treaty' (ENS 2001).

In the second group of countries identified above – rich core countries – compliance appears to be more regular once the rules have been agreed upon. In the last group of countries, those that are more passive in the process of transnational institution building, appropriation may be more of an issue. The process will likely be slower with a greater distance between the world of discourse and formal institutions and the world of action and practice that will remain very much structured by traditional patterns.

Without going too far in drawing conclusions at that stage, these observations would lead us to propose that the more reliable and stable driver of transnational institution building may in fact be the second group of countries – made up of rich and core countries with the EU at the centre. If the governance of globalization calls for a systematization of transnational institution building, then we should look – and hope – for leadership for that process in that second group as a collective. Relying on the US, as has tended to be the case throughout the second half of the twentieth century, may not in fact be an optimal strategy.

Other variables with an impact on trickle-down trajectories are the nature of incumbent rules and the degree of dependence of a particular country on external players. A country where local rules are weak, either because they lack legitimacy, have proven inefficient or a hindrance, are altogether absent or still at a pre-institutionalization stage as defined in the introduction to this volume, creates more space for rules constructed at a transnational level to trickle-down. This can only be reinforced in situations of dependence, where a country for example sees the granting of financial assistance it badly needs being conditioned upon compliance to a set of transnationally defined rules. This is not, after reflection, in contradiction with our precedent finding. Weak countries tend to belong to the group we have defined above as 'passive'. Weakness and dependence may compensate in part for passivity, which might lead to more rapid formal compliance than expected. Quite often, however, a significant gap will remain between the world of discourse and formal institutions on the one hand, and the world of practice on the other (this finds confirmation in earlier work by sociologists of global society, for example Meyer et al. 1997a, 1997b; Boli and Thomas 1999; Meyer and Ramirez 2000). The former might indeed be affected through a trickle-down trajectory by transnational challenger rules. The latter will tend to stay, at least for a while, embedded in local traditions and national institutional legacies. A special and quite different case of dependence should be added and mentioned here. Direct political dependence of national countries on a supranational construction, such as is the case in the European Union context, is an obvious path for trickle-down mechanisms. This situation naturally creates conditions where the rules defined at the supranational level are likely indeed to have a rapid and significant impact at the national level (Lilja and Moen; Plehwe with Vescovi; Midttun et al. in this volume).

Trickle-down trajectories and mechanisms

We now turn to the set of mechanisms that appear to be at work along what we have called here trickle-down trajectories. Chapters in Part II point to three main categories of mechanisms, parallel to the three categories identified for trickle-up trajectories. The first category is the coercive one. Within this category we find the granting of financial or, as a matter of fact, any form of assistance conditioned upon compliance to a set of transnationally defined rules of the game. Other coercive mechanisms, in the context in particular of supranational constructions such as the European Union, are political fiat, laws and decrees backed up by an enforcement apparatus. The mimetic category for this particular trajectory turns out to be even harder to disentangle and decouple from either the coercive or normative ones. Mimetic mechanisms in that case have to do with the voluntary adoption by a particular country of challenger rules of the game. This voluntary adoption, though, might sometimes be reflecting longer-term objectives – as, for example, with the case of Eastern European countries adopting European Union compatible sets of rules, just in case of and in order to be ready for future integration. Voluntary adoption may also be motivated by a conviction that adopted rules are indeed 'superior'.

The third category of mechanisms at work, finally, is the one we have labelled before normative. What we see, from the empirical evidence provided in Part II, are multiple and parallel processes of professionalization at the transnational level. Individuals and organizations are joining in, across and beyond national boundaries, around common preoccupations, goals or values and beliefs. They take it upon themselves to elaborate a set of norms and institutions in the sense of rules of the game. They virtually become, in the process, a transnational community (Morgan 2001) and, as such, they get actively involved in trying to push those common norms and rules down towards the national or even subnational levels. Here again, this type of mechanism is being reinforced by a worldwide process of standardization of institutions of socialization – whether schools, universities or the media in the wide sense of the term (Meyer et al. 1992; Meyer and Ramirez 2000; Byrkjeflot 2000; Amdam et al. 2002).

In Table C.2 below, we summarize the main features of what we have called here trickle-down trajectories. An important issue addressed in this volume has thus been how the transnational affects the local, and more particularly how the transnational may affect a nationally defined institutional constellation or system. One of the findings drawn from our collective endeavour has had to do with the nature of national institutional change. National institutional systems are changing quite significantly and enduringly, we argue, through a multiplicity and an aggregation of slow and incremental steps. We have identified two main types of trajectories – trickle-up and trickle-down – along which the transnational can effect, potentially in a quite significant way, a national institutional equilibrium or constellation. We see the combination of trickle-up and trickle-down trajectories, their mutual reinforcement and the incremental but significant institutional re-configuration they trigger through time, as an important and constitutive dimension of globalization.

This, however, is only one side of the story told in this book. At the same time that they look at how the transnational affects the local and the national, contributions to this volume also provide an understanding of how the local or the national shape the transnational. The transnational space, in our collective approach, is neither taken for granted nor treated as anomic or unstructured.

Table C.2   Trickle-down trajectories

Scenarios and actors	Conditions	Mechanisms
• Transnational organizations and supranational institutions as directing the process – essentially public and political process • Transnational fields or arenas – multiplicity of actors, public and private, involved	• Centrality and degree of openness • Weakness of local system and degree of dependence	• Coercive: conditional granting of assistance, political fiat, legal authority and enforcement apparatus (EU) • Normative: sharing of common cognitive frames through parallel socialization, processes of professionalization, responsabilization and collective self-monitoring

Rather, it emerges as an institutionalized arena in its own right. As Whitley argues in this volume and as others have systematically documented (for example Meyer et al. 1997a, 1997b) the structuration of that arena has made significant progress during the second part of the twentieth century. Such structuration has implied and concretely meant, we collectively argue, a process of institution building. And transnational institution building, we find, has often started from the local and the national or from the 'rubbing against each other' of multiple locals or nationals.

GLOBALIZATION AS INSTITUTION BUILDING

Collectively, the contributions to this volume provide evidence in fact of coevolution between the national and the transnational. A transnational rule or system of rules that is an offshoot of a local or national model or results from the interplay between multiple locals or national models may in time, in its own right and through either trickle-up or trickle-down trajectories, come to affect and impact local or national institutional arrangements. Time, here, is an important dimension. And so are, as argued above, a number of conditions that will either facilitate or constrain the process. A few chapters explicitly point to the circularity and self-reinforcing dimension of this process through time (McKenna et al.; Whitley; McNichol and Bensedrine). The others are more implicit about the diachronic interplay and present snapshots at particular points in time.

Institution Building: Scenarios and Actors

Transnational organizations
A first and obvious scenario historically for institution building in the transnational space has been the formal setting up of a transnational organization. This organization takes over a particular sphere or domain where cross-national interactions are significant and attempts to achieve its structuration through rule making and institution building. This, naturally, is an old scenario and with a little bit of a stretch the Roman Catholic Church could be used as an illustration, and a successful one at that.

Without going that far back in history and staying with transnational organizations that have been set up in the modern era, in the age of the nation-state, a number of other examples come to mind. The League of Nations was an important ancestor, although with ultimately little impact (Murray 1987; Knock 1995). The International Labour Organization is less known but is also worth mentioning. This transnational organization was created in the interwar period and was revived in 1948. In the few years following 1945, the project of structuring the transnational space regained significance after nearly two decades of strong nationalism and protectionism. In this postwar project, the transnational organization was undeniably the predominant scenario. The United Nations and its various divisions, the Organization for European Economic Cooperation (OEEC later to become the OECD), the International Monetary Fund (IMF) or the World Bank and the General Agreement on Tariffs and Trade (GATT, later to become the World Trade Organization) all proceeded from the same logic – although the GATT or WTO may have turned out to be more of an hybrid between this first scenario and the third one to be described below.

These organizations all had a centralized core, in charge of setting the rules and building institutions at a transnational level. And this centralized core was the direct reflection of the interests of national member states – naturally in varying mixes in each case. In other words, the attempt at rule-making and institution building in the transnational space was very much controlled, through these organizations, by public or semi-public types of actors – representatives of particular national governments and polities. In that context, such transnational organizations were in fact little more than the tools of particular nation-states and governments, mirroring at any one point in time the geopolitical balance of power. These types of transnational organizations have been more or less successful in their attempt at setting the rules of the game on a transnational scale. The more successful – the IMF, the World Bank and probably also the GATT or later the WTO – have been those with some control over compliance. Control could stem from a degree of dependence of member states on the transnational organizations as well as from the ability of these organizations to associate rewards with compliance and sanctions with non compliance.

Supranational constructions

A second scenario, historically, for institution building in the transnational space has come through the temptation to create a supranational market, or even a supranational state or nation. With a little bit of a stretch, once again, and some degree of historical anachronism since a number of them were constituted before the emergence of the nation-state, empires are the materialization of such a temptation. In our modern age, the most obvious illustrations of this second scenario are constructions such as the European Coal and Steel Community (ECSC), the European Economic Community (EEC) or the European Union. There are signs that NAFTA may also be travelling that road.

Here again, the process of rule setting and institution building stems from a political, top-down kind of initiative. Public or semi-public actors, governments or their representatives are instrumental in that process even though they may not always be as predominant as in the first scenario. The scope of those centrally engineered constructions goes well beyond, in general, what transnational organizations of the first type could do. The new rules and institutions are enforceable, in the sense of them being formally and efficiently associated with enforcement mechanisms that put member states under strong pressure to comply. In fact, the reality and strength of enforcement mechanisms combined with the scope of the domain controlled might be the key differentiating features between this type of supranational constructions and transnational organizations.

Several chapters in this book focus explicitly on institution building in the context of supranational constructions. The contributions by Lilja and Moen; Plehwe with Vescovi or Midttun et al. tell of the emergence of new rules of the game within the European Community or European Union space. They also show how these changes in rules of the game that are being initiated at the supranational level are then having an impact on national institutional configurations. This impact can be felt through trickle-up trajectories, where private and subsocietal actors change their behaviours and push these changes up towards their own national environments. The chapter by Lilja and Moen illustrates that, where an understanding of competition defined at the European Union level is transforming interactions in the Norwegian and Finnish forest industries and challenging, in the process, rules of the competitive game as they had until then been defined in these two countries.

The impact can also be felt through trickle-down trajectories, as documented in the chapters by Plehwe with Vescovi or Midttun et al. The process there is one where the supranational level imposes new rules of the game on national member states. And the path is from supranational authorities to national governments or political institutions. National governments and political institutions have in turn to push down and translate those supranational rules within their own national space, putting pressure in the process on actors at the subsocietal level to change their behaviours and ways of functioning. Both contributions clearly show that this trickling-down of new rules of the game is challenging national institutional configurations, leading to potentially quite significant transformations at that level. The trickle-down trajectory documented in these two contributions is made possible by the existence of enforcement mechanisms. A supranational construction such as the European Union is indeed characterized by the strength of enforcement mechanisms and thus by its potential clout and impact over member nations and states. One type of enforcement mechanisms are direct controls associated positively with rewards and negatively with sanctions. Another type of enforcement mechanism is the reliance on voluntary compliance where member states are aware of the overall benefits they draw from belonging to the supranational construction and, conversely, realize the dangerous consequences of not respecting the terms of a contract they entered of their own will.

Self-disciplining transnational communities

We now turn to a third scenario for institution building in the transnational space which, we argue, is progressively becoming more widespread. In this third scenario, all actors concerned by a particular type of transnational activity come together, generally in non-structured and little formalized settings, to elaborate and agree upon collective rules of the game. Little is known on transnational rule-making in such a context (but see Morgan and Engwall 1999; Djelic and Bensedrine 2001) and three chapters in this book – those by McNichol and Bensedrine; Ventresca et al. or Lehmkuhl – contribute to a better understanding of that process. In contrast to the first two scenarios, public or semi-public actors might be involved in rule setting but they are not the only ones. In fact, as documented in all three contributions, private actors might take the initiative and be quite instrumental for the elaboration of rules and the building of institutions as well as for monitoring compliance.

Another difference with the two previous scenarios is that the logic at work is not one of external control but rather one of self-disciplining. Instead of waiting for public actors to impose an institutional frame and thus orient private action, the actors concerned, and in particular non-governmental and private actors, take the initiative and set their own rules. Within an arena or a field of transnational activity lacking initially in structuration, all concerned actors collaborate in building institutional arrangements that will constrain their own actions, behaviours and interactions. The process is one of voluntary and relatively informal negotiations. A striking common finding, emerging from the contributions by McNichol and Bensedrine; Ventresca et al. or Lehmkuhl, is the relatively amorphous, fluid and multifocal nature of that process as well as of any kind of emerging structural arrangements.

A comparison of the chapters by McNichol and Bensedrine; Ventresca et al. and Lehmkuhl shows reliance on two main categories of enforcement mechanisms. One is voluntary compliance, but compliance this time not only of national states and governments but also directly of all actors involved in the process. Compliance is voluntary for the main reason that these actors define themselves the rules and inflict upon themselves the institutional constraints that will bound their own actions and interactions. From the empirical material, a second enforcement mechanism, socialization, can be identified – although probably more as a potential and an objective than as an already existing and concrete reality. Indeed, socialization can only emerge as an enforcement mechanism in a later stage. Rules and institutions have to be constructed and agreed upon (the habitualization or pre-institutionalization stage identified in the introduction to this volume), actors have to function within that frame for a while (codification), before the double process of socialization and self-reproduction through socialization can really become operative (sedimentation). The advantage of socialization as an enforcement mechanism is the decreasing need for direct controls, and thus for both external rewards and sanctions. Actors that are being socialized through a particular institutional frame or in a particular set of rules become their own watchdogs. Ultimately, the institutional frame and the set of rules should 'disappear', to the extent that, after a while, they have a tendency to become neutral and transparent for those actors that function within the space they structure.

This third scenario for institution building at a transnational level is not new. As argued in the chapter by Lehmkuhl, for example, the structuring of commercial arbitration at the transnational level by actors themselves – and in particular by private actors – has existed for a long time. One could also argue that international cartels, particularly during the interwar period but even after in some industries (Lilja and Moen this volume), fit within this type of scenario. The contemporary period of globalization, however, has been marked by an intensification of institution building at the transnational level (Whitley, this volume). And in the context of that intensification, we argue that this third scenario has become progressively more important particularly in recent years. Overall, a comparison of the various contributions to this book seem to show an historical evolution since 1945 in terms of which scenario has been predominant.

The early period, in the years following the war, was characterized by the multiplication of transnational organizations. Then came the time of supra-national constructions – particularly in Western Europe. This, naturally, is still going on and quite strongly in fact as the chapters by Lilja and Moen; Middtun et al. or Plehwe with Vescovi show. At the same time, the empirical evidence in the very last part of this book points for the recent period in the direction of an increasing role and place for self-disciplining transnational communities (see also Brunsson and Jacobsson 2000). Professions are one particular type of such communities but, as the last chapters in this book indicate, they are far from the only one.

Institution Building: Mode and Nature of the Process

In parallel to these three different scenarios, the chapters in this book also point to different modes for the process of transnational institution building.

Dominant mode

A first, obvious mode we label here 'dominant'. In that mode, the building of institutions at a transnational level simply reflects one dominant local or national model. The rules characteristic of one particular national space thus shape in a rather direct way the transnational space. In a second stage, this local turned transnational model is bound to have an impact on a number of other national institutional configurations. The latter are indeed being affected, to a greater or lesser extent, by transnational institutions and rules both through trickle-up and trickle-down trajectories as we have argued above.

This overall process generally reflects the objective and/or perceived strength of the 'dominant' nation, which itself depends on a combination of economic, military and geopolitical factors with some degree of ideological propping up. Quite a few of the contributions to this volume show that the United States has played the role of dominant model during the second half of the twentieth century. The chapters by Tainio et al.; Kleiner; McKenna et al. or Whitley do provide evidence of such a dominant mode or logic being at work in the process of transnational institution building, with a significant impact ultimately upon dependent or peripheral national institutional configurations. In most of those chapters in fact, the term 'Americanization' appears to fit better with the stories told than the apparently more neutral word 'globalization'.

Negotiated mode
A second mode emerging from the contributions to this volume we label the 'negotiated' mode. Institution building in the transnational space can come about through the confrontation or 'rubbing against each other' of multiple locals or nationals, leading to what can be described as a process of negotiation. The chapters by Plehwe with Vescovi; Midttun et al. or McNichol and Bensedrine or Ventresca et al. provide illustrations of that particular mode. In the contributions by McNichol and Bensedrine or Ventresca et al., though, what we see is in fact the interplay between the 'negotiated' and the 'dominant' mode. All participants to the negotiation are not created equal in that case and one of them – the United States – looms significantly larger than the others in the process. This underscores the ideal typical nature of the different modes we identify and the likelihood that they will coexist and interact in real life contexts.

While situations of negotiation are rarely perfectly balanced, a situation of dominance, on the other hand, is rarely so extreme as to leave no space for at least partial negotiation. In the context of what was described above as 'Americanization', for example, what the chapters by Tainio et al. and McKenna et al. documented was in fact both the transformation of a national model – the American one – into a transnational one and the partial alteration, translation and negotiation of that model when it came into contact with previously existing and established national institutional configurations (see also Djelic 1998).

Emergent mode
The contributions to this volume allow us to identify a third mode, although more as an overall trend and as a potential than as a really operative – at least as yet – mode of building transnational institutions. We label this third mode 'emergent'. Common to illustrations of both the 'dominant' and 'negotiated' modes is the fact that the actors involved – whoever and whatever they are –

remain strongly embedded in and shaped by the institutional contexts of their home countries. These actors tend in fact to extend the actions and strategies used in that context and shaped by it to the transnational arena (Whitley 2001 and this volume). What some of the contributions to this volume seem to show is that this is not necessarily always the case.

The chapters by Plehwe with Vescovi; McNichol and Bensedrine; Ventresca et al. or Lehmkuhl for example point to a blurring of identities – particularly national ones – amongst those actors involved in transnational institution building. Once transnational arenas have been structured for a little while, once transnational institutions and rules of the game shape behaviours and interactions, some of the actors concerned come to be more directly affected by these transnational institutions than by the institutions of the country they may originate from. The structures, strategies and even identities of these actors change, sometimes quite significantly, generally through the interplay between the national rules of the game of the country they come from and the transnational system that is being constructed. New actors may also sprout up and the only referent for these new actors will be the embryonic transnational institutional context in which they were born (for example some transnational NGOs, lobbying organizations created at the European level, see Salk et al. 2001).

Any further process of transnational institution building in that context cannot anymore fit under the categories of either the 'dominant' or the 'negotiated' mode. What takes place then is what we label, for lack of a better word, an emergent process. Multiple actors with no clear identities and functioning themselves at the interface of multiple rule systems, come in collision with each other. If we are to follow the metaphorical use of chaos theory in social sciences, the result in this case is bound to be unpredictable (Thietart and Forgues 1997). We call this result an 'emergent' construction.

The three modes identified here are clearly ideal types. There is bound to be, in other words, an interaction and an interplay between them in real life situations. At the same time, the chapters in this volume appear to document, collectively, a shift over time in their relative importance as a mode of transnational institution building. This shift parallels to quite a degree the evolution, in terms of scenario, that was identified above. In the immediate post-World War II years, we have argued, the main scenario for transnational institution building was the setting up of transnational organizations. During this period, the dominant mode – one national model, the American one, imposing itself on a transnational scale – was all but overwhelming. The dominant mode has not entirely disappeared with the attempts at supranational construction. But such projects, by their very nature, meant and required some degree of negotiation between the several member nations that were shaping them, generally on a world regional basis. Finally, the move towards the third scenario – transnational institution building by self-disciplining transnational communities – coincides quite closely with the slow assertion of an emergent mode. It seems, furthermore, to fit particularly with transnational institution building across world regions – in what gets close to being a 'global' space.

Table C.3 presents in summary form the variants of transnational institution building identified in this section.

Table C.3   Transnational institution building

Scenarios and actors	Mode
• Transnational Organizations. Actors: nations, states, governments and civil servants (almost exclusively)	• Dominant
• Supranational Constructions. Actors: nations, states, governments and civil servants (predominantly)	• Negotiated
• Self-disciplining transnational communities. Actors: multiple, public, semi-public but also non-governmental organizations and private	• Emergent

OUTCOMES AND FINAL REFLECTIONS

Globalization can be read as a double process of institutional change, at the national level, and institution building, in the transnational arena. As such, it emerges as a complex aggregation and constellation of multiple layers, each of which has to be contextualized, reflects particular contingencies and exhibits unique path dependencies. Behind this first level of extreme complexity, this volume has allowed us to point to a limited number of important patterns.

First, what clearly comes out of our collective findings is that globalization is in fact a world beyond convergence and divergence. And we could add that it is so in a structural way at least in the foreseeable future. The treatment of globalization layer by layer, facet by facet and dimension by dimension destroys the myth of clearcut convergence but we document in some cases multiple local reinterpretations of a 'dominant' model or of a common set of challenger rules (for example Tainio et al.; Kleiner; McKenna et al.). Still, although we do not document full convergence, we move away from the vision of stable systemic national models (Whitley 1999; Maurice and Sorge 2000; Hall and

Soskice 2001). We point instead to significant change affecting national institutional systems – what we call incremental but consequential change. Globalization is disrupting, we argue, the systemic stability and relative autonomy of national spaces. It is pushing along common logics and institutional rules of the game that coexist, compete, hybridize with or even replace incumbent national institutions.

Institutional rules of the game can be essentially of two kinds – structural and normative or ideational. We find that globalization is associated there with two main tendencies. First, a number of contributions in this volume document a significant intensification and the greater density of institutional rules in general. A second tendency seems to be the increasing importance and role, proportionally, of normative or ideational types of rules over more structural ones. This double tendency reflects both the demultiplication of levels at which rules are being produced – local, national, supranational (for example Europe) or global. It also reflects an explosion of and rising competition between centres and actors of rule production.

The traditional landscape – characteristic of modern world society – was one where relatively isolated and independent nation-states set the rules of the game that applied within their borders and had the coercive means to enforce them. The space in between remained relatively anomic. With respect to rule production, this volume points to a rather different story today. The landscape is one of loose and fluid but quite dense networks of 'actors' in the wide sense of the term, whether public, private or mixed, whether local, national, supranational or global, that compete and sometimes cooperate for the production of institutional rules. Many of those 'actors' do not have physical control over any form of territory. Some of them are in fact closer to being transnational or even virtual communities (Morgan 2001). Hence, instead of relying on coercion and external forms of control, the tendency there is to expect and foster socialization and the internalization of norms, self-discipline and peer regulation.

We would, naturally, benefit from having a much greater density of empirical building blocks of the type exemplified by the contributions to this book. It would, in particular, be interesting to move away from an overwhelming focus on traditional core countries and to observe the interactions of processes of institutional change and institution building in other parts of the world. However, we can nevertheless propose the following tentative conclusion. Globalization may be contributing to bringing about a radical change in the meaning of governance – reducing the importance of traditional coercive, external and centralized state power and increasing that of decentralized norm producing and self-regulating communities. Governance becomes less associated with downstream and external control, relying on coercion and repression. It becomes increasingly associated with upstream definition, voluntary adhesion to and appropriation of norms, policed by the risks of exclusion.

This second meaning of governance may be the only one available and acceptable within the transnational space. In that respect, calls for a world government do seem highly utopian and far fetched at least in the medium term (see for example Rodrick 2001). Interestingly, contributions to this volume seem to show that this particular meaning of governance is also making significant inroads in regional supranational constructions such as the European Union or even within nation-states. Globalization is not threatening governance – in fact we argue that globalization reflects a particular type of governance. However, what globalization may be doing is introducing within national polities and democratic arenas this second understanding of governance that can both coexist and compete with traditional state control. Globalization does not mean 'governance without governments' (Rosenau and Czempiel 1992) – it probably means, however, a partial reinvention and transformation of the role and place of governments in governance. As we have shown in this volume, this is naturally the case transnationally where nation-states have to contend with each other as well as with many other actors for both the structuration and the monitoring of governing institutions. This is also the case nationally we propose, with probably an important evolution to be confirmed in the coming years of national democratic landscapes that will come increasingly to incorporate logics of governance of the second type.

Through that reflection we suggest that the debates around globalization and its governance have to be somewhat reformulated. The dilemma is not between globalization and governance. The dilemma rather is between two different meanings of governance and the balance that should be reached between them. On the one hand, governance of the Westphalian or state control type has the advantage of being something that we are familiar with and that we can easily recognize. It is also both blunt and clear when it comes to the democratic game. In simplistic terms, it creates a separation between a government that makes the rules and civil society to which they apply (even though naturally governments are supposed to be direct representatives of civil society and the rules apply also in theory to governments and their members). The main shortcoming of the state control form or logic of governance is that it is tightly associated in its workings with a repressive apparatus that itself functions on a bounded territory. Hence it is difficult to extend that logic beyond the nation state – the European Union is a good laboratory to test this difficulty.

Governance of the community type, on the other hand, has the great advantage of potentially knowing no boundaries. It should be noted also that since it relies on voluntary adhesion rather than coercion it is less violent and probably less costly as a form of governance. On the other hand, this type of governance is associated with a rather different conception of the democratic game – more in line with Tocqueville's depiction of early America where civil society is much more directly active in rule building and enforcement through collective or organizational representatives (Tocqueville 1951). An issue with this type of democratic game, that comes out quite clearly in the last chapters of this volume, is its blurred, fuzzy and sometimes messy nature. While it brings many of the actors concerned around the table of negotiation, this type of democratic process does not ensure – far from – it that all actors are being created equal. The contributions by Lilja and Moen; Plehwe with Vescovi; McNichol and Bensedrine or Lehmkuhl point to significant power plays and imbalances behind what could appear at first sight to be egalitarian and neutral processes. What does not appear in those contributions and should be mentioned here is the total or partial exclusion of those groups, actors, nations, communities that either do not understand the change in game and rules of the game or else have not prepared or geared up to getting ready to play it. One obvious absence is that of labour and its representatives. It is clearly not the only one.

This reflection may contribute to explaining both the virulence of the anti-globalization movement and its repeated calls for governance. We have argued in this volume that globalization is in fact about governance and negotiations around governance, but the anti-globalization movement may be witness to the de facto exclusion from these negotiations of groups that do not play the game either because they do not have resources to play it or because they do not master its rules.

REFERENCES

Amdam, Rolv Petter, Ragnhild Kvalshaugen and Eirinn Larsen (eds) (2002), *Inside the Business Schools*, Oslo, Norway: Abstrakt Press.
Aslund, Anders (2001), *Building Capitalism*, NY: Cambridge University Press.
Berghahn, Volker (1986), *The Americanization of West German Industry*, Cambridge, New York: Cambridge University Press.
Boli, John and George Thomas (eds) (1999), *Constructing World Culture*, Stanford: Stanford University Press.
Byrkjeflot, Haldor (2000), *Management Education and Selection of Top Managers in Europe and the US*, Bergen, Norway: Los-Senteret Rapport.
Brunsson, Nils and Bengt Jacobsson (eds) (2000), *A World of Standards*, Oxford: Oxford University Press.
Campbell, John (1998), 'Institutional analysis and the role of ideas in political economy', *Theory and Sociology*, **27**, 377–409.
Campbell, John and Ove Kaj Pedersen (eds) (2001), *The Rise of Neoliberalism*, Princeton, NJ: Princeton University Press.
Clemens, Elizabeth and James Cook (1999), 'Politics and institutionalism: explaining durability and change', *Annual Review of Sociology*, **25**, 244–66.
Crouch, Colin and Henry Farell (2002), 'Breaking the path of institutional development? Alternatives to the new determinism', MPIfG discussion paper 02/5, Max Planck Institute for the study of Societies, Cologne.

Deeg, Richard (2001), 'Institutional change and the uses and limits of path dependency: the case of German finance', MFIfG discussion paper 01/6, Max Planck Institute for the Study of Societies, Cologne.

D'Iribarne, Philippe (1989), *La Logique de L'Honneur*, Paris: Editions du Seuile.

DiMaggio, Paul and Walter Powell (1983), 'The iron cage revisited: institutionalized isomorphism and collective rationality in organizational fields', *American Sociological Review*, **48**, 147–60.

Djelic, Marie-Laure (1998), *Exporting the American Model*, Oxford, New York: Oxford University Press.

Djelic, Marie-Laure (2001), 'From a typology of neo-institutional arguments to their cross-fertilization', research document, Paris: ESSEC Business School.

Djelic, Marie-Laure and Antti Ainamo (1999), 'The coevolution of new organizational forms in the fashion industry: a historical and comparative study of France, Italy and the United States', *Organization Science*, **10** (5), pp. 622–37.

Djelic, Marie-Laure and Jabril Bensedrine (2001), 'Globalization and its limits: the making of international regulation', in Glenn Morgan, Peer Hull Kristensen and Richard Whitley (eds), *The Multinational Firm*, Oxford, New York: Oxford University Press.

Dobbin, Franck (1994), *Forging Industrial Policy*, New York, Cambridge: Cambridge University Press, pp. 253–80.

Elster, John, Claus Offe and Ulrike Preuss (eds) (1998), *Institutional Design and Post Communist Societies*, Cambridge, New York: Cambridge University Press.

ENS (2001), 'US pulls out of Kyoto Protocol', *Environment News Service*, 28 March, Washington, DC, http://ens.lycos.com/ens/mar2001/2001L-03-28-11.html

Fligstein, Neil (1990), *The Transformation of Corporate Control*, Cambridge, MA: Harvard University Press.

Fligstein, Neil and Iona Mara-Drita (1996), 'How to make a market: reflections on the European Union's single market program', *American Journal of Sociology*, **102**, 1–33.

Giddens, Anthony (2000), *Runaway World*, NY: Routledge.

Granovetter, Mark (1985), 'Economic action and social structure: the problem of embeddedness', *American Journal of Sociology*, **91**, 481–510.

Guidry, John, Michael Kennedy and Mayer Zald (eds) (2001), *Globalizations and Social Movements*, Ann Arbor, MI: University of Michigan Press.

Guillén, Mauro (2001), 'Is globalization civilizing, destructive or feeble? A critique of five key debates in the social science literature', *Annual Review of Sociology*, **27**, 235–60.

Hall, Peter and David Soskice (2001), *Varieties of Capitalism*, Oxford: Oxford University Press.

Held, David, Anthony McGrew, David Goldblatt and Jonathan Perraton (1999), *Global Transformations*, Stanford, CA: Stanford University Press.

Hollingsworth, Rogers and Robert Boyer (eds) (1997), *Contemporary Capitalism*, Cambridge, UK: Cambridge University Press.

Institut de l'Entreprise (2001), 'Séminaire Benchmarking France–Allemagne', jointly run with the Institut Der Deutschen Wirtschaft, Köln, Paris: Palais du Sénat.

James, Harold (2001), *The End of Globalization: Lessons from the Great Depression*, Cambridge, MA: Harvard University Press.

Jones-Luong, Pauline (2001), *Institutional Change and Continuity in Post-Soviet Central Asia*, Cambridge, New York: Cambridge University Press.

Kitschelt, Herbert (1999), 'Constitutional Design and Postcommunist Economic Reform', working paper, November, Department of Political Science, Duke University.

Knock, Thomas (1995), *To End all Wars*, Princeton, NJ: Princeton University Press.

Kristensen, Peer Hull (2000), 'Unbundling battles over bounded rationalities', keynote speech 16th EGOS Colloquium, Helsinki.

Le Monde (7 November 2001), 'Le "Kodex", nouvelle bible du capitalisme Rhénan'.

Lane, Christel (1995), *Industry and Society in Europe: Stability and Change in Britain, Germany and France*, Aldershot: Edward Elgar.

Mahoney, James (2000), 'Path dependence in historical sociology', *Theory and Society*, **29** (4), 507–48.

Marks, Gary, Fritz Scharpf, Philippe Schmitter and Wolfgang Streeck (eds) (1996), *Governance in the European Union*, London: Sage.

Maurice, Marc and Arndt Sorge (eds) (2000), *Embedding Organizations*, Advances in Organization Studies (4), Amsterdam, NY: John Benjamin Publishers.

Meyer, John and Francisco Ramirez (2000), 'The world institutionalization of education', in J. Schriewer (ed.), *Discourse Formation in Comparative Education*, Frankfurt: Peter Lang Publishers.

Meyer, John and Brian Rowan (1977), 'Institutionalized organizations: formal structure as myth and ceremony', *American Journal of Sociology*, **83** (2), 340–63.

Meyer, John, Francisco Ramirez and Yasemin Soysal (1992), 'World expansion of mass education, 1870–1970', *Sociology of Education*, **65**, 128–49.

Meyer, John, John Boli, George Thomas and Francisco Ramirez (1997a), 'World society and the nation-state', *American Journal of Sociology*, **103** (1), 144–81.

Meyer, John, David Franck, Ann Hironaka, Evan Schofer and Nancy Tuma (1997b), 'The structuring of a world environmental regime, 1870–1990', *International Organization*, **51**, 623–51.

Moore, Karl and David Lewis (2000), *Foundations of Corporate Empire*, London: Financial Times – Prentice Hall.

Morgan, Glenn (2001), 'Transnational communities and business systems', *Global Networks: a Journal of Transnational Affairs*, **1** (2), 113–30.

Morgan, Glenn and Lars Engwall (eds) (1999), *Regulation and Organizations*, Advances in Management and Business Studies, 5, London: Routledge.

Murray, Gilbert (1987), *From the League to UN*, Westport, CT: Greenwood Publishing Group.

Murphy, Craig (1994), *International Organization and International Change*, Cambridge, UK: Polity Press.

Ohmae, Kenichi (1990), *The Borderless Economy*, NY: Harper.

Pierson, Paul (2000a), 'Increasing returns, path dependence, and the study of politics', *American Political Science Review*, **94**, 251–67.

Pierson, Paul (2000b), 'The limits of design: explaining the institutional origins and change', *Governance*, **13**, 475–99.

Polanyi, Karl (1944), *The Great Transformation*, Boston, MA: Beacon Press.

Robertson, Roland (1992), *Globalization, Social Theory and Global Culture*, London: Sage.

Rodrick, Dani (2001), 'Four simple principles for democratic governance of globalization', note for the Friedrich Ebert Foundation, May, Harvard: Kennedy School of Government.

Rodrick, Dani (2002), 'Reform in Argentina, take two', *The New Republic*, 14 January.

Rosenau, James and Ernst-Otto Czempiel (eds) (1992), *Governance without Governments*, NY: Cambridge University Press.

Salk, Jane, François Nielsen and Gary Marks (2001), 'Patterns of cooperation among regional offices in Brussels, homophily, complementarity and national embeddedness', CERESSEC Working Paper, Paris: ESSEC.

Sandholtz, Wayne and Alec Stone Sweet (eds) (1998), *European Integration and Supranational Governance*, Oxford: Oxford University Press.

Sassen, Saskia (1998), *Globalization and its Discontents*, NY: The New Press.

Schwartz, Thomas Alan (1991), *America's Germany*, Cambridge, MA: Harvard University Press.

Stark, David and Laszlo Bruszt (1998), *Postsocialist Pathways*, Cambridge, New York: Cambridge University Press.

Stiglitz, Joseph (2002), *Globalization and its Discontents*, NY: WW Norton & Co.

Stiglitz, Joseph and Pierre-Alain Muet (eds) (2001), *Governance, Equity and Global Markets*, Oxford: Oxford University Press.

Streeck, Wolfgang (2001), 'International competition, supranational integration, national solidarity: the emerging constitution of "Social Europe"', in Martin Kohli and Mojca Novak (eds) *Will Europe Work? Integration, Employment and the Social Order*, London: Routledge, pp. 21–34.

Thelen, Kathleen (2000), 'Timing and temporality in the analysis of institutional evolution and change', *Studies in American Political Development*, **14**, 101–8.

Thietart, Raymond-Alain and Bernard Forgues (1997), 'Action, structure and chaos theory', *Organization Studies*, **18** (1), pp. 119–43.

Tocqueville, Alexis (de) (1951), *De la Démocratie en Amérique*, Paris: Gallimard.

Wallerstein, Immanuel (1974), *The Modern World-System*, NY: Academic Press.

Weber, Max (1978), *Economy and Society*, Berkeley, CA: University of California Press.

Whitley, Richard (1992), *European Business Systems*, London: Sage

Whitley, Richard (1999), *Divergent Capitalisms*, Oxford: Oxford University Press.

Whitley, Richard (2001), 'How and why are international firms different? The consequences of cross-border managerial coordination for firm characteristics and behaviour', in Glenn Morgan, Peer Hull Kristensen and Richard Whitley (eds), *The Multinational Firm*, Oxford: Oxford University Press, pp. 27–68.

Williamson, Jeffrey (1996), 'Globalization, convergence, history', *Journal of Economic History*, **56** (2) (June), 277–306.

Williamson, Jeffrey (1997), 'Globalization and inequality, past and present', *The World Bank Research Observer*, **12** (2) (August), 117–35.

Zeitlin, Jonathan and Garry Herrigel (eds) (2000), *Americanization and Its Limits*, Oxford: Oxford University Press.

Index